BEST BOOKS
FOR YOUNG ADULTS

The Selections, the History, the Romance

Betty Carter

Young Adult
Library Services
Association

American Library Association
Chicago and London 1994

Acquisition Editor: Bonnie J. Smothers
Managing Editor: Joan A. Grygel
Production Manager: Dianne M. Rooney
Manufacturing Manager: Eileen Mahoney

Cover design by Harriett Banner
Text design by Dianne M. Rooney

The paper used in this publication meets the minimum
requirements of American National Standard for Information
Sciences—Permanence of Paper for Printed Library
Materials, ANSI Z39.48–1984. ∞

Composed by Alexander Graphics
    in Optima and Melior on a Datalogics Pagination System

Printed on 50-pound Arbor,
    a pH-neutral stock, and bound
    in 10-point cover stock by Edward Brothers, Inc.

Library of Congress Cataloging-in-Publication Data

Carter, Betty, 1944–
    Best books for young adults : the selections, the history, the
romance / by Betty Carter for Young Adult Library Services
Association.
        p.   cm.
    Includes index.
    ISBN 0-8389-3439-0
    1. Teenagers—United States—Books and reading. 2. Young adult
literature—Bibliography. 3. Best books for young adults. 4. Young
adult literature—Bibliography—Methodology. I. Young Adults
Library Services Association. II. Title.
Z1037.C34   1991
[PN1009.A1]
028.1'62—dc20   94-2640
                                                               CIP

Printed in the United States of America.

98 97 96 95   5 4 3 2

CONTENTS

PART ONE

Background

Betty Carter

Introduction

In 1978 I moved to Houston, Texas, with my husband, Don, and our daughter, Neta. Don's firm had offered him a new position in their Houston office and the three of us welcomed the transfer. Neta, then in first grade, needed the challenge of a progressive school district, and I was lucky enough to find a job as a school media specialist in a local junior high. Several years before, I had been a school librarian for a brief period, but more recently I had been working in a federal project designed to extend reading instruction in the high school social studies. I missed that mix of formal and informal contact with students, and I missed working with teachers to strengthen their instructional programs. In August of 1978, it felt good to be back home in a school media center.

Conditions appeared as good as they get: the district, both philosophically and financially, proudly supported school libraries; the campus principal, who may have absorbed his ideas from his librarian mother, thought that the school media center should be central to instruction; the faculty wanted the media center to change from a remote room far removed from the intellectual center of the school to a vibrant laboratory where learning took place; and the students represented that wonderful mix of sophistication and naiveté, excitement and indifference, and maturity and absurdity that so frequently characterizes young adults. Of course, I knew some disappointment lurked in the background; I just didn't know when I would discover it.

The moment of truth came early on the first day when I, eager to begin this dream job, took a serious look at the collection. It was old, stuffed with smelly, unattractive books. Shelves overflowed with the complete Beany Malone series, all the dated works of Rosmund DuJardin and Betty Cavanna, and elementary titles from Carolyn Haywood's Betsy and Eddie

3

books. There were adult classics by Dostoyevski and Tolstoy; the definitive collection on bargello; and a deadly dull nonfiction section that attempted to explicate answers to finite questions about imports and exports, diameters of the planets, and eating habits of Texas mammals. Satellite collections for classroom libraries contained outdated encyclopedias, some more than twenty years old, that praised the "white man for civilizing Oklahoma."[1] No paperback editions had ever been purchased. Here was the chance to make a difference in the development of lifetime readers and to implement a solid instructional program. But how could I do this without books? Plenty were available for checkout, but I could see little to read.

The simple solution was to weed and to order books, but because of the peculiarities of the funding procedures in this school system, money for the current budget would not be released until late September. Even with purchase orders in hand by that date, I could not expect campus delivery of any materials before November or December. So, two hours into the job, I went to the principal to requisition money for new books.

After listening politely for a few minutes, the principal conceded that there was some discretionary money. And, yes, he could see that books probably needed to be ordered. During the last year most of the book budget had been diverted for media purchases, but I could have around a thousand dollars. Because he was closing out budgets that very day (as principals always are when allocating funds), the money would need to be appropriated by that afternoon. I took the offer and returned to the library wondering how best to spend the small pittance allotted to tide me over until more funds were available.

I looked at the collection again. It wasn't a total loss. There was some updated material, books by Judy Blume, Paul Zindel, Milton Meltzer, and Richard Peck. But conspicuously absent were other fine authors such as Robert Cormier, Rosa Guy, Anne McCaffrey, and Sue Ellen Bridgers. I wrote down books by these authors and others I knew to be popular, but time was running out. Eager to turn in the order when requested, I went into the files, grabbed the most recent Best Books for Young Adults (BBYA) list available, and with no further selection tools, ordered the 1977 BBYA list as printed.

I'd heard about people like me in library school, those individuals who ordered rather than selected, and felt guilty about this guerrilla approach to collection development. Although I had heard of BBYA, I was still unfamiliar with many of the recommended titles. So it was with some unease that I awaited the shipment of books that would mark my new career.

When the books arrived, I quickly assigned two of my library helpers the job of unpacking them. As junior high students never are, they were neither silent nor efficient, but this time I wanted to hear their comments and listen to their reactions. Using those latent skills of an amateur detective I'd developed during my thirteen years in public schools, I watched them and listened to their comments. *One Fat Summer*, about the Crisco Kid who was fat in the can, looked "O.K." *Coma* held promise ("Check out that cover"); and *Madness, Magic, and Medicine*, according to my two junior critics, certainly addressed all faculty, or at least the first section did. Wil Huygen and Rien Poortvliet's *Gnomes* took a long time to unpack, as did Linda McCartney's *Linda's Pictures*. At least, I thought, these books look attractive, although I wondered if these surface reactions would encourage reading rather than curiosity. Finally, one junior critic, Mark Vivas, gave the shipment ultimate approval when he brought *Arnold*, an as-told-to biography of Arnold Schwarzenegger, to me and asked quite eagerly, "Can I check it out?" I silently thanked the committee.

If real life more closely resembled fairy tales, I could conclude this story with "and they read together happily ever after." But such a utopia didn't instantly materialize. Not all the books proved successful. Some, selected with high school students in mind, didn't appeal to these younger teenagers. I remember one girl who really enjoyed Dan Rather's *The Camera Never Blinks* because her sister, like Rather, had attended Sam Houston State University, located just ninety miles from Houston. She found a connection with that book that no others did, and I was glad to offer it to her. Still, after a year of single circulation, I shipped this book off to a high school where it found many more readers.

Some of the books on the 1977 list didn't hold mass appeal for this particular audience. But, then, many books never do. Only a few students checked out Nicholasa Mohr's *In Nueva York*, a strong collection of short stories that offered a dignified examination of a different culture peopled with multifaceted characters. Pauline Gedge's *Child of the Morning* failed to introduce large numbers of readers to fantasy, although for those already familiar with the genre it became another frequently read title in a long string of imaginative fiction selections. A few older readers began their foray into adult fiction with works like Brian Garfield's *Recoil*. Other books, like Robert Cormier's *I Am the Cheese*, didn't move quickly but over time built up a following. On the other hand, titles like Terry Brooks's *The Sword of Shannara*, Jay Anson's *The Amityville Horror*, Harry and Norma Fox Mazer's *The Solid Gold Kid*, Richard Petty's *King of the Road*, Richard Peck's *Ghosts I Have Been*, and Gary Gerani and Paul Schulman's *Fantastic Television* became instant hits. Additional books, such as Ilse Koehn's *Mischling, Second Degree* and Frank Uhlman's *Reunion*, not only proved popular but also found respected places in the curriculum.

This experience started my thinking about the Best Books for Young Adults Committee. How was it formed? How were books selected? Did young adults themselves have any input into the creation of the list? What should constitute a "best" book? What kinds of materials were considered? Were certain kinds of books slighted while others were favored?

In 1993, when Linda Waddle, deputy executive director for the Young Adult Library Services Association (YALSA) at the American Library Association (ALA) approached me about writing a history of the committee, these questions resurfaced along with two others. Did the list respond to that changing constituency the profession called young adults? Did publishers and authors appreciate this recognition? While searching for a structure, these questions stayed with me and eventually formed the basis of the discussion in the first part of this book.

My respect for those involved in BBYA began in 1977 and continues to grow over the years. Year after year this committee completes its charge: it produces an outstanding list of recommended titles for young adults. It isn't a perfect list, for, as Dorothy Broderick says, "There isn't any such animal unless you make the list just for you. Committee lists are lessons in compromise and in the art of win some, lose some graciously."[2] This annual list, like all other compilations, should not enjoy uncritical acceptance but should instead undergo the same professional evaluation as does any group of recommended readings. That evaluation can only begin by understanding the committee's composition, charge, and selection procedures. And that's the purpose of this book: to define the committee and provide some perspective on its work.

The process of learning about BBYA was an unusual one for me. Few traditional source materials, such as journal articles, exist on the committee, its selections, and its members. To gather that information, I had to visit the YALSA offices in Chicago and plow through association records: memos, committee reports, and board decisions. This trip was made possible by a grant from the School of Library and Information Studies at Texas Woman's University.

What I discovered in the archives were large gaps in BBYA history because both the quantity and the quality of the records varied from year to year. To broaden the picture concerning BBYA, I wrote each past committee chair, as well as the chairs of the three Best of the Best preconferences, and asked them to share their memories and their observations. Not surprisingly, knowing the spirit of cooperation within YALSA, these individuals responded graciously and thoughtfully.

In addition, I relied heavily on my own memories of BBYA. I had served on the committee as a member in 1984 and 1985 and as chair in 1986. I also had served on a 1989 task force that reexamined the workings of BBYA and had participated in the "Still Great in '88" preconference. While this involvement gave me a valuable perspective, it also led to strong opinions concerning some of the procedures. These opinions appear here but do not necessarily reflect the position of YALSA.

Part One is intended to provide some perspective on BBYA, but it is also designed to serve as background reading for those YALSA members participating in an ALA preconference during the summer of 1994. These individuals will gather in Miami, Florida, to compile a superlist of books from among the 1966 through 1993 BBYA lists. Consequently, these targeted years receive more attention than do those prior to the 1966 cutoff date. That is why early history of the committee is brief and why books appearing on lists before 1966 are not included in Part Two.

Even with all the cooperation of YALSA and its members, history and procedures are frequently sketchy. If you as a reader find discrepancies in the following chapters, please let either me or the YALSA offices know. BBYA deserves a history; it should be an accurate one.

ACKNOWLEDGMENTS

While working on this project, I've encountered numerous bests: the best books (1,257 of them), the best authors and editors (1,094 of them), the best Deputy Director of YALSA (Linda Waddle), the best editor (Bonnie Smothers), the best publishing assistant (Merri Monks), the best chairs (Joel Shoemaker, Deborah Taylor, Frances Bradburn, Judy Nelson, Eugene LaFaille, Jr., Barbara Lynn, Pam Spencer, Mike Printz, Deborah Kay Ashby, Nancy Rolnick, Jacqueline Brown Woody, Larry Rakow, Joni Bodart, Jan Guest Freeman, Penny Jeffrey, Jack Forman, Susan Tait, Eleanor Pourron, Rose Moorachian, Eileen Burgess, and Lora Landers), the best preconference organizers (Regina Minudri, Rhonna A. Goodman, and Penny Jeffrey), the best consultants (Barbara Duree and Sally Estes), the best columnists (Audrey Eaglen and Roger Sutton), the best watchdogs (Dorothy Broderick, Mary Kay Chelton, Cathi MacRae, and WASHYARG), the best researchers (Mary Cary, Michael Madden, and Penny Trosper), the best graduate assistants (Connie Kroll, Jennifer Kubenka, and Deanna Dodson), the best dean (Keith Swigger), and, as I always knew, the best husband (Don Carter). Each contributed to this monograph in a special and unique way. I thank you all.

Notes

1. I cannot give the precise reference for this quote. Published either in the 1950s or early 1960s, the encyclopedia has long ago been sent to weeders' heaven. I used the quote because it is an example of why even historical accounts needed updating.

2. Dorothy M. Broderick, "Good, Better, Best Or the Saga of YASD's Best Books Selection," *VOYA* 12 (Apr. 1989): 17.

History

Americans make lists. All kinds of lists. To-do lists, grocery lists, top-ten lists, even best and worst lists that apply to television programs or restaurants or hospitals or universities or cities. Once a list is established, it then becomes the perfect target for that related national pastime of second guessing someone else's pronouncements. We've all heard, and probably uttered, statements such as: the Academy Awards always favor epics; for her role of Jessica Fletcher, Angela Lansbury merits an Emmy; any given alma mater deserves a higher rating than a selected arch rival; and, surely, wherever a particular naysayer lives is more desirable than the site highlighted in the current compilation of Best American Cities.

The response to the annual Best Books for Young Adults (BBYA) list, now sponsored by the Young Adult Library Services Association (YALSA) of the American Library Association (ALA), reflects our infatuation with lists in general and with their individual components. A committee compiles the list; the list is criticized; the committee changes; the process starts anew. This pattern started in 1930. It continues today.

BBYA's coming-of-age spans sixty-five years, longer than most adults work and many governments last. Changes in both the committee and its annual list measure important trends in reviewing practices, publishing patterns, and professional concerns. More important, though, they reflect the continuing high standards held by young adult librarians—true professionals who just want to "get it right."

The BBYA committee started in 1930 with three members and then expanded from five to seven to nine before establishing its current total of fifteen. Today this group holds final responsibility for determining an annual list of those books deemed "best" for young adults. At one time, an extensive system of field input produced the nominations, and the chair retained the right of ultimate approval for all titles. Over the years, the number of final recommendations has grown with the size of the committee, amount of publishing output, and the definition of the intended audience. The 1930 list contained thirty titles; sixty-three years later the list more than tripled that number with ninety-seven final entries.

The definition of young adults, as well as the kinds of books recommended for them, has also changed. The current committee recognizes young adults as those teenagers between the ages of twelve and eighteen, and young adult literature as that literature read by them, but not necessarily published primarily for them. In earlier times, the list intended to serve readers of high school age and recognized only adult books or those books produced in adult departments from various publishing houses.

THE EARLY YEARS

Michael Madden details a thorough, early history of both the list and its ancestors in his 1967 master of arts dissertation, "An Analysis of the American Library Association's Annual List 'Best Books for Young Adults,' 1930 to 1967." The committee began in 1930 under the auspices of the School Libraries Section of ALA, and its first list, "Books for Young People, 1930" appeared in the July 1931 issue of *Booklist*.[1]

How the list was compiled remains a mystery, but its purpose and field of selection are clear: the committee focused on recreational reading and considered both juvenile and adult titles.[2] The thirty recommended books vary from Will James's autobiographical classic *Lone Cowboy* to Edna Ferber's popular adult release *Cimarron*. While such selections appear to be logical recommendations for teenage readers, the composition of the committee raises questions about the age level of the intended audience. During the first five years of the committee's existence, the association mandated that one member be an elementary school librarian while other members represent the association at large. Considering the times and grade-level configurations for public schools, though, the required presence of a children's librarian made sense. In the 1930s many elementary schools housed upper grades, such as six, seven, eight, or nine, that currently are included in modern junior and senior highs. At that time the concept of young adulthood was not an accepted or even a widespread one.

In the 1930s America was still moving from an agrarian to an industrial economy. Many youngsters went directly from childhood to adulthood, taking on the responsibilities of earning a living and raising a family during their teen years. Only when society demanded extended education or training for specialized jobs, which really didn't happen until the post–World War II years, did circumstances allow teenagers time for this transition, thus signaling the birth of adolescence. As part of their developmental processes, teenagers had always experienced those physical changes often equated with adolescence, but as Ken Donelson and Alleen Nilsen remind us, "Puberty is a universal experience but adolescence is not."[3]

Thus in 1930 young adult librarians, who in the most progressive of environments would have struggled with a limited constituency and an ill-formed charge, were an idea of the future, and their prospective populations were typically served by children's librarians.

For the next fourteen years, excluding 1932 when no such compilation appeared, the American Library Association supported annual lists entitled "Books for Young People." From 1930 to 1935 the School Libraries Section sponsored the lists; in 1936 ALA's Board on Library Service to Children and Youth in Public Libraries took on the responsibility for creating that year's list, and from 1937 to 1945 the Young People's Reading Round Table directed the project.[4]

Perhaps to protest the domination of public librarians on the selection committee (there were only three years between 1937 and 1945 when school librarians appeared on the committee, and then representation consisted of a single member), the School Libraries Section of the ALA compiled its own annual list and published it in the March 1, 1945, edition of *Booklist*. At this time the Young People's Reading Round Table decided to issue two annual lists instead of one, although this committee later agreed to develop a single list that would represent a collaborative effort between public and school librarians.

Clear differences concerning book selection policies existed among school and public librarians according to a 1945 letter from Margaret Ward, chair of the Young People's Reading Round Table: "It is my opinion that many titles are suitable for both school and public library collections, that a committee of school librarians would probably not limit themselves to factual or textbook types of books (although, of course, they would be likely to include more of this type than we who work mainly in recreational reading), and that both committees would often choose the same titles."[5] At this point, selection favored those overlapping books recognized by both school and public librarians—titles appropriate for recreational reading.

Although no recommendations appeared in either 1947 or 1950, from 1945 until 1950 the Booklist Committee of the Division of Libraries for Children and Young People compiled the list during the years it was published. Yet, while the committee remained fixed, the list changed names. For three years it was called "Books for Young People"; in 1948 the name switched to "Adult Books for Young People." The change in nomenclature reflects a clarification of the committee's charge. The proposal for the 1948 list came from Jane Roos, the president of the Young People's Reading Round Table, who wrote: "My own feeling about the books recommended for young people in the *Booklist* is that many of them are too juvenile. The majority are for the youngest group, eighth- and ninth-grade level. I think this is something to be considered by your committee. It seems to me that the easier part of the work is selecting titles from the juvenile lists. We need to select from the adult books for our readers, those that are beyond the children's reading level. . . . I think this list should be done jointly by the *Booklist* staff and our committee."[6]

This suggested change received widespread approval, both from librarians wanting to respond to young adult reading interests and from those seeking tacit ALA endorsement for popular books in their collections that might attract potential censors. As Margaret Edwards stated, "In these days when our very existence is threatened by narrow mental outlooks it seems to me it is high time to cease withholding valuable novels from young people because of a frank sex passage or two that after all have little new to tell them."[7]

The committee thought that the switch to recommending only adult titles called for a clarification of selection procedures. Winifred Jackson, from the Brooklyn Public Library, stated that good librarians would understand overall selection standards, thus eliminating the need to publish them.[8] But, she emphasized, when dealing with the "more mature books" suitable for "the older high school age," selection codes were in transition, and the

> whole issue of book selection for young people should be faced from a broader viewpoint than heretofore. In the case of controversial subjects we should ask:. . . Will it [a book] help our young people to develop critical faculties and encourage a sense of responsibility toward vital issues—not whom may this possibility offend? In judging debatable novels the committee took the position that a book should be considered as a whole and not discarded because of some frankness about sex or because of a few colorful words with which all, including young people, are undoubtedly familiar.[9]

No list appeared in 1950, but this omission did not signal lack of support for continuing the service. Elinor Walker, chair of the Association of Young People's Librarians, lobbied for a new list that would highlight the best books of the year for young adults. Her voice prevailed, though once again responsibility passed to yet another body, the Booklist Committee of the Association of Young People's Librarians, a group composed solely of public librarians.

Following a now-expected pattern, the name underwent several changes: In 1951, "1950 Books for Young People"; in 1952, "Some of the Best 1951 Books for Young People"; and, until 1960, "Interesting Adult Books of [year] for Young People." During this time, the list, with its exclusive attention to adult releases, addressed teenagers of high school age, and books were chosen on the basis of "general readability, integrity of presentation, and literary quality as well as appeal to young people."[10]

Prior to 1966, the various committees instituted a complicated process for nominating books and an autocratic method for selecting them. Michael Madden outlines the practice prior to 1966:

Initial Nominations
On or about October 1st letters are sent to committee members asking them to recommend about twenty titles (adult) published since January 1st.

First Ballot
These nominations are then placed on a ballot which is sent to all committee members. They are asked to pick 40 percent of the titles given.

Second Ballot
All titles receiving two or more votes on the first ballot appear on the second ballot. This time the committee is allowed to make comments.

Nationwide Ballot

A special ballot of all titles that received approximately eight votes from the committee on the second ballot was sent to young adult librarians of large, medium, and small public libraries and to school library administrators as well as school librarians. The names of those receiving a ballot were chosen at random. On this ballot they were asked to vote for twenty titles.

Third Ballot

The committee [voted] on the final titles to appear on the list. Their selections [were] based on their own voting.[11]

Although this procedure appears democratic, in reality the reverse was true. The nationwide balloting produced nominations rather than final selections, and often books with heavy outside support failed to make the final list, while those titles with limited field enthusiasm frequently did. In addition, the chair, who could override any votes, retained the final authority as to what books and how many titles appeared on any published list.

A second problem concerned the nationwide balloting. Elaine Simpson, the 1963 chair, wrote a memo detailing the shortcomings of the system. She stated that many librarians voted from reviews rather than from their own reading; that field voters frequently read less than 50 percent of the list; and that librarians outside the committee favored popular authors by automatically voting on the strength of the authors' reputations and, thus, slighted lesser-known writers.[12]

This system reflected young adult reading tastes as much as it did librarians' opinions about the books. These outside librarians frequently relied on the opinions of their young adult patrons when voting for books for the list. According to a 1964 press release, the "Significant Adult Books for Young People, 1963" were based on "reading interests among the 14–19 year age group . . . [from] a survey conducted among 100 specialists in big city high schools and public libraries. [Young adults'] reading tastes ranged over a broad area in concept and appeal."[13]

By 1958 the development of the list fell under the auspices of the newly created Young Adult Services Division (YASD) managed by three different committees: the Book Selection Committee from 1958 to 1960, the Committee on the Selection of Books and Other Materials from 1964 to 1966, and, finally, the now-familiar Best Books for Young Adults Committee from 1966 to the present.

Even with the now-established name in place, the committee, its procedures, and its charge still faced changes. Issues that plague the committee today, such as numbers and responsibilities of members, eligibility of nominated books, role of young adults in book selection, and procedures for nominating books, began to receive wide attention in 1966. In some cases dissatisfaction came from the committee; in other cases YASD (and later, YALSA) members generated controversy, prompting the characteristic description, "This is the committee everybody loves to hate." Although three formal task forces, appointed in 1979, 1983, and 1989, considered these issues, solutions have been neither quick nor long-lasting.

DEFINITION OF AUDIENCE

For years, the YASD and YALSA boards of directors wrestled with an age-level definition for young adults. Without such, BBYA committees operated under ambiguous criteria for recommending books. Were all young adults teenagers? Were they only teenagers over age fourteen, ALA's upper-level cutoff for the definition of children? Were the youngest young adults middle schoolers or junior high students? Were the oldest young adults students in secondary schools, or did high school graduates qualify?

In the fall of 1990, the YALSA board extended the term of the National Center for Education Statistics Task Force and "charged it to recommend an age and developmental definition of the term 'young adult.' "[14] A year later, the board adopted this task force's recommendation and officially defined young adults as those individuals from twelve to eighteen years old.

On the one hand, this standard definition eliminated discussion about the targeted BBYA audience. On the other, by legitimatizing the inclusion of books for younger readers, it opened the door to charges that the list was increasingly addressing a younger and younger audience.

On February 24, 1993, the Washington State Young Adult Review Group (WASHYARG) wrote the YALSA board expressing its displeasure over several characteristics of the 1993 list. One point of controversy was "the inclusion of so many titles intended for a very young audience."[15] To the casual observer, a list containing books such as *The Stinky Cheese Man and Other Fairly Stupid Tales*, *The House That Crack Built*, *Letters From Rifka*, and *Sojourner Truth: Ain't I A Woman?*, does indeed look young. A closer examination, however, reveals a more complicated picture of the age designations for this particular list.

Mary Cary, a high school librarian in Abilene, Texas, systematically analyzed the 1993 list in light of the WASHYARG criticisms. She located reviews for ninety-six of the recommended BBYA titles in five major review journals: *Booklist*, *Horn Book*, *Kirkus*, *School Library Journal*, and *VOYA*. (One book, *In Your Face: A Cartoonist at Work* by Doug Marlette, was not reviewed in any of these sources.) In order to evaluate age appropriateness, Cary noted the recommended levels designated by the various reviewers of each book. Since books appeal to readers over several age and grade levels, reviewers indicate that range in their recommendations. In a slight departure from that pattern, *VOYA* recommends by school configuration: M indicates middle school, grades 6–8; J indicates junior high, grades 7–9; and S indicates senior high, grades 10–12. In those cases where journals identified readers by grade rather than age, Cary added five years to the suggested grade level and used the resulting number as the targeted age. For example, a book recommended for readers in grade seven converted to a book recommended for twelve-year-olds by adding five to seven. Adult books recommended for young adults did not receive an age-level designation unless the review journal indicated one. In those instances where adult books were recommended without specifying a particular age or grade level (*Booklist* and *School Library Journal*, for example), Cary totaled the designations separately, labeling them simply "adult." Consequently, her final tally shows some adult books receiving a special "adult" designation while others receive a young adult (YA) age. Using her conversion figures, Cary recorded the lowest ages from each review of the ninety-six titles, averaged those figures, and arrived at the youngest mean recommendation. She repeated the process for the oldest mean recommendation. She then averaged these high and low ages and determined a mean age-level designation for each book. Table 1 shows the calculated means for three sample books.

TABLE 1   Calculated Mean Interest Levels for the 1993 BBYA List

Author/Title	Age					
	Booklist	Horn Book	Kirkus	SLJ	VOYA	Avg. Age
Armstrong, Jennifer Steal Away	12–15	9–12	11–15	10–13	—	13.3
Avi Blue Heron	10–13	—	11+	10–13	11–14	12.5
Berry, James Ajeemah and His Son	11–17	12–YA	12+	11+	12–17	14.6

Source: Mary Ruth Metcalf Cary, "An Analysis of the Critical Reception and the Age Level Designations for the 1993 Best Books for Young Adults List" (Professional paper, Texas Woman's University, 1993), 36.

From these calculations, Cary reports that 6 percent of the 1993 list is recommended for below age 12, 62 percent for readers from 12 to 15, and the remainder, or 32 percent, for more-mature readers ranging from age 15 to 18.[16] Such figures clearly indicate that the mean age-level recommendation for the 1993 list indeed skews toward the lower boundaries of young adulthood. What these figures fail to show, though, is the range of age-level recommendations covered by the list.

As one would expect, individual reviewers differ, sometimes drastically, in their recommendations. Jon Scieszka's *The Stinky Cheese Man and Other Fairly Stupid Tales* proves a case in point. *Kirkus* recommends the book for children as young as five years, while the *Horn Book* indicates ten-year-olds comprise the youngest suggested audience. Grade-level recommendations for this one book range from prekindergarten to twelfth grade. Similarly, Bruce Brooks's *What Hearts* is suggested as appropriate reading for elementary children as well as for older young adults. *Booklist* recommends this title for grades eight through twelve, *Horn Book* for ages twelve through young adult, *Kirkus* for ages eleven through fourteen, *School Library Journal* for grades five and up, and *VOYA* for both middle school and junior high school readers.[17] To picture this range, Cary noted all recommended ages for each book as shown in table 2.

Cary then totaled the frequency of recommendations for each age. This second tabulation (figure 1) indicates a more balanced age-level list than does the first. Although books recommended for twelve- and thirteen-year-olds clearly exceed suggestions for more-mature readers, the latter will also find a number of appropriate titles on the 1993 BBYA list.

TABLE 2   Recommended Audience for the 1993 BBYA List

Author/Title	Age														
	5	6	7	8	9	10	11	12	13	14	15	16	17	18	A
Brooks, Bruce *What Hearts*						X	X	X	X	X	X	X	X	X	
Edelman, Marian Wright *The Measure of Our Success:* *Letter to My Children* *and Yours*											X	X	X	X	X
Scieszka, Jon *Stinky Cheese Man*	X	X	X	X	X	X	X	X	X	X	X	X	X	X	X

Source: Mary Ruth Metcalf Cary, "An Analysis of the Critical Reception and the Age Level Designations for the 1993 Best Books for Young Adults List" (Professional paper, Texas Woman's University, 1993), 49, 56.

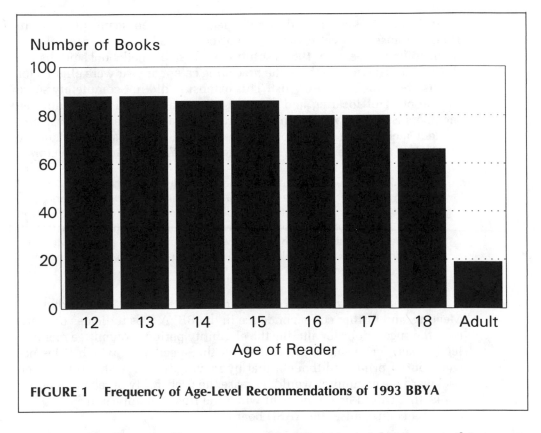

FIGURE 1   Frequency of Age-Level Recommendations of 1993 BBYA

Was the 1993 list too young, too old, or just right? In part, this answer depends on how one interprets the figures. Ultimately, the decision lies in the hands of young adult readers.

BBYA watchdogs will continue to monitor the age appropriateness of the list, realizing that each year's offerings reflect publishing output, the pool of nominations, and the committee's collaborative decisions. The official, expanded age definition sanctions recommendations for younger readers. In response to the growing middle-school movement across our nation, publishers now offer more titles for that population than ever before. Nonetheless, the committee must keep in mind that by the time a young adult reaches about sixteen years of age, he or she reads almost exclusively from adult offerings. These books, generally harder to obtain than juvenile publications (see "Issues" chapter), must remain as a viable part of any BBYA list.

Deborah Taylor, 1993 BBYA chair, addresses the underlying tension inherent in creating and evaluating each list: "When I think about the developmental needs of a twelve-year-old boy and those of an eighteen-year-old girl, I wonder can we make a list that addresses the best books for both of them and everyone in between? When I think about the process, I think yes, we can."[18]

ELIGIBILITY OF BOOKS

Early committees worried that fall releases received scant attention in BBYA because final voting needed to be completed in the first few weeks of the following year. By 1961 a solution was established: books published during the last two months of the preceding calendar year were eligible for inclusion on the next year's list. This extension did not completely solve the problem of locating and reading fall releases. In 1979, committee members Sue Tait and Eleanor Pourron worked with several past and present members of BBYA to address this and other issues. In January 1979, they recommended the following to the YASD board of directors:

> Books will be eligible for consideration for the list if they have been published between September 1st of one year and August 31st of the following year.
> This proposal means that the fall publishing lists would be considered early in the year, and the spring publishing lists would have an equal chance to be considered. The year would end with the summer publishing season, a somewhat lighter time. Additional flexibility could be built in by giving the option of accepting books published in the previous July or August.[19]

The board did not approve this document at the 1979 Midwinter Meeting, and further correspondence in the BBYA files indicates concern over the suggestions for altering the eligibility period. Committee member Jerri Baker, for instance, worried about the speed with which titles became out of print, and thought that by moving the allowable time frame backward the committee would increase the probability of recommending books that would be out of print when the final list appeared.[20]

As a compromise, the YASD board

> approved procedures so that the Best Books for Young Adults Committee will consider and vote on books copyrighted within their assigned calendar year, January 1 to December 31. Nominations are to be accepted from the field and committee up to November 1 of that calendar year. However, books published between September 1 and December 31 of the preceding calendar year may be nominated by Best Books for Young Adults committee members only and limited to titles not previously considered.[21]

The present BBYA committee operates under different nominating procedures, but the criterion that books published between September 1 and December 31 of the preceding calendar year are eligible for a current year's list remains in effect.

The tradition of the early lists including only adult books stayed in place until 1973 when the charge to the committee changed from "To select from the year's publications those *adult books* [my italics] significant for young adults"[22] to "select from the year's publications those *books* [my italics] significant for young adults."[23] This one-word alteration allowed books published in juvenile divisions to be eligible for the list. Not incidentally, this change also placed an additional reading and nominating burden on the committee by increasing the available pool of appropriate books.

NOMINATING BOOKS

With the institution of nationwide balloting, the committee signaled the profession that it wanted outside involvement and additional input in nominating books. When committee membership increased, this concept languished and apparently didn't resurface until the 1980s. Not surprisingly, the procedures for considering nominations from noncommittee members developed over time and through a combination of custom and official board policy. Only vague references to these practices appear in the BBYA files.

By the early 1980s, BBYA accepted field nominations, although they required additional approval from a committee member before becoming official. Later, only nominations from the preceding year's publications required such an endorsement.

The 1989 BBYA task force did not devote much time to the question of field nominations. Members informally checked on the frequency of these outside proposals; they concluded that since these nominations made up such a small percentage of considered books and rarely affected the workings of the committee they should be encouraged (mainly to downplay the growing perception of an imperial committee) and, for simplicity's sake, be treated just like any other nomination. In its haste, the task force failed to consider what might happen if the numbers of outside nominations increased beyond the token suggestions from previous years.

For a variety of reasons, ranging from increased visibility of the BBYA list to deliberate solicitations for potential best books from outside the committee, the number of field nominations mushroomed. The 1986 committee recorded six; the 1993 committee dealt with eighty. While these eighty additional nominations widened the pool of suggested books and allowed greater numbers of young adult librarians a voice in the composition of the list, they also increased the consideration file to an unwieldy number (307) and resulted in few (only 4) final selections.

If young adult librarians want a voice in the final list, then they must use that voice responsibly. In a 1988 article, Audrey Eaglen addresses this issue. She first outlines the problems inherent with nominations that come exclusively from the committee, such as the pressure to read already-nominated titles versus the luxury to search out new suggestions; the tendency for committee members to explore favored genres and neglect books with less-personal appeal; and the temptation to nominate from those readily available, publisher-donated books in place of less-accessible titles. She then admonishes noncommittee members who deal with new titles but fail to bring them to the committee's attention:

> Those of you out there in the field are exposed to all kinds of books, hundreds, even thousands, of new titles each year, many of which are potential candidates for YASD's Best Books list. But you don't *nominate* them.
>
> And the worst offenders, in my mind, are those of you who review new books for publications or newsletters. You glibly state, at the end of your reviews, that "this book is definitely one that should make the Best Books list," and then you forget about it. It would be a lot nicer and a lot more productive if you put your money where your mouth is and take just three minutes or so to fill out and fire off a nomination form.[24]

Eaglen does not suggest that YA librarians nominate all they see, nor does she imply that they blanket the committee with numerous ballots representing traditionally neglected genres. What she encourages, and encourages quite clearly, is responsible participation from the profession: "I believe that if everyone who works with young adults and their books would get into the habit of routinely sending in a nomination for any books that cross his or her desk that appear to be of *significance* [my italics] to young adults, the pool of books from which the committee performs its task of selecting for the list would result in the kind of best book lists we'd all like to see."[25] If librarians would follow this advice, then the problem of field nominations would reverse itself and turn into a bonanza of nationwide involvement.

Committee members also must heed this advice on judicious nominating. The more books nominated, the more reading each committee member must engage in; the higher the reading demands, the less likely each title will receive the complete committee's attention. This vicious circle will collapse only if nominators carefully weigh each book's merits *before* bringing it to the attention of the committee. Joel Shoemaker, the 1994 BBYA chair, urges such consideration in this early memo to that year's committee:

Dorothy Broderick kindly sent some helpful comments I'd like to share with you:

> I think no one should nominate a book until at least two weeks have passed since finishing it. If at the end of two weeks the reader can remember the basic plot and several memorable scenes, plus the *theme*, not just the plot, of the book, then it warrants bringing to the attention of other committee members.
>
> In my experience, this approach makes sense. I have nominated books immediately after reading the last page because they simply overwhelmed me (the Ryan White autobiography comes to mind), but I have found it helpful to let nominations "cool off" for a while to see if they hold up before sending them in. We all want *best* books to be only the *best*.[26]

MEMBERSHIP ON THE COMMITTEE

By 1966 both school and public librarians enjoyed representation on the BBYA committee, but the number of total representatives varied over the years. From 1966 to 1971 membership fluctuated between seven and nine voting participants. In 1971 the committee stabilized at nine voting members, and the cumbersome nationwide balloting involving more than 100 libraries was modified to involve only a few, select sites. This smaller number of school and public librarians participated in the process by nominating throughout each year's consideration period.

During the early 1970s, the committee created five affiliate members and encouraged them to send nominations and comments for discussion. Several associates attended the Midwinter Meetings, where the final decisions now took place, and offered insightful observations and passionate pleas for certain books. According to Eleanor Pourron, committee member (1974 and 1976) and chair (1975) during this period, "These affiliates eventually evolved into more members of the committee since they felt some frustration at not being actually able to vote on titles."[27]

The addition of five members (each representing a librarian who was former ad hoc adviser) to the committee of nine would have produced an even-numbered body. Consequently, when in 1978 the affiliate members had their roles changed from advisers to full-fledged members, six additional members were added and the total number of committee members jumped to fifteen. That number stands today.

In addition to their appointed members, modern committees have relied on the services of a permanent consultant from *Booklist*. Each of the former BBYA chairs mentions the importance of that adviser. Jack Forman, 1977 chair, writes:

> I have vivid recollections of the help Barbara Duree of *Booklist* gave to the committee in terms of her book knowledge and sensible judgment. All of us had a tendency to express our feelings about a nominated title in personal terms, but Barbara very often helped to bring us back to the context of the "young adult reader"—that mysterious creature to whom this list was supposed to be directed.[28]

Duree's tenure on the committee came with her appointment as editor of Young People's Books at *Booklist* in 1954. In the beginning, she served as a full voting member, but in 1966 her status changed to that of permanent consultant. Although she remained listed as BBYA consultant in the *Handbook of Organization* until 1986, Sally Estes, present editor of Books for Youth at *Booklist*, filled in for her in 1984 and 1985 and officially took over the role when Duree retired the next year.

The importance of Sally Estes's presence equals that of Barbara Duree's. Pam Spencer, 1987 chair, comments, "The best treat of chairing BBYA was working with Sally—another quiet person who has depths of information and caring and tact and expertise."[29] Mike Printz, 1985 chair, echoes those sentiments: "I think one of the things that has to be stressed is the real input brought to many of the committees by having someone with the professionalism and the knowledge of young adult books as Sally

Estes, who served as the representative from ALA *Booklist* on our committee. Her remarks and her insight were something—will be something—that I'll always sit in deep respect of.''[30]

Not only did the number of members fluctuate but so did the duration of their appointments. From 1966 to 1971, members served three-year, renewable terms. Appointments for 1971 ran for two years; these could be repeated, thus allowing four-year terms. This system ensured that as members rotated through their tenure, no single committee would contain either all novices or all veterans. Too many of the former, according to past chairs, hampers the work of the committee since first-year members require a settling-in time to adjust to the pace and expectations. On the other hand, these chairs emphasized that while seasoned members bring experience, they also lose their intensity as the constant reading eventually takes its toll. A committee balanced in terms of experience combines the best of both worlds: the enthusiasm of freshmen and the savvy of seniors.

Over time, both the reputation of the list and member participation in YASD grew. Young adult librarians eagerly sought what they considered prized appointments for the BBYA committee. In 1984 committee member Roger Sutton suggested that this jockeying for BBYA membership may have come from "the fact that YASD has only two selection committees—'Best Books' and 'High-Interest/Low-Literacy Level Materials Evaluation'—whose primary activity is discussing and evaluating books. And, at least in the restaurants I frequent, librarians still prefer to wrangle over books than bytes.''[31]

In 1983, an ad hoc task force was created to reexamine "the charge and structure of YASD's Best Books Committee [and] to explore the committee's current effectiveness, current needs in the YA field, and possible alternatives in the committee's structure, charge, membership, voting procedures, etc.''[32] The task force recommended that the two-year terms become nonrenewable. Now, more YASD members could participate in Best Books. The first group to operate under these guidelines was the 1986 committee. It welcomed six novices, while the 1987 committee saw nine new faces.

Concern over this system quickly surfaced. A task force created in 1989 to reevaluate BBYA heard repeated charges that the committee turned over too often and that sometimes members failed to perform their duties but were not removed from the committee because of the protection of the two-year tenure. In response to these concerns, the task force recommended, and the board accepted, a revised term of appointment: Members would receive initial appointments for a one-year term, which, depending on performance, was renewable for two more years. After a five-year hiatus from the committee, former members could reapply for appointment.[33]

ROLE OF COMMITTEE MEMBERS

For bibliophiles everywhere, the job description of a committee member, to read widely in the current year's publications, sounds like a dream. During the process, though, the dream often turns into a nightmare.

Reading for BBYA means reading everything possible—not just the complete works of Dickens, a large group of suspenseful mysteries, intelligent discussions of governmental policy, or well-developed fantasies that may reflect an individual's particular taste. The books a committee member reads must include first, all those titles that show promise for the list, and second, all books nominated by someone else.

Committee members read from January to October 31 to nominate appropriate titles. Suggestions for this pool come from professional journals, from authors' reputations, and from individual hunches. First, committee members search the review media and publishers' book announcements for possibilities for nomination. Then, they must find these targeted books and read them.

Some publishers send appropriate books to each committee member. This favor simplifies the process. As Penny Jeffrey, former BBYA chair, wrote to the YASD board, "No matter where we work, some titles just do not come through in time or are in such heavy demand that it takes a long time to get them."[34]

Other publishers, particularly those involved in adult-only or small houses, do not automatically blanket the committee with their new releases. When members request books from these less-visible publishers, the YALSA office must order the books and circulate them among the committee. Remember, many nominations come from galleys, and it takes several months for even the ALA to obtain a copy of some books. Add this delay to an estimated three-week turnaround for committee members to receive, read, and return books, and the resulting small readerships, particularly for those hard-to-get titles nominated late in the year, is understandable.

Even if books are readily available, the reading demands on committee members are fierce. In 1993, for example, more than 300 books were nominated. In order to read just the nominated list, each committee member would have averaged completing 82 percent of a book each day of the year.

Noncommittee members frequently analyze the reading patterns of individuals and of the committee as a whole. Occasionally these observations produce positive comments, such as these kudos from Dorothy Broderick for the 1986 committee: "The reason the list is longer than usual is because committee members read more books and were thus in a position to vote on more titles. The committee is to be congratulated for setting a high standard of responsibility all future committees should strive to match, if not exceed."[35] More frequently, though, negative observations concerning the committee's reading habits surface whenever BBYA discussions take place. Depending on the critic, these comments will vary: members read juvenile releases over adult books; they read fiction rather than nonfiction, they read realistic fiction over science fiction; they read what publishers send instead of ferreting out less available titles. While these criticisms are sometimes valid, they must be tempered with the enormous amount of reading each committee member generally accomplishes. Following the 1989 task force guidelines for weeding out the occasional, nonproductive member, chairs evaluate each member's reading and share these observations with the President-Elect of YALSA, who makes the final committee appointments for the next year (For YALSA policies and procedures on BBYA, see the Appendix.)

Committee reading carries an extra burden, for its purpose is neither diversionary nor casual. Typically, people read with an egocentric view, looking for personal identification or meaningful information within the pages of any given book. But BBYA readers must move outside that established pattern and read with a bifurcated eye. First, each member must read like a critic, paying attention to literary standards such as language, structure, and format. Second, these members must read like young adults, looking for the elements in a particular work that will speak to that particular audience. To further complicate the matter, these individuals can't read just like the young adult they remember themselves being, such as a teenager who just devoured science fiction but ignored historical accounts or who was attracted to action but repelled by quieter works. Instead, they must read as a reluctant reader, as a fantasy maven, as an information addict, and as a young adult just looking for a good book. Conscientious committee members adopt these various roles and ask the same questions brought up in 1948: "Will it [a book] appeal to young people? Will it increase their insight into human motives and behavior, or does it distort and confuse? Will it awaken the indifferent and encourage the sympathetic reader to think on wrongs that may be righted and on the ways and means of helping people to live together harmoniously on a little globe?"[36]

Beyond these general reading demands, BBYA members must develop some system for remembering each title. Very quickly the mass of books blurs, and without careful attention to detail, typically combined with some sort of notetaking procedure, all the reading comes to naught as members try to recall the particular features of an outstanding book. In addition, they must marshal cogent arguments for and against certain titles and be prepared to present them at both the Midwinter Meeting and Annual Conference of the ALA.

These discussions remain the lifeblood of the committee. They provide a forum for members to share that which they care about so passionately—books for young adults. They bond participants who discover much about themselves and their peers when discussing issues that really matter, and they produce the list, that never-to-be-forgotten purpose of the committee. Penny Jeffrey condenses these ideas: "The wonderful thing about the committee was not only doing all that reading, but having all those intelligent, intense discussions about books. That's professional work at a level few of us can participate in very often."[37]

ROLE OF THE CHAIR

Over the years, the role of the chair has expanded from that of moderator to one involving extended correspondence and clerical duties. Eleanor Pourron, 1975 BBYA chair, recalls "I could really have used this PC back then because I remember one of my biggest headaches, as chair, was getting the lists typed and produced and sent out to everyone. We did several versions during the year with the heaviest load coming late in the year, just before January and Midwinter ALA."[38]

These duties increased. Fifteen years ago, Penny Jeffrey, 1978 chair, commented on her appointment: "I would suggest that the term of the chairperson be limited to one year. It is very time consuming and expensive for a library. In order to keep the committee informed, frequent memos are necessary. This means copies for each committee member, one for *Booklist*, and one for the Executive Secretary [of YASD]. Sending ballots out to other librarians is also a problem. Hardly a day goes by without correspondence, which is unique to any YASD committee I have ever had anything to do with."[39]

Pam Spencer, 1987 BBYA chair, adds two other important, but frequently overlooked, dimensions to that role. She states, "The role of the chair is also that of cheerleader, to push committee members to read in particular genres and about certain topics. It also involves being a Mother Hen: rounding up nominations, sending out books, encouraging wide reading, and looking out for a variety of concerns."[40]

By the mid-1980s, the volunteer position of chair had mushroomed into a near full-time job. Chairs compiled nominations, served as a conduit channeling books to committee members, communicated with the committee, arranged meeting times for both Annual Conference and the Midwinter Meeting, spoke at various professional functions, and wrote to publishers and publicists informing them of the status of their nominated books. Just the duties involved with the last function could keep an experienced, full-time secretary busy several days a week. For example, by 1988, 248 books were nominated for the list. Of those 248 books, 78 came from various publishers or distinct imprints. Not only did Eugene LaFaille, the 1988 chair, have to write to these publishers and their representatives from both juvenile and adult departments but also he had to find out who in the ever-changing world of publishing to contact in each house. Add this to the responsibility of reading, and the chair's job quickly becomes an all-consuming monster.

The 1989 task force considered several solutions, including establishing the chair as a nonvoting committee member. Finally, however, they recommended, and the YALSA Board approved, the addition of a nonvoting, administrative assistant to the committee.[41] Although this person's role is currently evolving, the position includes administrative duties such as sending out notifications of nominated titles to publishers, keeping nominated lists up to date, tabulating straw votes throughout the year, double checking publication dates and bibliographic data, and counting final votes at Midwinter.[42] (See the Appendix for additional information.)

ANNOTATING BOOKS AND PREPARING THE BROCHURE

Not only does the committee select a group of books for the list but also it annotates them for a yearly brochure. Originally this annotated list appeared in the *NEA Journal*. By 1966 both the *Top of the News* and *Booklist* reprinted it. In 1981 *Top of the News* adopted the practice repeated in other professional publications, such as *School Library Journal*, of simply announcing the final titles. At present, *Booklist* stands as the only journal to reproduce the full, annotated list.

The annual BBYA brochure, with its snappy annotations, minimal bibliographic information, and appealing covers, addresses the young adults for whom the list is designed. This practice started with the 1979 task force. "Adults working with young people might wish to know such information as the intended audience of a book, the difficulty of reading, and the maturity level. These items, and others, may well be covered in some of the other printed reviews of most of the titles appearing on any list, and potential purchasers might be advised to check unfamiliar titles in other reviewing media."[43] These same concerns, about whom the list serves, surfaced with the 1989 task force. That group agreed to retain the established focus and continue the practice of not including suggested age or reading levels.

For many years, committee members left conference after a marathon reading and voting period and returned their annotations to Evelyn Shaevel (Executive Director of YASD) several days later, an onerous process somewhat akin to paying off your charge card a few months after you've enjoyed a meal. In 1985 Mike Printz suggested that the committee change the procedure by adding a meeting following all book discussion. This meeting was dedicated to tabulating the final vote and writing annotations. Through this system, committee members bought valuable time to distance themselves from the intensity of the previous days and to think undisturbed about their individual votes. After the votes were taken, they then had time to prepare the annotations before leaving conference, thus making the announcement available for the March 15 edition of *Booklist* (a month earlier than before).

Although this morning meeting reduced the final voting frenzy, the committee still worked under pressure to prepare annotations that would grab the young adult audience. This process frequently requires that members look at books in different ways, for the strengths they respect that place a book on the list are often not the elements that give it instant YA appeal. Sometimes they get it wrong. Once the committee sent little sister (*Little Sister*, BBYA 1983) to Singapore, a trip that caught the author completely by surprise.[44] Avi discovered another mistake in the annotation for *Wolf Rider*, and gently reminded the committee, "If you have occasion to republish your brochure, you might want to note that the book's protagonist is named Andy, not Jay."[45]

The brochure cover shed its 1950s line drawing for a bolder look in 1966. This dramatic design, a simple broad-lined border with the name of the list appearing in the lower right corner, held for three years. In 1969 it was replaced with a splatter-paint logo reminiscent of the popular tie-dying of the period. For three successive years the brochure sported the same design but altered color combinations annually.

The 1970s push for more youth participation resulted in annual brochures designed by teenagers. As Eleanor Pourron explained: "One place where we encouraged student participation was in the cover art for the list. For many years it was standard practice to encourage school and public librarians to seek student artwork for the cover. This artwork was then displayed at the committee discussions, and a choice was made, by the committee, on the cover art for that year's list. Entries did not pour in, and it was usually hard work to get the few entries that we did."[46]

The 1986 committee broke the fourteen-year tradition of having a young adult design the brochure cover for technical reasons: frequently the most appealing covers didn't reproduce well, and ALA's graphics department could provide a consistency in design and appeal frequently sacrificed with individual entries. Despite some isolated problems (in 1992, for instance, one title did not appear in an early brochure), production and printing remains the joint responsibility of the graphics department and YALSA. (See Part opener pages for selected brochure examples.)

SUMMARY

Over the years, the list has been the product of ten separate committees and has appeared under seven names. Changes in both charge and constituency have evolved over time. In all probability, the present system will be altered in the future. But that's the strength of the committee and the strength of the list. Both respond to current trends, both adapt to new situations, and both reflect the committee's charge: "to select from the year's publications those adult and young adult books significant for young adults."

Notes

1. Michael C. Madden, "An Analysis of the American Library Association's Annual List 'Best Books for Young Adults,' 1930–1967" (Master's thesis, University of Chicago, 1967), 3.
2. Madden, "An Analysis," 4.
3. Ken Donelson and Alleen Pace Nilsen, *Literature for Today's Young Adults* (Chicago: Scott, Foresman, 1980), 2.
4. Madden, "An Analysis," 5.
5. Margaret Ward, letter to Young People's Reading Round Table Committee, 19 July 1945, in Madden, "An Analysis," 6.
6. Winifred B. Jackson, "Selecting Adult Books for Young People," *Top of the News* 5 (Dec. 1948): 5.
7. Jackson, "Selecting Adult Books for Young People," 5–6.
8. Jackson, "Selecting Adult Books for Young People," 5.
9. Jackson, "Selecting Adult Books for Young People," 6, 31.
10. American Library Association, Press Release, 2 Feb. 1955, in Madden, "An Analysis," 9.
11. Madden, "An Analysis," 11.
12. Elaine Simpson, letter to Audrey Biel, 21 Jan. 1964.
13. Charles Carner, American Library Association Press Release, 1 Mar. 1964.
14. "Major Activities of the YASD Board," *Journal of Youth Services in Libraries* 4 (Fall 1990): 8.
15. Washington State Young Adult Review Group (WASHYARG), letter to YALSA Board, 24 Feb. 1993.
16. Mary Ruth Metcalf Cary, "An Analysis of the Critical Reception and the Age Level Designations for the 1993 Best Books for Young Adults List" (Professional paper, Texas Woman's University, 1993), 48.
17. Cary, "An Analysis of the Critical Reception," 36.
18. Deborah Taylor, letter to Betty Carter, 23 Apr. 1993.
19. Eleanor Pourron and Sue Tait, letter to YASD Board, 10 Jan. 1979.
20. Jerri Baker, letter to Jan Freeman, 19 May 1979.
21. "Letters," *Top of the News* 36 (Fall 1979): 18.

22. American Library Association, *ALA Handbook of Organization, 1972–73* (Chicago: American Library Association, 1973), 1087.

23. American Library Association, *ALA Handbook of Organization, 1973–74* (Chicago: American Library Association, 1974), 47.

24. Audrey B. Eaglen, "A Pox on Some of Your Houses," *School Library Journal* 34 (Jan. 1988): 45.

25. Eaglen, "A Pox," 45.

26. Joel Shoemaker, letter to 1994 BBYA Committee Members, 26 Mar. 1993.

27. Eleanor Pourron, letter to Betty Carter, 25 Mar. 1993.

28. Jack Forman, letter to Betty Carter, 15 Apr. 1993.

29. Pam Spencer, letter to Betty Carter, 12 May 1993.

30. Mike Printz, letter to Betty Carter, 20 Apr. 1993.

31. Roger Sutton, "Best Books for Young Adults," *School Library Journal* 30 (Mar. 1984): 125.

32. American Library Association, *ALA Handbook of Organization, 1983–84* (Chicago: American Library Association, 1974), 144.

33. "Major Activities of the YALSA Board," *Journal of Youth Services in Libraries* 5 (Fall 1991): 9.

34. Penny Jeffrey, letter to YASD Board of Directors, 19 Dec. 1978.

35. Dorothy M. Broderick, "Here's News," *VOYA* 10 (Apr. 1987): 6.

36. Jackson, "Selecting Adult Books for Young People," 31.

37. Penny Jeffrey, letter to Betty Carter, 15 Apr. 1993.

38. Pourron, letter to Carter, 25 Mar. 1993.

39. Jeffrey, letter to YASD Board, 19 Dec. 1978.

40. Pam Spencer, telephone interview by Betty Carter, 21 May 1993.

41. "Major Activities of the YALSA Board," *Journal of Youth Services in Libraries* 5 (Fall 1991): 9.

42. Young Adult Library Services Association, *A Manual for the Chair of the Best Books for Young Adults Committee* (Chicago: Young Adult Library Services Association, n.d.), 9.

43. Pourron and Tait, letter to YASD Board, Chicago, 10 Jan. 1979.

44. Margaret Gaan, letter to Evelyn Shaevel, 23 Nov. 1984.

45. Avi, letter to Evelyn Shaevel, 23 May 1987.

46. Pourron, letter to Carter, 25 Mar. 1993.

The Consultants Speak Out

A CONVERSATION WITH BARBARA DUREE AND SALLY ESTES

Although the collective members of the various committees have given BBYA its heart, the permanent *Booklist* consultants, first Barbara Duree (Young Adult Books editor, *Booklist*, 1953 to 1987) and then Sally Estes (who began as a reviewer for *Booklist* in 1965, became the Young Adult Books editor in 1987, and the Books for Youth editor in 1990), have maintained its stability and its memory. In May of 1993, with partial funding from the School of Library and Information Studies at Texas Woman's University, I went to Chicago to study the BBYA archives and to interview these two committee constants. Barbara and Sally feel passionate about young adults and their reading, and they enjoy a strong friendship based on mutual respect and common interests. Barbara and Sally lend a special perspective to the past and present workings of BBYA, for, between the two of them, they've truly "seen it all."

CARTER   *The archives indicate a strong connection between* Booklist *and BBYA. At one time the list responded to perceived weaknesses in* Booklist *policy, and at others it appears to complement the journal. Were you always a member of the BBYA Committee?*

DUREE   Yes, and that's interesting because ALA staff members were not supposed to be on committees. So there I was, sort of an honorary member. But, for years and years, I voted. Then there was a big uproar about how much influence ALA and, specifically, *Booklist*, was having on the Best Books List,

Conversation between Sally Estes (left) and Barbara Duree (right)—bibliophiles and cat lovers—flowed freely and covered a myriad of topics.

and I was ambivalent about my role. I really honestly felt I shouldn't vote. On the other hand, it was awfully good motivation to read everything.

CARTER   *I never realized that you were a voting member.*

DUREE   For eleven years. When I first came [to *Booklist*], one of the responsibilities of the Young People's Books editor was being on the Best Books Committee.

CARTER   *Why did you stay on after the committee decided you would no longer have a vote?*

DUREE   I chose to stay. I enjoyed helping create something.

ESTES   I think they [the committee] wanted you to stay.

DUREE   Nobody ever suggested that I depart.

CARTER   *I have written to all of the past chairs, asking them to share what they thought was important to the committee. To a person, every single one mentions your respective influence. I did receive one repeated complaint, though, probably the only one I'll ever see concerning Sally. Committee chairs said they wanted to hear more from her on the committee. How do you see your roles as advisers?*

DUREE   I really made an honest effort not to influence people. This is a committee where there's a lot of politicking and pressure. People get upset, . . . and I always felt that in my position it behooved me not to try to influence anybody. I thought my second duty was to keep discussions on an amicable, objective basis so people didn't hurt one another's feelings. You can offer objective criticism without being cutesy and . . .

ESTES   And personal.

DUREE   And personal. I have seen members in tears because of something somebody said.

ESTES   I haven't seen that. Most of the heated discussions I've seen have ended amiably. It's been the kind of discussion where members agree to disagree: They don't agree with each other, but they respect each other's opinion.

DUREE   I think that's true. We had some good discussions of books. People read and people were knowledgeable.

ESTES   There still are. This last year in Denver [Midwinter, 1993] the committee was "putting down" a lot of adult fiction, thinking kids wouldn't read it. Finally one committee member spoke up and said, "A lot of you are working in junior highs. But you've got to remember that this list includes seventeen- and eighteen-year-olds. You can't consider these books just for your own kids in junior high. Remember the older kids." And, by George, that turned the committee around, and that's the reason Alice Hoffman and a couple of other adult books got on the list. People started thinking, "Yes, I'm not dealing with seventeen- and eighteen-year-olds, but seventeen- and eighteen-year-olds will read these books." A comment like that from a committee member is good. It reminds me that Barbara said to me when I first came to *Booklist*: "You have to stop thinking about your collection at Dallas Public Library and your clientele. You can't do that. You have to think about a whole nation of kids." I've never forgotten that.

DUREE   I did?

ESTES   That's been my guiding light, Barbara! You should remember that. And I think that's what the committee has to do. They've got to think of both ends of the list and not be provincial.

DUREE   That's why you have committee members from different parts of the country, from different types of libraries, and from junior high and high school.

CARTER   *There was a note somewhere in one of the old files that mentioned a taboo of comparing books. Where did that come from, Barbara?*

DUREE   I don't know. The committee thought they shouldn't compare books.

ESTES   Were they to look at the book in a vacuum?

DUREE   Why not compare books? We should compare books—other books that have already been on or not been on.

ESTES   The committee still says, "I know I'm not supposed to compare books, but . . ." And then they go ahead and do it.

DUREE   But we should compare books. It's a part of the evaluation process. How do we know if one's better than another if we don't compare it with something else, either verbally or literally?

ESTES   I agree. I'm sure all the committee members, as they're reading and thinking about these books, are comparing them to other books that they're using with kids, other books that are in their collections, other books that have been nominated.

CARTER   *What do you think about audience participation in discussions?*

ESTES   I remember one impassioned plea for *Weetzie Bat.* I think this came from Patrick Jones. There's not that much discussion now. People come and read their kids' comments.

DUREE   Do they allow young people to speak at the discussions?

ESTES   Some have come in.

DUREE   This is a new development.

ESTES   Cathi [MacRae] brought her kids to Denver. A number spoke up, quite articulately, and the committee appreciated it. But the committee didn't vote on every book they wanted on the list.

DUREE   Aren't most kids going to be vastly influenced by each other? And for the two or three leaders in the group who say, "Hey, this book is great," there are going to be half a dozen other kids say, "Yeah, it is great," whether they would have said so individually or not. If you rely too heavily on young adult readers, how are you going to take into consideration the kids that don't get on that kind of committee because they're not reading enthusiastically?

ESTES   These kids will also not have read everything on the nomination list. They will have picked and chosen what they wanted to read. Or they may have been forced to read a nominated book by their librarian. But they don't have the balance of having read as widely as committee members.

DUREE   I agree with the input, but I don't see, with as little time as you have to gather everything together before the meetings are over, how much time you could devote to it.

CARTER   *I do know that there were times when the committee would specifically ask somebody to find out if there were readers for books like Margaret Atwood's* Handmaid's Tale, *where audience is a real problem.*

ESTES   For that kind of book you need to get a kid's response, because that is a very adult book. We think there are kids who are going to read and love that kind of book, but we can't be sure.

CARTER   *Were publishers always present for the discussions?*

DUREE   No, not always. I think publishers became more and more interested in being there when they discovered how important that list was to their sales.

ESTES   Well, of course, when the list first started out, when it was "Significant [or] Important Adult Books for Young Adults," the adult publishers didn't care. I think publishers probably started attending the discussions—now I wasn't there at that time, it was Barbara's bailiwick—when the committee began including juvenile books or young adult books.

CARTER   *Did publishers ever have any verbal input into the committee, or have they always attended as silent observers?*

DUREE   To my knowledge they've always been silent observers. The input they had, and again this was a big discussion, was whether or not they should be allowed to blanket members of the committee with books to consider.

Should committee members be allowed to accept books from publishers? There was a big, big discussion about that because some publishers gave everything, and some publishers were slow publishers, or didn't know about the committee, and didn't send anything. The duty I always had was rushing off to a library or to a bookstore to get a copy of something for everybody to read.

It also depends on how many committee members you have. We once had eight or nine committee members, but now that's practically doubled. If you're a small publisher, that could be a substantial number of review copies.

ESTES   That's a problem because these small presses cannot afford to print gigantic numbers of books. A lot of the review media don't cover the small presses. We never got for review *The Origin of Life on Earth: An African Creation Myth*, the book that won the Coretta Scott King Award for illustration, at *Booklist*. When we got a copy because we needed to use the illustration in our announcement, we saw that it was beautiful. We would have loved to have reviewed it. We've been in touch with the publisher and said, "If you do any more, be sure you send them to us."

CARTER   *I really wonder if we're doing readers a favor by putting a book with a print run of 1,300 copies on a major, national list? I don't think the large publishers should own the list, but I do remember one book we included in 1986 by John Fante (1933 Was a Bad Year) was published by a small press, and librarians simply couldn't get copies of it.*

ESTES   According to Charles Ferry, author and self-publisher of *Binge*, we are. He called and wanted to know if his was the first self-published book that had ever made Best Books. I went to the library and turned the question over to them.

DUREE   Another interesting point is to what extent distributors handle some of these small-press books. If a book is on a list, librarians must be able to order it. That's another consideration.

CARTER   *What particular books do you remember from your stint on BBYA?*

DUREE   I'll never forget Kin Platt's *Headman*. This book came up when I was still a voting member. I reluctantly voted for it because it would be a good book for reluctant readers. They only had to know about three or four words, and if they knew them, they could read it.

CARTER   *What kinds of differences have you seen with the books over the years? In your speech to the Still Alive in '75 Preconference, you talked about adult versus young adult books in particular.*

DUREE   And fiction versus nonfiction. The list became increasingly juvenile and increasingly fiction.

ESTES   I haven't done a real study since 1975, but my feeling is that, for the most part, except maybe when Mike Printz was on and was really pushing adult books, the list has been more juvenile fiction than anything else.

CARTER   *Of course, there are more juvenile books being published.*

DUREE   During the last couple of years, it seemed to me there was a preponderance of juvenile fiction that didn't need to be on any list. Is this list to promote reading among kids, or is it a buying guide for small libraries? Actually, of course, it's both.

CARTER   *In choosing best books, how do you define* best?

DUREE   When I was doing a study [for the Still Alive in '75 Preconference], it was fascinating to me to see the number of "Best" books from twenty-five years ago that kids were still reading twenty-five, thirty years after they had been on the list. I thought, "Well, there are some that really lasted and didn't go out of date." They were still popular, still in collections, still on New York Public Library's recommended *Books for the Teen Age*. That leads straight to the $64 question. For the purpose of this business, "best" should not be just popular. It seems to me you always start out with quality and then go to appeal. Quality should take priority. It's why you're doing this, for heaven's sake.

ESTES   Any librarian on the floor is trying to make readers out of kids. We may start them off with something simple, but we're trying to move them up into more sophisticated reading. And this is what this kind of list should do. We have to have a wide range because we have our reluctant readers who are reading *Headman*, and we have the more sophisticated ones who are reading *Handmaid's Tale*. What we're trying to choose for this list are the books that have quality and something to offer. They're not just light fluff. They have, I don't want to say "a message," but they have a certain significance or value. There are so many fantasies, so many science books, so many of every kind of book. What we're looking for is the best. There are so many whodunits that you read like you eat popcorn, that don't belong on the list. But then there is Mary Higgins Clark's best. That's where we want to move young adults to from Nancy Drew.

DUREE   There's another best in my mind, and it's not the best individual book. The list ought to reflect a variety of interests. I don't think we ought to have six teenage romances or twenty sports books. We ought to have one or two adult science, one or two historical, one or two adult fiction. The list itself ought to reflect a variety of interests and tastes.

CARTER   *I remember the first year I sat on the committee, Sally nominated a book that was a romance. It was a Regency romance, and a pretty good one at that. Committee members said, "What are we doing? This is not that wonderful." But it was a solid nomination for that genre.*

ESTES   Genre is low on the totem pole. But there's always room for romance.

CARTER   *How should the committee evaluate books that are published on high-demand topics? Should they treat the first book out on Bosnia or the Branch Davidians or a novel with previously neglected ethnic characters any differently from other books?*

DUREE   You ask, "Is it any good?" If the answer is no, then you wait for something that is authentic or worth reading. Let us not forget that magazines and newspapers have information on a topic. It doesn't have to be between the covers of a book—until it's a good book.

ESTES   Publishers hurried a lot of books out on the Persian Gulf War, but there's not one on the [Best] list.

DUREE   You wait till a good book comes along and you slap your knee and say "Thank God, it's here!"

ESTES   I agree.

CARTER   *How do you react when* Booklist *rejects make Best Books?*

ESTES   It's a rare list that doesn't contain a *Booklist* reject.

DUREE   The first thing I always did [after each Midwinter Meeting] was to go through the list to see how many books were included that *Booklist* had not recommended. And it's never been more than one or two, three at most.

CARTER   *What's your feeling about that?*

DUREE   Well, I would think that we're not doing a decent job at *Booklist* if there were a whole lot of books on the list that we hadn't recommended.

CARTER   *What about the reverse? What happens when you think a book is just super and the committee completely rejects it?*

DUREE   I remember Peter Beagle's *The Last Unicorn*. I thought it was such a delightful, lovely book. And the committee said, "Aaack."

CARTER   *What does that do to you?*

DUREE   You just go on.

ESTES   I don't expect to like every book the committee likes, either. Every year there's the list. It's a good list. There are many books on that I like, there are books on it I don't think should be on the list, there are books that I think should be on that weren't. I'm sure every committee member feels the same way.

DUREE   The important thing is that there is a list and that all these books are discussed. This committee and the discussions of this committee have done something to raise the level of juvenile publishing. Some of the editors come to those meetings and hear their books torn apart, or hear their books praised, and think, "Hey, got to remember that."

CARTER   *We've talked about adult and young adult fiction and nonfiction. Should there be separate lists?*

ESTES   I'd hate to see that. There are kids who are geared strictly to one or the other. And if they gravitated to just one or the other list, they might miss a chance to cross over—a nonfiction reader might miss a good fiction book, a fiction reader might miss *Adrift*. If they are introduced to these books, they might read something they wouldn't read otherwise.

DUREE   And a good book is a good book is a good book. I am no car racing enthusiast or horse racing enthusiast or art connoisseur or a million other things. But there are books in all these fields I could read and enjoy if they were well done and interesting. They might be on a subject I didn't really care about or knew nothing about. I'm no science fiction fan, but when a really good science fiction book comes along, I can enjoy it tremendously.

ESTES   And I think that's what it comes down to with a good book.

CARTER   *Should the committee consider every nominated book throughout the year, or should it be able to withdraw nominations?*

DUREE   This is backtracking, but did you know that books were once voted on at regular periods, and that we had a vast process of elimination? We grouped books into nonfiction science, nonfiction sports, Gothic romance, mystery, science fiction. And four, five, or six times during a year, members would get these lists of books, and they would read and vote. That eliminated many books before the committee met.

CARTER   *The latest task force talked about instituting some sort of elimination system.*

ESTES   Now a committee member who nominates a book can withdraw the nomination.

DUREE   That's sensible.

ESTES   But that doesn't mean someone else can't nominate it again.

CARTER   *What do you think would be the ideal membership on BBYA?*

DUREE   Nine members would be just fine. People in the field could feed to these nine committee members a whole bunch of nominations that [committee members] may not make themselves. Then that smaller group would be responsible for reading and discussing and making the final decisions. That seems better to me.

CARTER   *What about committee members being on BBYA for long periods of time?*

DUREE   There are two sides to that coin. I've always wondered whether people wanted to be on the committee because they loved books and enjoyed it and wanted to promote what they thought was best or whether they wanted to go up the ladder in YASD and get free copies from the publishers. There are always several good and bad reasons for everything. But finally YASD decided to let people get back on after they'd been off for a year.

ESTES   They're doing that now.

DUREE   The experience means a lot, too. People did a lot better the second or third year because they knew the ropes.

ESTES   Sometimes people flounder their first year. They've heard how much work it is, but until you actually have to deal with it, nobody knows what it's like. If four years—two two-year terms—is too long for people, then maybe each appointment should be a three-year term with one-third of the committee rolling over every year.

CARTER   *That's pretty much the system starting with the present [1994] committee.*

ESTES   Yes, but it hasn't really had a chance. This allows the chair to have two years of experience before he or she becomes a chair, which is important.

CARTER   *What do you remember as perennial problems for the committee?*

DUREE The time element, and I'm sure that's still true now that they've [YALSA] increased the number of librarians, the number of meetings and the length of the meetings. But the more people you have, the longer the discussions, the longer the list, the more time it takes. And when you get to the end, to that last night, everybody's frantic, everybody's staying up all night reading books. Then there's this criticism: the books people read the last night don't get a fair shake because everybody's too tired to think about what they're doing. I'll say one thing, it was never dull.

CARTER *Did you have that problem of committee members not reading the books? I always thought that was a problem that came with list length.*

DUREE It got worse with length obviously. If there were sixty, seventy books to read, then fine.

ESTES I've heard chairs over the years exhort people not to leave all the books they think they don't want to read till the last minute but to weave them in. Read something you really like, then pick up something you think you're not going to like as much. If you read a short book, make your next book a long book. And I think that is something individual committee members have to make themselves do. The committee's charge is to read the nominations. If you leave everything you don't want to read till the last minute, that's going to be sheer hell.

CARTER *What can be done about the amount of reading? It really is impossible.*

ESTES I wish I knew a way to whittle it down. We're making a stab at it now, with the person who nominated a book able to withdraw a nomination. But if someone has nominated something and feels strongly about it, even if a lot of others hate it, then it's not going to be withdrawn.

DUREE The only logical way—logic doesn't always work—but the only logical way is to have the criteria so clear and so impressed upon people that we cut down the numbers by the necessary qualifications. If we say: "You must not nominate a book just because it is by a popular young adult author. You should not nominate a book just because somebody in your library has read and loved it. You should not nominate a book that is so highly specialized that nobody will read it. You should not nominate a book that's really pretty trashy." Is there any way that books can be eliminated by virtue of the criteria?

CARTER *What do you think, Sally?*

ESTES Well, that one on the popular young adult author will have to be spelled out a little more clearly.

DUREE What about limiting the number of books a committee member could nominate? Say, "Look, friend, you're on this committee, and you cannot nominate more than twenty books. You'd better pick out your best twenty."

CARTER *That really is an interesting approach.*

DUREE Committee members tend to say, "I think this is pretty good, but I don't know; I'll see what somebody else thinks about it." Or, and I did this myself, "I'm not sure that this ought to go on, but I think it should be discussed."

CARTER   *I was guilty of that. Working with the committee seemed like the chance of a lifetime to listen to well-read professionals discuss some of the issues certain books raised. I wanted to know what others thought about a certain book.*

DUREE   That's right. But those books shouldn't be taking up committee members' time. I think you ought to nominate a book that you honestly feel should go on that list, not one that you'd like to hear somebody talk about.

ESTES   Committee chairs in recent years have told the committee, "Don't nominate a book as soon as you read it. Put it aside and let it sit, and a week later see if you still feel as strongly about it." You can read a book and get through with it and think, "Oh, that's the best book I've ever read and one I'm going to nominate." Then by the time you get around to discussing it, you can't even remember it.

CARTER   *When did the nominations become so big?*

DUREE   The last couple of years I was there, when you [Sally] weren't on, is when it began. I would tell Sally, "They have 125 books on this list they're trying to discuss. We can't discuss all these books." That was the transition time when we saw more and more nominations.

ESTES   Since I've been going to the committee, there have been a lot. It's been close to 200, then it inched over 200. This year it was over 300. The committee does get a lot of field nominations. I know I've always tried to nominate adult titles, mainly because I feel that I see them more often than the committee does.

DUREE   You could have two committees. One to deal with adult books and one to deal with juvenile books. And they could each meet and do their critique at the same time with their list of nominations, and then put the results together.

ESTES   There has been talk of dividing the list into adult and juvenile, but not combining them.

DUREE   You could even interlace them. You needn't separate them after they were done. But it would cut down on the number of nominations in each category, and the number of books to be read by each committee member.

CARTER   *There's been talk of splitting up, but it's always been with the idea that each committee will retain its own final list.*

DUREE   In a certain way you'd have a more valid list in each area because each committee member would be thinking in terms of that group of books. They wouldn't be comparing this M. E. Kerr with that Mary Higgins Clark. They would be comparing all the juvenile books ("this is the best of this year's juvenile stuff") and another group would be comparing all the adult books looking for what has appeal for young people.

ESTES   Two committees with nine members?

DUREE   You've got it. It might be worth a trial run. We've got to cut down on the reading to be fair to the books. People have to be able to read them in a reasonable atmosphere, with a reasonable absence of pressure. And in order to do that, you've got to cut down on numbers.

CARTER   *What final thoughts would you like to share?*

ESTES   Best Books for Young Adults is a valuable experience for committee members. They see what's published in a year. The members become experts on young adult literature. The committee promotes an interest in members in keeping up with reading the new books and shows them what is available. Since members are also reading reviews, they can see how accurately the reviews reflect the books. It keeps the consultants' feet on the ground, as we get tremendous feedback on what kids are reading and how books are being used with kids.

DUREE   I agree. Times change, and membership on the committee enables members to see changes in young adult interests and in publishing for young adults. The committee provides good training in formulating and articulating one's views. It becomes easier for members to speak publicly. In a time when so much emphasis is placed on video games and computers, anything that promotes better books and more reading is all to the good.

Issues

A lthough the mechanics of the Best Books for Young Adults committee, such as number of members, length of term, and voting procedures, presently appear as stable as those for any body of the American Library Association, several issues continue to plague the committee. These include the characteristics of the list, the length of the final list, and the role of young adults in book selection. None will be resolved in the near future, for each represents important theoretical considerations that divide the Young Adult Library Services Association members. Still, these issues warrant ongoing attention, and healthy debate underscores the seriousness with which the profession takes the list, young adult literature, and young adult readers.

CHARACTERISTICS OF THE LIST

Any historical examination of BBYA reflects changes in the business of publishing, charges to the committee, definition of audience, and concerns of society. Because of these and other influences, observed trends in BBYA lists do not stand as pure indicators of trends in either young adult literature or reading preferences. Still, a few noticeable characteristics of the lists deserve mention.

The most obvious, and frequently remarked upon, characteristic concerns the ratio of adult titles to young adult titles. The percentage of adult books appearing on BBYA has steadily declined since 1966. (See figure 2.) Like all other historical observations about the lists, this one deserves elaboration.

Prior to 1973, the committee officially considered only adult releases for inclusion on BBYA, although a few young adult books appeared on

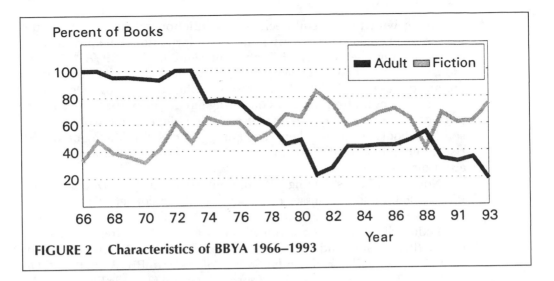

FIGURE 2   Characteristics of BBYA 1966–1993

pre-1973 lists. Figures indicating the percentage of adult books on early lists are high, while those numbers naturally drop after the 1973 change.

Without taking into account the eligibility of young adult books, some BBYA critics have used these declining numbers of adult books to conclude that the committee has dumbed down annual lists by including more and more juvenile titles. In addition, such critics fail to consider that many books once classified as adult would today be defined as young adult. Some titles such as Ann Head's *Mr. and Mrs. Bo Jo Jones* or Jean Thompson's *The House of Tomorrow*, both of which made the 1967 list, were published as adult books. If released today, those books would more than likely come from young adult imprints.

The decline in adult titles also reflects an increase in young adult publishing. After the groundbreaking success of S. E. Hinton's *The Outsiders* and Paul Zindel's *The Pigman* in the late 1960s (both of which failed to make BBYA lists, presumably because they originated in juvenile divisions), young adult publishing grew dramatically. Sophisticated books, such as Barbara Wersba's *Run Softly, Go Fast*, which slipped on the 1970 BBYA list, helped define this infant field as one worthy of respect and, consequently, as a genre with outstanding components deserving representation on any recommended reading list.

Another factor that led to the decline of the percentage of adult titles concerns the age-level definition of a young adult. Over the years, the range has broadened to include younger and younger adolescents. Currently, young adults are defined as those individuals between the ages of twelve and eighteen, and books recommended for them will naturally highlight more juvenile titles than did those early lists intended for teenagers between the ages of fourteen and eighteen.

Not only has BBYA changed from an almost exclusively adult list to a strongly juvenile one but it has also reversed from including mostly nonfiction books to containing a predominance of fiction titles. This trend is puzzling, especially in light of continued research that indicates that as young adults grow older, they increasingly prefer nonfiction reading selections.[1]

Along with the general decline of nonfiction selections comes the near disappearance of several kinds of informational books. How-to books, such as the *Woodstock Craftsman Manual* from BBYA 1972 and *Mother Nature's Beauty Cupboard*, which appeared the following year, are not represented in later lists. Presently, the sole acknowledgment of such books comes from volumes outlining environmental action, such as Jon Naar's 1991 selection, *Design for a Livable Planet*. On the other hand, self-help books, such as *When Your Parent Drinks Too Much*, are on the rise, although not nearly as popular as are comparable titles aimed at the adult market.

Nonfiction books dealing with the pure sciences (*The Double Helix*, BBYA 1968) appear in lesser numbers than those concerning the social sciences (*The Measure of Our Success*, BBYA 1993). Books from other nonfiction divisions, such as biographies of sports figures (*Go Up for Glory*, BBYA 1966, and *I Had a Hammer*, BBYA 1992), discussions of animal life (*The Shark: Splendid Savage of the Sea*, BBYA 1970, and *On the Wing*, BBYA 1990), and tales of pure adventure (*Time Is Short and the Water Rises*, BBYA 1967, and *Buried in Ice*, BBYA 1993) remain perennial favorites. Other nonfiction selections reflect both the concerns of society and those of young adult readers. A variety of nonfiction books about AIDS and HIV infection, ranging from pure informational texts to biographical accounts, frequently appear on more-recent lists.

Fiction increasingly dominates the list. In 1966, 33 percent of the recommended titles were fiction; in 1993, 75 percent of the books were fiction. Trends here are harder to pinpoint, for particular kinds of books will appear as strong components of one list and disappear on the following one. For example, prior to 1966, the postholocaust or doomsday novel first appeared with Neville Shute's *On the Beach* and Pat Frank's *Alas, Babylon*. While books with similar themes showed up on subsequent lists, 1985 produced a banner crop: *The Postman*, *Children of the Dust*, *Emergence*, and *Wolf of Shadows*. These selections did not mark the beginnings of a strong pattern, but rather reflected the 1984 publishing output.

General genre representation is also spotty. For instance, I tabulated those books of imaginative fiction listed from 1966 to 1993, because of vocal complaints about the lack of such books. In defining imaginative fiction, I included books of horror, ghost stories, time travel, high fantasy, and science fiction. What I discovered was that for ten years (1966, 1967, 1968, 1970, 1973, 1979, 1983, 1988, 1990, and 1993) imaginative fiction made up less than 1 percent of the final lists. For some of those early years, fiction representation in general was slight. Other years, though, contained strong showings of imaginative fiction consistently representing more than 10 percent of the list. In addition, lists from 1969 and 1982 show more than 27 percent of the total books as imaginative fiction.

Similar incidences occur throughout the history of the list. One year will feature historical fiction, another year realistic fiction, and another year science fiction. The next year, these genres will be replaced by mysteries, romances, and adventure, while the following year the selections will skew to either male or female readers. What BBYA fiction does represent, overall, is precisely what young adults tell us they want to read: good books.

LENGTH OF THE LIST

As the BBYA committee grew over the years, so did the number of recommended books. In 1966 twenty-seven titles were designated "the best," in 1976 the number had grown to thirty-nine, and by 1986 mushroomed to sixty-nine. (See Part Two: The Books by Year.)

Early attempts to limit the number of books proved unpopular, although an informal agreement to keep the recommendations between forty and fifty titles held until 1983. Prior to that time if more than fifty books were chosen, the committee faced the unwelcome challenge of eliminating some titles, a process dubbed "Wednesday night's massacre" by Jerry Stevens, a 1979 participant. Joni Bodart, chair of the 1980 committee, outlined these painful procedures:

> By the time the last meeting arrives, everyone is tense and exhausted after four nights of only three or four hours sleep. Now all the books that can be read have been read. The number of titles receiving eight or more votes is counted to see how many must be removed to make the list the required length. (Eight affirmative votes are necessary to put a book on the list, and traditionally the list ranges from about forty to fifty titles.) Everyone agrees that this is the worst part of the procedure. It is much easier to build a list than to cut it down. Each person painfully makes up a list of the five or ten or fifteen books he or she would vote to keep off the list. The number depends on how many titles need to be taken off and varies from year to year. Since they can vote, as always, only on titles that they've read, all members must now vote against titles they have spent several days fighting for. Usually the first five are not too hard, but the second group is excruciating. Everyone must vote five times.
>
> The last round takes place in silence. No comments from observers and no verbal protests from committee members are allowed. It's hard enough as it is to vote against the books you like—having to defend your choices would make it impossible. However, when a hotly contested item gets only three or four negative votes, there are smiles and sighs of relief. Disappointment is registered only with slumped shoulders, barely whispered "Oh no's," and the exchange of mutually despairing, defeated glances. But no one says anything.
>
> The negative votes are counted, titles are crossed off, and another vote is taken if more need to be removed. Finally, it's done. The list is finished. At last.[2]

The elimination of this step may have come as a result of the 1983 task force, but concern about the length of the list remained. By the mid-1980s, books receiving eight "yes" votes from the committee automatically made and remained on the final list.

When yet another task force was created in 1989 to reexamine the committee, its procedures, and its charge, one concern that reappeared was with the length of the list. On the one hand, a longer list allowed for more books from a variety of genres and addressed a variety of YA tastes and needs, while on the other hand, a longer list appeared less selective and diluted the concept of "best." Members of the task force examined voting records from the previous five years to see how BBYA composition would have been altered had nine and ten positive votes been required to put a book on the list. Concerned that requiring a two-thirds majority of ten votes for selection would eliminate the bulk of adult titles, nonfiction entries, and science fiction/fantasy recommendations but satisfied that establishing a nine-vote minimum would not, the task force recommended that the number of positive votes required for selection be increased from eight to nine.

The 1993 BBYA committee was the first to operate under these guidelines. Its list consisted of 97 titles, the longest ever in the history of BBYA. Not surprisingly, this list prompted complaints concerning merit of individual titles and quality of overall selections. What must be remembered in making such judgments is that any BBYA list is dependent on the quality of publications of any given year. Was 1992 a banner year in young adult literature, or did the list, in fact, recognize mediocre titles?

Mary Cary, high school librarian from Abilene, Texas, attempted to answer this question. She took the final selections from the 1993 list and looked at how each individual title was received by five major review journals: *Booklist*, *The Horn Book*, *Kirkus*, *School Library Journal*, and *VOYA*.[3]

One title, Doug Marlette's *In Your Face: A Cartoonist at Work*, was not reviewed by at least one of these journals. Ninety-two of the remaining books all received positive reviews from at least one of the sources. Three books (*Crossing Blood*, *Is Kissing a Girl Who Smokes Like Licking an Ashtray?*, and *Yaxley's Cat*) received a single negative review, while six other titles (*My Father the Nutcase*, *Binge*, *Crossing Blood*, *Bardic Voices*, *The Last Pendragon*, and *Where the Road Ends*) were not covered in *Booklist*, which in effect indicates a negative reception. In addition, fifteen (62.5 percent) of the twenty-four nonfiction titles and forty-seven (64 percent) of the seventy-three fiction titles received special recognition (a star in *Booklist*, *The Horn Book*, and *School Library Journal*; a pointer in *Kirkus*; a 5 Q [Quality] or 5 P [Popularity] in *VOYA*; and a boxed or focus review in *Booklist*). Almost a third of the titles (thirty books) received special recognition from more than one journal.

What these figures show, and show quite clearly, is that although the 1993 list was long, it was not necessarily indiscriminate, nor did it promote books generally discarded by the review media. Instead, the lengthy 1993 list might well reflect an honest attempt to address the multiple needs of all those young adults that the committee wished to serve.

Concentrating on the complexity of the audience, rather than the numbers of books on a particular list, former BBYA member Matthew Kollasch states: "I have never been too concerned about the length of the list because I thought, perhaps naively so, that there could be 80 to 90 'best' books for that ever-diverse 12- to 18-year-old age group."[4] Still, the question remains: How many best books are there? Joel Shoemaker, 1994 chair, offers this observation:

> At one end of the spectrum, "best" implies one book, a winner, a single book that stands alone as the ultimate example of the writer's art. ("That was the best pie I've ever eaten" or "He got the best grade in the class.") This position suggests that an absolute standard exists against which every other book can be compared. To these people [who hold with this definition], each additional title added to the list necessarily represents a diminution in quality and dereliction of duty.

To other minds, "best" suggests any book that's better than the average or the norm. ("Her paintings are all beautiful, but the best ones are from the sixties.") For these folks, standards are relative, and the more "bests" there are, the merrier.

Granting that each of the fifteen BBYA committee members falls somewhere along the continuum between the two extremes described above, five additional factors seem to interact in determining length of the list: (1) the number of books published, (2) the number of books read by the committee, (3) the number of committee members who read each title, (4) the perceived quality of those books, and (5) the policies and procedures governing the committee's work.[5]

Depending on the committee and the numbers of books available, then, the length of the list will continue to fluctuate from year to year. As Matt Kollasch concludes a thoughtful discussion concerning the length of the 1991 list, "During the two years that I was on BBYA, a long list was certainly never sought. Given the guidelines and number of books read and nominated, it just happened that way. . . . The problem may be that the committee is finally starting to hit its stride, what with the publishers' willingness to send review copies and the committee members' willingness to read them."[6] Judy Nelson, 1991 chair, adds: "It now seems as though the committee is doing too good a job of searching possible material available for YAs."[7]

Several YALSA members suggest that one solution to regulating the length of the list is to return to the system of predetermining the number of titles for any given year. Deborah Taylor, 1993 chair, comments:

> YALSA members need to decide, once and for all, if they want a list of a specific length. How long is too long? If the association wants the list a certain length, it needs to make that part of the charge. . . . The more books people examine, the more determined committee members are to search for books outside the standard young adult publishers' offerings, the greater chance there will be for long lists and healthy disagreement about the books that do and do not make the list.[8]

Like all other issues with BBYA, the question of limiting the length of the list is not a simple one and brings up several important points. First, how long is long enough? Should future lists cap at twenty-five titles, fifty titles, seventy-five titles?

Second, should these titles form some sort of balanced list? Should the books be restricted by genre so that a certain number will be imaginative fiction, a certain number biography, a certain number nonfiction, and a certain number realistic fiction? Should a preset percentage appeal to younger adolescents? Should a minimum number of books come from adult publishing houses? Should the list represent the literary equivalent of the Academy Awards with recognition being given to the best juvenile fiction, the best adult fiction, the best poetry, the best collection of essays, or the best realistic fiction?

At present the list is long. With that length comes a distinct plus: the more books, the greater the possibility that more young adults will be reached by the list. If current BBYA committees err on the length of the list, then they err on the side of relevance and service.

THE ROLE OF YOUNG ADULTS

With the abandonment of the nationwide balloting in the 1960s, the BBYA committee shifted from selecting those books young adults were actually reading to concentrating on titles that would foster "good reading," and have "general appeal, variety of interests, and literary merit."[9] In a 1963 memo, chair Elaine Simpson clarified the final criterion of literary merit by writing that this feature should be "good enough to warrant its [a book's] being singled out as one of the year's twenty to thirty adult titles for young adults." But she added a caution: "Do not . . . be so concerned with literary merit that the list loses its popular appeal for most young adults."[10] Simpson's memo indicates that although youth involvement in the final list had dwindled, young adults were not forgotten in the process.

Not all young adults were pleased with the BBYA books selected for them. Some disliked books that were intended for a younger, or an older, audience than themselves, while others just plain didn't care for the selections. A fourteen-year-old girl voiced her displeasure over the 1967 list by writing the YASD office:

> I have just gone over a copy of the 1967's "Best Books for Young Adults." I find it disgusting. I can't see, in the first place, why anyone writes them, in the second, why anyone would publish them, and third, why the American Library Association would recommend them to young people like myself to read and corrupt our minds with. There are enough problems in the world today without creating more. . . .
>
> I found "Mr. and Mrs. Bo Jo Jones" and "House of Tomorrow" particularly sickening and uncalled for.
>
> I hope you realize that there are a few decent kids left in the world today who like good reading. And I hope the next time you put out this folder, you will ask yourself if these are really the "best books" you can find for America's future leaders.[11]

This young writer offered no blueprint for creating a more acceptable list nor did she call for "America's future leaders" to have input in the creation of future lists. Her displeasure comes from the selections rather than from the selection policy.

Under Eleanor Pourron's BBYA leadership in the mid 1970s, youth participation again came to the attention of the committee.

> I had an active group of teens who served as the Teen Advisory Board. They were allowed to come to the discussions that were held during a Midwinter [Meeting] in Washington, D.C. There were still strong feelings about letting teens comment on the books during those committee discussions, so whenever the teens felt a comment coming on they would come whisper in my ear or pass me written comments and I became their surrogate speaker. They weren't stinting in their opinions.[12]

Although records concerning formal young adult involvement during the next decade remain spotty, it appears that individual committee members informally consulted the teenagers they worked with for opinions about various titles. Linda Waddle, committee member from 1981 to 1985, for example, asked the students at Cedar Falls (Iowa) High School to complete evaluation forms on each of the books they read, and she took these comments to the Midwinter Meetings and Annual Conferences, sharing them with the larger group when appropriate. Other committee members more informally polled young adults and considered their evaluations when making final decisions. It appears that no member relied exclusively on teen input when voting for books for any given BBYA list.

Gradually, librarians not on the BBYA committee began using the yearly nominations as a programming ploy to encourage the young adults they worked with to read and evaluate books. Frequently, these librarians held mock BBYA elections and shared the results, as well as the young adults' comments, with the committee chairs. The chairs, in turn, mailed these tabulations to members or announced the results before the formal balloting took place at the Midwinter Meeting. When the Midwinter Meeting was held in a site near one such participating library, those librarians brought interested young adults to the meeting to observe the workings of the committee they had been emulating all during the year.

Invariably, the young adults and the committee members disagreed about the merit of some titles. Such contradiction naturally occurs with any groups or individuals discussing books, whether they be young adults, librarians, publishers, or parents. By the early 1980s, though, that disagreement between young adult readers and committee members became a focal point for questioning the validity of several BBYA lists.

In 1982, young adults from Enoch Pratt Library in Baltimore registered their displeasure with the lack of youths' formal input in the final list. These avid readers believed that the final selections failed to reflect their true reading tastes. The concerned teenagers decided to produce their own alternative list for young adults, which they called "Youth to Youth Books: A List for Imagination and Survival." In addition, they formed a Young Adult Advisory Board (YAAB) and continued to read nominated titles and share their opinions with each year's BBYA committee.

In 1984, the Midwinter Meeting of ALA was held in Washington, D.C., and Cathi Edgerton (now MacRae), then the young adult librarian from Enoch Pratt, brought select members from YAAB to the BBYA deliberations. These young adults participated in discussion and shared their observations with the committee. Again, there was disagreement and disappointment. As MacRae later noted:

> Their [YAAB members'] most heartfelt favorites, especially Levoy's *Three Friends*, Kerr's *Him She Loves?*, Tenny's *Call the Darkness Down* and Hayden's *Sunflower Forest*, did not make the list. Adding insult to injury, some [titles] they thought were utterly dreadful did make it; they were livid about Patton Walsh's *A Parcel of Patterns*. . . . Two girls cried over the fate of *Sunflower Forest*. . . . The group had learned in past years to accept some disappointments, but these seemed overwhelming. They felt they had been completely ineffective at getting their message to the BBYA committee. Then they wondered if the committee bothered to listen or cared about their opinions at all.[13]

Speaking for this Enoch Pratt YAAB, Edgerton published an open letter to young adult librarians and young adults in the August 1985 issue of

VOYA. The group volunteered to act as a clearinghouse for national YA opinions of Best Books nominations. "We encourage all YA librarians reading this letter to show it to teenagers you know, asking interested YA readers to send us their opinions of books published in 1985. . . . We will organize all cards received into an opinion file to share with the Best Books Committee at their July and January meetings."[14] The hoped-for ground swell of youth opinions did not materialize, and, while Edgerton shared the comments of her YAAB with the 1985 committee, she had limited observations from other young adults around the country.

Still, the 1985 BBYA committee did not operate without youth input. Most members who were working with young adults shared their youths' opinions with the committee. In addition, committee chair Mike Printz organized a special meeting with BBYA members and young adults to discuss mutual interests. Printz remembers the occasion:

> We had a panel that I think we entitled "Seeing the Forest for the Trees" with the background that perhaps we needed to hear young adults speak about how they felt about all the sorts of issues in the world—not just books and libraries, but all sorts of issues. We got the young adult panel from Topeka and Chicago, and we based that panel discussion . . . [on] a questionnaire that had been sent out to approximately 800 young adults across the nation. . . . We had their votes and reactions, and then we heard actual young adults in the flesh and blood speak to us about those things.[15]

While this panel was well received, the question of how much direct input young adults should have on the final list remained unresolved in 1986 and 1987. One serious problem arose: ALA clearly dictates that only association members can participate in meetings, and since the young adults who wanted to speak during BBYA committee deliberations were not ALA members, they were denied the opportunities of physically voicing their opinions at conference. (Printz's panel was organized as a program, and non-ALA members are free to participate in programs when invited.) Nonetheless, in 1988, BBYA chair Gene LaFaille broke a three-year tradition and provided a forum for young adults to speak at the committee meeting. He shares his observations:

> Having youth participation at the meeting in the form of a YAAB group from Enoch Pratt . . . was definitely my most-enjoyable moment. Facing down the conservative elements of ALA . . . who tried to get me to scrap the plans to include the YAAB group made me feel like Gary Cooper in *High Noon*. The kids had their day, and I carved another notch on my six-shooter.[16]

At present, the issue of formalizing youth participation remains in limbo. ALA's policy that only ALA members can participate in meetings is still in effect. If young adults are to contribute personally to BBYA deliberations, this policy must change, and the impetus for change must come from the membership. Before advocating such change, several factors should be considered.

When the young adults from Enoch Pratt spoke in Washington in 1984, they left the meeting frustrated because the committee did not appear to hear their concerns. That, however, was their perception. As Roger

Sutton commented: "When those YAs spoke in Washington, I thought, 'They must know, they're, well, YAs.' But I also think: *Sunflower Forest*? Dramatic subject, drearily handled. *Him She Loves*? Second-rate Kerr. *Parcel of Patterns*? Loved it."[17] The committee did indeed listen; it just didn't agree. Unless the procedures change for choosing books for the list, the BBYA committee still retains the final decision. At present, youth participation does not guarantee youth selection.

The weight any group of young adults carries in determining the final list must be considered before establishing a policy concerning youth participation. If three youth groups love a book, does it automatically make the list? If the committee favors a title, but the young adult readers dislike it, should that book be eliminated? Without such considerations, it would appear that young adults who offer their opinions will find themselves in the same frustrating position as those librarians who participated in the nationwide balloting in the early 1960s: they work with the committee but have an ill-defined role in producing the final list.

Assuming the membership changes ALA regulations about speaking at meetings and conferences and, thus, opens the door for young adults to address the committee, then YALSA must set some guidelines concerning which young adults should speak to BBYA. Committees rotate members in part so that a select group won't control the list. Yet, if young adult advisory boards don't rotate, they in effect will begin to define the list. One respected tenet in examining reading interests and preferences is that information from various sites must be used. Should the same apply to youth participation in BBYA? In describing his massive reading-interest study of 1973, George Norvell points out, "Generally, we must expect data on young people's reading preferences secured in a single school or by a single teacher to be skewed by the special influences of the community, the school, and the teacher, regardless of the number of pupil records assembled."[18] Three years later E. Jane Porter came to the same conclusion. She concludes, "Teachers influence reading content by enthusiasm, by limiting and controlling choices, and by [the fact that] students [try] to please [their teachers]."[19] Even though these observations come from studies based in individual classrooms, the notion that adults may unconsciously influence reading preferences should be taken into consideration when examining youth participation in BBYA. Committee members cycle appointments on BBYA; young adult advisory groups should do the same.

Closely related to this issue is the question of how many young adult participants the committee can effectively handle during a single convention or meeting. While there is room in the deliberations for a few teenagers to share their observations, the committee's workings would be severely restricted if multiple YAAB groups decided to attend the Midwinter Meeting and speak for or against individual titles. Committee deliberations are an important part of the BBYA process. If twenty-five young adults choose to voice their opinions on twenty books, and even if they limit their comments to short, one-minute pleas, these teenagers would still take close to eight hours to present their views. How much time should BBYA devote to young adult comments during committee deliberations? Should the committee set aside certain periods of time for young adults to speak? Should young adults send their observations in writing instead of traveling to a convention site to share their opinions?

A third consideration lies with precisely what the young adults bring to the process of book selection. A 1984 study reports that young adults and librarians will select different fiction titles when using the same selection tools.[20] These results, however, do not mirror the process of a BBYA committee. Here, professionals each read the same books, rather than another's opinion about them, and allow their entire arsenals of literary criticism and knowledge about young adult reading to influence their votes for individual titles. How do young adults make similar decisions? How mature and reliable are their analyses of their own leisure-reading fare? When teenagers read for pleasure, are they cognizant of structural elements such as plot, character development, or theme, or do they simply react to such works on a naive, emotional level?

In an attempt to resolve these questions, Hollis Lowery-Moore, Barbara Samuels, and I applied for and received funding from ALAN (the Assembly on Literature for Adolescents of the National Council of the Teachers of English) to examine young adults' unsupervised responses to favored books.[21] Written student responses from the winning ballots in the 1987 and the 1988 Young Adults' Choices program were used as a basis for evaluating critical skills. Started in 1987, Young Adults' Choices is a project of the International Reading Association in which publishers send books that have had positive reviews to schools in four diverse geographical areas across the United States. In 1987, 146 such titles circulated among junior and senior high students; in 1988 the number of books increased to 253. Teenagers in the chosen sites were encouraged to read freely and to complete ballots for each title they read. In addition, young adults could, if they chose, respond to two open-ended questions: "I like the book because. . ." and "I didn't like the book because. . . ." This portion of the ballot allowed for freely offered, unstructured opinions on whatever aspect of each book teenagers see as significant.

We compared these comments with observations made by professional reviewers. Although problems exist with the design of the study (young adults generally favored the books they chose to read, for instance), we did discover anecdotal examples in these comparisons that point out features worth considering. An obvious one, but important enough to merit mention, is that individual readers and reviewers approach books with particular backgrounds and expectations, and what appeals to one will not appeal to another. Both teen and adult readers and reviewers complete books with subjective, personal, and often diverse opinions.

This observation is reinforced by the reality that adult reviews for a single title frequently differ. *Booklist* summed up Eve Bunting's *Face at the Edge of the World* by noting, "The narrative is leavened by enough humor to avoid being maudlin; characterizations, including that of Charlie, are sufficiently realized to make readers care about them; and the whole is uncluttered and satisfying."[22] *School Library Journal*, on the other hand, printed the antithesis, describing the characters as "wooden and not well developed," the plot as one lacking "tension and impact," and the novel on the whole as "a disappointment."[23] Predictably, neither did all young adults give identical responses to this book. One twelfth grader liked *Face at the Edge of the World* because "it kept you interested and I thought it could be a believable story," while another senior felt the book was "a little drawn out." Other young adults declared that the novel is "really facing the truth of life," showing "how a friend copes with his best friend's death and doesn't forget him until he solves what happened," and "was about something that could happen in life and wasn't fake." Running counter to these responses is the student who disliked the book for its lack of reality, because "most suicide mysteries go unsolved."

Although the purposes of the ballots and those of formal reviews differ, it became apparent that some particular books trigger equivalent responses from both adults and young adults. For example, one popular book with young adult readers that also received wide critical acclaim was Timothy Ferris's *Spaceshots: The Beauty of Nature Beyond Earth*. This volume is a collection of stunning photographs. Reviewers recommended it for this feature, and the students repeatedly, although not exclusively, remarked on the illustrations. Since text is limited to an introduction and explanatory captions, it would have been hard to ignore the visuals. This obvious example of reviewer/young adult agreement does not stand as an isolated one. The *School Library Journal* reviewer of Lynn Hall's *Just One Friend* felt that "Hall capture[s] Dorry's feelings of isolation and desperate loneliness."[24] So did an eleventh grader who wrote, "The girl in this book (of whom the story revolves around) is a slow learner, and although I am not able to sympathize with her in that way, I did understand her ways of thinking." Another student added, "It was a lonely book."

Reviewers and young adults also noticed similar structural characteristics. A seventh grade Houston student did not like T. Ernesto Bethancourt's *The Me Inside of Me* because "The plot was very common. . . . The only thing that was different was that the girl did not fall for him in the end, and they would live happily ever after." Similarly, Hazel Rochman from *Booklist* mentioned "formulaic style," "clichés," and "obvious lessons."[25] One reader particularly enjoyed the characterizations ("even the dog") from *The Blossoms Meet the Vulture Lady*, describing them as "warm and funny." Likewise, *Booklist* pointed out the warmth and humor in both characterization and tone. A *School Library Journal* reviewer remarked on the "poignant love story"[26] in *Abby, My Love*, while her teenage counterpart wrote, "It was a beautiful, touching love story, while most love stories for teenagers today are bubbly and sticky and silly." Stephanie Zvirin's *Booklist* review mentioned that in the same book the subject of incest is handled "with admirable restraint and sensitivity."[27] Agreeing with her, an eighth grader stated, "The theme, sexual abuse, is straightforward yet delicately handled."

At other times the young adults and the adults expressed divergent opinions. "Too full of individual incidences,"[28] described an adult reviewer's perception of *Count Me In*. The opposite view came from a seventh grader: "Many things happen in the book. In some books, too many things happen, it bugs me. In this book, the author puts things together so it seems natural that there be many problems. The book has so many thing[s] that can really happen to a person, that I really enjoyed the book, like being jealous of a baby, feeling left out, falling in love, and many other things. Overall, I *really* enjoyed the book."

One particular factor that separated the teenagers from the reviewers was the young adults' narrow breadth of reading, rather than a limited depth of response. Only once did a teenager compare a work to that of another author, mentioning that *Only Birds and Angels Fly* reminded her of S. E. Hinton's writing. The reviewers made such comparisons frequently.

In addition, reviewers commented on modest accounts, such as Rabo Rodgers' *The Rainbow Factor*, as pleasant reads but not unlike many other popular titles available to teens. Young adults, however, thought the book exciting and different, reminding us on the one hand of their lack of familiarity with formula fiction and on the other of the freshness each teenager brings to every reading experience.

The young adults' limited knowledge about available works surfaced with other titles. One reader of *Solitary Secret* shared: "I cried because some of the scenes were so unbelievably disgusting. Finally I have read a book that shows the bad side of life. Incest is something I would never expect to be explained in a book." Not only are books about incest readily available for young adults, but one, *Abby, My Love*, was also another title under consideration for that year's Young Adults' Choices project.

Young adults' responses indicated that when discussing books they were able to focus on distinct, contextual elements in order to make connections to their own lives and individual views of the world. They frequently approached books with the same critical eyes as did adult reviewers. Even though young adults clearly lacked sophistication and an extensive reading background, they recognized those qualities of a book that make it outstanding. On the other hand, often the opinions of the young adults reflected limited experiences with literature. In addition, they read what appealed to them—not what could hold meaning for their less sophisticated or more mature classmates or for their older or younger friends or for their peers of different sexes, interests, or abilities. Young adults know what they like at the moment but appear ill equipped to relate those preferences to who they were several years previously or who they might be in the future.

For example, we discovered that junior high students wanted familiar genres and predictable plots in their books but that the older students didn't. A twelfth grader commented on *Shanny On Her Own*: "It was boring. The whole story was about if she could get this boy to like her," while a seventh grader was impressed because "Shanny and Thor fall in love and at the end they all really care." Similarly, with *Baseball: It's Your Team*, a book with an interactive format, a seventh grader commented, "It was neat to make decisions and match them with the owner." In contrast, an eleventh grader wrote:

> I don't like the book because much like that of *Football: It's Your Team*, it lost originality and became much too repetitious. After the first five chapters it became boring and I began to lose interest. The choices became predictable, and again much like the other books in this series, it didn't contain human interest or the real things that the fans always see at the stadium or on television. It pertained too much to financial and strategic moves that would "make or break" a team.

Notice that in each of these examples, the older students responded in terms of their own tastes and were not able to see the possible value of these books for their younger counterparts. They simply looked at their own particular interests, found that the books did not meet them, and consequently dismissed the books.

Still, the question persists: Is there any agreement among those books chosen for BBYA and those favored by young adults? Again, data from the Young Adult Choices project provides the best insight into this query even though differences exist between the pool of books eligible for this youth-selected list and those considered for BBYA.

Books allowable for BBYA consideration must be published during a certain time frame and be nominated for the list. On the other hand, books eligible for the Young Adults' Choices project must first of all receive two positive reviews and second be accepted by a selection committee composed of adults. This committee chooses approximately one hundred books, places those in five different geographic school sites around the United States, and encourages students to read and vote for their individual favorites from among this pool. At the end of a year, the International Reading Association tallies the nationwide votes and declares these books (approximately thirty) with the most votes as Young Adults' Choices. Table 3 notes the major differences between the two lists.

TABLE 3   Differences between Young Adult Choices and BBYA Lists

Young Adult Choices	BBYA
Potential selections positively reviewed during eligibility period	Potential selections published during eligibility period
Nominations through committee deliberations	Individual nominations to committee
Books usually considered one year after publication	Books usually considered during year of publication
Approximately 100 titles formally nominated each year	Approximately 300 titles formally nominated each year
No minimum number of votes to appear on final list	Every book on final list receives at least 9 positive votes
Stable number of final selections each year	Fluctuating number of final selections each year

Despite these differences, each Young Adults' Choices List has also included books once designated as Best Books for Young Adults. Figure 3 shows that distribution since the inception of Young Adults' Choices in 1987. The overlapping titles, or those appearing on both BBYA and Young Adults' Choices lists, are listed in table 4 and certainly deserve our attention.

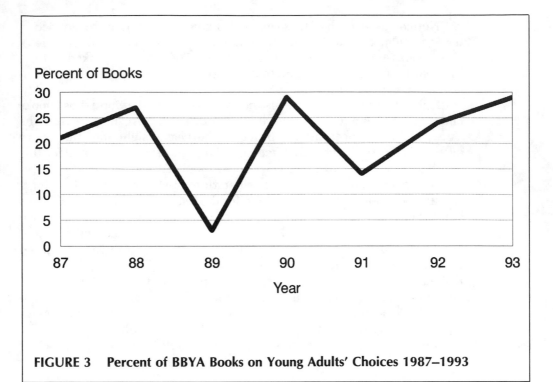

Percent of Books

FIGURE 3   Percent of BBYA Books on Young Adults' Choices 1987–1993

TABLE 4   Books Appearing on Both YA Choices and BBYA

Title/Author	Year on YA Choices	Year on BBYA
Abby, My Love by Hadley Irwin	1987	1985
Across the Grain by Jean Ferris	1992	1991
After the Dancing Days by Margaret I. Rostkowski	1988	1986
Bloods: An Oral History of the Vietnam War by Black Veterans by Wallace Terry	1987	1984
Boy Who Reversed Himself by William Sleator	1988	1987
Circle Unbroken by Sollace Hotze	1990	1988
Crosses by Shelly Stoehr	1993	1993
Dawn Rider by Jan Hudson	1992	1991
Dealing with Dragons by Patricia C. Wrede	1992	1991
Dear America: Letters Home from Vietnam edited by Bernard Edelman	1988	1986
Fade by Robert Cormier	1990	1988
Fallen Angels by Walter Dean Myers	1990	1988
Finder: The True Story of a Private Investigator by Marilyn Greene and Gary Provost	1990	1988
Finding David Delores by Margaret Willey	1988	1986
How It Feels to Fight for Your Life by Jill Krementz	1991	1990
Jason's Women by Jean Davies Okimoto	1988	1986
Just One Friend by Lynn Hall	1987	1985
Last Silk Dress by Ann Rinaldi	1990	1988

Title/Author	Year on YA Choices	Year on BBYA
Man from the Other Side by Uri Orlev	1993	1992
Midnight Hour Encores by Bruce Brooks	1988	1986
Night Kites by M. E. Kerr	1988	1986
No More Saturday Nights by Norma Klein	1990	1990
Pearl of the Soul of the World by Meredith Ann Pierce	1992	1991
Phoenix Rising; or, How to Survive Your Life by Cynthia D. Grant	1991	1990
Pictures of Adam by Myron Levoy	1988	1986
Predator! by Bruce Brooks	1993	1992
Rain Catchers by Jean Thesman	1993	1992
Rescue: The Story of How Gentiles Saved Jews in the Holocaust by Milton Meltzer	1990	1988
Ryan White: My Own Story by Ryan White and Ann Marie Cunningham	1993	1992
Say Goodnight, Gracie by Julie Reece Deaver	1990	1988
Scorpions by Walter Dean Myers	1990	1988
Shabanu: Daughter of the Wind by Suzanne Fisher Staples	1991	1990
Sing for a Gentle Rain by J. Alison James	1992	1991
Sirens and Spies by Janet Taylor Lisle	1987	1985
Skeeter by K. Smith	1991	1990
Smoke and Ashes: The Story of the Holocaust by Barbara Rogasky	1990	1988
Solitary by Lynn Hall	1988	1986
Solitary Blue by Cynthia Voigt	1987	1986
Solitary Secret by Patricia Hermes	1987	1985
Spaceshots: The Beauty of Nature Beyond Earth by Timothy Ferres	1987	1985
Sweetgrass by Jan Hudson	1991	1990
Tom Loves Anna Loves Tom by Bruce Clements	1992	1991
Trouble with Lemons by Daniel Hayes	1993	1992
We All Fall Down by Robert Cormier	1993	1992
What Daddy Did by Neal Shusterman	1993	1992
Woodsong by Gary Paulsen	1992	1991
Year of Impossible Goodbyes by Sook Nyul Choi	1993	1992
Year without Michael by Susan Beth Pfeffer	1989	1987
You Take the High Road by Mary K. Pershall	1992	1991

No compilation of recommended books will ever represent the perfect reading list for a specific audience. Certainly, future BBYA task forces will be directed to examine the role of young adults in compiling an annual list. These groups will have to ask themselves whether formal youth participation is desirable, feasible, and manageable. Should teenagers have voting power? Should their comments determine whether or not books make a particular list? Resolutions to these questions will not be simple; they must be thoughtful.

These and other issues will continue to come before the committee. As Deborah Taylor concludes, "I believe controversy about the BBYA lists is healthy. It's a good thing it is, since it will always be with us."[29]

Notes

1. R. F. Abrahamson and Betty Carter, "What We Know about Nonfiction and Young Adult Readers and What We Need to Do about It," *Publishing Research Quarterly* 8 (Spring 1992): 41–54.

2. Joni Bodart, "View from the Inside: How the Best Books for Young Adults Committee Really Works," *Top of the News* 38 (Fall 1981): 77.

3. Mary Ruth Metcalf Cary, "An Analysis of the Critical Reception and the Age Level Designations for the 1993 Best Books for Young Adults List" (Professional paper, Texas Woman's University, 1993).

4. Matthew Kollasch, "Professionalism and BBYA: A Lengthy Problem," *Wilson Library Bulletin* 66 (Sept. 1991): 69.

5. Joel Shoemaker, letter to Betty Carter, 13 Apr. 1993.

6. Kollasch, "Professionalism and BBYA," 69.

7. Kollasch, "Professionalism and BBYA," 69.

8. Deborah Taylor, letter to YALSA Board, 31 Mar. 1993.

9. Michael C. Madden, "An Analysis of the American Library Association's Annual List 'Best Books for Young Adults,' 1930–1967" (Master's thesis, University of Chicago, 1967), 14.

10. Elaine Simpson, letter to Audrey Beil, 21 Jan. 1964.

11. Brenda Nelson, letter to YASD, 17 May 1968.

12. Eleanor Pourron, letter to Betty Carter, 25 Mar. 1993.

13. Cathi Edgerton, letter to Mike Printz, Mar. 1985.

14. "Up For Discussion," *VOYA* 8, no. 3 (Aug. 1985): 169.

15. Mike Printz, letter to Betty Carter, Apr. 1993.

16. Eugene LaFaille, letter to Betty Carter, 19 Apr. 1993.

17. Roger Sutton, "Even Restaurants Have Menus," *School Library Journal* 31 (Aug. 1985): 36.

18. George Norvell, *The Reading Interests of Young People* (East Lansing: University of Michigan Press, 1973), 19.

19. E. Jane Porter, "Research Report," *Language Arts* 52 (Oct. 1975): 1025.

20. "Involving Young Adults in Fiction Selection," *Top of the News* 40, no. 2 (Winter 1984): 163–70.

21. Betty Carter, Hollis Lowery-Moore, and Barbara Samuels, "Readers' Choices: A Comparison of Critical Comments," *The ALAN Review* 20 (Spring 1993): 52–55.

22. Sally Estes, "Review of *Face at the Edge of the World* by Eve Bunting," *Booklist* 81, no. 13 (1 Mar. 1985): 102.

23. Nancy E. Black, "Review of *Face at the Edge of the World* by Eve Bunting," *School Library Journal* 32 (Dec. 1985): 98.

24. Li Stark, "Review of *Just One Friend* by Lynn Hall," *School Library Journal* 32 (Dec. 1985): 88.

25. Hazel Rochman, "Review of *The Me Inside of Me* by T. Ernesto Bethancourt," *Booklist* 82:10 (15 Jan. 1986): 75.

26. Maria B. Salvadore, "Review of *Abby, My Love* by Hadley Irwin," *School Library Journal* 31 (May 1985): 102.

27. Stephanie Zvirin, "Review of *Abby, My Love* by Hadley Irwin," *Booklist* 81, no. 13 (1 Mar. 1985): 945.

28. Ilene Cooper, "Review of *Count Me In* by Christine McDonnell," *Booklist* 81, no. 22 (Aug. 1985): 81.

29. Taylor, letter to YALSA Board, 31 Mar. 1993.

Authors

Since 1966, 1,094 individuals have contributed as either single authors, joint authors, editors, compilers, or selectors to the titles that make up the best books lists. Add to that total the individual essayists, poets, playwrights, short-story authors, and letter writers with entries in various volumes, and the number of outstanding contributors to young adult literature becomes a sizable segment of the modern literary scene.

The preceding numbers show that contributors to the BBYA list represent far more than a small group of select individuals. These authors and editors have varied backgrounds and different purposes for writing: some are new to young adult literature, others represent continued influence; some come from the entertainment or political world to tell their stories, while others draw heavily on personal, private experiences; and some cross over from children's literature, while others have their roots with an adult audience. From Henry Aaron to Roald Dahl to Will Hobbs to P. D. James to Mary Lyons to Kurt Vonnegut, each adds a distinct ingredient to the term *young adult author*.

ENCORE PERFORMERS

Each author brings new experiences to young adult readers in the form of memorable characters, meaningful information, challenging themes, provocative language, or powerful subjects. Jay Anson, Ruth Bell, Barbara Dana, Shelia Gordon, and Jim Miller each do so with one recognized entry on Best Books for Young Adults, while Maya Angelou, Barbara Cohen, Mildred Lee, Meredith Pierce, and Terry Pringle provide the same opportunities with multiple entries. Such repeated BBYA citations don't specify that certain authors speak more intensely to any individual young adult reader, but they do indicate that these particular writers have the opportunities to do so more frequently.

To date, forty authors and editors can each boast of having at least four separate commendations since 1966. As a group they deserve special mention for bringing untold hours of reading pleasure to the young adults we serve. These individuals are listed in table 5.

TABLE 5   Repeat Best Books for Young Adult Authors

Author	Book	Year on BBYA
Avi	*Blue Heron*	1993
	Nothing but the Truth: A Documentary Novel	1992
	True Confessions of Charlotte Doyle	1991
	Wolf Rider	1986
	Fighting Ground	1984
Bode, Janet	*Beating the Odds: Stories of Unexpected Achievers*	1992
	Voices of Rape	1991
	New Kids on the Block: Oral Histories of Immigrant Teens	1990
	Kids Having Kids: The Unwed Teenage Parent	1980
Bridgers, Sue Ellen	*Permanent Connections*	1987
	Sara Will	1985
	Notes for Another Life	1981
	All Together Now: A Novel	1979
	Home Before Dark	1976
Brooks, Bruce	*What Hearts*	1993
	Predator!	1992
	No Kidding	1990
	On the Wing	1990
	Midnight Hour Encores	1986
	Moves Make the Man	1985
Carter, Alden R.	*Up Country*	1990
	Sheila's Dying	1987
	Wart, Son of Toad	1985
	Growing Season	1984
Cormier, Robert	*Tunes for Bears to Dance To*	1993
	We All Fall Down	1992
	Fade	1988
	Bumblebee Flies Anyway	1983
	After the First Death	1979
	I Am the Cheese	1977
	The Chocolate War: A Novel	1974
Crichton, Michael	*Jurassic Park*	1992
	Electronic Life: How to Think about Computers	1984
	Terminal Man	1972
	Andromeda Strain	1969

Author	Book	Year on BBYA
Crutcher, Chris	*Athletic Shorts: 6 Short Stories*	1992
	Chinese Handcuffs	1990
	Crazy Horse Electric Game	1987
	Stotan!	1986
	Running Loose	1983
Dickinson, Peter	*AK*	1993
	Eva	1990
	Tulku	1979
(with Wayne Anderson)	*Flight of Dragons*	1979
Duncan, Lois	*Who Killed My Daughter? The True Story of a Mother's Search for Her Daughter's Murderer*	1993
	Don't Look Behind You	1990
	Chapters: My Growth as a Writer	1982
	Stranger with My Face	1981
	Killing Mr. Griffin	1978
Durrell, Gerald (with Lee Durrell)	*Amateur Naturalist*	1984
	Birds, Beasts, and Relatives	1969
	Rosy Is My Relative	1968
	Two in the Bush	1966
Freedman, Russell	*Indian Winter*	1993
	Wright Brothers: How They Invented the Airplane	1992
	Franklin Delano Roosevelt	1991
	Lincoln: A Photobiography	1988
	Indian Chiefs	1987
Greenberg, Joanne	*Of Such Small Differences*	1988
	Simple Gifts	1986
	Far Side of Victory	1983
	In This Sign	1970
Guy, Rosa	*Music of Summer*	1993
	Disappearance: A Novel	1979
	Edith Jackson	1978
	Ruby	1976
	Friends	1973
Hall, Lynn	*Flying Changes*	1992
	Solitary	1986
	Just One Friend	1985
	Uphill All the Way	1984
	Leaving	1980
	Sticks and Stones	1972
Hamilton, Virginia	*Cousins*	1991
	Anthony Burns: The Defeat and Triumph of a Fugitive Slave	1988
	In the Beginning: Creation Stories from Around the World	1988

Continued

TABLE 5   Continued

Author	Book	Year on BBYA
	Little Love	1984
	Magical Adventures of Pretty Pearl	1983
	Sweet Whispers, Brother Rush	1982
	M. C. Higgins, the Great	1974
Haskins, James (with Rosa Parks)	*Rosa Parks: My Story*	1993
	One More River to Cross: The Stories of Twelve Black Americans	1993
	Black Dance in America	1991
(with Kathleen Benson)	*60's Reader*	1988
	Black Music in America: A History Through Its People	1987
Hinton, S. E.	*Taming the Star Runner*	1988
	Tex	1979
	Rumblefish	1975
	That Was Then, This Is Now	1971
Janeczko, Paul B.	*Brickyard Summer*	1990
Janeczko, Paul B., ed.	*Place My Words Are Looking For: What Poets Say About and Through Their Work*	1991
	Music of What Happens: Poems That Tell Stories	1988
	Going Over to Your Place: Poems For Each Other	1987
	Pocket Poems: Selected for a Journey	1985
	Strings: A Gathering of Family Poems	1984
	Poetspeak: In Their Work, about Their Work	1983
	Don't Forget to Fly	1981
Jones, Diana Wynne	*Sudden Wild Magic*	1993
	Castle in the Air	1992
	Howl's Moving Castle	1986
	Archer's Goon	1984
	Homeward Bounders	1981
Kerr, M. E.	*Fell*	1987
	Night Kites	1986
	I Stay near You	1985
	Me Me Me Me Me: Not a Novel	1983
	Little, Little	1981
	Gentlehands	1978
	Is That You, Miss Blue?	1975
Koertge, Ron	*Harmony Arms*	1993
	Boy in the Moon	1991
	Arizona Kid	1988
	Where the Kissing Never Stops	1986
Mahy, Margaret	*Memory*	1988
	Tricksters	1987

Author	Book	Year on BBYA
	Catalogue of the Universe	1986
	Changeover: A Supernatural Romance	1984
Mazer, Harry	Girl of His Dreams	1987
	When the Phone Rang	1986
	I Love You, Stupid!	1981
	Last Mission	1979
	War on Villa Street: A Novel	1978
(with Norma Fox Mazer)	Solid Gold Kid	1977
Mazer, Norma Fox	Silver	1988
	After the Rain	1987
	Downtown	1984
	Someone to Love	1983
	Up in Seth's Room	1979
(with Harry Mazer)	Solid Gold Kid	1977
	Dear Bill, Remember Me?	1976
McKinley, Robin	Outlaws of Sherwood	1988
	Hero and the Crown	1985
	Blue Sword	1982
	Beauty: A Retelling of the Story of Beauty and the Beast	1978
Meltzer, Milton	Columbus and the World Around Him	1991
	Benjamin Franklin: The New American	1990
	Voices from the Civil War: A Documentary History of the Great American Conflict	1990
Meltzer, Milton, ed.	American Revolutionaries: A History in Their Own Words, 1750–1800	1987
	Rescue: The Story of How Gentiles Saved Jews in the Holocaust	1988
	Ain't Gonna Study War No More	1985
	Never Forget: The Jews of the Holocaust	1976
Meyer, Carolyn	Where the Broken Heart Still Beats: The Story of Cynthia Ann Parker	1993
	Denny's Tapes	1987
	Voices of South Africa: Growing Up in a Troubled Land	1987
	Center: From a Troubled Past to a New Life	1979
	C. C. Poindexter	1978
Michaels, Barbara	Be Buried in the Rain	1985
	Dark on the Other Side	1971
	Witch	1973
	Ammie, Come Home	1969
Myers, Walter Dean	Righteous Revenge of Artemis Bonner	1993
	Somewhere in the Darkness	1993
	Now Is Your Time! The African-American Struggle for Freedom	1992
	Mouse Rap	1991

Continued

TABLE 5   Continued

Author	Book	Year on BBYA
	Fallen Angels	1988
	Scorpions	1988
	Hoops	1981
	Legend of Tarik	1981
	Young Landlords	1979
Naylor, Phyllis Reynolds	*Send No Blessings*	1991
	Unexpected Pleasures	1987
	Year of the Gopher	1987
	Keeper	1986
	String of Chances	1982
Paulsen, Gary	*Haymeadow*	1993
	Cookcamp	1992
	Monument	1992
	Woodsong	1991
	Voyage of the Frog	1990
	Winter Room	1990
	Island	1988
	Crossing	1987
	Dogsong	1985
	Tracker	1984
	Dancing Carl	1983
Peck, Richard	*Princess Ashley*	1987
	Remembering the Good Times	1985
	Close Enough to Touch	1981
	Father Figure: A Novel	1978
	Ghosts I Have Been	1977
	Are You in the House Alone?	1976
	Representing Super Doll	1975
Rinaldi, Ann	*Break with Charity: A Story about the Salem Witch Trials*	1993
	Wolf by the Ears	1992
	Last Silk Dress	1988
	Time Enough for Drums	1986
Rylant, Cynthia	*Missing May*	1993
	Couple of Kooks and Other Stories about Love	1991
	Soda Jerk	1991
	Kindness	1988
	Fine White Dust	1986
Sleator, William	*Strange Attractors*	1991
	Duplicate	1988
	Boy Who Reversed Himself	1987
	Singularity	1985
	Interstellar Pig	1984
	House of Stairs	1974
Voigt, Cynthia	*On Fortune's Wheel*	1991
	Sons from Afar	1987
	Izzy, Willy-Nilly	1986

Author	Book	Year on BBYA
	Runner	1985
	Solitary Blue	1983
	Tell Me If Lovers Are Losers	1982
Wersba, Barbara	*Carnival in My Mind*	1982
	Tunes for a Small Harmonica	1976
	Country of the Heart	1975
	Run Softly, Go Fast	1970
Westall, Robert	*Stormsearch*	1993
	Yaxley's Cat	1993
	Kingdom by the Sea	1992
	Futuretrack 5	1984
	Devil on the Road	1979
	Wind Eye	1978
Yolen, Jane	*Briar Rose*	1993
Yolen, Jane, ed. (with Greenberg, Martin H., ed.)	*Vampires: A Collection of Original Stories*	1992
	Heart's Blood	1984
	Dragon's Blood	1982
	Gift of Sarah Barker	1981
Zindel, Paul	*Pigman and Me*	1993
	Begonia for Miss Applebaum	1990
	Pigman's Legacy	1980
(with Crescent Dragonwagon)	*To Take a Dare*	1982
	Confessions of a Teenage Baboon	1977
	Pardon Me, You're Stepping on My Eyeball!	1976
	Effects of Gamma Rays on Man-in-the-Moon Marigolds	1971

We can all manipulate the BBYA list in a number of ways and discover mystery, fantasy, science fiction, realistic fiction, and historical fiction writers; poets; anthologists; biographers; editors; adult authors and young adult authors; and African-American, feminist, and WASP authors. Instead, though, let's applaud this diverse group of *fine* authors and recognize that each one has made an enormous contribution to the reading lives of young adults.

BBYA APPRECIATED

We all like the recognition of a job well done, and authors prove no exception to this rule. Over the years, the Young Adult Services Division (YASD) and Young Adult Library Services Association (YALSA) offices have notified authors when one of their books appears on BBYA. In turn, many authors have responded, and this collected correspondence appears in the files. Some such as John Craig with the 1979 entry for *Chappie and*

Me find themselves at a loss for words: "I can't tell you—a terrible admission for a writer—just how pleased I am."[1] In 1975 Jeff Fields (*Cry of Angels*, BBYA 1974) simply wrote, in large letters:

OUT OF SIGHT![2]

Others, like Lloyd Alexander (*Westmark*, BBYA 1981), convey their enthusiasm in more conventional terms: "Excitement on top of excitement! *Westmark* is most honored by 'Best Books for Young Adults,' and you can be sure that its author is very proud indeed."[3] Nancy Larrick (*Crazy to Be Alive in Such a Strange World*, BBYA 1977) expressed her own quiet appreciation: "I am deeply honored to be on this list. I think it is the first time any publication of mine has been so honored by the ALA so I am basking in this recognition."[4] Similarly, Ed Spielman (*Mighty Atom*, BBYA 1980) wrote: "I have received some applause in my career, but this imparts a lasting satisfaction, a knowledge of having accomplished something worthwhile. . . . This selection embodies five years of work on my part, and a sense of completion in a most positive aspect."[5]

The special joys of finding the young adult audience don't escape authors. Barry Lopez (*Arctic Dreams*, BBYA 1986) shared his pleasure: "I would feel presumptuous, thinking that what I had to say in *Arctic Dreams* was said clearly enough to engage and inform young readers. I don't know what more marvelous thing you can say to a writer about a serious work of nonfiction than that he has reached beyond his own generation."[6] With that compliment comes responsibility, as Roger Caras (*Mara Simba*, BBYA 1986), indicated: "My first book way back in my wild youth (*Antarctica: Land of Frozen Time*) was a YA book and that audience has never been very far from my mind. In my fields of natural history and conservation if we don't 'get' them then we may never have a second chance."[7]

Some authors recognize and appreciate the work of the committee. In response to the selection of *Far Side of Victory* for BBYA 1983, Joanne Greenberg wrote:

> I was permitted to sit in on the deliberations last year in Los Angeles, and was moved as I listened to librarians wrangle, urge, fight for books that they love and defend the selection of these books. I saw the enthusiasm that they had for books and reading—the delight that they took in sharing what they thought were good books with friends.
>
> Sometimes when we read lackluster reviews or ponder the best seller list, some of my writing friends and I wonder who our audience is—who cares enough. I think you do, and it makes me very happy.[8]

W. E. Butterworth (*LeRoy and the Old Man*, BBYA 1980) extended his thanks beyond the committee to include a single librarian:

> I was, of course, flattered to have *LeRoy* singled out by you as a "Best Book for Young Adults," but I don't think I'm nearly as happy about it as is my old friend Mrs. Alice Doughtie, (now retired) Librarian of the Choctawatchee Regional Library (Dale, Barbour, and Henry Counties, Alabama) who fifteen years ago exerted her considerable powers of persuasion to force a very reluctant writer of paperback novels to try to write a book for young people.

She was right, of course, for I soon learned that it is a very rewarding thing to do, far more so than writing for adults. She has, whenever (too seldom) I still see her, rather smugly reminded me of this. She will now glow with self-satisfaction.[9]

At times, authors express their admiration for libraries, young adults, and librarians. Morgan Llywelyn, author of the 1982 BBYA *Horse Goddess*, paid solid tribute to all three with the following:

> This award means a great deal to me personally, as I feel I owe the libraries of America a tremendous debt. My library card was my ticket to an ongoing lifetime education; my ticket to adventure and knowledge, to entertainment and challenge, to growth and success. When the educational facilities available to me did not meet my needs, I practically moved into the nearest library to feed my insatiable curiosity about people and places, and found there, in books, my own future.
>
> As I remember my own life, the teenage years are a time when horizons seem endless . . . and sometimes frighteningly empty. Good literature can fill that void and get young minds in the habit of reading and learning for pleasure, not as a chore. There is no other period in a person's life when he or she is so vulnerable, so searching. All those questions seem to come bubbling out—"Who am I?" "What's important?" "Where do I come from?" "Where am I going?" I know I asked those questions, and so does Epona, the heroine of *The Horse Goddess*. She asks them in a different era twenty-seven hundred years ago, but the values she ultimately accepts are as important to young people today.[10]

One of the most eloquent thank-you notes comes from author Jacquie Gordon in an article that appeared in the 1990 issue of *SIGNAL*. Here Gordon describes the frustrations she experienced in trying to get her book, *Give Me One Wish* (BBYA 1988), to the proper audience. This book tells the story of Gordon's daughter's life and untimely death. Publicity appearances on television, radio, and in bookstores failed to establish an audience. Gordon wrote:

> But during this quiet time, unknown to all but fifteen people, voting members on the American Library Association's Nominating Committee for the best young adult books of 1988, something was happening through the normal channels of publishing.
>
> Colleen Macklin is the librarian in a small town of Tippecanoe, Wisconsin. She served on the ALA nominating committee in 1988. She read a review of *Give Me One Wish* in *Booklist*, the journal of the ALA, and ordered it for her library. She loved the book and says, "I carried it around with me like a gift, reading it on the bus, reading at night. I liked it better than *Eric*. It was perfect for teenagers." And it was she who decided to nominate it.
>
> When a book is nominated, the ALA asks the publisher to send fifteen review copies. Colleen never got hers, but she brought her copy with her to the conference in Washington D.C. in December where the final list was completed. She proposed the book as a finalist and was disturbed to find that the fifteen review copies had never been received. No other committee member had read it. This upset her because as she says, "The book belonged on our list." She found two more copies in the Washington D.C. public library and presented her case to the committee. "I told them how much we need a book like this. It deals with modern issues. It's about a teenager. It has to be on our list." Perhaps I should say the book is 350 pages long, not your usual slim volume. Says Colleen, "That was Saturday morning. The final vote was Tuesday. I asked the committee members to please take the

book back to their hotel rooms and read it and then pass it on to another member." This is a very dedicated group. Some of them read until late at night.

By the final vote, eight committee members had read the book, and eight votes were needed to have it on the final 1988 list. All eight voted yes.

So there it was. *Give Me One Wish*, the story of a spunky teenager who left her journals behind containing the bold message, "I want everyone to know me," was collecting dust in the Norton Warehouse, when one person in Tippecanoe with the courage of her convictions, stood up and said, "This is an important new book. We must not overlook it."

It's not the end of the story. Even this did not suddenly create a best seller. But because the American Library Association was wise enough to know where the book belonged, *Give Me One Wish* is finding its audience.

What teenagers have told me is they identify with Christine, the heroine in the story, and they like her. To young people the book is about them, which is exactly what Colleen Macklin had understood.[11]

While Gordon singles out one specific committee and its consideration of one particular book, she reminds all readers of the responsibility and influence of BBYA.

Notes

1. John Craig, letter to Jan Freeman, 8 May 1980.
2. Jeff Fields, letter to Eleanor K. Pourron, 11 Nov. 1975.
3. Lloyd Alexander, letter to Evelyn Shaevel, 20 May 1982.
4. Nancy Larrick, letter to Jack Forman, 2 June 1978.
5. Ed Spielman, letter to Evelyn Shaevel, 1 June 1981.
6. Barry Lopez, letter to Evelyn Shaevel, 7 July 1987.
7. Roger A. Caras, letter to Evelyn Shaevel, 14 May 1982.
8. Joanne Greenberg, letter to Evelyn Shaevel, 24 May 1984.
9. W. E. Butterworth, letter to Evelyn Shaevel, 14 May 1981.
10. Morgan Llywelyn, letter to Evelyn Shaevel, 27 May 1983.
11. Jacquie Gordon, "A Spark in Tippecanoe: Case Study of a Book That Would Not Die," SIGNAL 14 (Winter 1990): 10–12.

Influences of BBYA

At the conclusion of each Midwinter Meeting, weary committee members pack their belongings, head home, and vow that, for a few weeks at least, they will have a life unconnected to both reading and the American Library Association. But what happens to the books? In just a few short months the Best Books for Young Adults spotlight turns to new releases, and the previous year's selections fade from the pages of the review media, from the lips of the passionate defenders and dissuaders, and from the concerns of the literary equivalents of Monday morning quarterbacks.

AVAILABILITY OF BBYA BOOKS

While an enormous amount of attention goes into the creation of each list, relatively little concentrates on the aftermath. Once books appear on a BBYA list, are they purchased? Are they used?

In our May 1993 interview, Barbara Duree indicates that even though the list is designed to promote reading, it also serves as a buying guide for some institutions. Many library systems and school media centers will order some of the BBYA list books through their normal reviewing channels before they ever appear on a list. Others will take the list and check each title against review sources, looking for both topic and age appropriateness for their particular young adult audience. For a variety of reasons, a third group may simply ignore the list and its books. Still, for these recommendations to reach young adults, the books must be purchased and made available.

In the spring of 1993, Penny Trosper, MLS student at Texas Woman's University, elected to address the issue of availability. She wanted to determine which titles (out of a possible eighty-five) from the 1991 BBYA list were held by libraries within the Northeast Texas Library System (NETLS). To establish individual holdings, Trosper checked the Online Computer Library Center (OCLC) records. She identified four systems (Dallas, Irving, Plano, and Texarkana) within NETLS that also subscribed to OCLC and showed holdings from the 1991 list. The Dallas and Irving systems serve large metropolitan areas, the Plano system serves one of the suburban communities just north of Dallas, and the Texarkana system serves a more rural population on the Texas-Arkansas border.

Although Trosper reported her findings in the spring of 1993, she conducted her study during the latter part of 1992. Therefore, she chose to examine the 1991 list, assuming that libraries ordering books from that publication would have had time to receive them and include them in their holdings.

The larger NETLS systems, Dallas and Irving, showed that they owned the greater percentage of 1991 BBYA books with 92.9 percent (seventy-nine titles) and 84.7 percent (seventy-two titles) respectively. The smaller systems showed fewer holdings in the OCLC database. Plano recorded nineteen titles (22.3 percent), and Texarkana seventeen, or 20 percent.[1] One recommended book, *Children of the Dragon: The Story of Tiananmen Square*, did not appear in any of the records for the four systems, and only two titles, *The Cuckoo's Egg: Tracking a Spy Through the Maze of Computer Espionage* and *Tom Loves Anna Loves Tom*, were recorded for all four systems.[2]

As with any study, this one has limitations. Four participating library systems comprise a small database, thus producing imprecise generalizations. In addition, some of the other NETLS libraries do not subscribe to OCLC. Furthermore, books ordered but not yet received will not appear on the directory, which, not incidentally, records individual titles rather than numbers of books available. With these limitations in mind, librarians can still conclude that young adults within the metropolitan area of North Texas do not have immediate access to all recommended 1991 Best Books. Even though BBYA lists are not created as buying tools, they do exist to create demand for and interest in young adult literature. Libraries cannot meet that demand or interest without supplying the recommended books. Although interlibrary loan systems allow young adults to borrow the books from remote sites, such loans do not substitute for the immediate physical presence of suggested titles.

Trosper's findings address the original questions she raised. But the study also invokes several global issues that only the profession can address. Do young adult librarians use the BBYA list? If so, how? Have uses changed over the years? If so, why? How many of the 1992 or 1993 or 1994 books do particular libraries own? Do publishers see any value in the list? Do authors? Do young adults? Stop reading for a moment. Can you answer any of these questions from your own experiences, or can you provide statistical data from your own library? If you can, then do so. Write your responses and send them to Linda Waddle, Deputy Executive Director of YALSA, at the American Library Association, 50 East Huron, Chicago, IL

60611. Linda will compile your replies and share them with current committees. Only by working together and by doing so systematically and on a national level can the profession get an overall picture of the role of BBYA and use that information to better serve young adults.

THE BOOKS THAT LAST

The eyes of Texas, like those of much of the nation, currently focus on our past. When I walk across the Denton campus of Texas Woman's University, I see students dressed in the classic garb of the 1960s: miniskirts, bell-bottomed blue jeans, and tie-dyed shirts. Several major radio stations have now switched to an "oldies but goodies" format, playing songs by groups such as The Beach Boys and The Four Freshmen—songs that were recorded when the age of the singers accurately reflected the names of their bands. Despite the financial woes of small, independently owned businesses, established antique stores continue to thrive while newer co-ops, selling both antiques and memorabilia, are either opening or expanding across the state. Furniture styles, clothing fads, and musical scores return from our past, adding their own nostalgic mark on the present. Some items, particularly those such as comic books that identify the pop culture, have become financial windfalls. As Betty Thompson remarks in Marianne Gingher's novel *Bobby Rex's Greatest Hit*: "Everything always comes back in style. We'd be smart if we saved everything."[3] I suspect many of us share her sentiments—except when it comes to books.

Caught up in a growing emphasis to read the new titles, keep up with the latest trends, and learn today's hottest new authors, librarians often fail to remember those literary "oldies but goodies" that have been around for years. Nowhere is that tendency more evident than in young adult literature.

By nature, many young adult titles are trendy reflections of the day's popular culture, making it easy to forget those finer older works that have remained popular with teenagers over the years. Remembering those titles and highlighting them for another generation of YA librarians has been the thrust of three successful preconferences sponsored by YALSA.

In 1975, 1983, and 1988, YA bibliophiles signed up for three ALA preconferences ("Book You," "Best Books—and You!", and "Still Great in '88," respectively) to take a second (and sometimes a third and fourth) look at previous Best Books lists. They read through the greats and the not so greats from preceding years, they looked at titles that did not appear as Best Books but still held wide appeal for YA readers, and they compiled three superlists (entitled "Still Alive in '75," "The Best of the Best," and "Nothin' But the Best") of enduring books. (See Part Two: The Best of the Best by Preconference for a listing of these books.) In the summer of 1994, a fourth preconference in Miami repeats the process.

The concept for the preconference began in 1975 when Carol Starr was Young Adult Coordinator at the Alameda County (California) Library and Regina Minudri was Assistant County Librarian at the same library. They developed the idea for the first of these five-year programs:

> Carol Starr was YASD president that year. Neither of us [Starr and Minudri] can remember who came up with the idea. We believe it was simultaneous. I know that Carol wanted to do a preconference that focused on YA books, and after some discussion, we agreed to take a long look at Best Books for Young Adults to see how they had held up. She asked me if I would take responsibility for organizing the preconference and I agreed to be chair.
>
> Our intention was to revisit all the BBYA lists and reevaluate the titles. We wanted to come up with a "Best of the Best" list that would have titles that stood the test of time. Our focus was to select good books that had remained popular with young adults.
>
> . . . "Book You" was the title of the 1975 Best of the Best [preconference]. That came from a colleague in Alameda County who saw a four-letter word scrawled on the dust of the Bookmobile and was able to change it to "Book You" with just a few additions.[4]

When librarians registered to attend the preconference, they received assignments to locate, read, and evaluate books from a particular five-year segment from 1960 to 1974. They were encouraged to use BBYA lists as well as to look beyond those recommendations to find additional books young adults were still reading. Participants assigned to the more-recent lists located those books they thought tomorrow's young adults would be reading in the future. Enthusiasm ran high. One registrant, new to YASD, exemplified the spirit of the conference: "I decided that finances be damned and paid my way to San Francisco."[5]

Young adult librarians, authors, and reviewers examined trends in BBYA, in publishing, and in library services. But the real work and rewards of the preconference came when participants met with their respective groups and selected those books that were "Still Alive in '75." They borrowed from the Newbery-Caldecott balloting system, and each caucus worked independently of the others. Groups kept their individual tallies secret and turned them in to Regina Minudri an hour before a celebratory banquet. She recalls, "I remember well the feeling of excitement at the banquet when I walked in, after dessert, and had the final list in my hand. The [organizational] committee spent the hour between the end of the session and the beginning of dinner using pocket calculators to tabulate the results. As I read the list, from bottom to top, there were cheers from the audience as favorite authors and titles were mentioned."[6]

The results of the preconference extended far beyond the actual list. Participants Michael McCue and Evie Wilson shared their enthusiasm for the concept, the execution, and the outcome of "Book You":

> Just the having of this preconference was a hard-fought victory for YASD. Its quality is assuredly an indication of what the membership of this division can produce. There was an absolutely invaluable exchange of opinions on an informal, free-talking basis among publishers, librarians, and authors that will establish groundwork for better communication with all who serve young adults. "Book You" set somewhat of a precedent in the participation of those (though bodily absent) for whom the final list was intended. In many cases, surveys were taken in classrooms and libraries so that YAs could speak through the participants. Before the conference one might have expected people to be fighting tooth and nail over titles, but that was hardly the case. It was amazing as many a favorite name or title in one person's view got the ax with nary a whimper or snarl. Again and again in

the discussion groups, the heated conversation would be "OK, that's what you think, but are YAs really reading it?" This was the spirit of not BOOK ME, but BOOK YOU, resulting in what will predictably be one of the most popular YA lists in existence.[7]

Five years later, Barbara Newmark, the 1983 YASD president, planned a repeat performance. She appointed Rhonna Goodman as chair, and the program, "Best Books—and You!" focused on lists from the previous twelve years, 1970 to 1983. Panel discussions and invited speakers emphasized the "changing teenager but . . . the sameness of their interests."[8]

Again, participants registered for particular years and prepared themselves to discuss books and make recommendations, or denunciations, for a final list. As they had for the previous program, participants looked for those books still read and enjoyed by and relevant to young adults.

Goodman recalled the activities:

> The group meetings, which I observed, were very lively, and there was a lot of shouting and emotional pitches for favorite books. Each group developed a personality and real spirit. The great moment of excitement, however, was at the read-off. As I would read the titles on the list, people would cheer and/or shout.[9]

Trying for a charmed third and succeeding, Gerald Hodges, fleeting 1988 Young Adult Services Division (YASD) president (he had to resign this position when he took an administrative post at ALA) and Christy Tyson, 1989 YASD president, designed another preconference to reexamine young adult reading preferences. Penny Jeffrey agreed to chair. Following a now-established pattern, participants signed up for particular years (this time from 1966 to 1986), read widely in their assigned time periods, consulted young adults, and came prepared to formulate a list of books for the preconference "Still Great in '88."

Participant Cathi MacRae described the players in this third drama:

> Representing thirty states and Bermuda, over half of the preconference participants were public librarians, one quarter were school media specialists, and 10 percent were library school educators. The rest were a mixed bag of publishers, book reviewers, authors, and special librarians. Organized by publication year, they formed fifteen groups, each directed to choose, somehow, five top books within eight hours of discussion time.[10]

The majority of those selected books, or sixty-eight titles, came from previous BBYA lists. Since popularity was the dominant criterion, however, there were exceptions. The books singled out in the "Still Great in '88" program included titles hotly debated at the time of publication but not originally designated as BBYA, such as Judy Blume's perennial favorite *Forever*; selections not eligible for previous adult-books-only lists, such as S. E. Hinton's *The Outsiders* and Paul Zindel's *The Pigman*; and strong books appearing in annual YA popularity polls, such as Mary Higgins Clark's *Where Are the Children?*, that with the wisdom of hindsight should have been included on original BBYA lists but weren't.

Fiction dominates the 1988 list, and nine novelists (Robert Cormier, Chris Crutcher, Rosa Guy, S. E. Hinton, M. E. Kerr, Richard Peck, William

Sleator, Cynthia Voigt, and Paul Zindel) are represented with multiple entries. Nonetheless, this list is not the exclusive domain of such young adult authors: approximately one third of the selections are those special adult books that also appeal to a teenage audience.

The wide range of young adult reading tastes characterizes other divisions of the 1988 list. Biographical selections, such as Steven Callahan's *Adrift*, Lynda Van Devanter's *Home before Morning*, and Ilsa Koehn's *Mischling Second Degree*, reflect the persisting young adult interest in personal accounts. The inclusion of Raymond Briggs's adult picture book *When the Wind Blows*, informational works such as *The Rolling Stone Illustrated History of Rock and Roll* and *Under 18 and Pregnant*, drama (*The Effect of Gamma Rays on Man-in-the-Moon Marigolds*), short stories (*Sixteen*), and collections of letters (*Dear America: Letters Home From Vietnam*) all underscore the diversity in young adult book choices.

Do young adults change their reading from year to year? Of course they do, but they also stick with some special favorites. Although each preconference focused on different time periods, eight books appear on all three Best of the Best lists. Each deserves our respect; according to conference participants, table 6 lists the eight books that have received it from young adults.

TABLE 6   Books Appearing on Three "Best of the Best" Lists

Author	Title	BBYA Year
Angelou, Maya	*I Know Why the Caged Bird Sings*	1970
Childress, Alice	*A Hero Ain't Nothin' but a Sandwich*	1973
Cormier, Robert	*The Chocolate War: A Novel*	1974
Guy, Rosa	*Friends*	1973
Plath, Sylvia	*The Bell Jar*	1971
Sleator, William	*House of Stairs*	1974
Swarthout, Glendon	*Bless the Beasts and Children*	1970
White, Robb	*Deathwatch*	1972

These preconferences dramatically highlight good books, dedicated librarians, and young adult readers. But they are not perfect. Cathi MacRae discusses several weaknesses:

> While the Best of the Best Books lists are enjoyable, enlightening learning experiences for their compilers, they may not accurately depict what is "still great" among YA readers. Beyond the problem of merely being products of those who sign up for a preconference, there are other inconsistencies in their making. In 1988, fifteen groups selected their titles in fifteen different ways, sharing only the basic ground rules. Communication among groups was nonexistent, though some discussed the same titles, and no attempt was made to "balance" the final fragmentary product. All groups used their allotted five titles, with no way to judge which years' publications deserved more or less. Some groups, especially in the early years, found their choices easy; others were agonizingly difficult. These inequities account for such occurrences as the solo appearance of Stephen King's *Night Shift* (1975) in 1988, never his most popular work, so surely not "still greatest" of them all.

Of course any YA Best Books list is filtered through the perceptions of adults who are more (or less) aware of what young adults actually read, who fall on one side or another of the quality/popularity "perplex"—or wobble back and forth—and some of whom bring their personal agendas along, quite apart from the criteria. One 1988 conferee expressed disappointment with people who chose a certain year to crusade for personal favorites, with little concern for their use among YA readers. Some listmakers believe in prescribing books for kids, missing a not-so-subtle difference between annual Best Books lists and Best of the Best. Annual listmakers may hazard informed guesses about new books' appeal, but reevaluators must respond to those that have actually lasted."[11]

Despite these caveats, such programs have value. They bring young adult books and young adult reading to the discussion forefront and allow librarians opportunities to focus on those sometimes-forgotten older and less-flashy titles. These preconferences also give librarians a chance to think about how their preferences may have changed over the years. Jacquie Brown Woody, chair of 1982 BBYA, mentions that at the time of the voting her favorite title was Ford's *Quest for the Faradawn*, describing this book as "beautiful, lyrical, imaginative, and a pleasure to read." Yet, ten years later the book on the 1982 list that is now her favorite is one that has "staying power," and still stands as a "marvelous tribute to a great man," Paul Robeson's *Whole World in His Hands*.[12]

Some participants truly evaluate young adult preferences by checking circulation statistics, by conducting broad surveys, and by talking to great numbers of young adults. But much of the data shared in these sessions tends to be anecdotal, and that may well be of dubious value. Much of what we hear is what we want to hear. Young adults who frequent particular libraries know what their librarians like. Often, comments of the young adults mirror these adult librarian tastes, while the differences remain unspoken. To mitigate against this problem, future Best of the Best gatherings will have to encourage all participants to devote part of their preparation time to gathering solid data from young adult readers. Only then will such lists hold validity as reflections of reading preferences.

It also may be time to alter the focus in subsequent programs, although not as substitutes but rather as additions. Might not other preconferences examine touchstone books, such as Paul Janeczko's *Poetspeak* or Russell Freedman's *Lincoln: A Photobiography*, that may never garner the mass appeal of a Stephen King offering but, nonetheless, represent an important contribution in the development of young adult literature? While the strong emphasis on what young adults read remains important, it should always coexist with that which they might read by reaching beyond their familiar favorites.

POSTSCRIPT

So, what makes a best book? Throughout this project individuals and committees ask this over and over: "It's a good book, but is it a *best* book?" I've thought about this, and I've wrestled with it. And I've concluded that in the final analysis, a best book is one that not only challenges a reader to think about the world in a different way but one that stays with that reader—a book that becomes such an intimate part of his or her makeup that it turns into a welcomed friend. Individual readers discover their own friends, sometimes with outside help and sometimes independently. But for each young adult reader, I hope that somewhere among all these books resides a literary companion.

Nanette Burleson, a secondary education major at Texas Woman's University, understands the power of such a friendship:

> "Louden Swain is dead" I said.
>
> My spousal unit, unofficial representative of the common man, had been dozing.
>
> "Louden Swain the wrestler?" he replied.
>
> "Yes. He became an astronaut and was killed." His eyes grew large, searching my face for the telltale signs of a joke. "Louden Swain the wrestler—the guy that starved himself for the big match?"
>
> "Yes," I replied, somewhat impressed with the schemata he was displaying. The remark had actually been a test of sorts; I had thought he wouldn't know the name.
>
> "No, you can't be serious—let me see that," and grabbed the book out of my hands.* He read the lines himself and muttered, "No way. Not Louden. Not after all that . . ."
>
> Louden Swain was good, not what I had considered a universal modern day hero, but nonetheless, a contender in several other worthy categories on my list. But my common man's response was intriguing. Little usually woke him from slumber, let alone allowed for the display of sorrow and loss that followed. He was crushed. A gladiator had been slain.
>
> Several days passed and I became curious. How would the rest of the world handle the knowledge of Louden's untimely death? I began my own quite unscientific poll querying individuals that I knew and some that I didn't. Each time the questions were a bit different, sometimes direct: "Do you remember a character. . .?" Other times, "Did you ever read that book about the wrestler. . .?" "What was that guy's name, you know, the wrestler. . .?" Each time the respondents were correct in their answers, remembering names, plots, and even the villain.
>
> I attempted to get a wide variation in ages in my target audience. I accepted responses from individuals who had either read the book or seen the movie (since few people seem to separate the two experiences nowadays). Indeed, several mentioned that they had read the book after seeing the movie because they were so taken with the story.
>
> It became obvious that female respondents had different identifications with the character than did males, but each individual's memory was a vivid, fond, admirable one. Louden Swain had touched all of their lives. Each time I mentioned the fact that he was dead, looks of sorrow and loss would cross their faces. Some looked on me with disdain, I had brought the bad news of the death of a close friend.[13]

Louden Swain comes from *Vision Quest* by Terry Davis. And, yes, it's a best book.

*In Terry Davis's new book, *If Rock and Roll Were a Machine*, the reader is told of Louden Swain's death via a memorial plaque at David Thompson High School.

Notes
1. Penelope Lou Apple Trosper, "Holdings of the 1991 Best Books for Young Adult List Titles by Northeast Texas Library System Members Who Belong to Online Computer Library Center" (Professional paper, Texas Woman's University, 1993), 23.

2. Trosper, "Holdings of the 1991 Best Books," 21–22.

3. Marianne Gingher, *Bobby Rex's Greatest Hit* (New York: Atheneum, 1986), 286.

4. Regina Minudri, letter to Betty Carter, 14 Apr. 1993.

5. Michael McCue and Evie Wilson, "Book You—Book Now: A Survival Preconference," *Top of the News* 32 (Nov. 1975): 30.

6. Regina Minudri, letter to Betty Carter, 14 Apr. 1993.

7. McCue and Wilson, "Book You," 33.

8. Rhonna A. Goodman, letter to Betty Carter, 30 Mar. 1993.

9. Goodman, letter to Betty Carter, 30 Mar. 1993.

10. Cathi MacRae, "The Young Adult Perplex," *Wilson Library Bulletin* 63 (Nov. 1988): 98.

11. MacRae, "The Young Adult Perplex," 99.

12. Jacquie Brown Woody, letter to Betty Carter, 1 June 1993.

13. Nanette P. Burleson, "Terry Davis' Vision" (Unpublished paper, Texas Woman's University, 1993), 1–2, 6.

PART TWO

Book Lists 1966-1993

Young Adult Library Services Association

The Books by Author

Throughout the following complete listing of the Best Books for Young Adults, 1966 to 1993, some of the titles are noted with icons. These icons represent titles selected in three preconferences sponsored by the Young Adult Library Services Association and its predecessor, the Young Adult Services Division. The titles selected at the three preconferences were subsequently published in pamphlet form as "best of the best" lists. A ■ indicates selection in "Still Alive: The Best of the Best, 1960–1974." A ▲ indicates selection in "The Best of the Best Books: 1970–1983." A ◆ indicates selection in "Nothin' But the Best: Best of the Best Books for Young Adults, 1966–1986." Some titles were selected in more than one of the three preconferences and are so indicated. A complete roster of the titles and their authors appears in the section "The Best of the Best by Preconference."

Aaron, Henry, and Wheeler, Lonnie. *I Had a Hammer,* HarperCollins, 1992.
Henry Aaron, the man who broke Babe Ruth's home run record, found that his accomplishments brought cheers from some but unleashed racial hatred in others. (Nonfiction)

Abdul-Jabbar, Kareem, and McCarthy, Mignon. *Kareem,* Random, 1991.
Action and day-to-day routine are combined in Abdul-Jabbar's quiet reflections in a behind-the-scenes look at his last year in professional basketball. (Nonfiction)

Abel, Elie. *Missile Crisis,* Lippincott, 1966.
President Kennedy's decisive action during the 1962 nuclear confrontation between Russia and the U.S. over missile sites in Cuba is chronicled. (Nonfiction)

Abercrombie, Barbara. *Run for Your Life,* Morrow, 1984.
Writing a mystery that climaxes with a marathon while training for a similar contest, Sarah finds herself in a race with death as her fiction becomes reality. (Fiction)

Adams, Douglas. *Hitchhiker's Guide to the Galaxy,* Harmony, 1980. ◆
The hilarious journey of Arthur Dent and his friend Ford Prefect, a space hitchhiker, who escape from Earth seconds before it is demolished and travel to a variety of galactic civilizations while gathering information for a hitchhiker's guidebook. (Fiction)

————, and Carwardine, Mark. *Last Chance to See,* Crown/Harmony, 1992.
Adams, author of the Hitchhiker's trilogy, and zoologist Carwardine embark on a personal

journey filled with humor, irony, and frustations as they attempt to observe some of the earth's exotic endangered species. (Nonfiction)

Adams, Richard. *Watership Down,* Macmillan, 1974. ■ ▲
Follow the epic, Tolkienesque adventures of Fiver, Hazel and a ragtag lapin band. Rabbits will never seem the same again. (Fiction)

Adler, C. S. *Shell Lady's Daughter,* Coward, 1983.
Kelly, living with her disapproving grandmother and senile grandfather because of her mother's nervous breakdown, must decide whether her mother's needs or her own struggle for independence comes first. (Fiction)

Adoff, Arnold, ed. *Celebrations: A New Anthology of Black American Poetry,* Follett, 1978.
This outstanding compilation of poems by eighty-five black poets, familiar and new, is a celebration of black life as reflected in diverse themes, including "The Idea of Ancestry," "The Southern Road," "Young Soul," and "Make Music with Your Life." (Nonfiction)

Agard, John, comp. *Life Doesn't Frighten Me at All,* Holt, 1991.
A stimulating collection of poetry by writers from all over the world, from unknowns to Bob Marley and Maya Angelou. (Nonfiction)

Aldridge, James. *Sporting Proposition,* Little, 1973.
A poor teenage boy and the town's richest girl are pitted against each other for the ownership of a pony. (Fiction)

Alexander, Lloyd. *Beggar Queen,* Dutton, 1984.
As the kingdom of Westmark is torn by brutal civil strife, Theo must balance his personal and political responsibilities and face the monster in himself. (Fiction)

———. *Kestrel,* Dutton, 1982.
In this sequel to Westmark, Theo, along with his revolutionary friends, helps Mickie, now the queen, to victory when Westmark is invaded by the neighboring country. (Fiction)

———. *Westmark,* Dutton, 1981. ▲
Forced to leave town because of a murder he thinks he committed, Theo becomes involved with a medicine showman, a dwarf, and a beautiful girl—and with Cabbarus, who is influencing the king against him. (Fiction)

Ali, Muhammad, and Durham, Richard. *Greatest: My Own Story,* Random, 1975. ▲
Heavyweight boxing champ and outrageous poet, Muhammad Ali reveals the man behind the gloves. (Nonfiction)

Allen, Maury. *Jackie Robinson: A Life Remembered,* Watts, 1987.
A compassionate biography/oral history of the first black pro baseball player, who demonstrated competitiveness and courage. (Nonfiction)

Allen, Terry, ed. *Whispering Wind; Poetry by Young American Indians,* Doubleday, 1972.
The wind whispers and the heart soars with the eagle in these brief, moving poems on loneliness, love, and the search for self. (Nonfiction)

Amos, James. *Memorial: A Novel of the Vietnam War,* Crown, 1990.
Standing in front of the Vietnam War Memorial, Marine Lt. Jakes vividly recalls the horrors leading to its creation. (Fiction)

Amosov, Nikolai. *Open Heart,* Simon & Schuster, 1967.
Life and death drama fills this absorbing personal diary of two days and nights in the life of a compassionate Russian heart surgeon. (Nonfiction)

Anastos, Phillip. *Illegal: Seeking the American Dream,* Rizzoli, 1992.
Expressions of bleak desperation and tentative hope are captured in photographs of "illegal aliens" crossing the Rio Grande to seek a better life in America. (Nonfiction)

Anderson, Joan. *American Family Farm,* Harcourt, 1990.
Focusing on three separate families from Massachusetts, Georgia, and Iowa, this photo essay examines the typical joys and struggles of running the small family farm. (Nonfiction)

Anderson, Scott. *Distant Fires,* Pfeifer-Hamilton, 1991.
Risking both life and sense of humor, two young men re-create Eric Severeid's 1930 portage and canoe trip over 1,700 miles from the tip of Lake Superior to the shores of Hudson Bay. (Nonfiction)

■ Selected for "Still Alive: The Best of the Best, 1960–1974"

▲ Selected for "The Best of the Best Books, 1970–1983"

◆ Selected for "Nothin' But the Best: Best of the Best Books for Young Adults, 1966–1986"

Andronik, Catherine M. *Quest for a King: Searching for the Real King Arthur,* Atheneum, 1990.
Andronik unravels the mysteries of King Arthur's life and places the legends in historical and geographical perspective. (Nonfiction)

Angell, Judie. *One-way to Ansonia,* Bradbury, 1985.
At the turn of the century, Rose and her siblings emigrate from Russia to New York, where—with great determination—they fight to succeed in their new environment. (Fiction)

Angelou, Maya. *All God's Children Need Traveling Shoes,* Random, 1986.
The experience of finding a "home" where she has never before lived becomes the catalyst for insights about African and American blackness for this celebrated author. (Nonfiction)

_____. *Gather Together in My Name,* Random, 1974.
This sequel to *I Know Why the Caged Bird Sings* continues the autobiography of a dauntless young woman forced to take a variety of jobs to support herself and her infant son. (Nonfiction)

_____. *I Know Why the Caged Bird Sings,* Random, 1970. ■ ▲ ♦
Remarkable, poetic, and frank autobiography of a black girl who grew up in Arkansas, St. Louis, and San Francisco. For mature readers. (Nonfiction)

_____. *Swingin' and Singin' and Gettin' Merry like Christmas,* Random, 1976.
Angelou continues her autobiography, telling of her brief marriage, her efforts to raise her young son, and her beginning successes in show business. (Nonfiction)

Anonymous. *Go Ask Alice,* Prentice-Hall, 1971. ■ ▲
The true and painful diary of a young girl who accidentally falls into the contemporary drug scene. For mature readers. (Nonfiction)

Ansa, Tina McElroy. *Baby of the Family,* Harcourt, 1991.
Lena is special, not only because she is the baby of her middle-class African-American family but also because of the supernatural gifts she received at birth. (Fiction)

Anson, Jay. *Amityville Horror,* Prentice-Hall, 1977.
Bone-chilling cold, poltergeist activity, nauseating stench, unnatural noise, and green slime are only a few of the manifestations that terrify a family in their new home. Is this story a hoax or not? (Nonfiction)

Anson, Robert Sam. *Best Intentions: The Education and Killing of Edmund Perry,* Random, 1987.
This is the gripping story of events surrounding the death of black prep school student Edmund Perry at the hands of an undercover cop. (Nonfiction)

Anthony, Piers. *On a Pale Horse,* Ballantine/ Del Rey, 1984.
During his attempted suicide, Zane kills Death and thereafter must do Death's job of collecting souls. (Fiction)

Appel, Allen. *Till the End of Time,* Doubleday, 1991.
Transported back to the time of the bombing of Pearl Harbor, Alex Balfour uses his knowledge of contemporary history to try to stop the bombing of Hiroshima and Nagasaki. (Fiction)

_____. *Time after Time,* Carroll & Graf, 1986.
After traveling through time to 1917 Russia, Alex wonders if he should change history or simply escape. (Fiction)

Archer, Jeffrey. *Not a Penny More, Not a Penny Less,* Doubleday, 1976.
Discovering they have been conned by a fast-talking promoter, four strangers get together to recover their million dollars. (Fiction)

Archer, Jules. *Incredible Sixties: The Stormy Years That Changed America,* Harcourt, 1986.
Archer's thematic overview of the 1960s presents the important historical, political, and social events and personalities of the period. (Nonfiction)

Armor, John, and Wright, Peter. *Manzanar,* Times Books, 1990.
The tragic internment of Japanese Americans during World War II at one California relocation center is documented through Armor's evocative words and Ansel Adams's photos. (Nonfiction)

Armstrong, Charlotte. *Gift Shop,* Coward-McCann, 1967.
An exciting mystery in which Jean Cunliffe helps Harry Fairchild find and save a kidnapped child threatened with death. (Fiction)

Armstrong, Jennifer. *Steal Away,* Orchard/ Richard Jackson, 1993.
During a dangerous escape to the north, orphaned Susannah and her unwanted gift slave, Bethlehem, form a lifelong friendship. (Fiction)

Arnosky, Jim. *Flies in the Water, Fish in the Air: A Personal Introduction to Fly Fishing,* Lothrop, 1986.
Author, illustrator and trout fisherman Arnosky shares his knowledge of fly fishing,

his intimate acquaintance with water, and his love of nature. (Nonfiction)

Arrick, Fran. *God's Radar*, Bradbury, 1983. Roxie and her family, newcomers in a small town in Georgia, are seduced into joining a fundamentalist church by religious neighbors, and Roxie must make decisions, some of them against the tide. (Fiction)

———. *Steffie Can't Come Out to Play*, Dutton, 1978. When fourteen-year-old Steffie runs away to New York to be a model, she meets Favor and becomes one of his prostitutes before a concerned cop intervenes. (Fiction)

———. *What You Don't Know Can Kill You*, Bantam/Starfire, 1993. Ellen's agenda is exciting—graduation, college, lots of romance, and marriage. If it weren't for this "bug," everything would be perfect. Ellen is HIV-positive. (Fiction)

Arter, Jim. *Gruel and Unusual Punishment*, Delacorte, 1992. Always in trouble, Arnold jokes his way through school to hide the pain of repeating seventh grade, being friendless and fatherless, and protecting a mother whom others consider crazy. (Fiction)

Ash, Brian, ed. *Visual Encyclopedia of Science Fiction*, Crown/Harmony, 1978. A visually appealing compendium of SF info contains views on major themes by notable writers, a history of the genre, notes on fandom, science fiction art, movie tie-ins, and much more. (Nonfiction)

Ashabranner, Brent. *Always to Remember: The Vietnam Veterans Memorial*, Dodd, 1988. The story of Vietnam veteran Jan C. Scruggs's struggle to build a national monument honoring Americans who died or are missing in the Vietnam War. (Nonfiction)

———. *To Live in Two Worlds: American Indian Youth Today*, Dodd, 1984. Young American Indian men and women talk about their lives on and off the reservation and their hopes for the future. (Nonfiction)

Asimov, Isaac. *Fantastic Voyage*, Houghton, 1966. ■ How a miniaturized submarine carrying a team of doctors travels through the bloodstream of a brilliant scientist in order to save his life. (Fiction)

Asimov, Isaac, and others, eds. *Creations: The Quest for Origins in Story and Science*, Crown, 1983. Speculations on the creation of the universe and its part in fiction, scientific observation, and religious belief. (Nonfiction)

Atwood, Ann. *Haiku-Vision: In Poetry and Photography*, Scribner, 1977. The fusion of seeing and feeling is an experience of the spirit in an exquisitely illustrated book of haiku poetry and photography. (Nonfiction)

Atwood, Margaret. *Handmaid's Tale*, Houghton, 1986. Offred, a handmaid living in a near-future time, endures life in a society in which women able to bear children are used for procreation. (Fiction)

Auel, Jean. *Clan of the Cave Bear*, Crown, 1980. ▲ A Cro-Magnon girl-child, adopted by a tribe of Neanderthals, struggles to subdue her strong feminine creativity while growing up in a mystical and instinctive male-dominated society. (Fiction)

Avi. *Blue Heron*, Bradbury, 1993. A solitary blue heron becomes a symbol of strength and peace for thirteen-year-old Maggie when she discovers a troubling change has come over her father and his new family. (Fiction)

———. *Fighting Ground*, Lippincott, 1984. Jonathon sees his dream of heroic battle turn to a nightmare when he is captured by Hessian soldiers during the American Revolution. (Fiction)

———. *Nothing but the Truth: A Documentary Novel*, Orchard/Richard Jackson, 1992. It's against regulations to hum the national anthem in school. Philip decides to disobey the rule, and the whole nation watches what happens. (Fiction)

———. *True Confessions of Charlotte Doyle*, Watts/Orchard, 1991. The only passenger on a ship sailing from England to America in 1832, Charlotte finds herself accused of murder as she becomes in-

---

■ Selected for "Still Alive: The Best of the Best, 1960–1974"

▲ Selected for "The Best of the Best Books, 1970–1983"

♦ Selected for "Nothin' But the Best: Best of the Best Books for Young Adults, 1966–1986"

volved in a plot to overthrow the villainous captain. (Fiction)

_____. *Wolf Rider*, Bradbury, 1986.
When fifteen-year-old Andy gets a crank call from a man claiming to have murdered a woman, his life turns into a psychological nightmare. (Fiction)

Bach, Alice. *Waiting for Johnny Miracle*, Harper, 1980.
Twins Becky and Theo Maitland do everything together. But when cancer strikes Becky, they know that life will never be the same again. A sensitive portrait of a family in crisis. (Fiction)

Bach, Richard. *Biplane*, Harper, 1966.
Trading his modern plane for a 1929 open cockpit biplane, the author made a hazardous cross-country flight from North Carolina to California. (Nonfiction)

Bachman, Richard. *Long Walk*, Signet, 1979.
Of the one hundred boys who begin a grueling marathon walk, ninety-nine will die—and one will have his every wish granted. Or will he? (Fiction)

Bacon, Katherine Jay. *Shadow and Light*, Macmillan/Margaret K. McElderry, 1987.
During a summer at her beloved grandmother's farm in Vermont, fifteen-year-old Emma learns to cope with her grandmother's dying. (Fiction)

Bagley, Desmond. *Landslide*, Doubleday, 1967.
Amnesiac Bob Boyd struggles to find out who he really is in this adventure and suspense novel. (Fiction)

_____. *Vivero Letter*, Doubleday, 1968.
The discovery of a sixteenth-century golden plate leads to murder and an ancient Mayan city in Quintana Roo. (Fiction)

Balducci, Carolyn. *Is There a Life after Graduation, Henry Birnbaum?*, Houghton, 1971.
Henry Birnbaum and David Schoen, best friends in Queens, enroll in separate colleges and find life away from home almost overwhelmingly complicated by women and activists. (Fiction)

Baldwin, James. *If Beale Street Could Talk*, Dial, 1974. ■ ▲
A young black couple, separated by his unjust imprisonment, are bolstered by their love for each other and determination of her loyal family. (Fiction)

Baldwin, J., ed. *Whole Earth Ecolog: The Best of Environmental Tools and Ideas*, Crown, 1991.
A browser's delight, this is a catalog of the best ecological books, information, processes, tools, and ideas to help individuals make an environmental difference. (Nonfiction)

Ball, John Dudley. *Cool Cottontail*, Harper, 1967.
Virgil Tibbs, the black detective of *In the Heat of the Night*, is assigned to a case involving a murder committed in a nudist colony. (Fiction)

_____. *Johnny Get Your Gun*, Little, Brown, 1969.
Detective Virgil Tibbs is called into a case involving nine-year-old Johnny McGuire, who sets out to murder a schoolmate for breaking his radio but instead shoots a popular teenager. (Fiction)

Ballard, J. G. *Empire of the Sun*, Simon & Schuster, 1985.
Eleven-year-old Jim's orderly life in 1939 Shanghai turns into a nightmare when the Japanese attack, separate him from his family, and imprison him for three years. (Fiction)

Banfield, Susan. *Rights of Man, the Reign of Terror: The Story of the French Revolution*, Lippincott, 1990.
Do the ends justify the means? The French Revolution is chronicled in fascinating detail. (Nonfiction)

Banks, Lynne Reid. *Dark Quartet: The Story of the Brontes*, Delacorte, 1977.
The brilliant but tortured lives of the Brontës are presented in a biographical novel that is as dramatic as *Wuthering Heights* or *Jane Eyre*. (Fiction)

_____. *Writing on the Wall*, Harper/Charlotte Zolotow, 1982.
Tracy is bicycling through Holland with her "punk" boyfriend when she innocently becomes involved in drug smuggling. (Fiction)

Barjavel, Rene. *Ice People*, Morrow, 1971.
In a cryogenic vault under the polar ice cap an international team of scientists discovers a man and a woman who are 900,000 years old. (Fiction)

Barker, S. Omar. *Little World Apart*, Doubleday, 1966.
Two brothers find excitement and adventure while growing up on a small cattle ranch in New Mexico. (Fiction)

Barlow, Wayne Douglas, and Summers, Ian. *Barlow's Guide to Extraterrestrials*, Workman, 1980.
Have you ever wondered what a Puppeteer or a Vegan Mother Thing looks like? How Pegulas move or Polarians reproduce? This fascinating and meticulously detailed, illustrated guide to great science fiction aliens tells all that and more. (Nonfiction)

Bauer, Steven. *Satyrday: A Fable*, Putnam, 1981.

Evil Owl's attempt to rule the world requires that Matthew, a satyr, and Dairn, a boy, try to save the moon and all creatures. (Fiction)

Beattie, Owen, and Geiger, John. *Buried in Ice: The Mystery of a Lost Arctic Expedition*, Scholastic, 1993.

The story of Owen Beattie's discovery of the remains of Sir John Franklin's doomed 1845 expedition through the Northwest Passage. (Nonfiction)

Beck, Calvin. *Heroes of the Horrors*, Macmillan, 1975.

All those movie monster favorites—Karloff, Lugosi, Chaney, and Price—in a splendid brew of photos and text. (Nonfiction)

Begley, Kathleen. *Deadline*, Putnam, 1977.

The experiences of a young newspaper reporter, whose personal and professional lives become intertwined when, for example, she celebrates her birthday in a police station and writes her mother's obituary. (Nonfiction)

Bell, Clare. *Ratha and Thistle-chaser*, Macmillan/Margaret K. McElderry, 1991.

Ratha's encounter with outsider Thistle-chaser reunites her with her forgotten past as her tribe of intelligent cats fights for survival during a severe drought. (Fiction)

———. *Ratha's Creature*, Atheneum, 1983.

Ratha, born into a society of intelligent prehistoric felines, is banished from the Clan, rescued by an unnamed male cat, and helps the Clan when she learns to tame fire. (Fiction)

Bell, David, M.D. *Time to Be Born*, Morrow, 1975.

A two-pound "preemie" and a newborn addict were only two of the many babies that Dr. Bell, a young pediatrician, cared for and also deeply cared about. (Nonfiction)

Bell, Ruth, ed. *Changing Bodies, Changing Lives: A Book for Teens on Sex and Relationships*, Random, 1981. ▲ ♦

Everything you want to know about teenage sexuality, presented in an honest, explicit manner. Inspired by *Our Bodies, Ourselves* and written by some of the same people. (Nonfiction)

Benchley, Nathaniel. *Bright Candles: A Novel of the Danish Resistance*, Harper, 1974.

Two teenagers turn from pranks to sabotage in this tense story of a people pushed to their limits by the tyranny of the Nazi regime in Denmark. (Fiction)

Benedict, Helen. *Safe, Strong, and Streetwise*, Little, Brown/Joy Street Books, 1987.

Both men and women can learn how to protect themselves from sexual assault. (Nonfiction)

Bennett, James. *I Can Hear the Mourning Dove*, Houghton, 1991.

Struggling to recover from her father's death and her own suicide attempt, Grace meets Luke, a fellow patient and her first real friend. (Fiction)

Berry, James. *Ajeemah and His Son*, HarperCollins/Willa Perlman, 1993.

Snatched by African slave traders, Ajeemah and his soon-to-be-married son, Atu, are shipped to Jamaica, where, though separated, they never accept their status as slaves or give up their desire for freedom. (Fiction)

Bess, Clayton. *Tracks*, Houghton, 1986.

Eleven-year-old Blue Roan persuades his older brother to take him on the rails in Depression-era Oklahoma where their adventures range from vicious attacks by a hobo to an almost fatal encounter with KKKers. (Fiction)

Bickham, Jack M. *Katie, Kelly and Heck*, Doubleday, 1973.

A lady, a tough guy, and a kid clash in this funny, fast-moving tale set in a rough, raw frontier town of the 1880s. (Fiction)

Bing, Leon. *Do or Die*, HarperCollins, 1992.

A bone-chilling account of gang-banging in which Crips and Bloods, infamous rival Los Angeles gangs, speak for themselves. (Nonfiction)

Birmingham, John. *Our Time Is Now: Notes from the High School Underground*, Praeger, 1970.

In this stinging anthology, uncensored high school students speak out about injustices in the schools and in America, the home of the not-so-brave, and of changes needed now. (Nonfiction)

■ Selected for "Still Alive: The Best of the Best, 1960–1974"

▲ Selected for "The Best of the Best Books, 1970–1983"

♦ Selected for "Nothin' But the Best: Best of the Best Books for Young Adults, 1966–1986"

Blake, Jeanne. *Risky Times: How to Be AIDS-Smart and Stay Healthy,* Workman, 1991.
The author and six teens bring you a book of facts on AIDS: how you get it, how you don't, and the decisions you must make for a healthy life. (Nonfiction)

Blankfort, Michael. *Take the A Train,* Dutton, 1978.
After he becomes the protege of a black pimp and numbers man, Mr. Gilboa, "Doc" Henshel, a seventeen-year-old white boy, learns some hard facts about life, love, and friendship on the electric streets of Harlem. (Fiction)

Bleier, Rocky, and O'Neill, Terry. *Fighting Back,* Stein & Day, 1975. ▲
Rocky Bleier tells how he overcame the battle wounds of Vietnam through rigid self-discipline and played in the Super Bowl. (Nonfiction)

Block, Francesca Lia. *Cherokee Bat and the Goat Guys,* HarperCollins/Charlotte Zolotow, 1993.
Cherokee and the Goat Guys rock band descend into the excess of the drug-rock-punk scene and need to be rescued by Native American Coyote's wise spiritual friendship. (Fiction)

———. *Weetzie Bat,* HarperCollins/Charlotte Zolotow, 1990.
Lanky lizards! Punk teens Weetzie and Dirk search for love in a modern fairy tale that is funny, moving, and unlike any book you've read before. (Fiction)

Blue, Vida, and Libby, Bill. *Vida: His Own Story,* Prentice-Hall, 1972.
Baseball pitcher Vida Blue tells what it feels like to achieve instant stardom and then be expected to produce miracles on the field every day. (Nonfiction)

Blum, Ralph. *Old Glory and the Real-Time Freaks,* Delacorte, 1972.
Quintus Ells is encouraged by his grandfather to write, while stoned, a "map" of his seventeenth summer describing his relationships with family and friends for his future grandson. (Fiction)

———. *Simultaneous Man,* Little, Brown, 1970.
American scientists replace a man's mind with the memory and personality of another in this chilling tale of U.S. and Russian intrigue. (Fiction)

———, **and Blum, Judy.** *Beyond Earth: Man's Contact with UFO's,* Bantam, 1974.
A rational account documents the UFO sightings of 1973—the objects, the terrified people who saw or were taken aboard them, and the stories they told afterward. (Nonfiction)

Blume, Judy. *Letters to Judy: What Your Kids Wish They Could Tell You,* Putnam, 1986.
A popular author responds to a large variety of letters from many young fans who have confided in her. (Nonfiction)

———. *Tiger Eyes,* Bradbury, 1981.
After her father's murder, Davey moves to Los Alamos, where she meets Wolf, a college boy whose father is dying of cancer. (Fiction)

Bodanis, David. *Secret House: 24 Hours in the Strange and Unexpected World in Which We Spend Our Nights and Days,* Simon & Schuster, 1986.
The microbiological drama found within a house is explored from early morning to late evening. (Nonfiction)

Bode, Janet. *Beating the Odds: Stories of Unexpected Achievers,* Watts, 1992.
Racial discrimination, abuse, poverty, depression: teens and adults talk about dealing with the problems of life and making it in spite of them. (Nonfiction)

———. *Kids Having Kids: The Unwed Teenage Parent,* Watts, 1980.
Sexual conduct, the health risks associated with teenage pregnancy, birth control, and the options open to unwed mothers are covered in this guide for pregnant teenagers as well as those in danger of becoming pregnant through lack of information. (Nonfiction)

———. *New Kids on the Block: Oral Histories of Immigrant Teens,* Watts, 1990.
Eleven teenage immigrants reveal the trials, frustrations, and joys of making a new life in the United States after escaping poverty, repression, and even war in their native countries. (Nonfiction)

———. *Voices of Rape,* Watts, 1991.
Date and stranger rape are explored through interviews with victims, perpetrators, and those involved in the medical and justice systems. (Nonfiction)

Bogle, Donald. *Brown Sugar: Eighty Years of America's Black Female Superstars,* Harmony, 1980.
In a dazzling, informative portrait, selected black female performers are presented as individuals and as important social symbols. (Nonfiction)

Boissard, Janice. *Matter of Feeling,* Little, Brown, 1980.
From the safety of her suburban Paris family home, seventeen-year-old French schoolgirl Pauline Moreau reaches out, in a brief and ten-

der love affair, to forty-year-old artist Pierre. (Fiction)

Bond, Nancy. *Place to Come Back To,*
    Atheneum/Margaret K. McElderry, 1984.
As Charlotte finds herself strongly attracted to one of her childhood friends, she discovers how difficult it is to give and receive love. (Fiction)

Bonner, Cindy. *Lily,* Algonquin, 1993.
When hard-working farm girl Lily DeLony falls in love with Marion, the youngest member of the outlaw Beatty gang, the town of McDade, Texas, is set on its ear. (Fiction)

Booher, Dianna Daniels. *Rape: What Would
    You Do If . . .?,* Messner, 1981.
Clear guidelines on how to judge a potential rape situation, with specifics about what to do if a rape should occur. (Nonfiction)

Bosse, Malcolm. *Captives of Time,*
    Delacorte, 1987.
To escape not only plague but also the barbaric hordes that killed their parents, Anne and her mute brother make their way to their eccentric uncle in the city. (Fiction)

Boston Women's Health Book Collective.
    *Our Bodies, Ourselves: A Book by and for
    Women,* Simon & Schuster, 1976. ▲
New medical findings and rethought feminist attitudes are incorporated into a completely revised edition of the now classic handbook on the female body. (Nonfiction)

Boulle, Pierre. *Whale of the Victoria Cross,*
    Vanguard, 1983.
A blue whale, saved from killer orcas by a British destroyer bound for the Falkland Islands, becomes a friend to the entire fleet. (Nonfiction)

Bouton, Jim. *Ball Four: My Life and Hard
    Times Throwing the Knuckleball in the
    Big Leagues,* World, 1970.
Definitely not for hero worshippers, a lively, often funny but devastating account of the antics of baseball players, managers, and coaches by a former big leaguer. (Nonfiction)

Bova, Ben. *Multiple Man: A Novel of
    Suspense,* Bobbs-Merrill, 1976.
President James J. Halliday has a top level secret—several exact duplicates of himself have been mysteriously and secretly killed. Press secretary Meric Albano wants to know why. (Fiction)

_____. *Welcome to Moonbase,* Ballantine,
    1988.
From lunar cuisine to low gravity football, this handbook introduces new employees to Moonbase, Inc. (Fiction)

Boyd, Malcolm. *Are You Running with Me,
    Jesus?,* Holt, 1966.
Provocative prayers of a former campus chaplain who is concerned with all facets of modern life. (Nonfiction)

Bradbury, Ray. *I Sing the Body Electric!,*
    Knopf, 1969.
In this collection of 18 stories, the author writes of mechanical grandmothers and fourth-dimensional babies as well as the Irish Republican Army and Texas chicken farmers. (Fiction)

Bradford, Richard. *Red Sky at Morning,*
    Lippincott, 1968.
Joshua Arnold, a wise, wry man-child, must cope with an absent father and a sherry-tippling mother, and learn to live in a new town, make friends, and finish growing up. (Fiction)

Bradley, Marion Zimmer. *Hawkmistress!,*
    NAL/DAW, 1982.
Forbidden to use her gift for communicating with animals and pushed by her father to marry a man she hates, Romilly MacAran flees to the hills of Darkover. (Fiction)

Bradley, William Warren. *Life on the Run,*
    Quadrangle, 1976.
Knicks veteran Bradley talks about the sport he loves, his teammates, and the pressures of professional basketball. (Nonfiction)

Bradshaw, Gillian. *Beacon at Alexandria,*
    Houghton, 1987.
Charis flees ancient Ephesus to avoid an arranged marriage and makes her way to Alexandria to study medicine. (Fiction)

_____. *Hawk of May,* Simon & Schuster,
    1980.
The war between good and evil is portrayed in this fantasy in which King Arthur's nephew, Gwalchmai, a reluctant warrior, first turns to his mother, an evil sorceress, for knowledge and power, then sets out to join King Arthur. (Fiction)

Braithwaite, Edward. *Paid Servant,*
    McGraw-Hill, 1968.
Too white for a Negro family, too black for a white family, four-year-old Roddy poses a

---

■ Selected for "Still Alive: The Best of the Best, 1960–1974"

▲ Selected for "The Best of the Best Books, 1970–1983"

♦ Selected for "Nothin' But the Best: Best of the Best Books for Young Adults, 1966–1986"

problem for welfare officer Braithwaite, who tries desperately to find him a home. (Nonfiction)

Brancato, Robin F. *Come Alive at 505,* Knopf, 1980.
Danny Fetzer copes with senior-year anxiety through his imaginary radio station WHUP, 505 on the dial, and through it becomes involved and obsessed with classmate Mimi. Together, they begin to find themselves. (Fiction)

_____. *Sweet Bells Jangled out of Tune,* Knopf, 1982.
Everybody in Windsor laughs at Eva Dohrmann, the town eccentric—everybody but Ellen, her fifteen-year-old granddaughter. (Fiction)

_____. *Winning,* Knopf, 1977. ▲ ♦
After sustaining a paralyzing injury in a high school football game, Gary Madden is forced to face the fact that he may never walk again. (Fiction)

Brand, Stewart. *Last Whole Earth Catalog,* Random, 1971.
This supercatalog, a kind of counterculture *Consumer Reports*, lists everything from papoose packs to Moog synthesizers and all items are "useful as tools, relevant to independent education, high quality or low cost, and easily available by mail." (Nonfiction)

Branscum, Robbie. *Girl,* Harper, 1986.
Though left in the exploitive care of their grandmother, a girl and her siblings find strength in each other as well as hope in the dream of their mother's return. (Fiction)

Bredes, Don. *Hard Feelings,* Atheneum, 1977.
Explicit in language and incident, this is sixteen-year-old Bernie Hergruter's story of growing up—confronting a class bully, getting along with his family, and understanding his sexuality. (Fiction)

Brenner, Joseph H., Coles, Robert, M.D., and others. *Drugs and Youth: Medical, Psychiatric and Legal Facts,* Liveright, 1970.
The authors give clinical studies and young drug users equal time in an objective, informative report. (Nonfiction)

Bridgers, Sue Ellen. *All Together Now: A Novel,* Knopf, 1979. ♦
Twelve-year-old Casey befriends thirty-three-year-old retarded Dwayne and saves him from being sent to a home. (Fiction)

_____. *Home before Dark,* Knopf, 1976.
When her father takes his migrant family back to his childhood home in Florida, fourteen-year-old Stella Willis is determined to put down roots and never leave again. (Fiction)

_____. *Notes for Another Life,* Knopf, 1981. ▲
Caught between their father's recurrent bouts with mental illness and their mother's career ambitions, teenagers Kevin and Wren attempt to preserve their fragile identities and relationships. (Fiction)

_____. *Permanent Connections,* Harper, 1987.
While caring for an ill relative, Rob finds that spending his junior year in a rural town is living hell, until he meets equally unhappy Ellery. (Fiction)

_____. *Sara Will,* Harper, 1985.
In a story of acceptance and coming of age, Sara Will is disrupted forever by the arrival of her brother-in-law, his unwed teenage niece, Eva, and her baby. (Fiction)

Briggs, Raymond. *When the Wind Blows,* Schocken, 1983. ♦
In this grim, cartoon-style satire an elderly British couple innocently—and futilely—try to prepare for nuclear attack by following government directives. (Fiction)

Brin, David. *Postman,* Bantam, 1985.
Wearing the uniform of a long dead postman, Gordon Krantz travels among scattered communities in the western United States, struggling against survivalists and uniting people in a post-nuclear-holocaust America. (Fiction)

Brooks, Bruce. *Midnight Hour Encores,* Harper, 1986.
Arrogant and musically gifted Sib and her father travel across country so that she can audition for a musical genius and meet the "hippie" mother who deserted her at birth. (Fiction)

_____. *Moves Make the Man,* Harper, 1985.
As Jerome, a black athlete, shares his skills and interest in basketball with Bix, a white baseball player, their friendship grows and the game becomes a reflection of both their lives. (Fiction)

_____. *No Kidding,* Harper, 1990.
In a not-too-distant future where alcoholism is rampant, fourteen-year-old Sam must decide the fate of his alcoholic mother and younger brother. (Fiction)

_____. *On the Wing,* Scribner, 1990.
A companion to the PBS-TV series *Nature*, this beautifully written and illustrated book explores the life of birds—from feathers to flight. (Nonfiction)

_____. *Predator!,* Farrar, 1992.
Stunning color photographs and a fascinating text illuminate the never-ending quest for food that faces all animals in the wild. (Nonfiction)

_____. *What Hearts*, HarperCollins/Laura Geringer, 1993.
Follow Asa from age seven to age twelve as he learns how to appreciate his family. (Fiction)

Brooks, Earle, and Brooks, Rhoda. *Barrios of Manta*, NAL, 1966.
A young sales engineer and his schoolteacher wife describe their Peace Corps activities among the poverty-stricken people of Manta, Ecuador. (Nonfiction)

Brooks, Martha. *Two Moons in August*, Little, Brown, 1993.
Surrounded by a family unable to come to terms with the death of her mother, Sidonie conquers her self-doubts and faces the fact that survival means accepting life with all its tragedies and triumphs. (Fiction)

Brooks, Polly Schoyer. *Beyond the Myth: The Story of Joan of Arc*, HarperCollins/Lippincott, 1991.
Condemned as a witch, but later canonized as a saint, young Joan, inspired by her love of France, led her countrymen in their battle against the English. (Nonfiction)

Brooks, Terry. *Magic Kingdom for Sale— Sold!*, Ballantine/Del Rey, 1986.
In a funny fantasy adventure, a disillusioned sorrowing widower, Ben, buys a magic kingdom for one million dollars only to find a run-down castle operated by a motley group of inept courtiers. (Fiction)

_____. *Sword of Shannara*, Random, 1977.
A small band of humans, elves, and dwarfs must face the armies of an evil sorcerer in order to reach the sword that can destroy him. (Fiction)

Brown, Dee. *Bury My Heart at Wounded Knee: An Indian History of the American West*, Holt, 1971. ▲
Battle by battle, massacre by massacre, broken treaty by broken treaty, this is a documented chronicle of the Indian struggle from 1860 to 1890 against the white man. (Nonfiction)

_____. *Creek Mary's Blood*, Holt, 1980.
They called her Creek Mary, a proud and beautiful daughter of a Muskogee chief, who was a leader among her people. This story of her and her descendants begins with Revolutionary War Georgia and ends with Teddy Roosevelt's 1905 White House. (Fiction)

Brown, Michael. *Laying Waste: The Poisoning of America by Toxic Chemicals*, Pantheon, 1980.
The dumping of industrial chemical waste created a disaster at Love Canal. The reporter who broke the story warns that it can happen again. (Nonfiction)

Brown, Rita Mae. *Starting from Scratch: A Different Kind of Writers' Manual*, Bantam, 1988.
Unorthodox, funny, but very practical advice on how to write—plus the author's irreverent comments on life in general. (Nonfiction)

Brown, Turner, Jr. *Black Is*, Grove, 1969.
"Black is when somebody brings you home to lunch during Brotherhood Week—after dark" and other definitions of *black* not in the dictionary. (Nonfiction)

Bull, Emma. *War for the Oaks*, Berkley/Ace, 1987.
A mad phouka, the queen of the Faerie, and band leader Eddi McCandry battle the Dark Court's evil power in a tale of rock music in Minneapolis. (Fiction)

Bunting, Eve. *If I Asked You, Would You Stay?*, Lippincott, 1984.
Crow and Valentine step tentatively out of their private worlds of hurt and loneliness toward one another. (Fiction)

_____. *Jumping the Nail*, Harcourt, 1993.
Some teens see jumping off the Nail, a ninety-foot cliff above the bottomless sea, as a way to prove their love for another, but Elisa jumps for a more sinister reason. (Fiction)

Burch, Jennings Michael. *They Cage the Animals at Night*, NAL, 1984.
The author recalls the sometimes kind but often brutal treatment he received between ages eight and eleven when he was placed in a series of institutions and foster homes by his mother, who was ill and could no longer care for him or his brothers. (Nonfiction)

Burchard, Sue. *Statue of Liberty: Birth to Rebirth*, Harcourt, 1985.
Packed full of facts and anecdotes about Miss Liberty—from the statue's conception to its centennial reconstruction and plans for the future. (Nonfiction)

Burnford, Sheila. *Bel Ria*, Atlantic-Little, 1978.
How an abandoned but spunky circus dog, who survives the Nazi takeover of France, shipboard

---

■ Selected for "Still Alive: The Best of the Best, 1960–1974"

▲ Selected for "The Best of the Best Books, 1970–1983"

♦ Selected for "Nothin' But the Best: Best of the Best Books for Young Adults, 1966–1986"

life, and the bombing of England, affects the lives of those he encounters. (Fiction)

Burns, Olive Ann. *Cold Sassy Tree*, Ticknor & Fields, 1985.
As his rural Georgia hometown undergoes many changes in the year 1906, Will Tweedy survives family scandal, his first kiss, and being run over by a train. (Fiction)

Buss, Fran Leeper, and Cubias, Daisy.
Journey of the Sparrows, Dutton/Lodestar, 1992.
Maria makes the dangerous trip across the border to the United States where jobs are scarce and she must evade immigration officers. (Fiction)

Busselle, Rebecca. *Bathing Ugly*, Watts/Orchard, 1990.
When thirteen-year-old Betsy represents her cabin in the camp beauty and ugly contests, her absurd behavior causes peers and adults to reevaluate their attitudes toward outward appearance. (Fiction)

Butterworth, Emma Macalik. *As the Waltz Was Ending*, Scholastic/Four Winds, 1982.
The German occupation of Vienna interrupts a promising ballet career for Emma, and life becomes a desperate struggle to stay alive. (Nonfiction)

Butterworth, W. E. *LeRoy and the Old Man*, Four Winds, 1980.
After witnessing a gang mugging, LeRoy leaves his home in Chicago to live with his grandfather in Mississippi. When the victim dies, LeRoy must decide if he wants to continue to hide or if he should testify against the gang members. (Fiction)

Bykov, Vasil. *Pack of Wolves*, Crowell, 1981.
Paralyzed with fear and betrayed by comrades, a wounded Russian partisan leads his small band through swamps in a terrifying escape from German soldiers. (Fiction)

Cable, Mary. *Blizzard of '88*, Atheneum, 1988.
Shocked Easterners rally to survive the blizzard of 1888, still considered one of the most serious natural disasters in American history. (Nonfiction)

Cagin, Seth. *We Are Not Afraid: The Story of Goodman, Schwerner, and Chaney and the Civil Rights Campaign for Mississippi*, Macmillan, 1988.
Cagin describes the battle for civil rights in Mississippi—and the murders of three young activists, tragic casualties of that 1964 summer. (Nonfiction)

Callahan, Steven. *Adrift: Seventy-Six Days Lost at Sea*, Houghton, 1986. ♦
When his small sailboat sank in the Atlantic, Steve Callahan spent 76 days in a 5-foot inflatable raft, drifting 1,800 miles before rescue. (Nonfiction)

Calvert, Patricia. *Snow Bird*, Scribner, 1980.
Orphaned fourteen-year-old Willie Bannerman and her brother, T.J., come to the Dakota Territory in 1883 to live with an aunt and uncle. With the help of Snow Bird, a white mare, Willie begins to repair her life and discover her true strength. (Fiction)

————. *Yesterday's Daughter*, Scribner, 1986.
Hurt and resentful, sixteen-year-old Leenie vows to shut her returning mother out of her life—until a brief romantic interlude opens her mind and heart. (Fiction)

Campbell, Eric. *Place of Lions*, Harcourt, 1993.
After surviving a plane crash on the African Serengeti Plain, fourteen-year-old Chris sets off to find help for his father and the pilot, who are injured, and forges a magical relationship with an aging lion. (Fiction)

Campbell, Hope. *No More Trains to Tottenville*, McCall, 1971.
When her mother "splits the scene" to India, Jane finds herself woman of the house and involved with a strange young man named Scorpio. (Fiction)

Campbell, Wright R. *Where Pigeons Go to Die*, Atheneum, 1978.
While waiting for the overdue return of his racing pigeon, entered in a 600-mile competition, ten-year-old Hugh is forced to cope with the death of his beloved grandfather. (Fiction)

Cannon, A. E. *Amazing Gracie*, Delacorte, 1992.
When her mother remarries, Gracie's life changes: she moves away from her best friend, gets a weird six-year-old stepbrother, and watches her mother sink into total depression. (Fiction)

————. *Shadow Brothers*, Delacorte, 1991.
Marcus discovers that change is the only constant in his life when his Navajo foster brother Henry begins a search for his native American identity and the girl next door becomes more than a friend. (Fiction)

Capps, Benjamin. *Woman of the People*, Duell, 1966.
Captured by the Comanches as a child, Helen fights tribal customs until she falls in love with a young warrior. (Fiction)

Caras, Roger. *Mara Simba: The African Lion*, Holt, 1986.
The birth, maturation, and death of an African lion are fictionalized against the larger landscape of Africa, its people, and their interdependency. (Fiction)

Card, Orson Scott. *Ender's Game*, Tor, 1985. ♦
Andrew "Ender" Wiggin, a young genius in Battle School, where he is training to fight the alien Buggers, has to put his skills to the ultimate test much sooner than he expected. (Fiction)

———. *Seventh Son*, Tor, 1987.
Alvin, born seventh son of a seventh son, is destined for greatness, but something evil is trying to keep him from growing up. (Fiction)

———. *Speaker for the Dead*, Tor, 1986.
"Ender" Wiggin seeks a chance to redeem himself when Portuguese colonists on the planet Lusitania discover an intelligent species whose brutal customs threaten to start another war. (Fiction)

Carlson, Dale. *Girls Are Equal Too: The Women's Movement for Teenagers*, Atheneum, 1973.
How girls grow up, what is expected (and not expected) of them, how they get where they are, and what they can do about it are all covered in this book for younger readers. (Nonfiction)

———. *Mountain of Truth*, Atheneum, 1972.
In a remote Tibetan lamasery Michael finds his mystic destiny, but his brother Peter finds only questions that will haunt him the rest of his life. (Fiction)

Carrighar, Sally. *Home to the Wilderness*, Houghton, 1973.
An intimate self-portrait of the famous naturalist, who at the age of six learned to adjust to her mother's hatred and cruelty and eventually found a home in the wilderness. (Nonfiction)

Carson, Jo. *Stories I Ain't Told Nobody Yet: Selections from the People Pieces*, Watts/ Orchard, 1990.
Haunting, funny, and full of folk wisdom, these poems bring to life the colorful personalities and the life-style of the Appalachian region. (Nonfiction)

Carter, Alden R. *Growing Season*, Putnam/ Coward-McCann, 1984.
During his senior year in high school, Rick Simon moves to the country to help his family realize their lifelong dream of owning a farm. (Fiction)

———. *Sheila's Dying*, Putnam, 1987.
Basketball jock Jerry is planning to break up with his steady girl, Sheila, when he learns she is dying of cancer. (Fiction)

———. *Up Country*, Putnam, 1990.
Sent to live with relatives in the country while his alcoholic mother receives treatment, city kid Carl faces a serious problem from the past. (Fiction)

———. *Wart, Son of Toad*, Putnam/Pacer, 1985.
Nicknamed "Wart" by the school jocks, Steve, son of the most disliked teacher in his school, is constantly in conflict with his father about his grades, his friends, and his love of auto mechanics. (Fiction)

Carter, Peter. *Borderlands*, Farrar, 1991.
Heroes, villains, cowboys, and common settlers populate a tale of the 1870s in which thirteen-year-old Ben Curtis struggles to find his place in the vast frontier. (Fiction)

———. *Bury the Dead*, Farrar, 1987.
The lives of promising high jumper Erika and her family in East Berlin are changed when her grandmother's long-gone brother suddenly appears from West Germany. (Fiction)

Cary, Lorene. *Black Ice*, Knopf, 1992.
As a black scholarship student in a formerly all-white private school, the author struggled with racism, her family's expectations, peer pressure, and her own idealism. (Nonfiction)

Caseley, Judith. *Kisses*, Knopf/Borzoi, 1991.
Hannah is looking for answers: Why is her chest so flat? Why does everyone think she's a snob? Will anything ever turn out the way she wants? (Fiction)

———. *My Father, the Nutcase*, Knopf/ Borzoi, 1993.
Just when fifteen-year-old Zoe needs him the most, her father quits his job and leaves his family because he is clinically depressed. (Fiction)

■ Selected for "Still Alive: The Best of the Best, 1960–1974"
▲ Selected for "The Best of the Best Books, 1970–1983"
♦ Selected for "Nothin' But the Best: Best of the Best Books for Young Adults, 1966–1986"

Castaneda, Carlos. *Journey to Ixtlan: The Lessons of Don Juan,* Simon & Schuster, 1973.
The story of how the author became a "man of knowledge" through a long and arduous apprenticeship to the Yaqui Indian sorcerer, Don Juan Matus. (Nonfiction)

Cavagnaro, David, and Cavagnaro, Maggie. *Almost Home: A Life-style,* American West, 1975.
Through an appealing combination of photographs and narrative, the reader can identify with the author's down-to-earth harmony with nature. (Nonfiction)

Chambers, Aidan. *Dance on My Grave,* Harper/Charlotte Zolotow, 1983.
Hal, the romantic, and Barry, the cad, are lovers. When Barry is killed in a motorcycle accident, Hal cannot come to grips with his loss. (Fiction)

Cherry, Mike. *On High Steel: The Education of an Ironworker,* Quadrangle, 1974.
An articulate ironworker talks about his lifestyle in an absorbing book on his trade and his coworkers. (Nonfiction)

Chester, Deborah. *Sign of the Owl,* Scholastic/Four Winds, 1981.
Wint must recapture his father's land from an evil uncle in this medieval tale. (Fiction)

Chestnut, J. L. *Black in Selma: The Uncommon Life of J. L. Chestnut, Jr.,* Farrar, 1991.
The life of J. L. Chestnut is detailed against the dramatic backdrop of the civil rights movement in his native Selma, Alabama. (Nonfiction)

Chetwin, Grace. *Collidescope,* Bradbury, 1991.
When his space ship crashes on Earth, a highly advanced alien interferes in the lives of two teenagers living in Manhattan during different centuries. (Fiction)

Childress, Alice. *Hero Ain't Nothin' but a Sandwich,* Coward, 1973. ■ ▲ ♦
Benjie, a thirteen-year-old in Harlem, cannot face the reality of his drug addiction or the realization that someone cares for him. (Fiction)

_____. *Rainbow Jordan,* Coward, 1981. ♦
Frequently abandoned and neglected by her young and carefree mother, fourteen-year-old Rainbow suffers—until she learns to accept love and compassion from others. (Fiction)

Childress, Mark. *V for Victor,* Knopf, 1990.
Victor stumbles on a plot to land spies on the Alabama coast when his motorboat collides with a German U-boat sneaking into the harbor. (Fiction)

Chisholm, Shirley. *Unbought and Unbossed,* Houghton, 1970.
The first black woman to be elected to the U.S. Congress, Shirley Chisholm won this unique distinction against the odds of her race and sex, and by being "unbought and unbossed." (Nonfiction)

Choi, Sook Nyul. *Year of Impossible Goodbyes,* Houghton, 1992.
A North Korean family barely survives the Japanese occupation during World War II only to find that after the war they must flee Russian communists. (Fiction)

Claire, Keith. *Otherwise Girl,* Holt, 1976.
What can fifteen-year-old Matt do when he discovers that the beautiful redhead he befriends is really the ghost of a girl who drowned eight years before? (Fiction)

Clapp, Patricia. *Witches' Children: A Story of Salem,* Lothrop, 1982.
A frightening tale of the Salem witchcraft trials, based on historical fact and told from the perspective of one of the ten "afflicted girls." (Fiction)

Clarke, Arthur C. *Imperial Earth,* Harcourt, 1976.
Find out what happens to Duncan Makenzie when he is sent from Titan, a moon of Saturn, to Earth's quincentennial celebration. (Fiction)

_____. *Rendezvous with Rama,* Harcourt, 1973.
A brief encounter with an alien world, Rama, proves perilous and baffling to the humans who explore its mysteries. (Fiction)

Clarke, J. *Heroic Life of Al Capsella,* Holt, 1991.
Fourteen-year-old Al wants to be "like everyone else"—but with weird parents like his, he hasn't got a chance. (Fiction)

Cleary, Beverly. *Girl from Yamhill: A Memoir,* Morrow, 1988.
An honest and humorous account of the Depression-era childhood and adolescence of Beverly Cleary in Oregon, where she encountered many of the same situations that teens do today. (Nonfiction)

Cleaver, Eldridge. *Soul on Ice,* McGraw-Hill, 1968. ■
In a collection of essays and open letters written while in prison, Eldridge Cleaver talks about the inner feelings and drives of the outraged black man in the United States today. (Nonfiction)

Clements, Bruce. *Tom Loves Anna Loves Tom,* Farrar, 1991.
Tom and Anna fall in love at first sight and together face Anna's deepest secret. (Fiction)

Clifford, Francis. *Naked Runner,* Coward-McCann, 1966.
A former British intelligence agent has his Frankfurt vacation turned into a cold war nightmare. (Fiction)

Cohen, Barbara. *Unicorns in the Rain,* Atheneum/Argo, 1980.
Violence, pollution, and overcrowding have reached the point of no return. One family has built a large ship, an ark, and filled it with animals, and now it's starting to rain. . . . (Fiction)

_____, and Lovejoy, Bahija. *Seven Daughters and Seven Sons,* Atheneum, 1982.
In this retelling of a traditional Arabic tale, a poor merchant's daughter, disguised as a boy, makes a fortune and takes satisfying revenge on seven insulting male cousins. (Fiction)

Cohen, Susan, and Cohen, Daniel. *Six-pack and a Fake I.D.,* Evans, 1986.
An objective discussion of alcohol and its role in today's society of adults and young adults. (Nonfiction)

_____, _____. *When Someone You Know Is Gay,* Little, Brown, 1990.
The authors describe what it's really like and what it means to be gay. Includes a list of books and videos for more information. (Nonfiction)

Cohn, Nik. *Rock from the Beginning,* Stein & Day, 1969.
If you dig rock, Nik Cohn gives it to you straight—the lowdown and feel of the now sounds from folk to protest to psychedelic, from Elvis to Dylan to the Jefferson Airplane and beyond. (Nonfiction)

Cole, Brock. *Celine,* Farrar, 1990.
Casualties of divorce, independent teenager Celine and her seven-year-old neighbor, Jake, share an interest in television and Jake's father. (Fiction)

_____. *Goats,* Farrar, 1987.
Stripped naked by fellow campers and left on a deserted island, social misfits Laura and Howie survive humiliation, natural dangers, and each other. (Fiction)

Cole, Ernest, and Flaherty, Thomas. *House of Bondage,* Random, 1967.
The oppression suffered by blacks in South Africa is compellingly reported in text and photographs. (Nonfiction)

Coleman, Lonnie. *Orphan Jim,* Doubleday, 1975.
As if life in the Depression isn't hard enough, Trudy and her young brother choose to be "orphans" but avoid being sent to an orphans' home. (Fiction)

Collier, James Lincoln. *When the Stars Begin to Fall,* Delacorte, 1986.
Angry that he's treated as "thieving trash," Harry decides to prove himself by exposing a local carpet factory's illegal polluting. (Fiction)

Collins, Larry, and Lapierre, Dominique. *Or I'll Dress You in Mourning,* Simon & Schuster, 1968.
Manuel Benitez, an impoverished juvenile delinquent, fights tragedy and hunger to become the highest paid matador in the world and a symbol of the new Spain. (Nonfiction)

Collins, Max Allan. *Dark City,* Bantam, 1987.
After leaving Chicago, legendary gangbuster Eliot Ness goes to Cleveland to clean up a corrupt police force. (Fiction)

Coman, Carolyn. *Body and Soul: Ten American Women,* Hill, 1988.
Personal narratives and photo essays about unusual women, including Susan Butcher, two-time Iditarod winner, and "S & M businesswoman" Belle de Jour. (Nonfiction)

Comfort, Alex, and Comfort, Jane. *Facts of Love: Living, Loving and Growing Up,* Crown, 1979.
Birth control and respect for one's partner are stressed in a warm and readable guide to responsible sex for younger teens. (Nonfiction)

Conford, Ellen. *Alfred G. Graebner Memorial High School Handbook of Rules and Regulations: A Novel,* Little, Brown, 1976.
Humorous episodes of a girl's first year in high school as she copes with the school's unbelievable official handbook of regulations. (Fiction)

Conot, Robert. *Rivers of Blood, Years of Darkness,* Bantam, 1967.
The violent events before, during, and after the 1965 Watts riots in Los Angeles are told in vivid on-the-scene detail. (Nonfiction)

Conover, Ted. *Rolling Nowhere,* Viking, 1984.
Ivy League Denverite Ted Conover drops out of his safe existence and experiences life as a rail-

---

■ Selected for "Still Alive: The Best of the Best, 1960–1974"

▲ Selected for "The Best of the Best Books, 1970–1983"

♦ Selected for "Nothin' But the Best: Best of the Best Books for Young Adults, 1966–1986"

road hobo, scavenging for food, hopping trains, and making friends with other hobos who help him realize what people have in common. (Nonfiction)

Conrad, Pamela. *My Daniel*, Harper, 1990.
Years after treacherous and unscrupulous dinosaur hunters try to steal Daniel's discovery, Grandmother Julia reveals the exciting secrets of the now-famous bones. (Fiction)

_____. *Prairie Songs*, Harper, 1985.
Louisa idealizes Emmeline, the local doctor's beautiful, cultured wife, who, unable to adjust to the harsh and lonely pioneer life on the bleak Nebraska prairie, goes mad. (Fiction)

_____. *What I Did For Roman*, Harper, 1987.
Vulnerable Darcie becomes involved with a handsome, disturbed young man while working at the zoo. (Fiction)

Conrat, Maisie, and Conrat, Richard. *Executive Order 9066: The Internment of 110,000 Japanese Americans*, California Historical Society, 1972.
A nation's paranoia is strikingly revealed in this photographic view of World War II concentration camps, American style. (Nonfiction)

Conway, Jill Ker. *Road from Coorain*, Knopf, 1990.
Jill Ker Conway survives the physically harsh life of Australia's outback in the 1930s and becomes the first woman president of Smith College. (Nonfiction)

Cook, Robin. *Coma*, Little, Brown, 1977.
A young woman medical student discovers the horrifying truth—a black market in spare parts—about the rash of mysterious deaths of patients who have undergone surgery in a Boston hospital. (Fiction)

Cooney, Caroline B. *Don't Blame the Music*, Putnam/Pacer, 1986.
Susan's plans for an uneventful senior year are dashed when her older sister, Ashley, an embittered, failed rock musician, returns to cause her family anguish. (Fiction)

_____. *Flight #116 Is Down*, Scholastic, 1993.
A 747 crashes on the grounds of her family's estate, and sixteen-year-old Heidi, alone and terrified, pulls herself together to help rescue the survivors. (Fiction)

Cooper, Henry S. F., Jr. *Thirteen: The Flight That Failed*, Dial, 1973.
A minute-by-minute account of the intense efforts to save the ill-fated Apollo 13 and its three-man crew. (Nonfiction)

Cooper, J. California. *Family*, Doubleday, 1992.
From beyond the grave, Clora narrates the story of her family as she watches her children emerge from slavery during the Civil War. (Fiction)

Cooper, Louise. *Sleep of Stone*, Atheneum, 1993.
Shape-changer Ghysla is jealous of Prince Anyr's fiancee and tries to take her place, with tragic results. (Fiction)

Corman, Avery. *Prized Possessions*, Simon & Schuster, 1992.
Months after being raped during her first week in college, Elizabeth presses charges, precipitating a campus protest and her own healing. (Fiction)

Cormier, Robert. *After the First Death*, Pantheon, 1979. ▲ ◆
Ben tries unsuccessfully to balance his father's betrayal and his own failure after a busload of children is hijacked by a group of ruthless terrorists. (Fiction)

_____. *Bumblebee Flies Anyway*, Pantheon, 1983.
In an experimental hospital for the terminally ill, his memory shattered by mind-altering drugs, sixteen-year-old Barney is told that he is the "control" and should not get involved with the dying; but he cannot stop himself from reaching out to others as he slowly discovers the truth about himself. (Fiction)

_____. *Chocolate War: A Novel*, Pantheon, 1974. ■ ▲ ◆
"Sweets" abound at Trinity High while a schoolmaster feasts on his students' fear. A bitter story of one student's resistance and the high price he paid. (Fiction)

_____. *Fade*, Doubleday/Delacorte, 1988.
One boy in each generation of the Moreaux family inherits the power—and the curse—of invisibility. (Fiction)

_____. *I Am the Cheese*, Pantheon, 1977. ▲
A victim of amnesia, and under the influence of drugs administered by mysterious and unidentified questioners, teenager Adam searches through haunting memories that must not be recalled or revealed if he is to survive. (Fiction)

_____. *Tunes for Bears to Dance To*, Delacorte, 1993.
Henry discovers evil when his bigoted boss, Mr. Hairston, manipulates him into betraying his friend, an elderly Holocaust survivor. (Fiction)

_____. *We All Fall Down*, Delacorte, 1992.
All is not peaceful in small town Burnside—drunk teenagers trash a house, a young girl is

flung down the stairs, a murderer is quietly planning revenge, and Jane Jerome falls in love with a lost soul. (Fiction)

Counter, S. Allen.   *North Pole Legacy: Black, White and Eskimo,* Univ. of Massachusetts, 1992.

Counter's interest in black explorer Matthew Henson, who accompanied Robert E. Peary to the North Pole, triggers his search for Eskimo descendants of both men still living beyond the Arctic Circle. (Nonfiction)

Couper, Heather, and Pelham, David. *Universe,* Random, 1985.

Through pop-ups and pull tabs, paper mechanics provide three-dimensional illustrations of the Big Bang, star birth, and star death. (Nonfiction)

Courlander, Harold.   *African, a Novel,* Crown, 1968.

Captured by slavers in a village raid, Wes Hunu survives the ocean crossing from Dahomey and life on a Georgia plantation, eventually escaping with the hope that somewhere in America there is a future for him. (Fiction)

Cousteau, Jacques-Yves, and Cousteau, Philippe.   *Shark: Splendid Savage of the Sea,* Doubleday, 1970.

The Cousteaus present a world of beauty and danger as they study the shark and carry out research face to face with the most savage animal in the sea. (Nonfiction)

———, and Diole, Philippe.   *Life and Death in a Coral Sea,* Doubleday, 1971.

The authors guide the reader through the beautiful coral jungles of the Red Sea and Indian Ocean, introducing their inhabitants along the way. (Nonfiction)

Craig, John.   *Chappie and Me: An Autobiographical Novel,* Dodd, 1979.

Wearing blackface to play with Chappie Johnson and His Colored All Stars in the summer of 1939, a young white Canadian boy gains understanding of what being black means. (Fiction)

Craig, Kit.   *Gone,* Little, Brown, 1993.

Mrs. Hale's children are sure she'll have breakfast ready, but where is she? She's been kidnapped by a pyromaniac who is about to reunite the family in a modern-day chamber of horrors. Someone will soon die. (Fiction)

Craven, Margaret.   *I Heard the Owl Call My Name,* Doubleday, 1974. ■

Indian beliefs and nature lore enhance the poignant story of a dying young minister who wins the respect and friendship of the Indians with whom he lives while coming to terms with death. (Fiction)

Crew, Linda.   *Children of the River,* Delacorte, 1990.

Sundara struggles with the conflict between her Cambodian heritage and her growing love for Jonathan. (Fiction)

Crichton, Michael.   *Andromeda Strain,* Knopf, 1969. ■

Four scientists race against the clock to isolate a deadly microorganism from outer space that has killed all but two people in a small Arizona town. (Fiction)

———.   *Electronic Life: How to Think about Computers,* Knopf, 1984.

In this informal introduction to computers and the information society, a best-selling author explains computer terminology and considers what computers can and cannot do. (Nonfiction)

———.   *Jurassic Park,* Knopf, 1992.

Dinosaurs created from fossilized DNA for a fabulous theme park are not supposed to be capable of breeding, but they do—and they're hungry. (Fiction)

———.   *Terminal Man,* Knopf, 1972.

Terror spreads as a man wearing bandages, a bathrobe, and wires in his brain disappears from his hospital room. (Fiction)

Crispin, A. C.   *Starbridge,* Berkley, 1991.

Mahree Burroughs discovers her talent for languages and diplomacy when, on a routine flight to Earth, spaceship *Desiree* encounters intelligent beings from other planets. (Fiction)

Cross, Gillian.   *Chartbreaker,* Holiday, 1987.

Love and rage permeate the story of Janis Mary "Finch," a British rock star who sings "like concentrated danger." (Fiction)

———.   *On the Edge,* Holiday, 1985.

Tug, the son of a well-known British newswoman, is captured by terrorists in a story of relentless suspense. (Fiction)

Crutcher, Chris.   *Athletic Shorts: Six Short Stories,* Greenwillow, 1992.

Tales of love, death, bigotry, and heroism of real people with the courage to stand up to a world that often puts them down. (Fiction)

■ Selected for "Still Alive: The Best of the Best, 1960–1974"

▲ Selected for "The Best of the Best Books, 1970–1983"

♦ Selected for "Nothin' But the Best: Best of the Best Books for Young Adults, 1966–1986"

_____. *Chinese Handcuffs*, Greenwillow, 1990.
A winning triathlete's need to understand his older brother's suicide is complicated by memories and daring challenges. (Fiction)

_____. *Crazy Horse Electric Game*, Greenwillow, 1987.
Star athlete Willie Weaver's crippling accident forces him to leave his family and friends to rebuild his shattered life. (Fiction)

_____. *Running Loose*, Greenwillow, 1983. ◆
Louie takes a stand against his coach and playing dirty football, falls in love, and loses his girlfriend in a fatal accident—all in his senior year. (Fiction)

_____. *Stotan!*, Greenwillow, 1986.
A high school coach invites four members of his swimming team to a week of rigorous training that tests their moral fiber as well as their physical stamina. (Fiction)

Culin, Charlotte. *Cages of Glass, Flowers of Time*, Bradbury, 1979.
Abused by her mother (who in turn is still being beaten by her mother), fourteen-year-old Claire is afraid to trust anyone—until she meets kindness from some special friends. (Fiction)

Cullen, Brian. *What Niall Saw*, St. Martin's, 1987.
The misspelled fragments in a seven-year-old Irish boy's diary after the Bomb offer a chilling testament to the end of the world. (Fiction)

Currie, Elliott. *Dope and Trouble: Portraits of Delinquent Youth*, Pantheon, 1993.
This appeal to the social consciousness of America gives graphic and disturbing insight into the hopes and dreams of troubled teens. (Nonfiction)

Curtis, Edward S. *Girl Who Married a Ghost, and Other Tales from the North American Indian*, Scholastic/Four Winds, 1978.
Ghost stories, trickster tales, and other pieces of authentic native American folklore are combined with Edward Curtis's haunting Indian photographs. (Nonfiction)

Curtis, Patricia. *Animal Rights: The Stories of People Who Defend the Rights of Animals*, Four Winds, 1980.
The stories of seven people provide a thoughtful look at the rights of animals, ways in which they are abused, and what can be done to correct the abuse. (Nonfiction)

Cushman, Kathleen, and Miller, Montana. *Circus Dreams*, Little, Brown, 1991.
Follow Montana Miller through her first year at a circus school in France as she realizes her dream of becoming a trapeze artist. (Nonfiction)

Dahl, Roald. *Boy: Tales of Childhood*, Farrar, 1985.
A famous author recalls his struggle from school days to maturity in a humorous autobiography. (Nonfiction)

_____. *Going Solo*, Farrar, 1986.
Dahl's recollections become a collage of events from time spent in Africa to exciting flying experiences in Greece during World War II. (Nonfiction)

Dana, Barbara. *Necessary Parties*, Harper/ Charlotte Zolotow, 1986.
With the help of an offbeat lawyer-auto mechanic, fifteen-year-old Chris goes to court to fight his parents' divorce. (Fiction)

Dann, Patty. *Mermaids*, Ticknor & Fields, 1986.
In this quietly bizarre story, fourteen-year-old Charlotte wants to become a saint—if only she could stop lusting after the gardener at the nearby convent. (Fiction)

David, Jay, ed. *Growing Up Black*, Morrow, 1968.
Violence, hatred, and degradation mark the childhood of nineteen black Americans from the days of slavery to today's ghettos. (Nonfiction)

Davies, Hunter. *Beatles: The Authorized Biography*, McGraw-Hill, 1968.
John, Paul, George, and Ringo are seen as interesting, fallible human beings, each quite different from the others, each with his own history, hang-ups, and hopes. (Nonfiction)

Davis, Daniel S. *Behind Barbed Wire: Imprisonment of Japanese Americans during World War II*, Dutton, 1982.
An absorbing chronicle of an episode in American history when Japanese Americans were forcibly interned in "relocation" camps. (Nonfiction)

Davis, Jenny. *Checking on the Moon*, Orchard/Richard Jackson, 1992.
Thirteen-year-old Cab spends the summer with her grandmother in a decaying neighborhood, helping the area's residents, and learning to rely on her own resourcefulness. (Fiction)

_____. *Good-bye and Keep Cold*, Watts/ Orchard/ Richard Jackson, 1987.
The death of Edda's father in a strip-mining accident unleashes inexplicable currents of love and hate that threaten the family's fragile survival. (Fiction)

Davis, Lindsey. *Silver Pigs*, Crown, 1990.
The murder of a beautiful senator's daughter forces Marcus Didius Falco (Bogey in a toga) to

investigate a possible attempt to overthrow the emperor of ancient Rome. (Fiction)

Davis, Mildred. *Tell Them What's Her Name Called,* Random, 1975.
Three murders are all preceded by the same mysterious message—was it just coincidence? (Fiction)

Davis, Terry. *If Rock and Roll Were a Machine,* Delacorte, 1993.
After a teacher humiliates Bert, motorcycles, writing, racquetball, and a few caring adults help him regain his devastated self-confidence. (Fiction)

_____. *Vision Quest,* Viking, 1979.
As he prepares himself for adulthood, eighteen-year-old Louden finds a special joy in competitive wrestling, in the uniqueness of the Columbia River, and in his live-in girlfriend, Carla. (Fiction)

De Larrabeiti, Michael. *Borribles,* Macmillan, 1978.
The savage epic battle between the Borribles—strange children with pointed ears—and the Rumbles—intelligent ratlike creatures—is the focal point of an unusual, disconcerting fantasy set in London. (Fiction)

De Veaux, Alexis. *Don't Explain: A Song of Billie Holiday,* Harper, 1980.
The life of the incredibly gifted yet tragically insecure American jazz singer Billie Holiday, nicknamed Lady Day, is told in this free verse "song." (Nonfiction)

Dear, William. *Dungeon Master: The Disappearance of James Dallas Egbert III,* Houghton, 1984.
When computer genius James Dallas Egbert III disappears from Michigan State University in 1979, private investigator William Dear suspects that the fantasy world of "Dungeons & Dragons" has become too real for this 16-year-old. (Nonfiction)

Deaver, Julie Reece. *Say Goodnight, Gracie,* Harper/Charlotte Zolotow, 1988.
Sharing a zany sense of humor and anxieties about their futures, Jimmy and Morgan are best friends on the brink of love when Jimmy is killed by a drunk driver, leaving Morgan to cope with reality of death. (Fiction)

Decker, Sunny. *Empty Spoon,* Harper, 1969.
At a high school in Philadelphia's black ghetto, the school with the highest crime and drop-out rates in the city, Sunny Decker, a young white college graduate, attempts to overcome the hostility and belligerence of her students. (Nonfiction)

Del Rey, Lester. *Pstalemate,* Putnam, 1972.
When engineer Harry Bronson discovers he has psi powers, he vows that he will not become insane like other telepaths. (Fiction)

Demas, Vida. *First Person, Singular,* Putnam, 1974.
In a rambling diary-like letter to her psychiatrist, Pam recounts her struggles to find herself despite an unstable family and her own feelings of inadequacy. (Fiction)

Derby, Pat. *Visiting Miss Pierce,* Farrar, 1986.
For a school social concerns class project, Barry Wilson, a shy, awkward ninth-grader, regularly visits Miss Pierce, an eighty-three-year-old convalescent-hospital resident, and becomes intrigued by her tales of her older brother. (Fiction)

_____, **and Beagle, Peter.** *Lady and Her Tiger,* Dutton, 1976.
You can train wild animals by love rather than force, and Pat Derby proves it. One of her favorites is Chauncey, the Lincoln-Mercury cougar. (Nonfiction)

Deuker, Carl. *On the Devil's Court,* Little, Brown/Joy Street Books, 1990.
Seventeen-year-old Joe Faust must decide if it's worth selling his soul to the devil for one perfect season of basketball. (Fiction)

Dickinson, Peter. *AK,* Delacorte, 1993.
Paul, an orphaned twelve-year-old warrior in the 5th Commando Unit of the NLA, fights for freedom in his African homeland, both with and without his AK-47 assault rifle. (Fiction)

_____. *Eva,* Delacorte, 1990.
After a violent auto accident, thirteen-year-old Eva wakes up in a hospital to find she must learn how to live as a chimpanzee. (Fiction)

_____. *Tulku,* Dutton, 1979.
Surviving a Boxer massacre of a Christian mission in China, thirteen-year-old Theodore accompanies an eccentric British plant collector and her guide-lover through danger-laden territory to Tibet and a Buddhist monastery. (Fiction)

■ Selected for "Still Alive: The Best of the Best, 1960–1974"

▲ Selected for "The Best of the Best Books, 1970–1983"

♦ Selected for "Nothin' But the Best: Best of the Best Books for Young Adults, 1966–1986"

_____, **and Anderson, Wayne.** *Flight of Dragons*, Harper, 1979.
Dragons aren't real—or are they? This carefully constructed and beautifully illustrated case for the existence of dragons will convince even the skeptics. (Nonfiction)

Dickson, Margaret. *Maddy's Song*, Houghton, 1985.
Sixteen and musically gifted, Maddy Dow is abused by a brutal father who is seemingly a model citizen in their community. (Fiction)

Dixon, Paige. *May I Cross Your Golden River?*, Atheneum, 1975.
The rare, terminal disease that killed Lou Gehrig is also killing eighteen-year-old Jordan, but with his family's support he tries to lead a normal life. (Fiction)

Doherty, Berlie. *Dear Nobody*, Orchard, 1993.
High school seniors Chris and Helen are ready for love, but not for its responsibilities, which include a baby. (Fiction)

_____. *White Peak Farm*, Watts/Orchard, 1991.
As a teenager on her family's isolated Derbyshire farm, Jeannie Tanner faces secrets, change, and growth. (Fiction)

Dolan, Edward F. *Adolf Hitler: A Portrait in Tyranny*, Dodd, 1981.
An examination of the man, what he stood for, and how he came to assume power. (Nonfiction)

_____. *How to Leave Home—and Make Everybody Like It*, Dodd, 1977.
For the young person longing to get away from home—how to tell the family, find a job, manage money, and locate a place to live. (Nonfiction)

Dolmetsch, Paul, and Mauricette, Gail, eds. *Teens Talk about Alcohol and Alcoholism*, Dolphin/Doubleday, 1987.
Young people talk about how alcoholism affects their lives, families, and friends. (Nonfiction)

Donofrio, Beverly. *Riding in Cars with Boys*, Morrow, 1991.
Denied college, Beverly loses interest in everything but riding around, drinking and smoking, and rebelling against authority. After a divorce, she arrives in New York City with a young son and turns her life around. (Nonfiction)

Dorman, Michael. *Under 21: A Young People's Guide to Legal Rights*, Delacorte, 1970.
Legal advice for those under twenty-one is presented in a clear, straightforward manner on such subjects as dress, hair style, free speech, employment, driving, contracts, voting, criminal law, drug use, and parental problems. (Nonfiction)

Dorris, Michael. *Yellow Raft in Blue Water*, Holt, 1987.
Half-Indian, half-black Rayona's agonizing search for her true self is told from a three-generation perspective—Rayona's, her mother's, and her grandmother's. (Fiction)

Dowdey, Landon, comp. *Journey to Freedom: A Casebook with Music*, Swallow, 1970.
From the Bible to the Beatles, material gathered from poetry, plays, folk songs, and spirituals is combined in a joyous statement on the brotherhood of man and the celebration of life. (Nonfiction)

Dragonwagon, Crescent, and Zindel, Paul. *To Take a Dare*, Harper, 1982.
Thirteen-year-old Chrysta is already into drugs and sex when she runs away from home. After a couple of years on the road learning life the hard way, she meets several people who teach her about love, happiness, and giving. (Fiction)

Dribben, Judith. *Girl Called Judith Strick*, Cowles, 1970.
Judith Strick was seventeen when the Nazis occupied Poland, and this is her story of how she lured Germans into partisan traps, spied for the Polish underground, bamboozled and charmed her German captors, and survived three prisons, including Auschwitz. (Nonfiction)

Duder, Tessa. *In Lane Three, Alex Archer*, Houghton, 1990.
Overcoming injuries, Alex competes with her rival for a spot on the New Zealand Olympic swim team. (Fiction)

Due, Linnea A. *High and Outside*, Harper, 1980. ▲
Niki, the star pitcher on the girls softball team, has a drinking problem. Her catcher knows, her coach knows, but Niki won't admit it. (Fiction)

Dufresne, Frank. *My Way Was North*, Holt, 1966.
As a field agent for the U.S. Biological Survey, Dufresne spent twenty years in Alaska enjoying the frozen wastes, unusual animals, and individualistic people. (Nonfiction)

Duncan, Lois. *Chapters: My Growth as a Writer*, Little, Brown, 1982.
A popular author tells about her need and desire to be a writer from the time she was ten years old; examples of her early writing are used to demonstrate how life becomes fiction and to show how her career developed. (Nonfiction)

_____. *Don't Look behind You*, Delacorte, 1990.

April's life changes forever when her family must disappear into the federal witness protection program after her father testifies against members of a drug ring. (Fiction)

_____. *Killing Mr. Griffin*, Little, Brown, 1978. ▲ ♦

A group of high school students kidnaps a strict English teacher in order to get even with him—and what starts as a prank becomes a horror. (Fiction)

_____. *Stranger with My Face*, Little, Brown, 1981. ▲

Will Laurie's evil twin sister, Lia, already experienced in astral projection, succeed in taking over Laurie's body and comfortable life? (Fiction)

_____. *Who Killed My Daughter? The True Story of a Mother's Search for Her Daughter's Murderer*, Delacorte, 1993.

Determined to find her daughter's murderer, author Lois Duncan seeks the aid of psychics and uncovers startling parallels to her novels. (Nonfiction)

Durham, Marilyn. *Man Who Loved Cat Dancing*, Harcourt, 1972.

A western, a relentless character study, a violent tragedy, but—most of all—a love story. (Fiction)

Durham, Michael S. *Powerful Days: The Civil Rights Photography of Charles Moore*, Stewart, Tabori & Chang, 1992.

Graphic black-and-white photographs by a noted photojournalist vividly document events of the civil rights movement. (Nonfiction)

Durkin, Barbara Wernecke. *Oh, You Dundalk Girls, Can't You Dance the Polka?*, Morrow, 1984.

Fat but smart and gutsy Beatrice (Bebe) Schmidt becomes one of the crowd in her 1950s suburb of Baltimore. (Fiction)

Durrell, Gerald. *Birds, Beasts, and Relatives*, Viking, 1969.

An owl in the attic, a bear in the parlor, an overweight sister with acne, and a brother who collects eccentric humans are part of the Durrell "menagerie" which invades Corfu for a season and occupies it for five years. (Nonfiction)

_____. *Rosy Is My Relative*, Viking, 1968.

Adrian Rookwhistle inherits Rosy, a lovable beer-drinking elephant, and on their journey through the English countryside to find a circus home for Rosy, their progress is marked by many disquieting occasions. (Fiction)

_____. *Two in the Bush*, Viking, 1966.

A noted animal collector humorously relates his travels through New Zealand, Australia, and Malaysia to observe and photograph flying lizards, lyre birds, and other species close to extinction. (Nonfiction)

Durrell, Gerald, and Durrell, Lee. *Amateur Naturalist*, Knopf, 1984.

In seventeen "nature walks" the authors guide both amateur and seasoned naturalists from the beaches to the woodlands, suggesting observations and experiments that do not intrude on the natural world. (Nonfiction)

Eagan, Andrea Boroff. *Why Am I So Miserable If These Are the Best Years of My Life? A Survival Guide for the Young Woman*, Lippincott, 1976.

Straight talk on women's anatomy, sex, and legal rights. (Nonfiction)

Eckert, Allan. *Song of the Wild*, Little, 1981.

The unusual gift of being able to project his mind inside other living creatures separates Caleb Erikson from other fourteen-year-olds and causes tension between his parents and himself. (Fiction)

Edelman, Bernard. *Dear America: Letters Home from Vietnam*, Norton, 1985. ♦

In their personal letters, soldiers and civilians reveal the pain, frustration, confusion, and anger that were part of their daily lives in Vietnam. (Nonfiction)

Edelman, Marian Wright. *Measure of Our Success: A Letter to My Children and Yours*, Beacon, 1993.

A powerful mix of personal anecdote and moral conviction, Edelman's twenty-five lessons for life are an inspiration for everyone. (Nonfiction)

Edgerton, Clyde. *Floatplane Notebooks*, Algonquin, 1988.

The love and strength of the Copelands are portrayed generationally as they chronicle their adventures from a locked shed in rural Georgia. (Fiction)

■ Selected for "Still Alive: The Best of the Best, 1960–1974"

▲ Selected for "The Best of the Best Books, 1970–1983"

♦ Selected for "Nothin' But the Best: Best of the Best Books for Young Adults, 1966–1986"

Edmonds, Walter D.   *South African Quirt,* Little, Brown, 1985.
Natty Dunston, a young boy on a New York farm, is unwilling to give up his own standards to adjust to his father's tyrannical demands. (Fiction)

Einstein, Charles, ed.   *Fireside Book of Baseball,* 4th ed. Simon & Schuster, 1987.
A treasury of pictures, cartoons, history, and poetry in praise of "America's favorite pastime," by many of America's most talented baseball writers and literate fans. (Nonfiction)

Eisen, Jonathan, ed.   *Altamont: Death of Innocence in the Woodstock Nation,* Avon, 1970.
The Altamont Rock Festival, intended to be a West Coast Woodstock but instead a disaster, is clearly examined in relation to its meaning for the future of the counter-culture. (Nonfiction)

Elder, Lauren, and Streshinsky, Shirley.   *And I Alone Survived,* Dutton, 1978. ▲
The true story of a courageous young woman, sole survivor of a plane crash in the High Sierras, and her grueling ordeal in the mountains. (Nonfiction)

Elfman, Blossom.   *Girls of Huntington House,* Houghton, 1972. ■ ▲
"What can you teach pregnant girls that they do not already know," ask Blossom Elfman's friends when they learn she has accepted a teaching assignment in a school for unwed mothers. (Fiction)

_____.   *House for Jonnie O.,* Houghton, 1977.
Jonnie and her three friends—students at a school for pregnant unmarried teenagers—search for a "dream house" where they can be independent and support one another and their babies. (Fiction)

Ellison, Harlan.   *Deathbird Stories: A Pantheon of Modern Gods,* Harper, 1975.
In these tales set in some future time, the objects and rites of man's worship are stretched to the limits of their believability and horror. (Fiction)

Embury, Barbara.   *Dream Is Alive: A Flight of Discovery Aboard the Space Shuttle,* HarperCollins, 1991.
Based on three shuttle flights, with photographs taken on a 1984 mission, this photo essay describes what takes place on a typical space flight. (Nonfiction)

Epstein, Sam, and Epstein, Boryl.   *Kids in Court: The ACLU Defends Their Rights,* Scholastic/Four Winds, 1982.
Eleven case histories that involve the rights of young people who were defended by the American Civil Liberties Union during the 1950s and 1960s and that have become precedents for many of today's court cases. (Nonfiction)

Faber, Doris.   *Love and Rivalry: Three Exceptional Pairs of Sisters,* Viking, 1983.
A narrative examination of the relationships between Emily Dickinson, Charlotte Cushman, and Harriet Beecher Stowe and their respective sisters. (Nonfiction)

Fair, Ronald.   *We Can't Breathe,* Harper, 1972.
For Ernie Johnson life in Chicago's black ghetto in the 1930s meant roaches and rats, wine and grass, street games and violence, and even the "wow" of discovering a book. (Nonfiction)

Fall, Thomas.   *Ordeal of Running Standing,* McCall, 1970.
Running Standing, a Kiowa, and his girl-wife, Crosses-the-River, marry for love but part—she to help her people, he to search for success in the white man's world, a choice that inevitably leads to his betrayal and death. (Fiction)

Fante, John.   *1933 Was a Bad Year,* Black Sparrow, 1986.
High school senior Dominic Molise dreams of making it in the major leagues as a pitcher and of making out with his best friend's sister, in this witty and poignant story. (Fiction)

Fast, Howard.   *Hessian,* Morrow, 1972.
War is the awful villain and two boys are among the victims in this quiet, powerful novel of the American Revolution. (Fiction)

Feinstein, John.   *Season on the Brink: A Year with Bob Knight and the Indiana Hoosiers,* Macmillan, 1987.
The 1985–86 season of controversial coach Bob Knight and the Indiana Hoosiers is chronicled in detail. (Nonfiction)

Feldbaum, Carl B., and Bee, Ronald J.   *Looking the Tiger in the Eye: Confronting the Nuclear Threat,* Harper, 1988.
A passionate and clear look at the atom bomb, the way it has changed civilization, and—perhaps—will end it. (Fiction)

Ferazani, Larry.   *Rescue Squad,* Morrow, 1975.
What it's really like to be a member of a fire department rescue squad with all the joys and tragedies, the emotional and physical costs. (Nonfiction)

Ferris, Jean.   *Across the Grain,* Farrar, 1991.
Will is dragged from his beloved beach to live in the desert with his irresponsible older sister, where he adjusts with the help of new friends. (Fiction)

_____. *Invincible Summer*, Farrar, 1987.
While hospitalized with leukemia, Robin and Rick fall in love. (Fiction)

Ferris, Louanne.   *I'm Done Crying*, Evans, 1969.
For Louanne Ferris it takes a strong determination to raise a family in a hopeless ghetto neighborhood; but it takes more than determination to survive as a nurse in the world of a ghetto hospital. (Nonfiction)

Ferris, Timothy.   *Spaceshots: The Beauty of Nature beyond Earth*, Pantheon, 1985.
Spectacular photographs (with textual explanation) taken from space picture the Earth, moon, and a variety of planets, stars, and galaxies. (Nonfiction)

Ferry, Charles.   *Binge*, DaisyHill, 1993.
When his drunken joy ride kills several teenagers, eighteen-year-old Weldon must face the consequences. (Fiction)

_____. *Raspberry One*, Houghton, 1983.
Two young men, both of whom fall in love before shipping out to the Pacific to fight the Japanese, return home changed and scarred by their war experiences. (Fiction)

Fields, Jeff.   *Cry of Angels*, Atheneum, 1974.
The antics, adventures, and friendships of an assorted bunch of misfits are woven into a compelling story of a man's capacity for cruelty and love. (Fiction)

Fine, Judylaine.   *Afraid to Ask: A Book for Families to Share about Cancer*, Lothrop, 1986.
The terrifying subject of cancer is dispassionately explained in Fine's description of the causes, treatment, types, and emotional impact on victims and their families. (Nonfiction)

Fink, Ida.   *Scrap of Time: And Other Stories*, Pantheon, 1987.
Unforgettable stories evoke the horrific time when Polish Jews waited and suffered while the Nazis destroyed their lives. (Fiction)

Finnegan, William.   *Crossing the Line: A Year in the Land of Apartheid*, Harper, 1986.
While teaching in a "colored" high school in South Africa, Finnegan, a white Californian, witnesses extreme racial segregation and educational repression. (Nonfiction)

Finney, Jack.   *Time and Again*, Simon & Schuster, 1970.
As part of a top-secret government project, Simon Morley steps out of the twentieth century to take up residence in the New York of 1882, where he becomes involved in blackmail and romance. (Fiction)

Flanigan, Sara.   *Alice*, St. Martin's, 1988.
A nearly deaf, epileptic teen who has been abused by her family, Alice blossoms after two young neighbors rescue her from a locked shed in rural Georgia. (Fiction)

Fleischman, Paul.   *Borning Room*, HarperCollins/Charlotte Zolotow, 1992.
Births and deaths occur throughout generations of an Ohio farm family in their "borning room." (Fiction)

_____. *Joyful Noise: Poems for Two Voices*, Harper/Charlotte Zolotow, 1988.
"Book Lice" and the other delightful two-voice poems in this collection are direct, rhythmic, and great for reading aloud. (Nonfiction)

Fluek, Toby Knobel.   *Memories of My Life in a Polish Village, 1930-1949*, Knopf, 1992.
Intimate drawings and paintings portray Jewish life in Poland in the years before, during, and after the Russian and German WWII occupations. (Nonfiction)

Ford, Michael Thomas.   *100 Questions and Answers about AIDS: A Guide for Young People*, Macmillan/New Discovery, 1993.
With reliable and up-to-date research, Ford presents candid and comprehensive answers to questions about AIDS. (Nonfiction)

Ford, Richard.   *Quest for the Faradawn*, Delacorte/Eleanor Friede, 1982.
Nab, raised by forest animals from birth, begins a quest with Beth and several animal companions to save the world from destruction by mankind. (Fiction)

Forman, James D.   *Ballad for Hogskin Hill*, Farrar, 1979.
Deciding that big city life is not for him, David Kincaid returns to Kentucky, where he helps his father and grandfather do battle against a powerful coal company. (Fiction)

_____. *Becca's Story*, Scribner, 1993.
Becca can't decide which of her two beaus to choose—serious, secure Alex or exciting, unpredictable Charlie—but the Civil War takes away her choice. (Fiction)

■ Selected for "Still Alive: The Best of the Best, 1960–1974"

▲ Selected for "The Best of the Best Books, 1970–1983"

♦ Selected for "Nothin' But the Best: Best of the Best Books for Young Adults, 1966–1986"

Foster, Rory C. *Dr. Wildlife: A Northwoods Veterinarian*, Watts, 1985.
Founder of a hospital for orphaned or injured wild animals, Dr. Foster shows not only his reverence for animal life but also his struggles with the government to establish his practice. (Nonfiction)

Fox, Paula. *Monkey Island*, Orchard/Richard Jackson, 1992.
Awakening in a welfare hotel to find his mother gone, eleven-year-old Clay takes to the streets of New York City and finds shelter with two homeless men who help him survive. (Fiction)

_____. *One-Eyed Cat*, Bradbury, 1984. ♦
Sneaking out one night, young Ned Wallace shoots the air rifle his father has forbidden him to use and shortly thereafter becomes guilt-ridden with the appearance of a one-eyed cat. (Fiction)

Francke, Linda Bird. *Ambivalence of Abortion*, Random, 1978.
Adults and teenagers, both women and men, convey their honest feelings about the abortion experience and its effect on their lives. (Nonfiction)

Frazier, Walt, and Berkow, Ira. *Rockin' Steady: A Guide to Basketball and Cool*, Prentice, 1974.
"Clyde" explains how to get it all together and be cool on and off the basketball court. (Nonfiction)

Freedman, Russell. *Franklin Delano Roosevelt*, Clarion, 1991.
The complex and controversial life and times of FDR are revealed in Freedman's powerful photobiography. (Nonfiction)

_____. *Indian Chiefs*, Holiday, 1987.
Words and pictures tell the stories of six legendary Indian chiefs who are forced off their lands by westward expansion and the U.S. government. (Nonfiction)

_____. *Indian Winter*, Holiday, 1993.
Paintings by Karl Bodmer and journal entries by German prince Maximilian immerse you in their 1833–34 winter stay-over in Missouri River Indian country. (Nonfiction)

_____. *Lincoln: A Photobiography*, Clarion, 1988.
A skillfully written, appealing overview of Lincoln's life from boyhood to death, accompanied by carefully chosen photographs and prints. (Nonfiction)

_____. *Wright Brothers: How They Invented the Airplane*, Holiday, 1992.
Freedman tells the fascinating story of how two self-taught bicycle mechanics solve the problems that had baffled generations of scientists and engineers. (Nonfiction)

Freedman, Samuel G. *Small Victories: The Real World of a Teacher, Her Students and Their High School*, HarperCollins, 1991.
The neglected students at Stewart Park High School in Manhattan and their caring teacher, Jessica Siegel, find a way to beat the odds and make a future. (Nonfiction)

Freemantle, Brian. *Good-bye to an Old Friend*, Putnam, 1973.
A Russian space scientist appears to defect to England, but a British investigator, a scruffy and intelligent civil servant, has his doubts. (Fiction)

Fretz, Sada. *Going Vegetarian: A Guide for Teen-agers*, Morrow, 1983.
This complete guide includes the reasons why people become vegetarians and how to plan a healthy, meatless diet, along with wonderful recipes. (Nonfiction)

Friedman, Ina R. *Other Victims: First-Person Stories of Non-Jews Persecuted by the Nazis*, Houghton, 1991.
Would you be considered "unworthy of life"? Hitler's persecution extended beyond Jews; those often forgotten victims are remembered in these compelling first-person narratives. (Nonfiction)

Friedman, Myra. *Buried Alive: The Biography of Janis Joplin*, Morrow, 1973. ■
Janis Joplin, the great legendary rock singer of the 1960s, had a passion for life but was also a tortured and driven woman. (Nonfiction)

Friedman, Philip. *Rage*, Atheneum, 1972.
Dying, as is his son, from exposure to experimental nerve gas, Dan Logan uses the last reserves of his strength to take revenge. (Fiction)

Friel, Brian. *Philadelphia, Here I Come!*, Farrar, 1966.
Gar's last night at home, as dramatized in this contemporary play, exposes the lack of communication between generations. (Nonfiction)

Fuer, Elizabeth. *Paper Doll*, Farrar, 1991.
An amputee, Leslie has focused on becoming a concert violinist, but now her developing relationship with Jeff is forcing her to reevaluate her choices. (Fiction)

Fuller, John G. *Ghost of Flight 401*, Berkley, 1976.
Ghosts of crew members killed in the 1972 Eastern Airlines Everglades disaster haunt the crews and passengers of other flights. (Nonfiction)

———. *Incident at Exeter*, Putnam, 1966.
A journalist's investigation of unexplained UFO phenomena. (Nonfiction)

———. *Poison That Fell from the Sky*, Random, 1978.
Fuller dramatically reports the 1976 accident at a chemical factory that left a small Italian town permanently poisoned and its evacuated inhabitants physically and emotionally scarred. (Nonfiction)

Fussell, Samuel Wilson. *Muscle: Confessions of an Unlikely Bodybuilder*, Poseidon, 1992.
His muscles are like iron and ripple under the stage lights; steroids have made him perfect. But something is wrong! (Fiction)

Gaan, Margaret. *Little Sister*, Dodd, 1983.
Little Sister, a third-generation Chinese American, visits Shanghai at the beginning of a revolution and learns about her family from family members there. (Fiction)

Gaiman, Neil, and Pratchett, Terry. *Good Omens: The Nice and Accurate Prophecies of Agnes Nutter, Witch*, Workman, 1992.
In this zany romp, living on Earth is so much fun that Crowley the demon and Aziraphale the angel disobey orders and team up to prevent the Apocalypse. (Fiction)

Gaines, Ernest J. *Autobiography of Miss Jane Pittman*, Dial, 1971. ■
Born a slave in Louisiana before the Civil War, Jane Pittman lives to witness the struggle in the 1960s for civil rights in this fictional autobiography that reflects the courage and fortitude of America's blacks. (Fiction)

———. *Gathering of Old Men*, Knopf, 1983.
When a white man is killed by a black in Louisiana, more than a dozen aging black men and one young white woman each confess to the sheriff, each with a long-standing motive. (Fiction)

Gaines, William, and Feldstein, Albert, eds. *Ridiculously Expensive MAD*, World, 1969. ■
MAD is seventeen years old and this is a collection of the best of the worst from the magazine that takes on the Establishment with vigor and revels in its inanities. (Nonfiction)

Gale, Jay. *Young Man's Guide to Sex*, Holt, 1984.
A comprehensive and explicit guide to sex and sexuality, written specifically for young men. (Nonfiction)

Gallagher, Hugh Gregory. *FDR's Splendid Deception*, Dodd, 1985.
New insights into Roosevelt's life are provided as Gallagher reveals the way in which FDR refused to admit or expose his physical handicap—paralysis resulting from polio. (Nonfiction)

Gallery, Daniel. *Stand by-y-y to Start Engines*, Norton, 1966.
Ensign Willie Wigglesworth is the ringleader of monkey business in a series of salty anecdotes about life aboard the atomic carrier, *Guadalcanal*. (Fiction)

Gallo, Donald R., ed. *Sixteen: Short Stories by Outstanding Writers for Young Adults*, Delacorte, 1984. ♦
School, friendship, family, and love are all found within this unusual collection of humorous and serious short stories. (Fiction)

———. *Speaking for Ourselves: Autobiographical Sketches by Notable Authors of Books for Young Adults*, NCTE, 1991.
Popular young adult authors, from Lloyd Alexander to Paul Zindel, write brief sketches about their lives and work. (Nonfiction)

———. *Visions: Nineteen Short Stories by Outstanding Writers for Young Adults*, Delacorte, 1987.
Stories of youthful discoveries, among them Richard Peck's "Shadows," in which an orphan learns about love, and Todd Strasser's "On the Bridge," in which Seth learns about betrayal from a friend. (Fiction)

Garani, Gary, and Schulman, Paul. *Fantastic Television*, Harmony, 1977.
A pictorial history of the best of fifties and sixties television serials and science fiction, including "Star Trek," "Batman," "Twilight Zone," and "Superman." (Nonfiction)

Garden, Nancy. *Annie on My Mind*, Farrar, 1982. ▲ ♦
Lisa and Annie meet at New York's Metropolitan Museum of Art, fall in love, and then find that a public declaration is too threatening to their friends and relatives. (Fiction)

■ Selected for "Still Alive: The Best of the Best, 1960–1974"

▲ Selected for "The Best of the Best Books, 1970–1983"

♦ Selected for "Nothin' But the Best: Best of the Best Books for Young Adults, 1966–1986"

Garfield, Brian.   *Paladin*, Simon & Schuster, 1980. ◆
A fifteen-year-old boy, recruited by Winston Churchill to be his personal secret agent, is involved in murder, assassination, and sabotage on both sides of the front lines in this World War II novel. (Fiction)

_____. *Recoil*, Morrow, 1977.
With his government-manufactured cover blown and syndicate men closing in, a former star government witness decides to turn the tables on his pursuers. (Fiction)

Garland, Sherry.   *Song of the Buffalo Boy*, Harcourt, 1993.
Running away to Ho Chi Minh City with the boy she loves after being promised in marriage to a menacing old man, seventeen-year-old Loi tries to find out about her American father. (Fiction)

Gaylin, Willard, M.D.   *In the Service of Their Country: War Resisters in Prison*, Viking, 1970.
Six imprisoned war resisters tell their stories in compelling case histories as recorded by Dr. Gaylin, a psychiatrist. (Nonfiction)

Gedge, Pauline.   *Child of the Morning*, Dial, 1977.
Reared by her Pharaoh father to assume his throne upon his death, Hatshepsut—a real historical figure—has to contend with her weak half-brother before she can realize her dream. (Fiction)

Gelman, Rita Golden.   *Inside Nicaragua: Young People's Dreams and Fears*, Watts, 1988.
The fear and danger surrounding the war between the Sandinistas and the contras are reflected in the lives of Nicaragua's youth. (Nonfiction)

Geras, Adele.   *Voyage*, Atheneum, 1983.
A group of young Jewish immigrants share love, friendship, hope, and fears during their two-week voyage to America, the land of freedom. (Fiction)

Gibbons, Sheila.   *Ellen Foster*, Algonquin, 1987.
After her mother's untimely death, young Ellen must survive despite her abusive father and other relatives who want no part of her. (Fiction)

Giddings, Robert.   *War Poets*, Orion, 1988.
The work of a variety of World War I poets, many of whom died in that conflict, is reinforced with illustrations, biographical notes, and a brief history of "the war to end all wars." (Nonfiction)

Gies, Miep, and Gold, Alison Leslie.   *Anne Frank Remembered: The Story of Miep Gies, Who Helped to Hide the Frank Family*, Simon & Schuster, 1987.
A story of personal courage by the woman who hid the Frank family and retrieved Anne's diary so that the world would never forget. (Nonfiction)

Gilman, Dorothy.   *Clairvoyant Countess*, Doubleday, 1975.
Exotic Madame Karitska and her psychic powers help the police handle some of their more distressing dilemmas: robbery, murder, voodoo possession, and a missing person. (Fiction)

_____. *Unexpected Mrs. Pollifax*, Doubleday, 1966.
Volunteering her services to the CIA, the irrepressible Mrs. Pollifax accepts a job as courier to Mexico where her safe assignment suddenly becomes sinister. (Fiction)

Gilmore, Kate.   *Enter Three Witches*, Houghton, 1991.
Sixteen-year-old Bren finds living with witches hard enough, but how can he prevent his girlfriend from discovering their existence? (Fiction)

Gingher, Marianne.   *Bobby Rex's Greatest Hit*, Atheneum, 1986.
A suggestive hit song by a small North Carolina town's heartthrob catapults its namesake, Pally Thompson, into the national limelight and passionate disavowal. (Fiction)

Giovanni, Nikki.   *Gemini*, Bobbs, 1972.
A dynamic young black writer explores her life and times with the fierce intensity of a poet. (Nonfiction)

_____. *My House: Poems*, Morrow, 1973.
A well-known black author celebrates love in all its many facets with gentle, compelling immediacy. (Nonfiction)

_____. *Women and the Men*, Morrow, 1975.
Poems from the heart and soul of a spirited young woman that speak directly to the lives of young and old, women, and men. (Nonfiction)

Girion, Barbara.   *Handful of Stars*, Scribner, 1982.
Julie Meyers, fifteen, must learn to cope with epilepsy as her resentment mounts against the thoughtless cruelties of her family and friends. (Fiction)

_____. *Tangle of Roots*, Scribner, 1979.
When her mother's unexpected death forces sixteen-year-old Beth Frankle to cope with grief and sorrow, her relationships with family and friends are affected. (Fiction)

Glass, Frankcina. *Marvin and Tige,* St. Martin's, 1978.
Tige, an orphaned eleven-year-old street-wise black youth, and Marvin, a white alcoholic executive dropout, establish a friendship based on caring for and needing each other. (Fiction)

Glasser, Ronald J. *Ward 402,* Braziller, 1973.
While treating a child dying of leukemia, a young intern is forced to reexamine his attitudes and those of his colleagues toward their daily dealings with life and death. (Nonfiction)

Glenn, Mel. *Class Dismissed! High School Poems,* Clarion, 1982. ■ ▲
Glenn's poems, accompanied by photographs, mirror the agony and the ecstasy of high school as experienced by young people. (Nonfiction)

_____. *My Friend's Got This Problem, Mr. Candler,* Clarion, 1992.
Poems, both serious and funny, express the thoughts and emotions of students and their families as they speak to a high school guidance counselor. (Nonfiction)

Godden, Rumer. *Thursday's Children,* Viking, 1984.
Neglected Doone Penny and his pampered older sister, Crystal, both strive to be the best in the competitive world of ballet. (Fiction)

Golden, Frederic. *Trembling Earth: Probing and Predicting Quakes,* Scribner, 1983.
A clear and concise statement of present knowledge concerning earthquakes—brief enough to be exciting but complete enough to cover the facts. (Nonfiction)

Goldman, Peter, and Fuller, Tony. *Charlie Company: What Vietnam Did to Us,* Morrow, 1983.
Men who served in Vietnam talk with poignancy, pain, and bitterness about their experiences. (Nonfiction)

Goldston, Robert. *Sinister Touches: The Secret War against Hitler,* Dial, 1982.
Dramatic accounts of covert activities and espionage during World War II that read like a spy novel. (Nonfiction)

Gordon, Jacquie. *Give Me One Wish,* Norton, 1988.
A mother tells the bittersweet story of the short life of her daughter Chris, who, despite being stricken with cystic fibrosis, eagerly participated in high school activities. (Nonfiction)

Gordon, Ruth, ed. *Under All Silences: Shades of Love: An Anthology of Poems,* Harper/Charlotte Zolotow, 1987.
From e. e. cummings and Sappho to Emily Dickinson and Yosan Akiko, this collection of poems celebrates the universal experience of love and passion. (Nonfiction)

Gordon, Sheila. *Waiting for the Rain,* Watts/ Orchard/ Richard Jackson, 1987.
On a South African farm, Tengo, black, and Frikkie, white, forge a friendship that is later challenged by the injustices of apartheid. (Fiction)

Gordon, Sol, and Conant, Roger. *You! The Teenage Survival Book,* Quadrangle, 1976.
A positive, practical, lively approach to learning about "you." Comic book sections include "Ten Heavy Facts about Sex" and "Juice Use." (Nonfiction)

Gordon, Suzanne. *Off Balance: The Real World of Ballet,* Pantheon, 1983.
Behind the glittering facade of ballet lies a darker world of pain, rivalry, and exploitation. (Nonfiction)

Goro, Herb. *Block,* Random, 1970.
The struggle for survival by young blacks in a decaying Bronx neighborhood is told in pictures and text to show the underlying pride and hope of people trapped in a hopeless situation. (Nonfiction)

Goulart, Ron. *What's Become of Screwloose? and Other Inquiries,* Scribner, 1971.
A computer turned author, a homicidal dishwasher, an evil pet dog who is also a cyborg, and a totally automated house are just four of the malign machines which populate these stories. (Fiction)

Gould, Steven. *Jumper,* Tor, 1993.
Davy jumps for the first time when he escapes a beating by teleporting to the library. Now he's on the run from his alcoholic father, the police, and a secret government agency—but who can catch a jumper? (Fiction)

Grace, Fran. *Branigan's Dog,* Bradbury, 1981.
After the loss of his beloved dog, Casey Branigan is forced out of his self-imposed isolation and must confront the reason for his impulse to set fires. (Fiction)

■ Selected for "Still Alive: The Best of the Best, 1960–1974"

▲ Selected for "The Best of the Best Books, 1970–1983"

♦ Selected for "Nothin' But the Best: Best of the Best Books for Young Adults, 1966–1986"

Graham, Robin Lee, and Gill, Derek L.T.
  Dove, Harper, 1972. ■
Setting out in his sloop to encircle the globe, a
sixteen-year-old boy finds adventure and romance. (Nonfiction)

Granatelli, Anthony. *They Call Me Mister
  500,* Regnery, 1969.
Andy Granatelli, daring automobile racer and
builder, tells how he made it through poverty
and crashes to become a millionaire at age
thirty. (Nonfiction)

Grant, Cynthia D. *Phoenix Rising; or, How
  to Survive Your Life,* Atheneum, 1990.
Reading her sister Helen's diary of her yearlong
bout with cancer helps Jenny cope with her
feelings of pain and anger about Helen's death.
(Fiction)

Gravelle, Karen, and Peterson, Leslie.
  Teenage Fathers, Messner, 1993.
Thirteen teenage fathers talk about their
parenthood with feelings that range from total
alienation and irresponsibility to complete devotion to the children they have fathered.
(Nonfiction)

Gray, Martin, and Gallo, Max. *For Those I
  Loved,* Little, Brown, 1973.
A Polish Jew survives the horrors of wartime
Warsaw and a Nazi death camp only to be de-
prived of peace and happiness by a cruel twist
of fate. (Nonfiction)

Green, Connie Jordan. *War at Home,*
  Macmillan/Margaret K. McElderry, 1990.
Chauvinistic Virgil infuriates cousin Mattie
when he comes to live with her family in Oak
Ridge, Tennessee, during the secretive and se-
curity-ridden days of World War II. (Fiction)

Greenbaum, Dorothy, and Laiken, Deidre S.
  Lovestrong, Times Books, 1985.
Dorothy Greenbaum, wife and mother, struggles to get through medical school and become
a doctor. (Nonfiction)

Greenberg, Jan. *No Dragons to Slay,* Farrar,
  1984.
A high school soccer star afflicted with cancer
finds the courage to fight back while working at
an exciting archaeological dig. (Fiction)

Greenberg, Joanne. *Far Side of Victory,*
  Holt, 1983.
Paroled after being sentenced for "driving
under the influence," Eric Gordon meets
Helen, the woman whose husband and chil-
dren his car had killed. (Fiction)

_____. *In This Sign,* Holt, 1970. ▲ ◆
The isolation and the often frenzied rage of the
deaf in trying to cope in a hearing world are
vividly portrayed in this story of Abel and

Janice Ryder and their hearing daughter, Margaret. (Fiction)

_____. *Of Such Small Differences,* Holt,
  1988.
Immersed in the world of twenty-five-year-old
blind and deaf John Moon, the reader experiences not only John's attempts to survive alone,
but also the turmoil, passion, and love brought
into his life by Leda, a sighted, hearing actress.
(Fiction)

_____. *Simple Gifts,* Holt, 1986.
A simple poor family of engaging misfits turns
their ranch into a place where visitors pay to
sample "authentic" 1880s homestead life.
(Fiction)

Greenburger, Ingrid. *Private Treason: A
  German Memoir,* Little, Brown, 1973.
Rejecting Nazism completely, this gentile girl
left her country and family and fled to France
where she fell in love with a young French Resistance worker. (Nonfiction)

Greene, Constance C. *Love Letters of
  J. Timothy Owen,* Harper, 1986.
Tim thinks he will finally have a successful romance when he sends anonymous love letters,
but the results are unexpected and discourag-
ing. (Fiction)

Greene, Marilyn, and Provost, Gary. *Finder:
  The Story of a Private Investigator,* Crown,
  1988.
The story of Marilyn Greene, no hard-boiled
detective but a housewife who found a career
through years of search and rescue training,
hard work, and caring. (Nonfiction)

Greenfield, Josh, and Mazursky, Paul.
  Harry and Tonto, Saturday Review Press,
  1974.
Forcibly evicted from his condemned apartment house, seventy-two-year-old Harry and
his cat, Tonto, set off on a hilarious cross-country jaunt to a new life in California. (Fiction)

Gregory, Kristiana. *Earthquake at Dawn,*
  Harcourt/Gulliver, 1993.
Experience being a survivor of one of the worst
earthquakes in American history. (Nonfiction)

Gregory, Susan. *Hey, White Girl!,* Norton,
  1970.
Susan Gregory attends a black ghetto high
school in her senior year and becomes more
than another "whitey" in this rare and honest
book. (Nonfiction)

Grisham, John. *Pelican Brief,* Doubleday,
  1993.
When the wrong people find Darby Shaw's legal brief outlining her theory about who killed
two Supreme Court justices, she must use all

her wits to outrun them and save her own life. (Fiction)

Grunwald, Lisa. *Summer*, Knopf, 1986.
Summers with her artistic family on a Massachusetts island have always been perfect. Now Jennifer must bear her dying mother's last summer. (Fiction)

Guest, Judith. *Ordinary People*, Viking, 1976. ▲ ♦
Seventeen-year-old Conrad returns home from a mental institution, where he was sent after his brother's accidental death and his own ensuing suicide attempt. To begin a new life he must learn to accept himself and those close to him. (Fiction)

Guffy, Ossie, and Ledner, Caryl. *Ossie: The Autobiography of a Black Woman*, Norton, 1971.
A black woman, who is not famous, smart, or rich but just loves her children and wants the best she can get for them, tells a moving story. (Nonfiction)

Gurney, James. *Dinotopia: A Land Apart from Time*, Turner, 1993.
A newly discovered, illustrated journal reveals life on the lost island of Dinotopia, where shipwrecked survivors work and play in harmony with dinosaurs. (Fiction)

Guy, David. *Football Dreams*, Seaview, 1981.
Dan Keith desperately wants to succeed as a high school football player—mostly to please and to prove himself to his dying father. (Fiction)

_____. *Second Brother*, NAL, 1986.
High school freshman Henry underestimates his own special talents in the shadows of his superachieving older brother and his daredevil "Renaissance man" best friend. (Fiction)

Guy, Rosa. *Disappearance: A Novel*, Delacorte, 1979. ♦
Released from jail in the custody of the Aimsley family, Imamu Jones immediately becomes a prime suspect when Perk, their youngest daughter, disappears soon after his arrival. (Fiction)

_____. *Edith Jackson*, Viking, 1978. ▲
Though Edith fails in her struggle to hold her orphaned family of three younger sisters together and has an unhappy love affair, she eventually begins to discover her own identity. (Fiction)

_____. *Friends*, Holt, 1973. ■ ▲ ♦
Rejected by her classmates because she "talks funny," Phyllisia Cathy, a young West Indian girl, is forced to become friends with poor, frazzled Edith, the only one who will accept her. (Fiction)

_____. *Music of Summer*, Delacorte, 1993.
Spending the summer on Cape Cod, talented pianist Sara, who is ostracized by Cathy and her "light skinned" friends, overcomes racism with courage and the help of a new love. (Fiction)

_____. *Ruby*, Viking, 1976.
Ruby, daughter of a West Indian restaurant owner in Harlem, fights her loneliness by forming a relationship with the beautiful Daphne. (Fiction)

Habenstreit, Barbara. *"To My Brother Who Did a Crime. . .": Former Prisoners Tell Their Stories in Their Own Words*, Doubleday, 1973.
Taped interviews with prisoners who were allowed to enroll and live at Long Island University in a rehabilitation experiment. Some made it. Some did not. (Nonfiction)

Hailey, Kendall. *Day I Became an Autodidact: And the Advice, Adventures, and Acrimonies That Befell Me Thereafter*, Doubleday, 1988.
This journal records the joys and pitfalls of Kendall Hailey's life after she decided, at fifteen, to graduate early and stay home to educate herself. (Nonfiction)

Haing, Ngor, and Warner, Roger. *Cambodian Odyssey*, Macmillan, 1988.
Cambodian doctor Haing Ngor chronicles the destruction of his homeland and family under the brutal rule of the Khmer Rouge. (Nonfiction)

Halberstam, David. *Amateurs*, Morrow, 1985.
By providing an in-depth look at the Olympic rowing team, Halberstam defines what is involved in "going for the gold." (Nonfiction)

Haley, Alex. *Roots*, Doubleday, 1976.
Poignant and powerful narrative of the descendants of Kunta Kinte, who had been snatched from freedom in Africa and brought by ship to America and slavery. (Nonfiction)

■ Selected for "Still Alive: The Best of the Best, 1960–1974"
▲ Selected for "The Best of the Best Books, 1970–1983"
♦ Selected for "Nothin' But the Best: Best of the Best Books for Young Adults, 1966–1986"

Hall, Barbara. *Dixie Storms*, Harcourt, 1991.
Spending all her fourteen years in a small Virginia farming town, Dutch Peyton has found life to be pretty good until the drought-plagued summer when her sophisticated cousin Norma arrives and family secrets surface, bringing trouble. (Fiction)

_____. *Fool's Hill*, Bantam, 1993.
Summer is usually long, hot, and boring in Libby's small town, but when two new girls with a convertible move into the area, Libby discovers that excitement also brings frightening choices. (Fiction)

Hall, Elizabeth. *Possible Impossibilities: A Look at Parapsychology*, Houghton, 1977.
What's possible and what's impossible about telepathy, clairvoyance, precognition, psychokinesis, and other psychic phenomena. (Nonfiction)

Hall, Lynn. *Flying Changes*, Harcourt, 1992.
The Kansas prairie sizzles as seventeen-year-old Denny faces the aftermath of her first love affair, her rodeo-rider father's crippling injury, and her mother's sudden reentry into her life. (Fiction)

_____. *Just One Friend*, Scribner, 1985.
Unattractive and slightly retarded, Dory is desperate for just one friend when she is mainstreamed—with tragic results—into a regular high school. (Fiction)

_____. *Leaving*, Scribner, 1980.
After graduation from high school Roxanne believes it is time to leave the familiar home and family farm. A job in the big city may be her ticket to happiness—or is it? (Fiction)

_____. *Solitary*, Scribner, 1986.
Unwilling to accept the support of others, Jane returns to her backwoods childhood home to become independent and self-reliant. (Fiction)

_____. *Sticks and Stones*, Follett, 1972. ■
Sixteen and a newcomer to tiny Buck Creek, Iowa, Tom Naylor suddenly realizes that the hostility of his fellow students and teachers is due to his friendship with Ward Alexander. (Fiction)

_____. *Uphill All the Way*, Scribner, 1984.
Callie, seventeen, learns that being a horseshoer is easier than helping a troubled delinquent friend. (Fiction)

Hallet, Jean-Pierre. *Congo Kitabu*, Random, 1966.
Astounding adventures of a Belgian civil servant working with the people and animals in the jungles of the Congo. (Nonfiction)

Hamanaka, Sheila. *Journey*, Watts, 1991.
Hamanaka's mural presents a capsule history of Japanese-American oppression before and during World War II, and the slow healing after the war. (Nonfiction)

Hambly, Barbara. *Dragonsbane*, Ballantine/ Del Rey, 1986.
John, the Dragonsbane, fights the dreaded Black Dragon, but Jenny, a half-taught sorceress and mother of John's two sons, pays the price of the dragon's surrender. (Fiction)

_____. *Those Who Hunt the Night*, Ballantine/Del Rey, 1988.
The tombs of London's Highgate Cemetery and the gaiety of 1906 Paris are the setting when James Asher is forced to investigate the mystery of who is killing the vampires of London. (Fiction)

Hamilton, Eleanor. *Sex with Love: A Guide for Young People*, Beacon, 1978.
Candid and liberal, though advising some restraints, this handbook takes a positive approach to human sexuality. (Nonfiction)

Hamilton, Virginia. *Anthony Burns: The Defeat and Triumph of a Fugitive Slave*, Knopf, 1988.
Anthony Burns escaped from slavery only to be returned to it under the Fugitive Slave Law—until he regained his freedom through the efforts of the antislavery movement. (Nonfiction)

_____. *Cousins*, Putnam/Philomel, 1991.
In trying to cope with her grandmother's aging and death, Cammy overlooks the terrifying knowledge that younger people die as well—in deaths that seem to have no reason. (Fiction)

_____. *In the Beginning: Creation Stories from Around the World*, Harcourt, 1988.
A visually stunning treatment of creation myths, told by people from around the world, reminds us of the spirit and the vivid imagination of the human race. (Nonfiction)

_____. *Little Love*, Putnam/Philomel, 1984.
Sustained by the love of her boyfriend and her grandparents, Sheema searches for her father and discovers that, although she feels fat, insecure, and slow, she is strong and beautiful. (Fiction)

_____. *M. C. Higgins, the Great*, Macmillan, 1974.
M.C.'s illusions and fantasies of escaping the dreary hill country are shattered, but he gains new insights into his own future and that of his warm but tough family. (Fiction)

_____. *Magical Adventures of Pretty Pearl*, Harper/Charlotte Zolotow, 1983.
The god-child Pretty Pearl meets the doomed hero, John Henry, when she joins a hidden community of blacks who are closely in touch with a Cherokee band deep in the forests of Georgia during Reconstruction times. (Fiction)

_____. *Sweet Whispers, Brother Rush,* Philomel, 1982. ▲

Fourteen-year-old Tree learns a lot about her family and the interconnections between their past and present tragedies from Brother Rush, her uncle's ghost. (Fiction)

Hamlin, Liz. *I Remember Valentine,* Dutton, 1987.

A seriocomic view of the Depression through the eyes of an eleven-year-old girl who learns about four-letter words and sex when she moves next door to the infamous Hart family. (Fiction)

Hammer, Richard. *One Morning in the War: The Tragedy at Son My,* Coward-McCann, 1970.

Without attempting to condemn or excuse, the author presents carefully researched documentation of the 1968 Son My massacre and tries to understand why Americans, sent to protect the Vietnamese, should end up slaughtering them. (Nonfiction)

Hanckel, Frances, and Cunningham, John. *Way of Love, a Way of Life: A Young Person's Introduction to What It Means to Be Gay,* Lothrop, 1979.

This positive guide to what being homosexual means—physically, emotionally, and socially—includes profiles of twelve diverse gay lives. (Nonfiction)

Hardy, William Marion. *U.S.S. Mudskipper: The Submarine That Wrecked a Train,* Dodd, 1967.

A psychopathic World War II submarine captain takes his crew on shore and blows up a tiny Japanese train to add one more trophy to his collection. (Fiction)

Harris, Marilyn. *Hatter Fox,* Random, 1973. ■ ▲

Seventeen-year-old Hatter Fox, a spirited Navajo loner, is befriended by a young white doctor, Teague Summer, who never stops questioning his involvement with her. (Fiction)

Harris, Rosemary. *Zed,* Faber & Faber, 1984.

Held hostage by a group of terrorists, Zed finds courage, cowardice, kindness, and cruelty in unexpected places and discovers his own strength. (Fiction)

Harrison, Sue. *Mother Earth Father Sky,* Doubleday, 1991.

Chagak, the only survivor of a brutal massacre, endures starvation, cold, and forced marriage as she struggles to find her father's family in prehistoric America. (Fiction)

Hartman, David, and Asbell, Bernard. *White Coat, White Cane,* Playboy, 1979.

The true story of David Hartman, M.D., blind since the age of eight, whose only ambition was to become a doctor. (Nonfiction)

Hartog, Jan De. *Captain,* Atheneum, 1967.

Gripping story of a Dutch tug boat captain facing personal conflict and awesome danger in the North Atlantic during World War II. (Fiction)

Haskins, James. *Black Dance in America,* Harper/Crowell, 1991.

Haskins explores the development of black dance from the forced dancing on slave ships through the era of music video. (Nonfiction)

_____. *Black Music in America: A History through Its People,* Harper, 1987.

Haskins demonstrates the unique place of Afro-American music in American culture. (Nonfiction)

_____. *One More River to Cross: The Stories of Twelve Black Americans,* Scholastic, 1993.

Haskins presents the lives of twelve black Americans and their impact on American society. (Nonfiction)

_____, **and Benson, Kathleen.** *60's Reader,* Viking Kestrel, 1988.

The authors describe in depth the major movements of the 1960s and how they changed the direction of American history. (Nonfiction)

Hathorn, Libby. *Thunderwith,* Little, Brown, 1992.

Rejected after her mother's death by her father's new wife in the Australian outback, Laura seeks solace in a strange dog she discovers during a storm. (Fiction)

Haugaard, Erik Christian. *Chase Me, Catch Nobody!,* Houghton, 1980.

Hitler's prewar Germany is the destination for a group of Danish schoolboys on holiday, among them fourteen-year-old Erik who, through the anti-Nazi underground, becomes involved in an adventure filled with intrigue and danger. (Fiction)

■ Selected for "Still Alive: The Best of the Best, 1960–1974"

▲ Selected for "The Best of the Best Books, 1970–1983"

♦ Selected for "Nothin' But the Best: Best of the Best Books for Young Adults, 1966–1986"

Hautzig, Deborah. *Hey, Dollface,* Greenwillow, 1978.

As Val and Chloe share their home and school experiences during one eventful year, Val becomes concerned that their relationship is becoming something more than friendship. (Fiction)

Hay, Jacob, and Keshishian, John M. *Autopsy for a Cosmonaut,* Little, Brown, 1969.

Sam Stonebreaker, M.D., is chosen by computer to be the first doctor in space and his assignment is to find out what killed the Russian cosmonauts in a marooned space vehicle. (Fiction)

Hayden, Torey L. *Ghost Girl: The True Story of a Child Who Refused to Talk,* Little, Brown, 1992.

Torey Hayden finds that eight-year-old Jadie's bizarre behavior is a result of sexual abuse and a satanic cult. (Nonfiction)

_____. *Murphy's Boy,* Putnam, 1983.

Will therapist Torey Hayden be able to help fifteen-year-old Kevin, who is autistic and whose life has been filled with abuse and violence? (Nonfiction)

_____. *One Child,* Putnam, 1980. ▲

It's not easy to work with emotionally disturbed children when your youth and blue jeans mean more to the administration than your rapport with your class—but Torey Hayden manages it. (Nonfiction)

Hayes, Billy, and Hoffer, William. *Midnight Express,* Dutton, 1977.

A young man's hellish captivity in a Turkish prison after his conviction on a drug charge, and his adventurous escape to freedom. (Nonfiction)

Hayes, Daniel. *Trouble with Lemons,* Godine, 1992.

When Tyler and Lymie discover a body floating in the quarry where they are taking a forbidden midnight swim, they fear for their lives. (Fiction)

Hayes, Kent, and Lazzarino, Alex. *Broken Promise,* Putnam, 1978.

Abandoned by their parents en route to California, five children (the oldest eleven years old, the youngest eighteen months old) learn to subsist on their own and to defy a juvenile court system that threatens to separate them. (Fiction)

Hayslip, Le Ly, and Wurts, Jay. *When Heaven and Earth Changed Places: A Vietnamese Woman's Journal from War to Peace,* Doubleday, 1990.

The haunting memoir of a young Vietnamese girl who survived the brutal Vietnam War and learned to forgive. (Nonfiction)

Head, Ann. *Mr. and Mrs. Bo Jo Jones,* Putnam, 1967. ■ ♦

When July, sixteen and pregnant, rushes into marriage with her high school steady, the two must cope with parental interference and personal problems. (Fiction)

Hearne, Betsy. *Love Lines: Poetry in Person,* Macmillan/Margaret K. McElderry, 1987.

Passionate, wryly humorous, and gently regretful lines about love in all its guises. (Nonfiction)

Hedgepeth, William, and Stock, Dennis. *Alternative: Communal Life in New America,* Macmillan, 1970.

Communes as a way of life for "quiet revolutionaries," who feel alienated from the established world and seek the humanness of man, are pictured almost poetically in photographs and text. (Nonfiction)

Heidish, Marcy. *Secret Annie Oakley,* NAL, 1983.

Told in flashback, this is a novelization of Annie Oakley's cruel and abused childhood. (Fiction)

Hellman, Peter, and Meier, Lili. *Auschwitz Album: A Book Based upon an Album Discovered by Concentration Camp Survivor, Lili Meier,* Random, 1982.

A powerful and unique visual presentation of the extermination process at Auschwitz, viewed through candid photographs of its victims. (Nonfiction)

Helms, Tom. *Against All Odds,* Crowell, 1979.

Twice paralyzed by accidents, Tom Helms fought back—not only against his body but against the attitudes of the physically whole. (Nonfiction)

Helprin, Mark. *Swan Lake,* Houghton, 1990.

A totally new and surprising version of a famous ballet, this is a timeless and awesomely beautiful book. (Fiction)

Henderson, Zenna. *Holding Wonder,* Doubleday, 1971.

Some of these twenty science fiction tales deal with "The People," but others treat more mundane subjects such as murder and almost all take place in the author's favorite arena—the classroom. (Fiction)

Hendry, Frances Mary. *Quest for a Maid,* Farrar, 1991.
Young Meg is pitted against political forces and her sister's powerful sorcery when she is chosen to be companion to the Maid of Norway on her journey to Scotland to ascend to the throne. (Fiction)

Henry, Sue. *Murder on the Iditarod Trail,* Atlantic Monthly Press, 1992.
Money, dogs, and reputation are at stake during the intense competition of the Iditarod. As mushers are murdered, state trooper Jensen looks at the race with new eyes. (Fiction)

Hentoff, Nat. *American Heroes: In and out of School,* Delacorte, 1987.
First Amendment rights become part of everyday lives when students and other ordinary people resist infringements on basic freedoms. (Nonfiction)

_____. *Does This School Have Capital Punishment?,* Delacorte, 1981.
While fighting false charges for possessing dope, Sam makes friends with a famous black jazz trumpeter. (Fiction)

Herbert, Frank. *Soul Catcher,* Putnam, 1972.
Transformed into a mystical spirit named Katsuk, a young American Indian sets out to avenge the injustices suffered by his people by performing a ritual murder. (Fiction)

Hermes, Patricia. *Solitary Secret,* Harcourt, 1985.
Abandoned by her mother, a lonely and frightened fourteen-year-old girl becomes the victim of her father's sexual abuse. (Fiction)

Herring, Robert. *Hub,* Viking, 1981.
In this story reminiscent of Huckleberry Finn, flood waters trap Hub and Hitesy on an island with a man they saw commit a murder. (Fiction)

Herriot, James. *All Things Bright and Beautiful,* St. Martin's, 1974.
The completely captivating continuation of *All Creatures Great and Small* relates episodes in the life of a veterinarian and the human and animal characters he encounters. (Nonfiction)

Herzog, Arthur. *Swarm,* Simon & Schuster, 1974. ■
Killer bees, moving up from South America, terrorize citizens and baffle scientists who are trying to prevent a national disaster. (Fiction)

Hesse, Karen. *Letters from Rifka,* Holt, 1993.
In letters to her cousin, twelve-year-old Rifka describes what happens when she flees to the United States with her family to escape religious persecution in Russia. (Fiction)

Heyerdahl, Thor. *Ra Expeditions,* Doubleday, 1971.
The spirit of *Kon-Tiki* lives on in the author's dramatic tale of crossing the Atlantic in a papyrus reed boat to prove that the ancient Egyptians beat Columbus. (Nonfiction)

Heyman, Anita. *Exit from Home,* Crown, 1977.
Opposing the demands of a dictatorial father, the oldest son of a Jewish family in czarist Russia follows his own commitment to social revolution. (Fiction)

Higa, Tomiko. *Girl with the White Flag: An Inspiring Tale of Love and Courage in War Time,* Kodansha, 1992.
Inspired by a World War II photograph, Higa recounts her harrowing childhood ordeal wandering Okinawa alone at the end of the war. (Nonfiction)

Higgins, Jack. *Eagle Has Landed,* Holt, 1975.
In a small English town, a reporter uncovers the hidden grave of German soldiers and a suspenseful story of a Nazi plot to kidnap Churchill. (Fiction)

Highwater, Jamake. *Anpao: An American Indian Odyssey,* Lippincott, 1977.
American Indian legends are combined in the story of Anpao's love for a girl promised to the Sun and of his search to find proof of the Sun's agreement to let him marry her. (Nonfiction)

_____. *Ceremony of Innocence,* Harper/Charlotte Zolotow, 1985.
In the early nineteenth-century Northwest, Amana, a Blackfoot Indian, strives to survive in a white world that refuses to accept her friendship with a French-Cree prostitute and causes Amana's daughter to lose her pride in the culture of her people. (Fiction)

_____. *Legend Days,* Harper/Charlotte Zolotow, 1984.
Amana struggles to maintain her heritage even as she witnesses the disintegration of her Indian civilization as a result of famine, disease, and the encroaching presence of white settlers. (Fiction)

■ Selected for "Still Alive: The Best of the Best, 1960–1974"

▲ Selected for "The Best of the Best Books, 1970–1983"

♦ Selected for "Nothin' But the Best: Best of the Best Books for Young Adults, 1966–1986"

Hill, Susan. *Woman in Black,* Godine, 1986.
An old-fashioned ghost story of quiet horror is set on the desolate English moors. (Fiction)

Hillerman, Tony. *Blessing Way,* Harper, 1970.
Navajo detective Joe Leaphorn must solve the riddle of a mysterious death and an Indian spirit, part wolf, part man, who is frightening the people on a lonely reservation. (Fiction)

_____. *Dance Hall of the Dead,* Harper, 1973.
When a Navajo policeman, Lt. Joe Leaphorn, is called upon to investigate the murder of the young fire god, Ernesto Cata, he becomes involved in the world of Zuni religious beliefs. (Fiction)

_____. *Thief of Time,* Harper, 1988.
The disappearance of an anthropologist propels Navajo tribal policemen Jim Chee and Joe Leaphorn into mysteries of ancient cultures and modern murders. (Fiction)

Hinton, S. E. *Rumblefish,* Delacorte, 1975.
Brothers, caught in an environment of violence, are as incapable of changing their behavior as are the fighting fish who battle to their death. (Fiction)

_____. *Taming the Star Runner,* Doubleday/ Delacorte, 1988.
Travis attacks his stepfather and is sent to live with his uncle Ken on a ranch, where he learns how to make friends and deal with his inner conflicts. (Fiction)

_____. *Tex,* Delacorte, 1979. ▲ ♦
The life of easygoing Tex is complicated by his older brother's serious outlook and the frequent absences of his father. Simply surviving becomes a real challenge. (Fiction)

_____. *That Was Then, This Is Now,* Viking, 1971. ■ ♦
In this sequel to *The Outsiders,* Bryon and Mark at sixteen are still inseparable, but Bryon is beginning to care about people while Mark continues to hot-wire cars, steal, and do things for kicks. (Fiction)

Hirshey, Gerri. *Nowhere to Run: The Story of Soul Music,* Random/Times Books, 1984.
Interviews with the artists who produced the music that exploded in the 1960s are interwoven with research results and personal recollections. (Nonfiction)

Ho, Minfong. *Rice without Rain,* Farrar, 1991.
Events ranging from changes in her rural village to the student protests in Bangkok propel seventeen-year-old Jinda toward choices that she must make about her own life. (Fiction)

Hobbs, Anne, and Specht, Robert. *Tisha: The Story of a Young Teacher in the Alaskan Wilderness,* St. Martin's, 1976.
True account of a young girl who went to Chicken, Alaska, in 1927 and was beset with all the problems of frontier living and prejudice. (Nonfiction)

Hobbs, Will. *Bearstone,* Atheneum, 1990.
Coming to terms with his Indian heritage, Cloyd learns to accept himself in a battle for survival in the mountains of Colorado. (Fiction)

_____. *Big Wander,* Atheneum, 1993.
A compelling adventure story that takes Clay on his "big wander" through Arizona's canyon country in search of his missing uncle. (Fiction)

_____. *Downriver,* Atheneum, 1992.
Fifteen-year-old Jesse and other rebellious teenage members of a wilderness survival team abandon their adult leader, steal his van and rafts, and run the dangerous whitewaters of the Grand Canyon. (Fiction)

Hodges, Margaret. *Making a Difference: The Story of an American Family,* Scribner, 1990.
Hodges tells the extraordinary story of the Sherwoods, a family whose belief in social responsibility effected change in women's rights, politics, medicine, and conservation. (Nonfiction)

Hoffman, Alice. *At Risk,* Putnam, 1988.
When eleven-year-old Amanda Farrell is diagnosed as having AIDS, her family, friends, and neighbors react in unexpected ways in spite of their best intentions. (Fiction)

_____. *Turtle Moon,* Putnam, 1993.
Keith Rosen, the meanest boy in Verity, Florida, runs away, steals a baby, and does other peculiar things, none of which are very strange—considering that it is May and the time of the Turtle Moon. (Fiction)

Hogan, William. *Quartzsite Trip,* Atheneum, 1980. ▲ ♦
1962 was the year of the seventh Quartzsite Trip, when P. J. Cooper took thirty-six assorted high school seniors from Los Angeles into the Arizona desert to learn that the Great Equalizer cannot always be ignored. (Fiction)

Holland, Isabelle. *Man without a Face,* Lippincott, 1972. ▲ ♦
Not much affection has come Charles's way until the summer he is fourteen when he meets McLeod and learns that love has many facets. (Fiction)

_____. *Of Love and Death and Other Journeys*, Lippincott, 1975.
The death of her lovable, easygoing mother forces fifteen-year-old Meg to adjust to a new life with the father she has resented but never known. (Fiction)

Holliday, Laurel, ed. *Heart Songs: The Intimate Diaries of Young Girls*, Bluestocking Books, 1978.
Spanning several centuries and different countries, the writings of these ten young girls reflect the same joys and fears of approaching womanhood as those experienced by young women today. (Nonfiction)

Hollinger, Carol. *Mai Pen Rai Means Never Mind*, Houghton, 1966.
A foreign-service wife who became a university teacher in Bangkok, Mrs. Hollinger crashed head-on with the unfamiliar customs of the Thai people but soon succumbed completely to their charm. (Nonfiction)

Holman, Felice. *Slake's Limbo*, Scribner, 1974. ▲ ◆
A loser and loner picked on by everyone, Slake finds refuge in a subway, which becomes his home for 121 days. (Fiction)

_____. *Wild Children*, Scribner, 1983.
Overlooked in the arrest of his family, Eric runs with outlawed and homeless children trying to survive in the bleak aftermath of the Bolshevik revolution. (Fiction)

Homes, A. M. *Jack*, Macmillan, 1990.
Still dealing with his parents' divorce and a wacko friend, fifteen-year-old Jack is hit with another bombshell—his father's revelation that he's gay. (Fiction)

Honeycutt, Natalie. *Ask Me Something Easy*, Orchard/Richard Jackson, 1992.
Addie feels like an outsider as her older sister, Dinah, and their angry mother cling to each other following the parents' divorce. (Fiction)

Hoover, H. M. *Another Heaven, Another Earth*, Viking, 1981.
Survivors of an unsuccessful attempt at colonization must choose between primitive life on a doomed planet or return to a mechanized, crowded Earth. (Fiction)

_____. *Dawn Palace: The Story of Medea*, Dutton, 1988.
Denied the inheritance of Dawn Palace, Medea marries Jason and helps him secure the Golden Fleece, only to endure the dissolution of their marriage and his murder of her children. (Fiction)

Horan, James David. *New Vigilantes*, Crown, 1975.
Eight Vietnam veterans released from prison camp return to the United States to find justice a travesty. They decide to take the law into their own hands. (Fiction)

Horner, John R., and Gorman, James. *Digging Dinosaurs*, Workman, 1990.
The discovery of a baby dinosaur's bones during a six-year dig in Montana results in a revolutionary theory about cold-blooded creatures. (Nonfiction)

Horrigan, Kevin. *Right Kinds of Heroes: Coach Bob Shannon and the East St. Louis Flyers*, Algonquin, 1993.
Coach Bob Shannon of the East St. Louis Flyers isn't the easiest guy to play football for. But whoever said anything in East St. Louis was easy? (Nonfiction)

Horwitz, Elinor. *Madness, Magic, and Medicine: The Treatment and Mistreatment of the Mentally Ill*, Lippincott, 1977.
How mentally ill people have been treated from ancient times to the present is a bizarre, tragic, and inhumane chapter of history. (Nonfiction)

Hotchner, A. E. *Looking for Miracles: A Memoir about Loving*, Harper, 1975.
Results are hilarious and poignant when Aaron masquerades as an experienced camp counselor to get himself and his younger brother into a summer camp. (Fiction)

Hotze, Sollace. *Acquainted with the Night*, Clarion, 1993.
During a Maine island summer, seventeen-year-old Molly and her cousin Caleb, wounded in Vietnam, resist their romantic feelings for each other as they help a ghost find peace. (Fiction)

_____. *Circle Unbroken*, Clarion, 1988.
Recaptured by her father after living with Sioux Indians for seven years, Rachel faces prejudice and needs great courage to find happiness. (Fiction)

■ Selected for "Still Alive: The Best of the Best, 1960–1974"

▲ Selected for "The Best of the Best Books, 1970–1983"

◆ Selected for "Nothin' But the Best: Best of the Best Books for Young Adults, 1966–1986"

Hough, John. *Peck of Salt: A Year in the Ghetto*, Little, Brown, 1970.
A very personal, moving story of a young white VISTA volunteer and his honorable failure to help black junior high school students in Detroit. (Nonfiction)

Houriet, Robert. *Getting Back Together*, Coward, 1971.
The rambling odyssey of one man who sets out to discover whether or not "the simple life" is to be found in the more stable communes and communities throughout the country. For mature readers. (Nonfiction)

Houston, James. *Ghost Fox*, Harcourt, 1977.
Kidnapped by the Abnaki Indians in colonial times, sixteen-year-old Sarah Wells gradually adopts the Abnaki way of life and must eventually choose between it and returning to the life from which she was taken. (Fiction)

_____. *White Dawn*, Harcourt, 1971.
Based on a real incident in the 1890s, three lost white whalers are rescued by Eskimos and taken into their community where their lack of appreciation for and understanding of Eskimo tradition leads to tragedy. (Fiction)

Howard, Jane. *Please Touch: A Guided Tour of the Human Potential Movement*, McGraw-Hill, 1970.
A *Life* magazine writer subjected herself to many forms of encounter group and sensitivity-training programs before making this shrewd and delightfully witty assessment. (Nonfiction)

Howker, Janni. *Badger on the Barge and Other Stories*, Greenwillow, 1985.
In each of five beautiful, long short stories, a young person encounters an older stranger who helps to shed light on the problem posed. (Fiction)

_____. *Isaac Campion*, Greenwillow, 1987.
The death of his older brother forces young Isaac to assume the entire burden of working on his vicious father's horse farm in turn-of-the-century England. (Fiction)

Hudson, Jan. *Dawn Rider*, Putnam/Philomel, 1991.
Though she has hidden her early morning encounters with her Blackfoot tribe's first horse, sixteen-year-old Kit's riding experience proves vital during battle. (Fiction)

_____. *Sweetgrass*, Philomel, 1990.
A fifteen-year-old Blackfoot girl of the 1830s must prove herself a capable woman before she can marry Eagle Sun. (Fiction)

Huffaker, Clair. *Cowboy and the Cossack*, Trident, 1973.
Confronted by nearly insurmountable odds—including a Tartar raid—fifteen American cowboys with a Cossack escort drive 500 cattle across several thousand miles of Russian wilderness in 1880. (Fiction)

Hughes, Monica. *Hunter in the Dark*, Atheneum, 1983.
In this rites-of-passage novel, Mike, a fifteen-year-old leukemia patient, comes to terms with his illness during a solitary camping trip. (Fiction)

_____. *Keeper of the Isis Light*, Atheneum, 1981.
Never having seen another human, Olwen does not know how different she is until Earth settlers come to Isis and she falls in love. (Fiction)

Human Rights in China. *Children of the Dragon: The Story of Tiananmen Square*, Macmillan/Collier, 1991.
Never before published photographs and words of student activists vividly re-create the 1989 Tiananmen Square massacre. (Nonfiction)

Hunter, Kristin. *Survivors*, Scribner, 1975.
Each was a survivor—Miss Lena, independent businesswoman, and B.J., a tough, appealing street kid—but they learned that they needed each other. (Fiction)

Hunter, Mollie. *Cat, Herself*, Harper/Charlotte Zolotow, 1986.
Cat finds ways to blend an old Scottish "on the road" life-style with her own needs. (Fiction)

Huygen, Wil, and Poortvliet, Rien. *Gnomes*, Abrams, 1977.
Everything anyone ever wanted to know about gnomes, plus colorful illustrations identifying these unusual little creatures. (Nonfiction)

Inouye, Daniel Ken, and Elliot, Lawrence. *Journey to Washington*, Prentice-Hall, 1967.
An exciting and inspiring autobiography of the first Japanese-American to become a U.S. Senator. (Nonfiction)

Ipswitch, Elaine. *Scott Was Here*, Delacorte, 1979.
In a moving record of personal and family courage, Ipswitch tells the story of her son Scott, whose battle with Hodgkin's disease ended with his death at the age of fifteen. (Nonfiction)

Irwin, Hadley. *Abby, My Love*, Atheneum/Margaret K. McElderry, 1985. ♦
Chip loves Abby and can't understand why she keeps him at a distance—until she reveals that she has been sexually abused by her father. (Fiction)

_____. *What About Grandma?*, Atheneum/Margaret K. McElderry, 1982.
When Grandmother Wyn refuses to stay in a nursing home, sixteen-year-old Rhys and her

mother spend the summer with her. It is a time of conflict, discovery, and Rhys's first love affair. (Fiction)

Ives, John.   *Fear in a Handful of Dust,* Dutton, 1978.
Four kidnapped psychiatrists, one a woman, manage to survive the rigors and horrors of the desert after being left to die by a psychotic killer. (Fiction)

Jacobs, Anita.   *Where Has Deedie Wooster Been All These Years?,* Delacorte, 1981.
Because of her English teacher's faith in her, Deedie blossoms, finds herself, and realizes that she no longer needs to beg for her mother's love. (Fiction)

Jacopetti, Alexandra.   *Native Funk and Flash: An Emerging Folk Art,* Scrimshaw, 1974.
Beautiful color photos with brief text describing functional, unique, lovingly hand-decorated objects: clothes, puzzles, furniture, and fine embroidery. (Nonfiction)

Jacot, Michael.   *Last Butterfly,* Bobbs, 1974.
A half-Jewish clown is forced to entertain Jewish children at Terezin. When the International Red Cross team departs, children board carefully concealed cattle trains. Destination: Auschwitz. (Fiction)

Jacques, Brian.   *Redwall,* Putnam/Philomel, 1987.
With the help of animal allies, peace-loving mice defend their medieval abbey when it is besieged by Cluny the Scourge and his fierce band of rats. (Fiction)

Jaffe, Rona.   *Mazes and Monsters,* Delacorte, 1981.
Fantasy becomes terrifyingly real when four college students discover underground caverns near their campus and one of them confuses game strategy with reality. (Fiction)

James, J. Alison.   *Sing for a Gentle Rain,* Atheneum, 1991.
Disturbing dreams pull James into the past where a lonely young Indian girl and the timeless mystery of the Anasazi beckon. (Fiction)

James, P. D.   *Unsuitable Job for a Woman,* Scribner, 1973.
When Cordelia Gray, slight but savvy, inherits a shabby detective agency after the suicide of her partner, her first case involves the appar-

ently motiveless suicide of a Cambridge student. (Fiction)

Janeczko, Paul B.   *Brickyard Summer,* Watts/ Orchard, 1990.
These poems set in a New England mill town evoke the feelings of growing up during the summer between eighth and ninth grades. (Nonfiction)

Janeczko, Paul B., ed.   *Don't Forget to Fly,* Bradbury, 1981.
A panorama of modern poems, by a variety of poets, that spans the range of human experience. (Nonfiction)

_____.   *Going Over to Your Place: Poems for Each Other,* Macmillan/Bradbury, 1987.
Contemporary poems that tease the emotions of each of us. (Nonfiction)

_____.   *Music of What Happens: Poems That Tell Stories,* Watts/Orchard/Richard Jackson, 1988.
Poems that are stories—and stories that are poems—about ghosts and lovers, triumph and tragedy. (Nonfiction)

_____.   *Place My Words Are Looking For: What Poets Say about and through Their Work,* Bradbury, 1991.
Writers share their poems and give insights into their craft and life. (Nonfiction)

_____.   *Pocket Poems: Selected for a Journey,* Bradbury, 1985.
A pocket-size collection of 120 short, modern poems, by some 80 poets, with titles ranging from "Song against Broccoli" to "An Elegy." (Nonfiction)

_____.   *Poetspeak: In Their Work, about Their Work,* Bradbury, 1983.
Sixty-two living North American poets select and comment on their works for a teenage audience. (Nonfiction)

_____.   *Strings: A Gathering of Family Poems,* Bradbury, 1984.
More than 70 modern poets present a multifaceted view of families and their special relationships—husbands, wives, parents, children, etc.—in a 127-poem anthology. (Nonfiction)

Jenkins, Peter.   *Walk across America,* Morrow, 1979.
The author begins his 1,500-mile hike from New York to Louisiana with disdain for American life-styles and ends it with a feeling of expectation and discovery. (Nonfiction)

- ■ Selected for "Still Alive: The Best of the Best, 1960–1974"
- ▲ Selected for "The Best of the Best Books, 1970–1983"
- ♦ Selected for "Nothin' But the Best: Best of the Best Books for Young Adults, 1966–1986"

Jenner, Bruce, and Finch, Philip. *Decathlon Challenge: Bruce Jenner's Story*, Prentice-Hall, 1977.
The 1976 American Olympic champion's story of his rigorous training and the many ups and downs he experienced before winning the decathlon gold medal. (Nonfiction)

Johnson, Earvin "Magic." *What You Can Do to Avoid AIDS*, Times Books, 1993.
Facts, questions and answers, and interviews make up a thorough teen guide on AIDS. (Nonfiction)

Johnson, LouAnne. *Making Waves: The Story of a Woman in This Man's Navy*, St. Martin's, 1987.
This bittersweet, raunchy, and eye-opening look at one woman's military experience in today's navy sprints from recruiting promises and basic training to a hitch overseas. (Nonfiction)

Johnson, Scott. *One of the Boys*, Atheneum, 1993.
Being part of the in-crowd is fun for Eric, until his new friend Marty's pranks become serious and criminal. (Fiction)

Johnston, Jennifer. *How Many Miles to Babylon? A Novel*, Doubleday, 1974.
A friendship between two young Englishmen from different social classes continues despite parental objection and leads to tragedy. (Fiction)

Jones, Adrienne. *Hawks of Chelney*, Harper, 1978.
Siri, a wild young outcast who takes refuge near the hawks that obsess him, incurs the wrath of superstitious villagers who fear his difference and blame the birds for their empty fishing nets. (Fiction)

Jones, Diana Wynne. *Archer's Goon*, Greenwillow, 1984.
A menacing, oversized Goon joins Howard's unusual family and refuses to leave until Howard's father has met the demands of his unrelenting master. (Fiction)

———. *Castle in the Air*, Greenwillow, 1992.
Abdullah is whisked away to a magic kingdom when he falls asleep on a magic carpet he has just bought. But is he really sleeping? (Fiction)

———. *Homeward Bounders*, Greenwillow, 1981.
When Jamie discovers a group of spectres warring with real people, he is condemned to wander the outer boundaries forever. (Fiction)

———. *Howl's Moving Castle*, Greenwillow, 1986.
When a witch turns seventeen-year-old Sophie into an old woman, Sophie goes to live with the feared wizard Howl in his castle and becomes embroiled in the zany events that lead to her happiness. (Fiction)

———. *Sudden Wild Magic*, Morrow, 1993.
The good witches of Earth band together to stop the magicians of Arth from stealing Earth's technology and creating disasters. (Fiction)

Jones, Douglas C. *Gone the Dreams and Dancing*, Holt, 1985.
Defeated but not beaten, the Comanche chief Kwahadi bargains with the whites to achieve a place for his people without betraying their past. (Fiction)

Jordan, June. *His Own Where*, Crowell, 1971. ▲
Refusing to be trapped by the hopelessness of life in a black ghetto, sixteen-year-old Buddy Rivers escapes with his girl Angela to a deserted cemetery shed. Short, honest, and poignant, this is an inner city love story for mature readers. (Fiction)

Jordan, June, ed. *Soulscript: Afro-American Poetry*, Doubleday, 1970.
The black experience seen through the prism of poetry—some poems are angry and bitter; others are eerie and enigmatic; some lash out reflexively; others brood philosophically. (Nonfiction)

Jordan, Robert. *Eye of the World*, St. Martin's, 1991.
Three teenagers take on a classic fantasy quest in this epic struggle between good and evil. (Fiction)

Kaplan, Helen Singer. *Making Sense of Sex: The New Facts about Sex and Love for Young People*, Simon & Schuster, 1979.
Addressing older teens, a leading sex therapist provides knowledgeable and detailed information, including some of the latest scientific findings, on human sexual functioning. (Nonfiction)

Katz, William Loren. *Breaking the Chains: African American Slave Resistance*, Atheneum, 1991.
The myth that black slaves wore their chains quietly is shattered by this account of how slaves actually fought for their freedom before, during, and after the Civil War. (Nonfiction)

Kavaler, Lucy. *Freezing Point: Cold as a Matter of Life and Death*, John Day, 1970.
Cold, once considered an enemy, is revealed as one of man's greatest allies when utilized in such areas as diet, medicine, and research to defer death. (Nonfiction)

Kaye, Geraldine. *Someone Else's Baby,* Hyperion, 1993.
Terry, seventeen, single and pregnant, tells the truth in her journal as she fights to do what's right. (Fiction)

Kazimiroff, Theodore L. *Last Algonquin,* Walker, 1982. ♦
Joe Two Trees, an Algonquin Indian, orphaned at age thirteen, first tries to make his way in the hostile white man's world, but finally returns to a traditional Indian life-style. (Nonfiction)

Keane, John. *Sherlock Bones: Tracer of Missing Pets,* Lippincott, 1979.
Pet detective Keane describes his funny, sad, and suspenseful adventures tracking down lost and stolen pets with his sidekick Paco, an old English sheep dog. (Nonfiction)

Kellogg, Majorie. *Tell Me That You Love Me, Junie Moon,* Farrar, 1968. ■
Junie Moon, an acid-scarred girl, Warren, a paraplegic, and Arthur, who is suffering from a progressive neurological disease, decide to leave the hospital and set up housekeeping together. (Fiction)

Kelly, Gary F. *Learning about Sex: The Contemporary Guide for Young Adults,* Barron's Educational Series, 1978.
A down-to-earth, nonjudgmental discussion of values, relationships, love, and sex. (Nonfiction)

Kennedy, William P. *Toy Soldiers,* St. Martin's, 1988.
When Arab terrorists take over an exclusive American boarding school in Rome, they face an implacable foe—high school student Billy Tepper, practical joker and computer whiz. (Fiction)

Kerr, M. E. *Fell,* Harper, 1987.
Being paid $20,000 to impersonate another boy at a private school seems like child's play to John Fell, until he has to cope with the Sevens, a mysterious club that dominates the entire school. (Fiction)

_____. *Gentlehands,* Harper, 1978. ♦
Buddy's world is turned upside down when he falls in love and then, catastrophically, when he discovers that his refined and cultured grandfather is a notorious Nazi war criminal. (Fiction)

_____. *I Stay near You,* Harper/Charlotte Zolotow, 1985.
Family members fall in love, cope with sudden death, and survive numerous separations in linked stories that follow three generations from the big-band forties to the hard-rock eighties. (Fiction)

_____. *Is That You, Miss Blue?,* Harper, 1975.
Ups and downs in the lives of three teenage girls in a boarding school where the unforgettable Miss Blue is "the best teacher" in spite of her unusual habits. (Fiction)

_____. *Little Little,* Harper, 1981.
Teenage dwarfs Little Little La Belle and Sidney Cinnamon try to find romance in spite of a mother's matchmaking. Part serious drama, part comedy, part satire. (Fiction)

_____. *Me Me Me Me Me: Not a Novel,* Harper/Charlotte Zolotow, 1983.
A series of autobiographical anecdotes from Kerr's youth as related to their use in her novels. (Nonfiction)

_____. *Night Kites,* Harper, 1986.
Seventeen-year-old Jim's relationships with his family and friends change when his older brother reveals he has AIDS. (Fiction)

Kilworth, Garry. *Foxes of Firstdark,* Doubleday, 1991.
Human encroachment makes survival in Trinity Woods a struggle for O-ha the she-fox, her mate, and her kits. (Fiction)

Kim, Richard. *Lost Names: Scenes from a Korean Boyhood,* Praeger, 1970.
A famous Korean writer tells what it was like to grow up during the oppressive Japanese regime of the 1930s and 1940s. (Nonfiction)

Kimble, Bo. *For You, Hank: The Story of Hank Gathers and Bo Kimble,* Delacorte, 1993.
Bo and Hank were inseparable friends and teammates who knew that basketball was the road up. But Hank was in trouble—then dead. All of Bo's memories lead to the same question—why? (Nonfiction)

Kincaid, Jamaica. *Annie John,* Farrar, 1985.
Growing up on the island of Antigua, Annie changes from happy child to defiant teenager in a fiercely painful separation from her strong, loving mother. (Fiction)

■ Selected for "Still Alive: The Best of the Best, 1960–1974"

▲ Selected for "The Best of the Best Books, 1970–1983"

♦ Selected for "Nothin' But the Best: Best of the Best Books for Young Adults, 1966–1986"

Kincaid, Nanci. *Crossing Blood*, Putnam, 1993.

In the 1960s South, Lucy Conyers is fascinated by the people in the house across the way, and especially by Skippy, the handsome, clever son of their black maid—a fascination that is not only forbidden but dangerous. (Fiction)

King, Coretta Scott. *My Life with Martin Luther King, Jr.*, Holt, 1969.

With dignity but emotion, Coretta Scott King tells her story of being black, of devotion to the movement, and of marriage to the man who said, "I have a dream." (Nonfiction)

King, Stephen. *Firestarter*, Viking, 1980.

Eight-year-old Charlie can set things on fire just by looking at them, but will she use her awesome power against The Shop, the secret government agency pursuing her and her father? (Fiction)

_____. *Night Shift*, Doubleday, 1978. ♦

The author of *Carrie* serves up a horrifying collection of short stories packed with vampires, bogeymen, a cellar full of rats, and a fatal can of beer. (Fiction)

Kingsolver, Barbara. *Animal Dreams*, HarperCollins, 1992.

When Codi returns after fourteen years to the small Arizona town of her childhood, she finds a new career, a cause to fight for, and a man to love again. (Fiction)

_____. *Bean Trees*, Harper, 1988.

Attempting to break away from her harsh life in Appalachia, Taylor Greer finds herself in a small Oklahoma town, with a new name, a new life, and strangest of all, a new Cherokee baby girl whom she names Turtle. (Fiction)

Kisor, Henry. *What's That Pig Outdoors? A Memoir of Deafness*, Hill & Wang, 1991.

The autobiography of a Chicago journalist who never let deafness prevent him from doing what he wanted. (Nonfiction)

Kittredge, Mary. *Teens with AIDS Speak Out*, Messner, 1993.

In the most important fight of their lives, teenagers confront past and current behaviors as they tell their AIDS stories. (Nonfiction)

Klass, David. *Wrestling with Honor*, Dutton/Lodestar, 1990.

Ron Woods's anticipation of a championship wrestling season is complicated when he fails a drug test and refuses to take another. (Fiction)

Klass, Perri Elizabeth. *Not Entirely Benign Procedure: Four Years as a Medical Student*, Putnam, 1987.

A young woman's witty description of four years at Harvard Medical School. (Nonfiction)

Klass, Sheila Solomon. *Page Four*, Scribner, 1987.

When his father deserts the family, David channels his feelings of confused betrayal into his college application essay. (Fiction)

Klause, Annette Curtis. *Silver Kiss*, Delacorte, 1991.

Feeling alienated from everyone during her mother's terminal illness, Zoe comes under the spell of Simon, a vampire doomed to live until he avenges the death of his mother 300 years earlier. (Fiction)

Klein, Norma. *No More Saturday Nights*, Knopf, 1990.

Seventeen-year-old Tim's life is turned upside down when he decides to raise his baby alone while attending college. (Fiction)

Knowles, John. *Peace Breaks Out*, Holt, 1981.

Returning to teach at Devon School after World War II, Pete Hallam finds violence and tragedy among his students. (Fiction)

Knudson, R. R., and Swenson, May, eds. *American Sports Poems*, Watts/Orchard, 1988.

Representing a wide variety of sports from skateboarding to baseball, this treasury of nearly 200 poems conveys the vigor of American sports and their heroes and heroines. (Nonfiction)

Koehn, Ilse. *Mischling, Second Degree: My Childhood in Nazi Germany*, Greenwillow, 1977. ♦

A young woman grows up in Nazi Germany not knowing until after the war that she is part Jewish. (Nonfiction)

_____. *Tilla*, Greenwillow, 1981.

Two young German survivors of World War II, Tilla and Rolf, flee to Berlin and slowly attempt to create a new life in the occupied, war-torn city. (Fiction)

Koertge, Ron. *Arizona Kid*, Little, Brown/Joy Street Books, 1988.

Summer work at a racetrack, living with his gay uncle, and falling madly in love make wimpy, short, tenth-grader Billy Kennedy more self-confident and wiser in the ways of the world. (Fiction)

_____. *Boy in the Moon*, Little, Brown/Joy Street Books, 1991.

Senior year changes everything for Nick, who copes with acne, love, and changing relationships while pondering the meaning of his essay, "Who Am I?" (Fiction)

_____. *Harmony Arms*, Little, Brown, 1993.
Gabriel struggles to survive the culture shock
he suffers when he moves from small-town
Bradleyville to Los Angeles. (Fiction)

_____. *Where the Kissing Never Stops*,
Atlantic Monthly Press, 1986.
In a warmly humorous first-person narrative,
seventeen-year-old Walker deals with his father's death, his mother's new job as a stripper,
and his attraction to Rachel. (Fiction)

Kogan, Judith. *Nothing but the Best: The
Struggle for Perfection at the Juilliard
School*, Random, 1987.
A profile of the Juilliard School reveals the ec-
stasy and disappointment of the exceptional
musicians, singers, and others who study there.
(Nonfiction)

Kohner, Hanna. *Hanna and Walter: A Love
Story*, Random, 1984.
Separated during the Nazi invasion of Czecho-
slovakia, Walter Kohner went to America and
Hanna Bloch to Holland. At the end of the war,
learning that Hanna was still alive after enduring concentration camps and her husband's
death, Walter searched throughout Europe until they were finally reunited. (Nonfiction)

Koller, Jackie French. *Primrose Way*,
Harcourt, 1993.
In seventeenth-century America, sixteen-year-
old Rebekah Hall defies her missionary father's
beliefs and embraces the gentle ways of the
Pawtuckets—especially the wise and handsome Mishannock. (Fiction)

Komunyakaa, Yusef. *Dien Cai Dau*,
Wesleyan University, 1988.
In these powerful poems, Komunyakaa remembers the agony of the Vietnam War. (Nonfiction)

Konecky, Edith. *Allegra Maud Goldman*,
Harper, 1976.
A sensitive, funny, and at times sad story of a
precocious, strong-minded girl's struggle to
find her identity while growing up in Brooklyn
during the 1930s. (Fiction)

Konigsburg, E. L. *Father's Arcane Daughter*,
Atheneum, 1976.
Overprotected children of wealthy parents get
a chance to grow up normally because of the
efforts of their mysterious half sister. (Fiction)

Koontz, Dean R. *Watchers*, Putnam, 1987.
Travis takes in a very special golden retriever
that is being stalked by The Outsider, a hide-
ous, evil monster. (Fiction)

Kopay, David, and Young, Perry. *David
Kopay Story: An Extraordinary Self-
Revelation*, Arbor House, 1977.
A pro football player candidly relates his agonizing journey in coming to terms with his ho-
mosexuality and making public his sexual pref-
erence. (Nonfiction)

Korman, Gordon A. *Losing Joe's Place*,
Scholastic, 1991.
Convinced his older brother Joe is the
"coolest," Jason had been looking forward to
spending an unchaperoned summer with two
friends in Joe's apartment. But he didn't figure
on his brother's best friend, 300-pound Root-
beer, moving in, too. (Fiction)

_____. *Semester in the Life of a Garbage
Bag*, Scholastic, 1987.
Will Sean's sabotage of the school's solar
power plant thwart Raymond's hilarious
schemes to earn a trip to a Greek island?
(Fiction)

_____. *Son of Interflux*, Scholastic, 1986.
A hilarious, improbable tale of high school students challenging Interflux, a major corpora-
tion. (Fiction)

Korschunow, Irina. *Night in Distant Motion*,
Godine, 1983.
Regine questions her loyalty to the Nazi party
after she meets Jan, a Polish prisoner considered "sub-human." Only then she begins to notice the injustice and horror, the muted rebellion, and fear of the people around her.
(Fiction)

Kotlowitz, Alex. *There Are No Children
Here: The Story of Two Boys Growing Up
in the Other America*, Doubleday, 1992.
This searing portrait of life in Chicago's public
housing projects depicts the love and the terror
in the lives of two brothers. (Nonfiction)

Kovic, Ron. *Born on the Fourth of July*,
McGraw, 1976.
Beginning with the battle that leaves him paralyzed from the chest down, Kovic tells of his
struggle to reenter American society—a struggle that leads him to become a leading antiwar
activist. (Nonfiction)

■ Selected for "Still Alive: The Best of the Best, 1960–1974"
▲ Selected for "The Best of the Best Books, 1970–1983"
♦ Selected for "Nothin' But the Best: Best of the Best Books for Young Adults, 1966–1986"

Kozol, Jonathon. *Rachel and Her Children: Homeless Families in America*, Crown, 1988.
Kozol's look at families living on the streets challenges everyone who takes home for granted. (Nonfiction)

Kramer, Jerry. *Instant Replay; the Green Bay Diary of Jerry Kramer*, World, 1968.
In this day-by-day account, the physical wear and tear on the field and the business deals off it are equally important to this player. (Nonfiction)

Krementz, Jill. *How It Feels to Be Adopted*, Knopf, 1983.
Kids from eight to sixteen share their feelings about being adopted. (Nonfiction)

_____. *How It Feels to Fight for Your Life*, Little, Brown, 1990.
Fourteen courageous young people suffering from life-threatening illnesses talk about what it's like to live with constant pain. (Nonfiction)

_____. *How It Feels When a Parent Dies*, Knopf, 1981.
Feeling lonely, frightened, and betrayed by death, eighteen young people talk candidly about the continuation of their lives after losing a parent. (Nonfiction)

Krents, Harold. *To Race the Wind: An Autobiography*, Putnam, 1972. ■
He was totally blind, but Harold and his parents determined that he would not be limited by his blindness. (Nonfiction)

Kropp, Lloyd. *Greencastle*, Freundlich Books, 1987.
The difficulties faced by a bright, awkward high school student are captured in this haunting 1950s coming-of-age novel. (Fiction)

Kuklin, Susan. *Fighting Back: What Some People Are Doing about AIDS*, Putnam, 1990.
A moving look—in words and inspired photographs—at a team of volunteers fighting the war against AIDS by offering practical and emotional support to patients. (Nonfiction)

_____. *Reaching for Dreams: A Ballet from Rehearsal to Opening Night*, Lothrop, 1987.
Kuklin details the activities and emotions of the choreographer and dancers involved in Alvin Ailey's production of the ballet *Speeds*. (Nonfiction)

_____. *What Do I Do Now? Talking about Teenage Pregnancy*, Putnam, 1992.
"I can't believe how frightened I am," admits one young woman in this collection of honest interviews with pregnant teenagers, expectant fathers, and those who care for them. (Nonfiction)

Kullman, Harry. *Battle Horse*, Bradbury, 1981.
A modern-day joust, played in the magnificent style of Ivanhoe, goes astray when a young contender is compelled to beat a mysterious black knight. (Fiction)

Kunen, James Simon. *Strawberry Statement: Notes of a College Revolutionary*, Random, 1969.
An ex-varsity crew member at Columbia joins the 1968 confrontation over the university's indifference to war, racism, and poverty and records the struggle on the spot. (Nonfiction)

Kuper, Jack. *Child of the Holocaust*, Doubleday, 1968.
Jankel, a young Jewish boy, escapes Nazi persecution (in Poland) by posing as a Christian. When the war ends he begins a harrowing odyssey to find his family and his faith. (Nonfiction)

Kurtis, Bill. *Bill Kurtis on Assignment*, Rand McNally, 1984.
Danger, intrigue, power, and compassion are fact, not fiction, as CBS news-anchor Kurtis presents sensitive, on-the-scene investigative reports of Agent Orange, Vietnam, the Iranian hostages, and the plight of Amerasian children. (Nonfiction)

Kuznetsov, Anatolli Petrovich. *Babi Yar*, Dial, 1967.
The German occupation of Kiev in 1941 seen through the eyes of a Ukrainian boy who witnessed Nazi barbarity. (Fiction)

L'Engle, Madeleine. *Many Waters*, Farrar, 1987.
Intruding in their father's lab, twins Sandy and Dennys are flung across time to a desert where Noah's family lives among mythical creatures. (Fiction)

Lackey, Mercedes. *Arrows of the Queen*, NAL/DAW, 1987.
Discovered by a telepathic steed, Talia, a misfit in her society, is taken to be educated as herald to the queen. (Fiction)

_____. *Bardic Voices: The Lark and the Wren*, Baen, 1993.
No risk is too daunting for fourteen-year-old Rune, daughter of a tavern wench, as she pursues her dream of joining the Bardic Guild. (Fiction)

Laird, Elizabeth. *Kiss the Dust*, Dutton, 1993.
It's Iraq, and Tara's family are Kurds. "He" has put out the word, and they must flee for their lives. (Fiction)

_____. *Loving Ben*, Delacorte, 1990.
When Ann's hydrocephalic brother Ben is born, she finds herself overcome with ambivalent emotions—love, embarrassment, anger, and eventually acceptance. (Fiction)

Lamb, Wendy, ed.   *Meeting the Winter Bike Rider and Other Prize Winning Plays*, Dell/Laurel-Leaf, 1986.
A wide range of topics and moods is explored by playwrights ages ten to eighteen in eight compelling works performed at the Young Playwrights Festival in New York. (Nonfiction)

Langone, John.   *AIDS: The Facts*, Little, Brown, 1988.
By an experienced science writer, this comprehensive, understandable, and well-researched study presents a nonjudgmental overview of current knowledge about AIDS. (Nonfiction)

Lanker, Brian.   *I Dream a World: Portraits of Black Women Who Changed America*, Stewart, Tabori & Chang, 1990.
Photographs and text highlight the strength of black women who have prevailed in the face of adversity and prejudice. (Nonfiction)

Larrick, Nancy, ed.   *Crazy to Be Alive in Such a Strange World: Poems about People*, Evans, 1977.
Tinged with humor and irony, a collection of poems written by both well- and little-known poets about people of varied backgrounds and ages. (Nonfiction)

Larson, Gary.   *Prehistory of The Far Side: A 10th Anniversary Exhibit*, Andrews & McMeel, 1991.
In cartoons and words not for the "humorously squeamish," Larson describes his life as creator of "The Far Side." (Nonfiction)

Lasky, Kathryn.   *Beyond the Divide*, Macmillan, 1983.
Meribah runs away to join her father on a trek to California—and ends up surviving alone in the Sierra Nevada mountains. (Fiction)

_____. *Pageant*, Macmillan/Four Winds, 1986.
Sarah's years at an exclusive high school are full of self-awareness, humor, and conflict with the teachers. (Fiction)

_____. *Prank*, Macmillan, 1984.
While trying to determine her future plans, Birdie Flynn confronts her brother about his

involvement in vandalizing a synagogue. (Fiction)

Lauber, Patricia.   *Seeing Earth from Space*, Watts/Orchard, 1991.
Lauber's photo essay shows how scientists use various photographic methods to study the earth. (Nonfiction)

_____. *Summer of Fire: Yellowstone, 1988*, Orchard, 1992.
In an account enhanced by stunning photographs, Lauber clearly describes the effects, both positive and negative, of the awesome fires that roared through our oldest national park in 1988. (Nonfiction)

Laure, Jason, and Laure, Ettagale.   *South Africa: Coming of Age under Apartheid*, Farrar, 1980.
Eight young people talk about their lives and their aspirations in a country where color rules one's place in society. (Nonfiction)

LaVallee, David.   *Event 1000*, Holt, 1971.
A nuclear-powered submarine is marooned in more than 1,200 feet of water, 160 miles from New York City, where for over a month the rescue team fights political and business interests to get an outmoded diving bell altered to rescue the trapped men below. (Fiction)

Lawick-Goodall, Jane Van.   *In the Shadow of Man*, Houghton, 1971.
A young Englishwoman writes about the ten years she spent in Tanzania studying chimpanzees and describes with loving care each facet of their lives from birth to death. (Nonfiction)

Lawrence, Louise.   *Calling B for Butterfly*, Harper, 1982.
Six young survivors of a destroyed starliner must depend on their own wits, a fragile radio link, and a mysterious alien presence. (Fiction)

_____. *Children of the Dust*, Harper, 1985.
The story of three generations of the same family representing the two human factions—those who mutated due to exposure to a nuclear holocaust and those who were sheltered. (Fiction)

Lawson, Don.   *United States in the Vietnam War*, Crowell, 1981.
Traces U.S. involvement beginning with the use of advisers through the fall of Saigon and the final peace treaty. (Nonfiction)

Lawson, Donna.   *Mother Nature's Beauty Cupboard: How to Make Beautiful, Money-*

■ Selected for "Still Alive: The Best of the Best, 1960–1974"
▲ Selected for "The Best of the Best Books, 1970–1983"
♦ Selected for "Nothin' But the Best: Best of the Best Books for Young Adults, 1966–1986"

Saving Natural Cosmetics and Other Beauty Preparations, Crowell, 1973.
Strawberries and avocados are just two foods that you can turn into natural and inexpensive beauty aids that are fun to make. (Nonfiction)

Le Guin, Ursula K.   *Beginning Place,* Harper, 1980.
Irena and Hugh each follow a hidden path to Tembreabrezi, a fantasy place, where they struggle to save their friends and make peace with the real world. (Fiction)

———.   *Dispossessed,* Harper, 1974.
Shevek, the Dispossessed, a brilliant but politically naive scientist, attempts to establish interplanetary relations between two disparate societies, neither of which shares his utopian dream. (Fiction)

———.   *Very Far Away from Anywhere Else,* Atheneum, 1976. ▲
In a brief and unique Le Guin story, Owen and Natalie, two gifted seventeen-year-olds, find friendship and love by sharing their dreams: one to be a scientist, the other, a musician. (Fiction)

Leder, Jane M.   *Dead Serious: A Book about Teenagers and Teenage Suicide,* Atheneum, 1987.
What to do for and not to do for friends and parents of those who are considering suicide. (Nonfiction)

Lee, Mildred.   *Fog,* Seabury, 1972.
In October Luke Sawyer's life was going great; in December everything in his comfortable world started to fall apart. (Fiction)

———.   *People Therein,* Houghton/Clarion, 1980.
A turn-of-the-century love story set in southern Appalachia joins together Lanthy, resigned to life without marriage because she is crippled, and Drew, a botanist who comes to the Great Smoky Mountains from Boston to cure his fondness for alcohol. (Fiction)

Lee, Tanith.   *Black Unicorn,* Atheneum, 1992.
Bored with her lonely life as the no-talent daughter of a quirky sorceress, Tanaquil reconstructs a unicorn and, when it comes to life, takes off for adventure. (Fiction)

———.   *Red as Blood; or, Tales from the Sisters Grimmer,* NAL/DAW, 1983.
Bizarre and chilling new twists to old fairy tales by a master fantasy writer. (Fiction)

Leekley, Sheryle, and Leekley, John.   *Moments: The Pulitzer Prize Photographs,* Crown, 1978.
Dramatic, prizewinning photographs from 1942 to the present illuminate small everyday human happenings and make important historical events come alive again. (Nonfiction)

Leffland, Ella.   *Rumors of Peace,* Harper, 1979.
Growing up in California, a young girl finds the anxieties of childhood and adolescence complicated by the turmoil of World War II. (Fiction)

LeFlore, Ron, and Hawkins, Jim.   *Breakout: From Prison to the Big Leagues,* Harper, 1978.
A former thief, drug addict, and ex-con recalls the people and events that led him from the prison baseball team to the Detroit Tigers and the All-Star game. (Nonfiction)

Lehrman, Robert.   *Juggling,* Harper, 1982.
In this touching novel, affluent high school student Howie Berger not only suffers the agonies of first love but also is frustrated as he tries to become an accepted member of an all-Jewish-immigrant soccer team. (Fiction)

Leitner, Isabella.   *Fragments of Isabella: A Memoir of Auschwitz,* Crowell, 1978. ▲
The strength of the human spirit and the passionate will to survive the degradation and death of Auschwitz are portrayed with searing intensity through Leitner's fragmented memories. (Nonfiction)

LeRoy, Gen.   *Cold Feet,* Harper, 1979.
Attempting to give her life new direction, Geneva draws away from family and school and becomes involved in a gambling ring . . . disguised as a boy! (Fiction)

Leslie, Robert.   *Bears and I: Raising Three Cubs in the North Woods,* Dutton, 1968.
While panning for gold in Canada the author is "adopted" by three orphan bear cubs whom he has to teach to find food, recognize danger, and share his cabin. (Nonfiction)

Lester, Julius.   *Search for the New Land,* Dial, 1969.
Combining autobiography, contemporary history, and "found" poetry, a sensitive black militant reveals the frustrations of his life, the sickness in American society, and a revolutionary hope for the future. (Nonfiction)

———.   *This Strange New Feeling,* Dial, 1982.
Three black slave couples reach freedom by different paths, but all experience an emancipation made richer by their dangerous struggle. (Fiction)

Levenkron, Steven.   *Best Little Girl in the World,* Contemporary Books, 1978. ▲
Obsessive dieting and bizarre rituals with food are symptoms of Francesca's battle with anorexia nervosa in a novel about the disorder

that afflicts one out of every three hundred teenage girls. (Fiction)

LeVert, John. *Flight of the Cassowary*, Atlantic Monthly Press, 1986.
More and more obsessed with the animal characteristics of people, sixteen-year-old Paul—bright, normal, and athletic—comes to believe that he can fly. (Fiction)

Levin, Betty. *Brother Moose*, Greenwillow, 1991.
Survival takes on new meaning for orphans Louisa and Nell, as they trek through the Maine woods with an old Indian and his grandson. (Fiction)

Levin, Ira. *Boys from Brazil*, Random, 1976.
Nazis living in Brazil have an ingenious plot for establishing a Fourth Reich. (Fiction)

Levit, Rose. *Ellen: A Short Life Long Remembered*, Chronicle, 1974.
Told at fifteen that she has cancer, Ellen for two years finds the inner strength to live each day as fully as she can. (Nonfiction)

Levitin, Sonia. *Return*, Atheneum, 1987.
Desta, an Ethiopian Jew, and her family make a courageous and tragic journey across Ethiopia to Israel with the help of Operation Moses. (Fiction)

———. *Silver Days*, Atheneum, 1990.
Escaping from Nazi Germany, the Platts struggle to find a home in America and pursue their own dreams. (Fiction)

Levitt, Leonard. *African Season*, Simon & Schuster, 1967.
A swinging Peace Corps volunteer in Tanganyika quickly becomes "broo," meaning brother, to the villagers. (Nonfiction)

Levoy, Myron. *Pictures of Adam*, Harper/ Charlotte Zolotow, 1986.
Though fourteen-year-old camera bug Lisa is drawn to class misfit Adam, she is dismayed when he claims to be an alien from the planet Vega-X. (Fiction)

———. *Shadow like a Leopard*, Harper, 1981.
Ramon Santiago, a street punk and gifted poet, forms an unlikely friendship with an elderly artist, and each helps the other face his private fears. (Fiction)

Liang, Heng, and Shapiro, Judith. *Son of the Revolution*, Knopf, 1983.
Liang Heng recounts his growing up during the Chinese Cultural Revolution, which fragmented his family and changed his life. (Nonfiction)

Lieberman, James E., and Peck, Ellen. *Sex and Birth Control: A Guide for the Young*, Crowell, 1973.
Mature, responsible sexual behavior is the cornerstone of a candid, comprehensive handbook offering facts about sex and sexual relationships. (Nonfiction)

Lindall, Edward. *Northward the Coast*, Morrow, 1966.
Having agreed to hide two political refugees, hard-boiled Lang Bowman takes them across the Australian wasteland with the police in pursuit. (Fiction)

Lipsyte, Robert. *Brave*, HarperCollins/ Charlotte Zolotow, 1992.
Sonny Bear, half-white and half-Moscondaga Indian, wants to be a boxer but has difficulty controlling his anger until he meets Alfred Brooks, a New York City cop and former contender. (Fiction)

———. *One Fat Summer*, Harper, 1977. ▲ ♦
Overweight Bobby Marks confronts the ridicule of friends and sheds his excess pounds in a comical story of his last fat summer. (Fiction)

Lisle, Janet Taylor. *Sirens and Spies*, Bradbury, 1985.
Fourteen-year-old Elsie feels betrayed when she discovers that her beloved violin teacher, Miss Fitch, has a dark and painful secret she has been hiding since her girlhood in World War II France. (Fiction)

Llewellyn, Chris. *Fragments from the Fire: The Triangle Shirtwaist Company Fire of March 25, 1911*, Viking, 1987.
This slim volume of poetry tells the story of the women and children who died when fire destroyed the Triangle shirtwaist factory. (Nonfiction)

Llywelyn, Morgan. *Horse Goddess*, Houghton, 1982.
A young Celtic woman and a savage warrior journey throughout the ancient world pursued by a Druid priest, the horrible Shapechanger. (Fiction)

■ Selected for "Still Alive: The Best of the Best, 1960–1974"

▲ Selected for "The Best of the Best Books, 1970–1983"

♦ Selected for "Nothin' But the Best: Best of the Best Books for Young Adults, 1966–1986"

Lockley, Ronald. *Seal Woman*, Bradbury, 1975.
Truth and fantasy blend in this haunting story of an Irish girl who became a princess of the seals and of the man she chose as her prince. (Fiction)

Logan, Jane. *Very Nearest Room*, Scribner, 1973.
Fifteen-year-old Lee Kramer's life is bounded by family—a hard-working doctor father, boy-crazy younger sister, frail younger brother, and, especially, her dying mother. (Fiction)

London, Mel. *Getting into Film*, Ballantine, 1978.
An award-winning filmmaker shares the "inside dope" on career opportunities in all aspects of the film industry. (Nonfiction)

Lopes, Sal, ed. *Wall: Images and Offerings from the Vietnam Veterans Memorial*, Collins, 1988.
Images of peace, war, and remembrance are evoked in this photographic essay about the healing force of the Vietnam Veterans Memorial. (Nonfiction)

Lopez, Barry. *Arctic Dreams: Imagination and Desire in a Northern Landscape*, Scribner, 1986.
An enchanting, literate, challenging account of the animals, people, geology, and history of the Arctic. (Nonfiction)

Lord, Bette Bao. *Legacies: A Chinese Mosaic*, Knopf, 1991.
These unique portraits of life in China during the past forty years form an affecting picture of events that led to Tiananmen Square. (Nonfiction)

Lord, Walter. *Incredible Victory*, Harper, 1967.
The crucial World War II battle of Midway stirringly re-created from both the American and Japanese points of view. (Nonfiction)

Lowenfels, Walter, ed. *Writing on the Wall: 108 American Poems of Protest*, Doubleday, 1969.
Martyrdom, inhumanity, war, and death confront the conscience of the reader in this anthology of protest poetry. (Nonfiction)

Lueders, Edward, and St. John, Primus, comps. *Zero Makes Me Hungry: A Collection of Poems For Today*, Lothrop, 1976.
Poems in a contemporary vein—with eye-catching modern graphics. (Nonfiction)

Lund, Doris Herold. *Eric*, Lippincott, 1975.
Told at seventeen that he has leukemia, Eric crowds his dreams for the future—college, sports, love—into the short time he has left. (Nonfiction)

Lydon, Michael. *Rock Folk: Portraits from the Rock 'n Roll Pantheon*, Dial, 1971.
These sketches bring to life the personality, life-style, and music of rock stars Chuck Berry, Carl Perkins, B. B. King, Smokey Robinson, Janis Joplin, the Grateful Dead, and the Rolling Stones. (Nonfiction)

Lynd, Alice. *We Won't Go*, Beacon, 1968.
Told with utter sincerity, these are the personal accounts of Vietnam protesters, some of whom are pacifists. (Nonfiction)

Lynn, Elizabeth A. *Sardonyx Net*, Putnam, 1982.
Star captain Dana Ikoro becomes Rhani Yago's slave, bodyguard, and lover, as well as her pilot, after he is convicted of smuggling dorazine. (Fiction)

Lyons, Mary E. *Letters from a Slave Girl: The Story of Harriet Jacobs*, Scribner, 1993.
Through letters to family and friends, Harriet Jacobs describes her life as a young slave girl in North Carolina and her daring escape to freedom. (Fiction)

_____. *Sorrow's Kitchen: The Life and Folklore of Zora Neale Hurston*, Scribner, 1992.
A biography of Zora Neale Hurston who, wanting to preserve the cultural heritage of black Americans, achieved fame and triumph through her stories and plays, only to die poor and, until recently, almost forgotten. (Nonfiction)

Maas, Peter. *Rescuer*, Harper, 1967.
How Charles Momsen, utilizing his previously untried diving bell, succeeded in rescuing thirty-three men entombed in the sunken submarine *Squalus*. (Nonfiction)

_____. *Serpico*, Viking, 1973. ■
Believing cops should be honest, New York policeman Frank Serpico attempts to get action from the top against corrupt fellow officers. (Nonfiction)

Macaulay, David. *Motel of the Mysteries*, Houghton, 1979.
"Plastic is forever" in an illustrated catalog of the wonderful things discovered by archaeologists in the year 4022, when they excavate the ruins of the Toot 'n' C'mon Motel. (Nonfiction)

_____. *Way Things Work*, Houghton, 1990.
Little woolly mammoths help you learn everything you always wanted to know about machines and how they work. (Nonfiction)

MacCracken, Mary. *Circle of Children,* Lippincott, 1974. ▲
Involving herself in a school for emotionally disturbed children, Mary MacCracken learns that these children can be helped through the love, trust, and compassion of those who teach them. (Nonfiction)

_____. *Lovey: A Very Special Child,* Lippincott, 1976.
A profoundly disturbed child, Hannah was trapped in the prison of her emotions until a gifted teacher helped her to break free. (Nonfiction)

MacInnes, Helen. *Salzburg Connection,* Harcourt, 1968.
Tension mounts steadily as Bill Mathison, a young attorney sojourning in the Alps, finds himself facing a dangerous group of international agents. (Fiction)

Mackay, Donald A. *Building of Manhattan,* Harper, 1988.
Ever wonder how the Empire State Building was built, how the New York subway works, or what happened to the farmland on Manhattan Island? Mackay explains it all. (Nonfiction)

MacKinnon, Bernie. *Meantime,* Houghton, 1984. ♦
Told through the eyes of their son, this story concerns a middle-class black family living in a white suburb and facing the hostility of neighbors and schoolmates. (Fiction)

MacLachlan, Patricia. *Journey,* Delacorte, 1992.
Journey's grandparents find a way to restore his family to him after his mother abandons him and his sister. (Fiction)

MacLaine, Shirley. *You Can Get There from Here,* Norton, 1975.
Invited to visit the People's Republic of China, the author and a group of American women were not prepared for what they saw and learned. (Nonfiction)

MacLean, Alistair. *Circus,* Doubleday, 1975.
It took a five-man circus act with a psychic tightrope artist to get in and out of an East European prison safely. (Fiction)

_____. *When Eight Bells Toll,* Doubleday, 1966.
Philip Calvert, a ruthless agent for Britain's secret service, outwits a gang of modern pirates operating on the Irish Sea. (Fiction)

MacLean, John. *Mac,* Houghton, 1987.
Mac's world, which centers on sports, school, and girls, crumbles when he is molested by a physician—and he tries to act as if it never happened. (Fiction)

MacLeish, Roderick. *First Book of Eppe: An American Romance,* Random, 1980.
Sherborne Eppe, a lovable bungler, reentering the world after seven years in an "insane asylum," encounters several opportunities to do good as he flees from his mother, searches for his father, and tries to find himself. (Fiction)

Madaras, Lynda. *Lynda Madaras Talks to Teens about AIDS: An Essential Guide for Parents, Teachers, and Young People,* Newmarket, 1988.
The curious, worried, or scared will find information, help, and hope in this honest look at how AIDS affects teens today. (Nonfiction)

_____, **and Madaras, Area.** *What's Happening to My Body? A Growing Up Guide for Mothers and Daughters,* Newmarket, 1983.
An illustrated guide discusses body image, body changes, menstruation, puberty in boys, and sexuality. Emphasizes the importance of liking and knowing one's own body. (Nonfiction)

Magorian, Michelle. *Back Home,* Harper/ Charlotte Zolotow, 1984.
When Virginia (Rusty) Dickinson returns to England after being evacuated to America during World War II, she feels lonely and alienated until she and her mother grow toward mutual understanding and acceptance. (Fiction)

_____. *Good Night, Mr. Tom,* Harper, 1982.
A badly battered and frightened young boy evacuated from London during World War II fills an empty void in the heart of a dour old man. (Fiction)

_____. *Not a Swan,* HarperCollins/Laura Geringer, 1993.
Spending an unchaperoned summer in a seaside English town during World War II, three sisters discover their lives will never be the same. (Fiction)

Magubane, Peter. *Black Child,* Knopf, 1982.
The sad, harsh realities of life in South Africa are sensitively revealed in photographs of children's faces. (Nonfiction)

■ Selected for "Still Alive: The Best of the Best, 1960–1974"
▲ Selected for "The Best of the Best Books, 1970–1983"
♦ Selected for "Nothin' But the Best: Best of the Best Books for Young Adults, 1966–1986"

Maguire, Gregory. *I Feel like the Morning Star*, Harper, 1990.
Pioneer Colony's three dissidents—Ella, Mort, and Sorb—plot to escape their underground post-nuclear holocaust community. (Fiction)

Mahy, Margaret. *Catalogue of the Universe*, Atheneum/Margaret K. McElderry, 1986.
Angela's search for the father she has never met leads to a surprising new relationship with her best friend, Tycho Potter. (Fiction)

_____. *Changeover: A Supernatural Romance*, Atheneum/Margaret K. McElderry, 1984.
With the help of an older boy who loves her, Laura "changes over" into a witch to fight the evil forces that are attacking her little brother. (Fiction)

_____. *Memory*, Macmillan/Margaret K. McElderry, 1988.
After a wild, drunken night seeking the truth behind his confused memories of his sister's death, teenage Jonny meets Sophie, an old woman who has lost her memory but has retained her zest for life. (Fiction)

_____. *Tricksters*, Macmillan/Margaret K. McElderry, 1987.
Three strangers from nowhere are catalysts in the lives of Harry and her family when reality and fantasy merge to expose unexpected secrets. (Fiction)

Maiorano, Robert. *Worlds Apart: The Autobiography of a Dancer from Brooklyn*, Coward, 1980.
A soloist with the New York City Ballet recounts his first sixteen years by presenting the two contrasting worlds in which he grew up—the tough streets of Brooklyn and the demanding and exciting world of ballet. (Nonfiction)

Manchester, William. *One Brief Shining Moment: Remembering Kennedy*, Little, Brown, 1984.
Twenty years after John F. Kennedy's assassination, friends, family, and associates offer sentimental, yet candid reminiscences in words and pictures. (Nonfiction)

Mandela, Winnie. *Part of My Soul Went with Him*, Norton, 1986.
Battered but unyielding, Winnie Mandela reveals brutal facts about apartheid through her personal account of life in South Africa. (Nonfiction)

Mann, Peggy, and Hersh, Gizelle. *"Gizelle, Save the Children!"*, Everest, 1981.
Gizelle Hersh, inspired by her mother's parting words, attempts to save her three younger sisters and a brother from death in the Auschwitz

concentration camp at the close of World War II. (Nonfiction)

Manry, Robert. *Tinkerbelle*, Harper, 1966.
A copy editor of the *Cleveland Plain Dealer* realized a lifelong goal when he sailed his 13½-foot sloop across the Atlantic alone. (Nonfiction)

Margolies, Marjorie, and Gruber, Ruth. *They Came to Stay*, Coward, 1976.
The heartwarming story of how a single woman adopted two daughters—one Korean and the other Vietnamese—and the problems they had until the three strangers became a family. (Nonfiction)

Marlette, Doug. *In Your Face: A Cartoonist at Work*, Houghton, 1993.
"Kudzu" creator and political cartoonist Doug Marlette describes—in words and art—his sometimes offbeat life. (Nonfiction)

Marsden, John. *So Much to Tell You*, Little, Brown/Joy Street Books, 1990.
In her diary, Marina, a young Australian girl locked in a self-imposed silence, reveals her deepest feelings and the family problems that led to her muteness. (Fiction)

Marsh, Dave. *Born to Run: The Bruce Springsteen Story*, Doubleday, 1979.
An illustrated biography of a rock star—from his beginnings to the top of the rock and roll charts. (Nonfiction)

Marshall, Kathryn. *In the Combat Zone: An Oral History of American Women in Vietnam, 1966-1975*, Little, Brown, 1987.
Dramatic, thoughtful, often tragic accounts by a few of the thousands of women who served in Vietnam and, years later, are unable to forget. (Nonfiction)

Martin, Valerie. *Mary Reilly*, Doubleday, 1991.
Intrigued by the mysterious Dr. Jekyll, housemaid Mary Reilly finds life taking a different twist as she learns more about his late-night prowling in Victorian England. (Fiction)

Marzollo, Jean. *Halfway down Paddy Lane*, Dial, 1981.
Kate experiences a drastic change in life-style when she is transported back in time to 1850 as the daughter of an Irish immigrant family that lives and works in a New England mill town. (Fiction)

Mason, Bobbie Ann. *In Country*, Harper, 1985. ♦
Sam, a recent high school graduate who is trying to understand the strange behavior of her uncle Emmett and the death of the father she never knew, both victims of the Vietnam War, explores the war and its consequences while

on a pilgrimage to the Vietnam War Memorial. (Fiction)

Mason, Robert C.   *Chickenhawk*, Viking, 1983.
The account of an American helicopter pilot in Vietnam, who recalls his military training, the horror of Vietnam combat, and the pain of coming home. (Fiction)

Mather, Melissa.   *One Summer in Between*, Harper, 1967.
Harriet Brown, a Negro college student, working temporarily for a white family in Vermont, is shocked when she recognizes her own prejudice. (Fiction)

Mathis, Sharon Bell.   *Listen for the Fig Tree*, Viking, 1974.
In spite of her blindness and an alcoholic mother, Muffin, with the help of a kind neighbor, celebrates Kwanza and is able to face the future. (Fiction)

_____.   *Teacup Full of Roses*, Viking, 1972.
Into the lives of a middle-class black family reach the tragedies of drugs, demolished dreams, and sudden death. (Fiction)

Matsubara, Hisako.   *Cranes at Dusk*, Doubleday/Dial, 1985.
Like her defeated country of Japan, ten-year-old Saya faces painful readjustments after World War II. Her mother, who can neither abandon tradition nor accept changes, attempts to turn Saya against her wise and progressive father. (Fiction)

Matthew, Christopher.   *Long-Haired Boy*, Atheneum, 1980.
War, self-pity, endless skin grafts, and long hospitalizations face Hugh Fleming, a young British fighter pilot, as he learns about life and finds a purpose for living. (Fiction)

Mayhar, Ardath.   *Soul Singer of Tyrnos*, Atheneum, 1981.
Though only a novice at singing souls, Yeleeve becomes the singer chosen to help combat the great evil threatening to overpower the land. (Fiction)

Maynard, Joyce.   *Looking Back: A Chronicle of Growing Up Old in the Sixties*, Doubleday, 1973.
Writing at age eighteen, the author takes a nostalgic look at what it was like to grow up in middle-class, white America in the 1960s. (Nonfiction)

Mazer, Harry.   *Girl of His Dreams*, Harper/Crowell, 1987.
Runner Willis Pierce has to reconcile his fantasy about the "girl of his dreams" with reality when he meets Sophie, a girl who makes the world a less lonely place. (Fiction)

_____.   *I Love You, Stupid!*, Crowell, 1981.
Marcus Rosenbloom wants to love a girl but isn't sure he knows how—until he meets Wendy Barrett. (Fiction)

_____.   *Last Mission*, Delacorte, 1979. ▲ ◆
When fifteen-year-old Jack Raab lies his way into becoming a tail gunner during World War II, he has no idea of the terrifying experiences that await him. (Fiction)

_____.   *War on Villa Street: A Novel*, Delacorte, 1978.
Thirteen-year-old Willis, who has turned to running as an escape from an unhappy home, coaches a retarded boy in athletics, an experience that helps both gain self-respect. (Fiction)

_____.   *When the Phone Rang*, Scholastic, 1986.
When their parents are killed in an air crash, Billy, Lori, and their older college-age brother, Kevin, struggle against adults and among themselves to avoid separating the family. (Fiction)

_____, **and Mazer, Norma Fox.**   *Solid Gold Kid*, Delacorte, 1977.
When five teen-agers accept a ride from strangers, they become the victims of a kidnap plot and experience six horror-filled days that change their lives. (Fiction)

Mazer, Norma Fox.   *After the Rain*, Morrow, 1987.
Rachel tells the story of her growing understanding of her eighty-three-year-old grandfather, a cantankerous old man she finds hard to love and almost impossible to like. (Fiction)

_____.   *Dear Bill, Remember Me?*, Delacorte, 1976.
Eight short stories, all featuring strong female characters, ranging from a sensitive portrayal of an eighteen-year-old dying from cancer to the tale of a turn-of-the-century immigrant girl who defied tradition by getting an education and not getting married. (Fiction)

_____.   *Downtown*, Morrow, 1984.
When his mother reappears after eight years, Pete Connors, son of antiwar activists who have been in hiding, must reconcile his desire

---

■   Selected for "Still Alive: The Best of the Best, 1960–1974"

▲   Selected for "The Best of the Best Books, 1970–1983"

◆   Selected for "Nothin' But the Best: Best of the Best Books for Young Adults, 1966–1986"

for normalcy with an understanding of his parents' ideals and acts. (Fiction)

_____. *Silver*, Morrow, 1988.
When fourteen-year-old Sarabeth Silver transfers to a new school, she is thrilled to find herself a part of the in crowd, until she becomes privy to an awful secret. (Fiction)

_____. *Someone to Love*, Delacorte, 1983.
When Nina and Mitch fall in love, it seems only natural for them to live together until Nina finishes college. (Fiction)

_____. *Up in Seth's Room*, Delacorte, 1979.
Though Finn's parents forbid her relationship with nineteen-year-old Seth, the two develop a real attachment that helps them understand more about themselves and each other. (Fiction)

McCaffrey, Anne. *Dragonsinger*, Atheneum, 1977.
With the help of Master-harper, Menolly and her fire lizards overcome the prejudice against a woman's becoming a harper on the planet Pern. (Fiction)

_____. *Pegasus in Flight*, Ballantine/Del Rey, 1992.
In a future where the psychically talented are both exploited and shunned, quadriplegic Peter and slum-kid Tirla join forces to build a new space station and infiltrate a child-smuggling ring. (Fiction)

McCammon, Robert R. *Boy's Life*, Pocket Books, 1992.
Cory and his dad find a corpse handcuffed to the steering wheel of a sinking car and search for the killer. (Fiction)

McCartney, Linda. *Linda's Pictures: A Collection of Photographs*, Knopf, 1977.
Large-size color photographs of the Beatles—especially McCartney and family—and other rock groups. (Nonfiction)

McConnell, Joan. *Ballet as Body Language*, Harper, 1977.
A vivid and realistic introduction to the behind-the-scenes sweat and pain—as well as the onstage glamour—of ballet. (Nonfiction)

McCorkle, Jill. *Ferris Beach*, Algonquin, 1991.
Katie Burns is caught in the conflict between the conventional life of her family and the daring, romantic lives of her beautiful cousin Angela and her lively neighbor, Mo Rhodes. (Fiction)

McCoy, Kathy, and Wibbelsman, Charles. *Teenage Body Book*, Pocket Books, 1979. ▲
Everything you ever wanted to know about teenage health and physical and mental development—sex, diseases, skin, feelings, pregnancy, relationships, etc. (Nonfiction)

McCullough, Frances, ed. *Earth, Air, Fire and Water*, Harper/Charlotte Zolotow, 1990.
What is a poem? This revised edition of a memorable collection of poems by 125 poets from all over the world may change your definition in surprising and intriguing ways. (Nonfiction)

_____. *Love Is like the Lion's Tooth: An Anthology of Love Poems*, Harper, 1984.
Passion, not romance, is the theme of this diverse anthology of love poems from various times and places. (Nonfiction)

McFarlane, Milton C. *Cudjoe of Jamaica: Pioneer for Black Freedom in the New World*, Ridley Enslow, 1978.
A retelling of the story of General Cudjoe, who led the proud Maroons of Jamaica in their successful eighteenth-century fight against enslavement by the British. (Nonfiction)

McGuire, Paula. *It Won't Happen to Me: Teenagers Talk about Pregnancy*, Delacorte, 1983.
Interviews with fifteen young women who have faced unwanted pregnancies. (Nonfiction)

McIntyre, Vonda N. *Dreamsnake*, Houghton, 1978. ▲ ♦
Snake, a young healer in a dangerous post-holocaust world, undertakes an arduous search for Grass, the slain dreamsnake vital to her profession. (Fiction)

McKibben, Bill. *End of Nature*, Random, 1990.
McKibben explores and explains the environmental cataclysms and global climate changes facing planet Earth. (Nonfiction)

McKillip, Patricia A. *Fool's Run*, Warner, 1987.
Masked musician The Queen of Hearts and her band entertain in an orbiting prison and create an intergalactic emergency. (Fiction)

McKinley, Robin. *Beauty: A Retelling of the Story of Beauty and the Beast*, Harper, 1978. ▲ ♦
Fantasy and romance are beautifully blended in an evocative, much-expanded version of the classic fairy tale. (Nonfiction)

_____. *Blue Sword*, Greenwillow, 1982. ▲
Harry Crewe, bored with her dull and sheltered life, finds new magic, love, and her destiny as a woman warrior when kidnapped by a handsome king who has mysterious powers. (Fiction)

_____. *Hero and the Crown*, Greenwillow, 1985.
Struggling to become a dragon killer, Aerin almost dies subduing the Black Dragon—only to face the evil mage, Agsded. (Fiction)

_____. *Outlaws of Sherwood*, Greenwillow, 1988.
In a retelling that transcends the centuries, Newbery medalist Robin McKinley gives readers a lively, romantic new version of Robin Hood and his merry band. (Fiction)

McKissack, Patricia C., and McKissack, Fredrick. *Sojourner Truth: Ain't I a Woman?*, Scholastic, 1993.
A slave for the first thirty years of her life, Sojourner Truth achieved freedom and became an eloquent orator for the abolition of slavery and the emancipation of women—in spite of never learning to read or write. (Nonfiction)

Meltzer, Milton. *Ain't Gonna Study War No More*, Harper, 1985.
A lively account of the individuals and groups that have protested against the wars in which the United States has been involved—people convinced that there are peaceful solutions to conflict. (Nonfiction)

_____. *Benjamin Franklin: The New American*, Watts, 1990.
The life story of an American original—a self-made man of many interests and talents and one of the revolutionaries who bucked the establishment to found a new country. (Nonfiction)

_____. *Columbus and the World around Him*, Watts, 1991.
Meltzer's "no holds barred" biography of Columbus details the explorer's voyages in search of Asia and describes the tragic impact of the Spaniards upon the native Americans. (Nonfiction)

_____. *Never to Forget: The Jews of the Holocaust*, Harper, 1976. ■ ▲
Based on diaries, letters, songs, and history books, a moving account of Jewish suffering in Nazi Germany before and during World War II. (Nonfiction)

_____. *Rescue: The Story of How Gentiles Saved Jews in the Holocaust*, Harper, 1988.
In an account of individuals who risked their own lives to save thousands of others during the Holocaust, Meltzer shows the quiet but impressive courage of those who chose to stand firm in the face of evil. (Nonfiction)

_____. *Voices from the Civil War: A Documentary History of the Great American Conflict*, Harper/Crowell, 1990.
Details and excerpts from letters, diaries, and other primary sources make the Civil War come alive through the voices of those who fought, died, and survived its ravages. (Nonfiction)

Meltzer, Milton, ed. *American Revolutionaries: A History in Their Own Words, 1750-1800*, Harper/Crowell, 1987.
Letters, journals, etc., provide the personal views of people living in a turbulent time. (Nonfiction)

Meriwether, Louise. *Daddy Was a Number Runner*, Prentice-Hall, 1970.
Francie, a twelve-year-old black girl, faces the daily hazards of life in the Harlem of the 1930s. (Fiction)

Messing, Shep, and Hirshey, David. *Education of an American Soccer Player*, Dodd, 1978.
One of the North American Soccer League's great goalies, Messing relates anecdotes about his Bronx childhood, Harvard education, participation in the Munich Olympics, and career with the New York Cosmos. (Nonfiction)

Meyer, Carolyn. *C. C. Poindexter*, Atheneum, 1978.
In this zany story, C.C. (Cynthia Charlotte) Poindexter, who at age fifteen is 6'1" and still growing, tells how she coped with her own problems and family conflicts during one chaotic summer. (Fiction)

_____. *Center: From a Troubled Past to a New Life*, Atheneum/Margaret K. McElderry, 1979.
David, who smokes marijuana, pops pills, cuts school, and steals, is sent to the Center, where teenagers help each other. (Fiction)

_____. *Denny's Tapes*, Macmillan/Margaret K. McElderry, 1987.
Ejected by his stepfather, Dennis goes across country in search of his real father, detouring to visit both his grandmothers, from whom he learns about his biracial heritage. (Fiction)

_____. *Voices of South Africa: Growing Up in a Troubled Land*, Harcourt, 1987.
Meyer recounts her journey to South Africa in a moving record of life in that beautiful and violent country. (Nonfiction)

_____. *Where the Broken Heart Still Beats: The Story of Cynthia Ann Parker*, Harcourt/Gulliver, 1993.
Discovered and forced to return to her own family in 1836, twenty-four years after her capture by Comanche Indians, Cynthia Ann Parker is tragically unable to adjust to life away from the tribe that she now claims as her own. (Fiction)

Michaels, Barbara. *Ammie, Come Home*, Hawthorn, 1969.
A ghost that never quite materializes and the spirit of "Ammie" Campbell haunt an old Georgetown house, threatening the lives of its occupants. (Fiction)

_____. *Be Buried in the Rain*, Atheneum, 1985.
Medical student Julie Newcomb rediscovers love as well as the terrors of her childhood when she goes to care for her sinister grandmother in a southern mansion that is—perhaps—haunted. (Fiction)

_____. *Dark on the Other Side*, Dodd, 1971.
Writer Michael Collins did not believe in supernatural powers until he too saw the savage black dog that was driving Linda Randolph to the brink of insanity. (Fiction)

_____. *Witch*, Dodd, 1973.
Ellen's beautiful house, rumored to be haunted by a witch and her cat, changes from a refuge to a prison as she tries to understand the strange and threatening events that crowd around her. (Fiction)

Michelson, Maureen R., ed. *Women and Work: Photographs and Personal Writings*, NewSage, 1987.
Handsome black-and-white photographs together with women's personal testimony capture the depth and breadth of American working women. (Nonfiction)

Mickle, Shelley Fraser. *Queen of October*, Algonquin, 1990.
Sent to her grandparents while her parents contemplate divorce, Sally comes to terms with herself and her life in a story set in the 1950s. (Fiction)

Miller, Frances A. *Truth Trap*, Dutton/Unicorn, 1980.
Mathew McKendrick is fifteen and a nonconformist. When their parents are killed in an automobile accident, he and his nine-year-old, deaf sister Kathie run away to Los Angeles where Mat finds himself unjustly accused of murder. (Fiction)

Miller, Jim Wayne. *Newfound*, Watts/Orchard, 1990.
Newfound Creek in Tennessee is home to teenager Robert Wells and his extended family in this haunting story of what it is really like to grow up in Appalachia. (Fiction)

Miller, Jonathan, and Pelham, David. *Facts of Life*, Viking, 1985.
Six three-dimensional, movable models illustrate the human reproductive system and fetal development from conception to birth. (Nonfiction)

Mills, Judie. *John F. Kennedy*, Watts, 1988.
This biography reveals President John F. Kennedy's failures and faults as well as his moral courage and political successes. (Nonfiction)

Moeri, Louise. *Forty-third War*, Houghton, 1990.
Forced to join a Central American army, twelve-year-old Uno learns firsthand about soldiering and war. (Fiction)

Mohr, Nicholasa. *In Nueva York*, Dial, 1977.
Interrelated stories of love, friendship, and the struggle to survive show the tragic and comic sides of life in a Puerto Rican community on New York's Lower East Side. (Fiction)

Mojtabai, A. G. *400 Eels of Sigmund Freud*, Simon & Schuster, 1976.
Summer at a scientific community for gifted teenagers ends in tragedy for Isaiah, the rebel among them, who prefers music to science. (Fiction)

Moll, Richard. *Public Ivys: A Guide to America's Best Public Undergraduate Colleges and Universities*, Viking, 1986.
Assuming that some state-supported colleges offer programs equivalent to those of the higher-priced Ivy League, Moll's thoughtful evaluations of the "public ivys" are right on target. (Nonfiction)

Monk, Lorraine. *Photographs That Changed the World*, Doubleday, 1990.
Fifty-one memorable photographs, with short essays that explore their enduring meaning. (Nonfiction)

Montalbano, William D., and Hiaasen, Carl. *Death in China*, Atheneum, 1984.
Romance and murder lead a former Vietnam Special Forces officer on spectacular chases through thousands of clay soldiers who guard a Chinese emperor's tomb at Xi'an—where he finds clues to the mysterious death of his friend. (Fiction)

Montandon, Pat. *Intruders,* Coward-McCann, 1975.
A San Francisco television star becomes perplexed and terrified by the intrusion of unexplained violence into her glamorous hilltop home. (Nonfiction)

Montgomery, Sy. *Walking with the Great Apes: Jane Goodall, Dian Fossey, Birute Galdikas,* Houghton, 1992.
The fascinating stories of three intrepid women who left civilization to study and share the lives of primates. (Nonfiction)

Moody, Anne. *Coming of Age in Mississippi: An Autobiography,* Dial, 1969.
■
This is what it's like to grow up poor and black in Mississippi; although flawed by the Southern racial system, Anne Moody refused to be broken by it. (Nonfiction)

Moody, Raymond A., Jr. *Life after Life: Investigation of a Phenomenon, Survival of Bodily Health,* Stackpole, 1976.
What is it like to die? Here are speculations by Dr. Moody and reports on interviews with people who had clinically died but lived to relate their comforting near-death experiences. (Nonfiction)

Moore, Gilbert. *Special Rage,* Harper, 1971.
A black *Life* reporter assigned to the Huey Newton trial in 1968 writes convincingly of Oakland ghetto conditions, Newton's background, the Panthers, and the trial. (Nonfiction)

Morpurgo, Michael. *Waiting for Anya,* Viking, 1992.
In World War II France, young Jo helps Benjamin hide Jewish children from the Germans and conduct them over the mountains to safety in Spain. (Fiction)

Morrison, Lillian, Selector. *Rhythm Road: Poems to Move You,* Lothrop, 1988.
The essence of motion is captured in this collection of poetry by classic and contemporary writers. (Nonfiction)

Mowry, Jess. *Way Past Cool,* Farrar, 1993.
Struggling to survive the streets of Oakland, California, thirteen-year-old Gordon and his gang of "friends" join forces with a neighboring gang to run the local drug dealer off their turf but are hindered rather than helped by the police. (Fiction)

Murphy, Barbara Beasley, and Wolkoff, Judie. *Ace Hits the Big Time,* Delacorte, 1981.
A black eye patch and a dragon-emblazoned jacket help transform Horace Hobart into "Ace"—gang member, movie star, and cool guy. (Fiction)

Murphy, Jim. *Boy's War: Confederate and Union Soldiers Talk about the Civil War,* Clarion, 1992.
Riveting photographs, diaries, and painfully honest letters tell the little-known story of hundreds of thousands of boys who fought in the Civil War. (Nonfiction)

_____. *Death Run,* Clarion, 1982.
Four high school boys try to evade the police after a malicious prank accidentally causes the death of a fellow student. (Fiction)

_____. *Long Road to Gettysburg,* Clarion, 1993.
The personal journals of two young soldiers, one from each side, illuminate the events leading up to this pivotal battle, the bloody fighting, and the aftermath. (Nonfiction)

Murphy, Pat. *City, Not Long After,* Doubleday/Foundation, 1990.
Following a devastating plague, a teenage girl leads the surviving residents of San Francisco, all artists and dreamers, against an invasion by a cruel despot. (Fiction)

Murrow, Liza Ketchum. *Fire in the Heart,* Holiday, 1990.
Molly realizes that to reunite her family she must uncover the secret surrounding her mother's death. (Fiction)

Myers, Walter Dean. *Fallen Angels,* Scholastic, 1988.
Seventeen-year-old Richie Perry's stint in Vietnam brings home to him the agony and futility of war as he learns to kill and watches his comrades die. (Fiction)

_____. *Hoops,* Delacorte, 1981. ♦
Lonnie and the rest of his Harlem ghetto basketball team learn the fine art of playing and winning like pros from Cal, who once was one. (Fiction)

_____. *Legend of Tarik,* Viking, 1981.
Having witnessed the annihilation of his West African family and tribesmen at the hands of El Muerte, young Tarik seeks justice after proving himself worthy. (Fiction)

■ Selected for "Still Alive: The Best of the Best, 1960–1974"

▲ Selected for "The Best of the Best Books, 1970–1983"

♦ Selected for "Nothin' But the Best: Best of the Best Books for Young Adults, 1966–1986"

_____. *Mouse Rap*, Harper, 1991.
Fourteen-year-old rapper Mouse, his ace Styx, and other friends search for money hidden by a 1930s gangland leader, finding friendship and romance along the way. (Fiction)

_____. *Now Is Your Time! The African-American Struggle for Freedom*, HarperCollins, 1992.
Blending well-known facts, obscure incidents, and his own family stories into a telling of African-American history, Myers brings the past to life. (Nonfiction)

_____. *Righteous Revenge of Artemis Bonner*, HarperCollins, 1993.
Wanting to recover his Uncle Ugly Ned's lost fortune for his widowed aunt, Artemis tracks evil Catfish Grimes through the Old West in a chase that turns into a wild, hilarious romp. (Fiction)

_____. *Scorpions*, Harper, 1988.
Jamal's ability to be a good student and to live up to his father's expectations is challenged by his role as a gang leader. (Fiction)

_____. *Somewhere in the Darkness*, Scholastic, 1993.
Jimmy is shocked when an unexpected visitor turns out to be his father; he has been in prison for eight years and now wants Jimmy to drive with him to Chicago. (Fiction)

_____. *Young Landlords*, Viking, 1979.
In an amusing story, Paul, his girlfriend Gloria, and their friends inadvertently become landlords of a slum apartment building inhabited by some unusual tenants. (Fiction)

Naar, Jon. *Design for a Livable Planet*, HarperCollins, 1991.
In an environmental handbook for the nineties, Naar explains the causes and effects of pollution, offering practical solutions for individuals and groups. (Nonfiction)

Nabokov, Peter. *Native American Testimony: An Anthology of Indian and White Relations/First Encounter to Dispossession*, Crowell, 1978.
Authentic illustrations, most of them photographs, and historical documents expressing the Indian view provide insight into native American and white relationships through the nineteenth century. (Nonfiction)

Nader, Ralph. *Unsafe at any Speed*, Grossman, 1966.
A young lawyer's effective exposé of "the designed-in dangers of the American automobile." (Nonfiction)

Naidoo, Beverley. *Chain of Fire*, HarperCollins/Lippincott, 1991.
The South African government uses psychological abuse and physical brutality to force Naledi and others to relocate to a desolate township. (Fiction)

Namioka, Lensey. *Island of Ogres*, Harper, 1990.
An out-of-work samurai has to solve the mystery of an island's ogres before a political plot to free the deposed ruler is successful. (Fiction)

_____. *Village of the Vampire Cat*, Delacorte, 1981.
Two young masterless samurai, Zenta and Matsuzo, solve the mystery of the vampire cat that has been terrorizing the villagers and Zenta's tea ceremony master. (Fiction)

Naughton, Jim. *My Brother Stealing Second*, Harper, 1990.
Grief-stricken Bobby, coming to terms with his brother's death, is devastated to learn the truth about the fatal accident. (Fiction)

Naylor, Phyllis Reynolds. *Keeper*, Atheneum, 1986. ♦
His father's mental illness paralyzes the entire family, forcing Nick to make an agonizing decision. (Fiction)

_____. *Send No Blessings*, Atheneum/Jean Karl, 1991.
A proposal from Harless Prather looks like the best escape from the cramped trailer sixteen-year-old Beth shares with her family, but she fears marriage will ultimately end her dreams of a better life. (Fiction)

_____. *String of Chances*, Atheneum, 1982.
When she goes to spend the summer with her less religiously oriented cousin and her husband, sixteen-year-old Evie Hutchins is confronted with an unexpected tragedy that turns her life around. (Fiction)

_____. *Unexpected Pleasures*, Putnam, 1987.
A heartwarming romance between a thirty-two-year-old Tidewater, Maryland, bridgeworker and a sixteen-year-old girl fleeing a shiftless family. (Fiction)

_____. *Year of the Gopher*, Atheneum, 1987.
Fed up with college-application writing and parental nagging, George Richards opts for a blue-collar job. (Fiction)

Nelson, Theresa. *And One for All*, Watts/Orchard, 1990.
The time is 1967, and young men are struggling to make it to college to avoid the Vietnam War—except for Wing, whose decision affects his whole family. (Fiction)

_____. *Beggar's Ride*, Orchard/Richard Jackson, 1993.
Fleeing an alcoholic mother and a sexually abusive stepfather, Clare joins a gang of young runaways in Atlantic City and learns to survive by depending on this new family. (Fiction)

Newth, Mette. *Abduction*, Farrar, 1990.
An Inuit woman kidnapped by brutal whalers, Osugo finds friendship and understanding from her Norwegian jailer, Christine. (Fiction)

Newton, Suzanne. *I Will Call It Georgie's Blues*, Viking, 1983.
Neil has a secret escape in music from the dark tensions beneath his family's smooth public facade—but the strain pushes his little brother Georgie over the edge of sanity. (Fiction)

Nicholls, Peter. *Science in Science Fiction*, Knopf, 1983.
Presents the scientific basis for many of the "what ifs?" raised in science fiction—from Jules Verne's submarines to extraterrestrials. (Nonfiction)

Nicol, Clive W. *White Shaman*, Little, Brown, 1979.
A young student undergoes a spiritual rebirth as he discovers a mystical kinship with the Inuit or Eskimo people of northern Canada. (Fiction)

Niven, Larry, and Jerry, Pournelle. *Mote in God's Eye*, Simon & Schuster, 1974.
Who will win out in man's first extragalactic contact with an alien civilization, totally different in life and culture but equal in technology, cunning, and suspicion? (Fiction)

Nolen, William. *Making of a Surgeon*, Random, 1971.
An account of a young surgeon's training at New York's Bellevue Hospital told with wit and honesty. (Nonfiction)

Nomberg-Prztyk, Sara. *Auschwitz: True Tales from a Grotesque Land*, Univ. of North Carolina Press, 1985.
Forced to work for Dr. Josef Mengele as a teenage hospital attendant at Auschwitz during World War II, the author gives a firsthand account of the cruel medical experiments that left nearly one-half million Jews dead. (Nonfiction)

Noonan, Michael. *McKenzie's Boots*, Watts/Orchard, 1988.
Getting into the Australian army by lying about his age, sixteen-year-old Rod McKenzie finds himself alone, unarmed, and face-to-face with the enemy in the person of soldier and butterfly collector Hiroshi Ohara. (Fiction)

Norman, David, and Milner, Angela. *Dinosaur*, Knopf, 1990.
Representative of the outstanding Eyewitness series, this account traces the history of dinosaurs through photographs, other illustrations, and text. (Fiction)

North, James. *Freedom Rising*, Macmillan, 1985.
A young white journalist's 25,000-mile clandestine travels through southern Africa reveal the daily reality of apartheid. (Nonfiction)

O'Brien, Robert C. *Report from Group 17*, Atheneum, 1972.
A strange zoo in the Russian embassy, an ex-Nazi biologist, and a missing twelve-year-old girl—it is Fergus's job to find out how they all fit together. (Fiction)

_____. *Z for Zachariah*, Atheneum, 1975. ▲
In a peaceful valley, two survivors of an atomic holocaust are brought together—one a self-sufficient young girl, the other a killer bent on killing again. (Fiction)

O'Brien, Tim. *If I Die In a Combat Zone, Box Me Up and Ship Me Home*, Delacorte, 1973.
This introspective memoir of a foot soldier in Vietnam is a perceptive statement on courage, cowardice, and morality in war. (Nonfiction)

_____. *Things They Carried*, Houghton, 1991.
In these candid short stories based on O'Brien's Vietnam experiences, heartaches, dreams and terror were among the things soldiers in Vietnam carried. (Fiction)

O'Leary, Brian. *Making of an Ex-Astronaut*, Houghton, 1970.
A NASA "dropout" tells about his seven months as an astronaut and why he was the first scientist to resign. (Nonfiction)

Okimoto, Jean Davies. *Jason's Women*, Atlantic Monthly Press, 1986.
Jason fights his "wimpy tendencies" by getting a hot date through a newspaper ad and by working for a feisty old woman running for mayor. (Fiction)

■ Selected for "Still Alive: The Best of the Best, 1960–1974"
▲ Selected for "The Best of the Best Books, 1970–1983"
♦ Selected for "Nothin' But the Best: Best of the Best Books for Young Adults, 1966–1986"

Olsen, Jack. *Black Is Best: The Riddle of Cassius Clay,* Putnam, 1967.
A sportswriter describes the controversial career of Cassius Clay and tells why the great fighter believes that "black is best." (Nonfiction)

_____. *Night of the Grizzlies,* Putnam, 1969.
On the night of August 12, 1967, grizzlies attacked a campground in Glacier National Park—a violent clash between a vanishing species and the humans invading its territory. (Nonfiction)

Oneal, Zibby. *Formal Feeling,* Viking, 1982. ▲
A year after the death of her mother, Anne Cameron gradually comes to terms with their past relationship while adjusting to a new life with her stepmother. (Fiction)

_____. *In Summer Light,* Viking Kestrel, 1985.
Reluctantly returning to her island home to recuperate from mono, Kate hates the dominance and power her famous artist father holds over her, but her love for graduate art student Ian Jackson helps her to understand her father and herself. (Fiction)

_____. *Language of Goldfish,* Viking, 1980.
Afraid of growing up, thirteen-year-old Carrie Stokes suffers a mental breakdown when she retreats to the childhood world where life was uncomplicated and unthreatening. (Fiction)

Orlev, Uri. *Man from the Other Side,* Houghton, 1992.
Knowing the way through the sewers, Marek leads a Polish Jew, who wants to die among Jews, back to the doomed Warsaw ghetto. (Fiction)

Page, Thomas. *Hephaestus Plague,* Putnam, 1974.
An eccentric entomologist, charged with finding a way to destroy flame-throwing roaches, develops an affinity for them and breeds them while others work to save the East Coast from the destructive insects. (Fiction)

Page, Tim. *Nam,* Knopf, 1983.
UPI photographer Tim Page utilizes the photo essay to demonstrate the reality and the horror found on the front lines of the Vietnam conflict. (Nonfiction)

Palmer, David R. *Emergence,* Bantam, 1985.
Heroic deeds become the daily routine for eleven-year-old Candy Smith-Foster who, as a member of a new human species, begins a trek with her pet macaw, Terry D., across an American landscape scarred by bionuclear war. (Fiction)

Palmer, Laura. *Shrapnel in the Heart: Letters and Remembrances from the Vietnam Memorial,* Random, 1987.
Who can forget those who died in 'Nam? Not the buddies, sweethearts, families, and friends who leave remembrances at the Vietnam Memorial in Washington. (Nonfiction)

Parini, Jay. *Patch Boys,* Holt, 1986.
In a small Pennsylvania mining town in the 1920s, fifteen-year-old Sammy di Cantini learns about maturity and friendship and takes on responsibility when his brother is killed in a miners' protest. (Fiction)

Park, Ruth. *Playing Beatie Bow,* Atheneum, 1982.
When she is transported backward in time, Abigail must survive in nineteenth-century Australia while struggling to return home. (Fiction)

Parks, David. *G.I. Diary,* Harper, 1968.
A frank diary of a young Negro draftee's service in the Army during which he experienced a rough year in boot camp and a grim tour of Vietnam. (Nonfiction)

Parks, Gordon. *Born Black,* Lippincott, 1971.
The celebrated author-photographer interviews Malcolm X, Muhammed Ali, Eldridge Cleaver, and other black notables and concludes with the statement: "America is still a racist nation. It has not learned much from the turbulent decade just passed." (Nonfiction)

_____. *Choice of Weapons,* Harper, 1966.
With love, dignity, and hard work *Life* photographer Gordon Parks won his battle against the debasement of poverty and racial discrimination. (Nonfiction)

_____. *Voices in the Mirror: An Autobiography,* Doubleday, 1991.
Breaking one racial barrier after another to rise above bitter poverty, this celebrated black filmmaker, photographer, and renaissance man expands our views of life's possibilities. (Nonfiction)

Parks, Rosa, and Haskins, Jim. *Rosa Parks: My Story,* Dial, 1993.
Rosa Parks tells in her own words what it was like to defy the system and, in the process, become a symbol of freedom for African Americans. (Nonfiction)

Parnall, Peter. *Daywatchers,* Macmillan, 1985.
A beautiful illustrated, nontechnical narrative of Parnall's observations of and experiences with various birds of prey. (Nonfiction)

Pascal, Francine. *My First Love and Other Disasters,* Viking, 1979.
Fifteen-year-old Victoria humorously describes the summer of her first love, when she comes to realize that there's more to real affection than outward appearances. (Fiction)

Patent, Dorothy Hinshaw. *Quest for Artificial Intelligence,* Harcourt, 1986.
Patent examines the nature of intelligence and traces attempts to make machines duplicate human behavior. (Nonfiction)

Paterson, Katherine. *Jacob Have I Loved,* Crowell, 1980.
Growing up among the "water people" on an island off the coast of eastern Maryland during the 1940s, Louise searches for her identity while fighting lifelong jealousy of her talented, fragile, and beautiful twin sister. (Fiction)

_____. *Lyddie,* Dutton/Lodestar, 1992.
Unable to pay off the debt on the family farm, feisty, single-minded Lyddie survives the dangers of the textile mills in 1840s Massachusetts, determined not to forfeit her dreams. (Fiction)

Paton Walsh, Jill. *Parcel of Patterns,* Farrar, 1984.
Vividly and dramatically, Mall Percival writes in her journal of the tragic events that befell her and the other villagers of Eyam during the disastrous plague of the 1660s in England. (Fiction)

Patterson, Sarah. *Distant Summer,* Simon & Schuster, 1976.
Set in England during World War II, the story of seventeen-year-old Kate who is courted by two young fliers—a sensitive, serious Englishman and a happy-go-lucky American. (Fiction)

Paulsen, Gary. *Cookcamp,* Orchard/Richard Jackson, 1992.
What would cause a mother to pin a note to her five-year-old son's jacket, put him on a train, and send him far away to live in the north woods? (Fiction)

_____. *Crossing,* Watts/Orchard/Richard Jackson, 1987.
An alcoholic army sergeant and a homeless Mexican orphan come together in an unlikely friendship. (Fiction)

_____. *Dancing Carl,* Bradbury, 1983.
Carl came to McKinley, Minnesota, in the winter, drunk and maybe crazy, but he soon held the attention of the entire town with his power and strange dance. (Fiction)

_____. *Dogsong,* Bradbury, 1985.
Fourteen-year-old Russell, an Eskimo boy, borrows a neighbor's sled and dog team for a 1,400-mile journey, encounters a mammoth from earlier times and a pregnant girl from the present, and discovers his own relationship to his Eskimo culture. (Fiction)

_____. *Haymeadow,* Delacorte, 1993.
This survival story pits John, only fourteen, against 6,000 sheep, four dogs, two horses, and uncooperative Mother Nature. (Fiction)

_____. *Island,* Watts/Orchard/Richard Jackson, 1988.
The island in the middle of Sucker Lake gives fifteen-year-old Wil Newton the opportunity to discover himself and the harmony of nature. (Fiction)

_____. *Monument,* Delacorte, 1992.
Rocky, a mixed-race teen, has her life changed by an unusual artist who comes to her small town to design a war memorial. (Fiction)

_____. *Tracker,* Bradbury, 1984.
The dramatic journey of an orphan, John, who, in tracking a deer through the Minnesota wilderness, comes to terms with his grandfather's approaching death. (Fiction)

_____. *Voyage of the Frog,* Watts/Orchard, 1990.
Lost at sea without a radio, David fights for survival in his small sailboat during a fierce storm. (Fiction)

_____. *Winter Room,* Watts/Orchard, 1990.
Seated around a cozy fire in "the winter room," Elton and his brother Wayne challenge the truth of Uncle David's almost mythological stories about death and survival during his earlier life in Norway. (Fiction)

_____. *Woodsong,* Bradbury, 1991.
Through his dogsledding adventures in the Minnesota wilderness where there are wolves, deep snow, and minus-30-degree temperatures, the author comes to understand nature's ways and harrowing surprises. (Nonfiction)

Peck, Richard. *Are You in the House Alone?,* Viking, 1976. ▲ ♦
After receiving a series of threatening notes, Gail Osburne is raped by one of the richest and most popular boys in her school—but nobody believes her story. (Fiction)

■ Selected for "Still Alive: The Best of the Best, 1960–1974"

▲ Selected for "The Best of the Best Books, 1970–1983"

♦ Selected for "Nothin' But the Best: Best of the Best Books for Young Adults, 1966–1986"

_____. *Close Enough to Touch*, Delacorte, 1981.
How do you recover from your girlfriend's sudden death? Matt's solution is Margaret, who helps change his pain into love. (Fiction)

_____. *Father Figure: A Novel*, Viking, 1978. ▲
The security that Jim finds in his role as surrogate father to his eight-year-old brother is threatened when, after their mother's suicide, the boys are packed off to spend the summer with their father, who long ago abandoned them. (Fiction)

_____. *Ghosts I Have Been*, Viking, 1977.
In a hilarious sequel to *The Ghost Belonged to Me*, Alexander Armsworth meets his match in Blossom Culp, whose wits and psychic powers save the day. (Fiction)

_____. *Princess Ashley*, Delacorte, 1987.
"New girl" Chelsea must decide what price she is willing to pay to win popular Ashley Packard's acceptance. (Fiction)

_____. *Remembering the Good Times*, Delacorte, 1985.
Meeting at a time of change in their lives, Kate, Buck, and Trav developed a special friendship—but even their mutual caring couldn't keep the gap from widening or avert the tragedy of Trav's suicide. (Fiction)

_____. *Representing Super Doll*, Viking, 1975.
Darlene Hoffmeister, the beautiful but dumb Miss Hybrid Seed Corn, sets out on the Beauty Contest Road and runs into some unexpected traffic. (Fiction)

Peck, Robert Newton. *Day No Pigs Would Die*, Knopf, 1973. ■
Through his relationship with his hard-working father, twelve-year-old Rob learns to cope with the harshness of Shaker life and emerges a mature individual. (Fiction)

Pei, Lowry. *Family Resemblances*, Random, 1986.
Visiting her unconventional aunt, fifteen-year-old Karen becomes aware of the complexities of adult relationships and also experiences a love affair of her own. (Fiction)

"Pele", do Nascimento, Edson A., and Fish, Robert. *My Life and the Beautiful Game: The Autobiography of Pele*, Doubleday, 1977.
An intimate and touching autobiography of the world's most famous soccer player on the eve of his retirement from "the beautiful game." (Nonfiction)

Pershall, Mary K. *You Take the High Road*, Dial, 1991.
Samantha is delighted to have a new baby brother, but her life is torn apart when the baby is killed in a tragic accident. (Fiction)

Peters, Ellis. *Black Is the Colour of My True-Love's Heart*, Morrow, 1967.
A folk song festival in rural England goes awry when a thwarted romance erupts into violence and murder. (Fiction)

Peterson, P. J. *Nobody Else Can Walk It For You*, Delacorte, 1982.
Eighteen-year-old Laura desperately tries to lead a group of young backpackers to safety as they are pursued by three threatening motorcyclists through isolated mountainous country. (Fiction)

_____. *Would You Settle For Improbable?*, Delacorte, 1981.
Just released from juvenile hall, Arnold is befriended by a student teacher and some of his ninth-grade classmates, with unexpected results. (Fiction)

Petty, Richard. *King of the Road*, Macmillan, 1977.
An American race car driver and his family share their team spirit in a winning photographic documentary. (Nonfiction)

Pevsner, Stella. *How Could You Do It, Diana?*, Clarion, 1990.
Bethany struggles to understand why her pretty, popular sister committed suicide. (Fiction)

Peyton, K. M. *Prove Yourself a Hero*, Collins, 1979.
After being released by kidnappers, sixteen-year-old Jonathan feels guilty for having acted like a coward and for having cost his family the ransom money. (Fiction)

Pfeffer, Susan Beth. *About David*, Delacorte, 1980.
When Lynn finds out that David, whom she has known since childhood, has murdered his adoptive parents and killed himself, she must confront new feelings about David before she can recover from this loss. (Fiction)

_____. *Family of Strangers*, Bantam/Starfire, 1993.
Abby feels so alone and unloved that she attempts suicide. It takes a sympathetic therapist to help her recover from the damage done by her family of strangers. (Fiction)

_____. *Year without Michael*, Bantam, 1987.
The unexplained disappearance of high school student Michael throws his family into a state of uncertainty and agony. (Fiction)

Phipson, Joan. *Hit and Run*, Atheneum/
   Margaret K. McElderry, 1985.
After stealing a Ferrari and running from an accident, sixteen-year-old Roland has to decide
whether or not to abandon the injured consta-
ble who has followed him into the Australian
bush. (Fiction)

Pierce, Meredith Ann. *Darkangel*, Atlantic
   Monthly Press, 1982. ▲
Though both fascinated and repelled by the
vampyre, Aeriel tries to save her mistress and
the other vampyre brides. (Fiction)

————. *Pearl of the Soul of the World*, Little,
   Brown/Joy Street Books, 1991.
In the conclusion to the Darkangel Trilogy,
Aeriel must carry the Pearl of the Soul of the
World to the witch Irrylath, who seeks to de-
stroy her. (Fiction)

————. *Woman Who Loved Reindeer*,
   Atlantic Monthly Press, 1985.
The daimon child that her sister-in-law brings
Caribou to rear in the cold lands of the North
grows into her unearthly companion and helps
Caribou serve as the leader of her people.
(Fiction)

Pierce, Ruth. *Single and Pregnant*, Beacon,
   1971.
Here is a blunt, cautionary, never judgmental
discussion by a social worker on the medical,
financial, and social problems facing the single, pregnant, and young. (Nonfiction)

Pinkwater, Jill. *Buffalo Brenda*, Macmillan,
   1990.
The outrageous team of India Ink Teidlebaum
and Brenda Tuna takes on the high school and
its cliques. (Fiction)

Plath, Sylvia. *Bell Jar*, Harper, 1971. ■ ▲ ◆
During a queer, sultry summer in New York,
Esther Greenwood works as a junior editor on
Mademoiselle, quarrels with her mother and
boy friend, and is gradually aware of her de-
scent into madness. (Fiction)

Platt, Kin. *Headman*, Morrow, 1975. ▲
Owen's desperate fight for survival through the
streets of Los Angeles, in a "rehabilitative"
youth camp, and as "headman" of a gang is
told in swift, sharp, and realistic street language. (Fiction)

Plimpton, George. *Paper Lion*, Harper, 1966.
A writer-by-trade played the part of a rookie
quarterback with the Detroit Lions in order to

write this entertaining inside view of pro football. (Nonfiction)

Plummer, Louise. *My Name Is Sus5an
   Smith: The 5 Is Silent*, Delacorte, 1992.
When Susan leaves her small town to study art
in Boston, she loses her illusions of life and
love but rediscovers herself and her independence. (Fiction)

Pohl, Frederik. *Man Plus*, Random, 1976.
To survive without mechanical help on the surface of Mars, Roger Torraway must become a
biological monster and yet stay sane until he
reaches his destination. (Fiction)

Pollack, Dale. *Skywalking: The Life and
   Times of George Lucas*, Harmony/Crown,
   1983.
All about the man who created such spectacu-
lar movies as *Star Wars* and *Raiders of the Lost
Ark*. (Nonfiction)

Popham, Melinda Worth. *Skywater*,
   Graywolf, 1991.
Brand X never intended to be a savior, and indeed most of his fellow coyotes never reach
their destination. But their quest for the unpol-
luted water source Skywater leads to a deeper
understanding of their desert world. (Fiction)

Portis, Charles. *True Grit: A Novel*, Simon &
   Schuster, 1968.
With her papa's pistol tied to her saddlehorn
and a supersized ration of audacity, fourteen-
year-old Mattie Ross sets out to avenge her father's murder. (Fiction)

Postman, Neil, and Weingartner, Charles.
   *Soft Revolution: A Student Handbook for
   Turning Schools Around*, Delacorte, 1971.
Here is a treatise on how students can change
their schools without violence through innova-
tive suggestions, persuasion, and gentle manip-
ulation. (Nonfiction)

Potok, Chaim. *The Chosen*, Simon &
   Schuster, 1967. ◆
Two Jewish boys growing to manhood in
Brooklyn discover that differences can
strengthen friendship and understanding.
(Fiction)

————. *My Name Is Asher Lev*, Knopf, 1972.
Asher Lev is an ordinary Jewish boy from
Brooklyn until his passion and genius for
painting create a furor in the art world and
alienate him from the parents he loves.
(Fiction)

■ Selected for "Still Alive: The Best of the Best, 1960–1974"

▲ Selected for "The Best of the Best Books, 1970–1983"

◆ Selected for "Nothin' But the Best: Best of the Best Books for Young Adults, 1966–1986"

———. *Promise*, Knopf, 1969.
In this sequel to *The Chosen*, rabbinical student Reuven confronts his dogmatic teacher, and his friend Danny undertakes his first case as a clinical psychologist, one requiring a drastic, experimental treatment. (Fiction)

Powell, Randy. *Is Kissing a Girl Who Smokes Like Licking an Ashtray?*, Farrar, 1993.
Eighteen-year-old Biff looks 14, and he gets tongue-tied around girls, so he can't speak to Tommie, whom he's loved for two years. But he's about to meet Heidi, and his life will never be the same again. (Fiction)

Powers, John R. *Do Black Patent Leather Shoes Really Reflect Up?*, Regnery, 1975.
Doing battle with an army of pimples, being a teenager, and spending four years in a south side Chicago high school far exceed Eddie's worst suspicions. (Fiction)

———. *Unoriginal Sinner and the Ice-Cream God*, Contemporary Books, 1977.
The irreverently humorous adventures and misadventures of a Catholic teen-ager growing up on Chicago's South Side. (Fiction)

Powers, Thomas. *Diana: The Making of a Terrorist*, Houghton, 1971.
An examination of the tragic forces in the life of Diana Oughton which led her from a comfortable home to a commitment to revolution and finally her death in a "bomb factory" town house explosion in 1970. (Nonfiction)

Prince, Alison. *Turkey's Nest*, Morrow, 1980.
Eighteen-year-old Kate rejects the father of her unborn child for the security of her aunt's farm in Suffolk. There she comes to terms with herself and her future. (Fiction)

Pringle, Terry. *Fine Time to Leave Me*, Algonquin, 1990.
Chris and Lori experience ups and downs, joys and ordeals, as they discover the hard realities of marriage. (Fiction)

———. *Preacher's Boy*, Algonquin, 1988.
The community keeps an eagle eye on Michael's blossoming romance with Amy as her career and his first college year complicate his struggles for a better relationship with his father. (Fiction)

Prochnik, Leon. *Endings: Death, Glorious and Otherwise, as Faced by Ten Outstanding Figures of Our Time*, Crown, 1980.
Exploration of the lives and often unusual deaths of ten fascinating people, from Freud and Houdini to Isadora Duncan and Malcolm X. (Nonfiction)

Pullman, Philip. *Broken Bridge*, Knopf, 1993.
During her sixteenth summer, Ginny must come to terms with a brother she never knew she had, secrets her father won't share with her, and a tale of a long-ago kidnapping. (Fiction)

———. *Ruby in the Smoke*, Knopf, 1987.
Sally, sixteen and an orphan, must find her way through a maze of nineteenth-century villains to claim her inheritance and her independence. (Fiction)

———. *Shadow in the North*, Knopf, 1988.
In an attempt to protect a client's investment, Sally Lockhart, a financial consultant in nineteenth-century London, comes up against an evil, rich industrialist who seeks to win her by any means. (Fiction)

———. *Tiger in the Well*, Knopf, 1991.
Did Sally Lockhart marry Arthur Parrish? Sally's certain that she didn't, but his legal evidence proves the contrary. What protection does Sally have against the evil forces that are threatening her? (Fiction)

Ramati, Alexander. *And the Violins Stopped Playing: A Story of the Gypsy Holocaust*, Watts, 1986.
Based on a young survivor's account, this gripping story tells of the Nazi massacre of the Gypsies during World War II. (Nonfiction)

Rappaport, Doreen. *American Women: Their Lives in Their Words*, HarperCollins/Crowell, 1992.
The vital and changing roles women have played in American history from colonial times to the present are vividly portrayed through their diaries, letters, photos, etc. (Nonfiction)

Rather, Dan, and Herskowitz, Mickey. *Camera Never Blinks: Adventures of a TV Journalist*, Morrow, 1977.
A controversial autobiography by one of the best known and most respected TV newscasters. (Nonfiction)

Ray, Delia. *Nation Torn: The Story of How the Civil War Began*, Dutton/Lodestar, 1991.
An accessible, well-illustrated account of events leading up to the fateful firing on Fort Sumter. (Nonfiction)

Read, Piers Paul. *Alive: The Story of the Andes Survivors*, Lippincott, 1974. ■
A compassionate account of sixteen young rugby players who survived a plane crash in the Andes and lived for 10 weeks on faith, finally choosing to use the bodies of their dead comrades for sustenance. (Nonfiction)

Reader, Dennis J.   *Coming Back Alive*,
   Random, 1981.
Because Bridget's parents are dead and Dylan
is in conflict with his, the two seek refuge in
the rugged Trinity Mountains and in each
other. (Fiction)

Reaver, Chap.   *Little Bit Dead*, Delacorte,
   1993.
After Reece saves Shanti from being lynched,
information from a dance hall girl saves Reece
from the marshal and his posse. (Fiction)

Reed, Kit.   *Ballad of T. Rantula*, Little,
   Brown, 1979.
Because his mother has left his father and his
best friend is committing suicide by not eating,
Futch hides in the monstrous alter ego of T.
Rantula. (Fiction)

Reese, Lyn.   *I'm on My Way Running:
   Women Speak on Coming of Age*, Avon,
   1983.
Young women come of age in autobiography,
poetry, fiction, and anthropological accounts
from around the world. (Nonfiction)

Reidelbach, Maria.   *Completely Mad: A
   History of the Comic Book and Magazine*,
   Little, Brown, 1993.
Mad magazine is funny and offensive. No won-
der teens love it and parents hate it! Read all
about it in this illustrated history. (Nonfiction)

Reiss, Kathryn.   *Time Windows*, Harcourt,
   1993.
Moving into a mysterious old house, Miranda
finds that she can see the horrifying things that
happened there in the past. Can she do anything now to change history? (Fiction)

Rendell, Ruth.   *Heartstones*, Harper, 1987.
A victim of anorexia and bonded to her father,
teenage Elvira leads her family to total destruction. (Fiction)

Renvoize, Jean.   *Wild Thing*, Atlantic-Little,
   1971.
Morag, a foster child, runs away to the isolated
wilderness of the Scottish mountains, where
she is happy for a time but soon realizes that no
one can survive alone. (Fiction)

Rhodes, Richard.   *Farm: A Year in the Life
   of an American Farmer*, Simon &
   Schuster, 1990.
Everything you didn't think you needed to
know about the real life of a family earning its
livelihood from the land. (Nonfiction)

Rice, Robert.   *Last Pendragon*, Walker, 1993.
Sir Bedwyr disobeys Arthur's dying wish and
hides the sword Caliburn instead of returning it
to the lake, but when he returns to help Arthur's grandson fight the Saxons, the sword has
disappeared. (Fiction)

Richards, Arlene Kramer, and Willis, Irene.
   *Under 18 and Pregnant: What to Do If You
   or Someone You Know Is*, Lothrop,
   1983. ♦
Information for teens on all aspects of pregnancy, including single parenting, adoption,
abortion, marriage, and infant care. (Nonfiction)

Riddles, Libby.   *Race across Alaska: The
   First Woman to Win the Iditarod Tells Her
   Story*, Stackpole, 1988.
A true tale recounts how Libby Riddles over-
came all odds to become the first woman to win
the Iditarod. (Nonfiction)

Ridgway, John M., and Blyth, Chay.
   Fighting Chance, Lippincott, 1967.
Two young British paratroopers undertake a
harrowing voyage across the Atlantic in a 20-
foot rowboat. (Nonfiction)

Riley, Jocelyn.   *Only My Mouth Is Smiling*,
   Morrow, 1982.
Merle desperately tries to hide her mother's
mental illness from the whole world and especially from her own family. (Fiction)

Rinaldi, Ann.   *Break with Charity: A Story
   about the Salem Witch Trials*, Harcourt/
   Gulliver, 1993.
Susanna, fearful for the safety of her family,
keeps silent about the motives of her friends
who are accusing the Salem townspeople of
witchcraft. (Fiction)

_____. *Last Silk Dress*, Holiday, 1988.
As teenage Susan Chilmark champions the
Confederate cause by collecting the last silk
dresses in Richmond to build a hot air balloon,
she examines her loyalty to family, friends, and
country. (Fiction)

_____. *Time Enough for Drums*, Holiday,
   1986.
Fifteen-year-old Jemima, torn by her growing
love for a supposed Tory sympathizer during
the American Revolution, matures through her
father's murder and her brothers' fight for independence. (Fiction)

- ■ Selected for "Still Alive: The Best of the Best, 1960–1974"
- ▲ Selected for "The Best of the Best Books, 1970–1983"
- ♦ Selected for "Nothin' But the Best: Best of the Best Books for Young Adults, 1966–1986"

_____. *Wolf by the Ears,* Scholastic, 1992. Harriet Hemings, rumored to be Thomas Jefferson's daughter, faces the choice of passing as white or remaining a slave in the sheltered but restricted life at Monticello. (Fiction)

Ritter, Lawrence S. *Babe: A Life in Pictures,* Ticknor & Fields, 1988. The life of Babe Ruth, the orphan who became the greatest legend in baseball history, is captured in this photobiography. (Nonfiction)

Robertson, Dougal. *Survive the Savage Sea,* Praeger, 1973. ■ ▲ Having survived the wreck of their boat by killer whales, the Robertson family and a friend face an incredible thirty-eight-day battle for life in a secondhand raft, 1,000 miles from land. (Nonfiction)

Robertson, James I. *Civil War! America Becomes One Nation,* Knopf, 1993. A vivid portrayal of the Civil War—on both the battlefield and the home front. (Nonfiction)

Robeson, Susan. *Whole World in His Hands: A Pictorial Biography of Paul Robeson,* Citadel, 1982. ◆ A memoir of the brilliant, talented, and controversial black singer, lovingly told in words and pictures by his granddaughter. (Nonfiction)

Robinson, Spider. *Callahan's Crosstime Saloon,* Ridley Enslow, 1977. The misfits of earth and elsewhere who belly up to Callahan's bar tell some of the wildest and funniest stories in the galaxies. (Fiction)

Rochman, Hazel, ed. *Somehow Tenderness Survives: Stories of Southern Africa,* Harper, 1988. Ten short stories and autobiographical sketches by both whites and blacks from southern Africa reveal how it is to grow up under apartheid. (Fiction)

Rodowsky, Colby. *Julie's Daughter,* Farrar, 1985. Slug meets the mother who deserted her when she was a baby and finally learns to accept the past. (Fiction)

Rogasky, Barbara. *Smoke and Ashes: The Story of the Holocaust,* Holiday, 1988. Revealing photographs and a graphic text trace the annihilation of the Jews before and during World War II. (Nonfiction)

***Rolling Stone Illustrated History of Rock and Roll,* Rolling Stone Press, 1977.** In-depth portraits (with large black-and-white photographs) of the most important movers of rock and roll from the 1950s to the present. (Nonfiction)

Rose, Louise Blecher. *Launching of Barbara Fabrikant,* McKay, 1974. A witty, empathetic, and earthy first-person story about the freshman college year of the overweight daughter of a rabbi. (Fiction)

Rosten, Leo. *Most Private Intrigue,* Atheneum, 1967. A sophisticated and intriguing novel in which former espionage agent Peter Galton attempts to bring three important scientists out of Russia. (Fiction)

Rostkowski, Margaret I. *After the Dancing Days,* Harper, 1986. Thirteen-year-old Annie befriends hideously disfigured Andrew, a World War I veteran. (Fiction)

Rothenberg, Mira. *Children with Emerald Eyes: Histories of Extraordinary Boys and Girls,* Dial, 1977. Heartrending case histories of autistic and schizophrenic children, told by a psychologist who works closely with them. (Nonfiction)

Roueche, Berton. *Feral,* Harper, 1975. What happens to a fictional, rural Long Island community when stray cats turn wild and terrorize the town's residents? (Fiction)

Ruby, Lois. *Arriving at a Place You've Never Left,* Dial, 1977. Seven moving short stories deal with such personal crises as coping with a mother's nervous breakdown; being seventeen, pregnant, and unmarried; and facing anti-Semitism. (Fiction)

Ruskin, Cindy. *Quilt: Stories from the Names Project,* Pocket Books, 1988. The lovers, friends, and relatives of the thousands who have died from AIDS express their love and loss in handcrafted 3-by-6-foot panels sewn into an enormous memorial quilt. (Nonfiction)

Russell, Bill, and McSweeney, William. *Go Up for Glory,* Coward-McCann, 1966. The Boston Celtics' superstar highlights his career and gives his opinions on subjects ranging from coaches to civil rights. (Nonfiction)

Ryan, Cheli Duran, ed. *Yellow Canary Whose Eye Is So Black,* Macmillan, 1978. A rich bilingual collection of poems by more than forty poets reflects the variegated tapestry of life in Latin America. (Nonfiction)

Ryan, Cornelius. *Last Battle,* Simon & Schuster, 1966. An exciting day-by-day chronicle, based on eye-witness accounts, of the twenty-one days before the fall of Berlin in 1945. (Nonfiction)

Ryden, Hope. *God's Dog,* Coward, 1975. A naturalist's two-year field study of coyotes results in a compassionate plea for changes in our attitudes toward these misunderstood creatures. (Nonfiction)

Ryerson, Eric.   *When Your Parent Drinks Too Much: A Book for Teenagers*, Facts On File, 1985.
In addition to letting young adults know they are not alone, Ryerson provides hope: "You can't control your parent's drinking, but you can make changes that will make your life better." (Nonfiction)

Rylant, Cynthia.   *Couple of Kooks and Other Stories about Love*, Watts/Orchard, 1991.
Many faces of love are found in these short stories—from love for an unborn child to romantic love and love that can never be reciprocated. (Fiction)

———.   *Fine White Dust*, Bradbury, 1986.
When the traveling preacher comes to town, Peter's religious beliefs find a focus—but is running away with the preacher the answer to Peter's needs? (Fiction)

———.   *Kindness*, Watts/Orchard/Richard Jackson, 1988.
Chip must cope with conflicting emotions when his mother reveals that she is pregnant and refuses to name the father. (Fiction)

———.   *Missing May*, Orchard/Richard Jackson, 1993.
After the death of her beloved Aunt May, Summer is afraid that she will also lose her Uncle Ob to his grief, but a quirky boy and the remembrance of May's love help them to heal and to reaffirm life. (Fiction)

———.   *Soda Jerk*, Watts/Orchard/Richard Jackson, 1991.
The poetic observations of a young drug store soda jerk in a small Virginia town, who comments on the people and activity around him. (Fiction)

Sachs, Marilyn.   *Fat Girl*, Dutton, 1984.
Jeff Lyons is obsessed with creating a new person out of an unhappy fat girl, but loses control of the situation when the girl begins to think for herself. (Fiction)

Sagan, Carl.   *Cosmos*, Random, 1980.
Based on the PBS series, this chronicle of the life of our galactic backyard includes history, science, astronomy, and philosophy in a format that can be enjoyed in bits and pieces or from cover to cover. (Nonfiction)

Salassi, Otto R.   *Jimmy D., Sidewinder, and Me*, Greenwillow, 1987.
In jail, fifteen-year-old Dumas Monk is writing—on the judge's orders—the story of how he became a pool hustler and a murderer. (Fiction)

Saleh, Dennis.   *Rock Art: The Golden Age of Record Album Covers*, Ballantine, 1978.
Printed in full color from original negatives, this is a lavish collection of the best rock album covers from the preceding decade. (Nonfiction)

Salisbury, Graham.   *Blue Skin of the Sea*, Delacorte, 1993.
In a series of eleven stories, Sonny Mendoza faces fear, love, and challenges as he comes of age in a small Hawaiian fishing village. (Fiction)

Sallis, Susan.   *Only Love*, Harper, 1980.
The adversity of a wheelchair existence does not overwhelm Fran, and the knowledge that she is dying leads her to live each day to the fullest with humor, adventure, and love. Fran's love affair with Lucas, another wheelchair occupant at Thornton Hall, is full of surprises. (Fiction)

Salzman, Mark.   *Iron and Silk*, Random, 1987.
A young Yale graduate describes his two years in China teaching English to medical students, perfecting his Chinese, and studying martial arts with a master. (Nonfiction)

Samson, Joan.   *Auctioneer*, Simon & Schuster, 1976.
What begins as a harmless Saturday pastime becomes sinister when the auctioneering stranger in town becomes its most influential and evil citizen. (Fiction)

Samuels, Gertrude.   *Run, Shelley, Run!*, Crowell, 1974. ■ ▲
Runaway Shelley, a victim of family neglect and juvenile injustice, finally gets the help she needs through the concern of a sympathetic judge and the intercession of a kind neighbor. (Fiction)

Sanders, Dori.   *Clover*, Algonquin, 1991.
When her father is killed in an automobile accident in rural South Carolina, ten-year-old Clover is left to be reared by her white stepmother within the black community. (Fiction)

■ Selected for "Still Alive: The Best of the Best, 1960–1974"

▲ Selected for "The Best of the Best Books, 1970–1983"

♦ Selected for "Nothin' But the Best: Best of the Best Books for Young Adults, 1966–1986"

Sanders, Scott R.   *Bad Man Ballad,*
Bradbury, 1986.
In the early 1800s, two unlikely partners, a
backwoods boy and a Philadelphia lawyer, go
in search of a frontier "bigfoot" who has been
accused of murder. (Fiction)

Sanderson, Ivan.   *Uninvited Visitors: A
Biologist Looks at UFO's,* Cowles, 1968.
Using exacting scientific methodology, the author delves deep into problems such as what
could UFOs be, where do they come from,
when did they start coming, and what would
they want from us? (Nonfiction)

Sandler, Martin.   *Story of American
Photography: An Illustrated History for
Young People,* Little, Brown, 1979.
From daguerreotypes to Polaroid, an illustrated
history of the men and women who shaped the
course of a major art and industry. (Nonfiction)

Santiago, Danny.   *Famous All over Town,*
Simon & Schuster, 1983.
Chato, a young Mexican-American growing up
in a Los Angeles barrio, has an IQ of 135 but
gets bad grades in school because his first loyalty is to his family and gang. (Fiction)

Santoli, Al.   *Everything We Had: An Oral
History of the Vietnam War as Told By 33
American Soldiers Who Fought It,*
Random, 1981. ▲
Thirty-three veterans of the Vietnam war re-
count its impact on their lives one decade later.
(Nonfiction)

Sargent, Pamela.   *Earthseed,* Harper, 1983.
Ship has created and raised a generation of
Earth children as it carries them through space
toward a new planet where they must survive
alone without Ship's care. (Fiction)

Sargent, Pamela, ed.   *Women of Wonder:
Science Fiction Stories by Women about
Women,* Vintage, 1975.
These exceptional stories show that science fic-
tion is no longer a field completely reserved for
men. (Nonfiction)

Saul, John.   *Creature,* Bantam, 1990.
Seemingly perfect Silverdale hides a horrible
secret brought to light only when the coach's
boys begin turning into monsters—both on and
off the football field. (Fiction)

Savage, Georgia.   *House Tibet,* Graywolf,
1992.
After she is raped by her father, Vicky and her
autistic younger brother run away, learn survival skills from street kids in an Australian
beach town, and are befriended by some unusual people. (Fiction)

Say, Allen.   *Ink-Keeper's Apprentice,* Harper,
1979.
Living on his own in post-World War II Tokyo,
thirteen-year-old Kiyoi begins a new life when
he becomes an apprentice to a famous
cartoonist. (Fiction)

Scaduto, Anthony.   *Bob Dylan,* Grosset,
1972.
What makes Dylan tick—from his early days in
Hibbing, Minnesota, to his current silent
stance. (Nonfiction)

Schaap, Richard.   *Turned On: The Friede-
Crenshaw Case,* NAL, 1967.
At nineteen Celeste Crenshaw was dead of an
overdose and her wealthy, socially prominent
boyfriend was on his way to prison. (Nonfiction)

Schami, Rafik.   *Hand Full of Stars,* Dutton,
1991.
A young teenage boy in modern Damascus
faces career choices, political ferment, and romance. (Fiction)

Schell, Jonathan.   *Fate of Earth,* Knopf,
1982.
The possibility of human extinction because of
nuclear disaster is discussed in this frightening
and important book. (Nonfiction)

Schiff, Ken.   *Passing Go,* Dodd, 1972.
A curious blend of the real and surreal, this is
an eighteen-year-old boy's day-by-day account
of four bleak months in a mental hospital.
(Fiction)

Schirer, Eric W., and Allman, William F.
Newton at the Bat: The Science in Sports,
Scribner, 1984.
From Schirer's sports column in *Science 84*
magazine, these essays survey the part that
physics, physiology, and aerodynamics play in
baseball, Frisbee, skiing, sailing, and many
other sports. (Nonfiction)

Scholl, Hans, and Scholl, Sophie.   *At the
Heart of the White Rose: Letters and
Diaries of Hans and Sophie Scholl,*
Harper, 1988.
The personal writings of a brother and sister
beheaded by the Nazis for their opposition to
the Hitler terror. (Nonfiction)

Schulke, Flip.   *Martin Luther King, Jr.: A
Documentary . . . Montgomery to Memphis,*
Norton, 1976.
Striking pictures and text graphically recapitu-
late the entire civil rights movement through
the story of Dr. King's struggle to fulfill his
dream. (Nonfiction)

Schulz, Charles. *Peanuts Treasury,* Holt, 1968. ∎

Lucy, the natural-born fussbudget turned amateur psychiatrist, Charlie Brown, much maligned but dedicated manager of the world's most defeated baseball team, and Snoopy, the only dog in existence with a split personality, devise their own inimitable philosophies to cope with life's adversities. (Nonfiction)

Schwarz-Bart, Andre. *Woman Named Solitude,* Atheneum, 1973.

Understated and suffused with imagery and irony, this is the tale of a beautiful mulatto slave girl who is eventually driven into a zombie-like state of madness. (Fiction)

Schwarzenegger, Arnold, and Hall, Douglas Kent. *Arnold: The Education of a Bodybuilder,* Simon & Schuster, 1977.

The six-time winner of the Mr. Olympia title and star of *Pumping Iron* recounts his life and presents a program for successful body building. (Nonfiction)

Scieszka, Jon. *Stinky Cheese Man and Other Fairly Stupid Tales,* Viking, 1993.

A wickedly hysterical parody of childhood stories, complete with wild illustrations and a "surgeon general's warning." (Fiction)

Scoppettone, Sandra. *Happy Endings Are All Alike,* Harper, 1978.

Traditional values are questioned and love is tested when Jaret is raped by a disturbed boy and everyone learns of her lesbian relationship with Peggy. (Fiction)

_____. *Trying Hard to Hear You,* Harper, 1974. ∎ ▲

Sixteen-year-old Camilla recalls the tumultuous summer of 1973 when her best friend, Jeff, and Phil, the boy she had a crush on, fell in love with each other. (Fiction)

Scortia, Thomas N., and Robinson, Frank G. *Prometheus Crisis,* Doubleday, 1975.

Prometheus, a nuclear power station: Did human error, sabotage, or carelessness cause the final breaking point? (Fiction)

Searls, Hank. *Sounding,* Random, 1982.

As an old sperm whale seeks his former pod, a disabled Russian submarine teeters on a reef; perhaps the ancient cetacean hope that man can communicate will come true. (Fiction)

Sebestyen, Ouida. *Far from Home,* Atlantic-Little, 1980.

After the death of his mother, fourteen-year-old Salty, following the words in a note his mother left him, finds a home for himself and his elderly grandmother at the Buckley Arms Hotel where he begins to learn about love and family. (Fiction)

_____. *IOU's,* Atlantic Monthly Press, 1982.

Stowe Garrett is torn between the loyalty and love he feels for his mother and his longing to break free and experiment with life. (Fiction)

_____. *Words by Heart,* Atlantic-Little, 1979.

Lena learns what it means to be black in a white world, but, helped by her father, she also learns how to be a real person. (Fiction)

Seed, Suzanne. *Fine Trades,* Follett, 1979.

In photographs and words, ten craftspersons explain their trades—ranging from violin making to bookbinding—and tell of the personal satisfaction they get from their work. (Nonfiction)

Segal, Erich. *Love Story,* Harper, 1970.

Oliver Barrett IV, a rich, cocky Harvard senior, and Jennie Cavilleri, a Radcliffe music type, poor and serious, discover they are made for each other in this funny but touching love story. (Fiction)

Senn, Steve. *Circle in the Sea,* Atheneum, 1981.

After wearing a special ring, Robin dreams that she is the dolphin Breee. In fact, her mind actually inhabits the body of Breee, who is involved in a fight against those who are polluting the seas. (Fiction)

Severin, Tim. *Sinbad Voyage,* Putnam, 1983.

In a hand-sewn boat, Severin follows the trading routes, attributed to Sinbad, to China by way of the Indian Ocean. (Nonfiction)

_____. *Ulysses Voyage: Sea Search for the Odyssey,* Dutton, 1988.

Severin tells how he and a crew of scholars and adventurers sailed the Mediterranean in a Bronze Age-style galley in an attempt to follow the path of Ulysses and identify sites made famous by Homer. (Nonfiction)

∎ Selected for "Still Alive: The Best of the Best, 1960–1974"

▲ Selected for "The Best of the Best Books, 1970–1983"

♦ Selected for "Nothin' But the Best: Best of the Best Books for Young Adults, 1966–1986"

Shannon, George. *Unlived Affections,*
Harper/Charlotte Zolotow, 1990.
Discovering a box of old letters, Willie learns
the truth about his parents' relationship.
(Fiction)

Sharpe, Roger C. *Pinball!,* Dutton, 1977.
For players and lovers of the pinball machine—
a vicarious experience enlivened by full-page
color photos of the real thing. (Nonfiction)

Shaw, Arnold. *World of Soul: Black
America's Contribution to the Pop Music
Scene,* Cowles, 1970.
The brothers and sisters of soul—Otis Redding,
James Brown, and Aretha Franklin—are all
here in this full story of blues and R & B. (Non-
fiction)

Sheehan, Carolyn, and Sheehan, Edmund.
Magnifi-Cat, Doubleday, 1972.
When a cat appears at the gates of heaven with
an extraordinary halo, the whole computerized
admissions process grinds to a halt. (Fiction)

Sheehan, Susan. *Ten Vietnamese,* Knopf,
1967.
Revealing interviews with men and women
representing a cross section of the Vietnamese
people, including the Viet Cong. (Nonfiction)

Sheldon, Mary. *Perhaps I'll Dream of
Darkness,* Random, 1981.
Effie is dead now, and her sister Susan, through
her diary, asks why. The answer lies with
David Angel, the self-destructive rock star
whom Effie idolized. (Fiction)

Sherman, D. R. *Brothers of the Sea,* Little,
Brown, 1966.
A simple and moving tale about a fisherman's
son whose friendship with a dolphin leads to
tragedy. (Fiction)

_____. *Lion's Paw,* Doubleday, 1975.
An obsessed white hunter, a young Bushman,
and a crippled lion confront one another in the
conflict for survival. (Fiction)

Sherman, Josepha. *Child of Faerie, Child of
Earth,* Walker, 1993.
Percinet, the son of the queen of Faerie, is in
love with a mortal girl, but can she accept his
love and the presence of magic in her life?
(Fiction)

Shilts, Randy. *And the Band Played On:
Politics, People, and the AIDS Epidemic,*
St. Martin's, 1987.
The shocking and frightening story of the failure of the U.S. government, the medical establishment, and the American people themselves
in the face of the devastating modern AIDS
plague. (Nonfiction)

Shreve, Susan. *Masquerade,* Knopf, 1980.
After their father is arrested for embezzlement
and their mother has a nervous breakdown, the
Walker family—especially seventeen-year-old
Rebecca—must learn to cope with the dis-
turbing truth and begin to sort out their lives.
(Fiction)

Shusterman, Neal. *What Daddy Did,* Little,
Brown, 1992.
After the murder of his mother, Preston must
find a way to face, and even forgive, his father—the man who killed her. (Fiction)

Sieruta, Peter D. *Heartbeats and Other
Stories,* Harper, 1990.
Depicting joy and pain, love and sorrow, family
conflicts and relationships, these nine short stories feature teenagers dealing with life's problems and issues. (Fiction)

Silverberg, Robert. *Lord Valentine's Castle,*
Harper, 1980. ◆
Joining a troupe of itinerant jugglers, young
Valentine gathers a motley and many-specied
party of supporters and journeys across the
continent of Majipoor to regain the rightful
throne. (Fiction)

Simak, Clifford D. *Enchanted Pilgrimage,*
Putnam, 1975.
A strange, enchanted, allegorical journey in a
world where elves, gnomes, and goblins are as
normal as bacon and eggs. (Fiction)

_____. *Werewolf Principle,* Putnam, 1967.
Strange adventure follows when Andrew Blake
is found frozen in a space capsule and brought
back to earth after 200 years. (Fiction)

Simon, Neil. *Brighton Beach Memoirs,*
Random, 1984.
Sex and baseball are the primary preoccupa-
tions of fifteen-year-old Eugene in this story
about lower middle-class Jewish family life in
New York City during the Depression. (Nonfiction)

_____. *Lost in Yonkers,* Random, 1993.
Two young brothers rely on their sense of humor when they are sent to live with their fear-
some, irascible grandmother during World War
II. (Nonfiction)

Simon, Nissa. *Don't Worry, You're Normal:
Teenager's Guide to Self Health,* Crowell,
1982.
This brief but thorough guide answers many
questions about physical and psychological
changes occurring during the teen years.
(Nonfiction)

Singer, Marilyn. *Course of True Love Never
Did Run Smooth,* Harper, 1983.
While acting the role of lovesick Helena in a
high-school production of *A Midsummer*

Night's Dream, Becky is infatuated with the handsome lead, until she discovers that she loves her longtime friend Nemi. (Fiction)

Skurzynski, Gloria.   *Manwolf*, Houghton/Clarion, 1981.
Adam's heritage as the son of a masked knight and a serf in medieval Poland results in some unearthly tendencies and the need to turn to Kasia, the witch, for survival and true identity. (Fiction)

_____. *Tempering*, Clarion/Ticknor & Fields, 1983.
Karl faces a decision to stay in school or go to work in a Pennsylvania steel mill, in the early twentieth century. (Fiction)

Sleator, William.   *Boy Who Reversed Himself*, Dutton, 1987.
How strange is Omar? Laura's question is answered when this high school friend takes her into the fourth dimension. (Fiction)

_____. *Duplicate*, Dutton, 1988.
When David needs to be in two places at once, he duplicates himself with a machine he picked up on the beach—and finds his life in danger. (Fiction)

_____. *House of Stairs*, Dutton, 1974. ■ ▲ ♦
Five sixteen-year-old orphans find themselves alone in an experimental nightmare—where stairs and landings stretch as far as the eye can see and a strange red light trains them to dance for their food. (Fiction)

_____. *Interstellar Pig*, Dutton, 1984.
Barney's strange new neighbors invite him to play a bizarre board game called Interstellar Pig, which actually spans the universe and can destroy worlds. (Fiction)

_____. *Singularity*, Dutton, 1985.
Rivalry between sixteen-year-old twins Barry and Harry Krasner intensifies after their discovery of a foreboding playhouse on their family's inherited property leads them to the gateway of a universe that accelerates time's passage 3,600-fold and may unleash a monster. (Fiction)

_____. *Strange Attractors*, Dutton, 1991.
With a time travel phaser in his pocket and no memory of how it got there, Max must determine where it belongs without sending himself into oblivion. (Fiction)

Slepian, Jan.   *Night of the Bozos*, Dutton, 1983.
George, a teenaged electronic musician, and his young uncle see their lives change when they meet a strange carnival girl and the Bozo, the clown who dares passersby to knock him into a tub of water. (Fiction)

Slesar, Henry.   *Thing at the Door*, Random, 1974.
Haunted by memories of her mother's suicide when she was a child, Gail Gunnison at twenty-six is driven to the edge of suicide by strange events. (Fiction)

Smith, Dennis.   *Report from Engine Co. 82*, Saturday Review Press, 1972.
On crowded, angry city streets firemen respond when no one else does—to fire alarms, heart attacks, childbirth, mob violence. (Nonfiction)

Smith, K.   *Skeeter*, Houghton, 1990.
Hoping to enhance their hunting skills, two boys stumble on the best hunting terrain while trespassing on the property of an ornery black man. (Fiction)

Smith, Martin Cruz.   *Nightwing*, Norton, 1978.
A young Hopi Indian searches desperately for the cave of the vampire bats that have swarmed into the Southwest, bringing the threat of bubonic plague. (Fiction)

Smith, Mary-Anne Tirone.   *Book of Phoebe*, Doubleday, 1985.
In a novel that is hilarious and moving, Yale senior Phoebe, who goes to Paris to have her illegitimate baby, finds a man who loves her and tells him a bizarre story from her adolescence—the time she and a friend held Grant's tomb hostage. (Fiction)

_____. *Lament for a Silver-eyed Woman*, Morrow, 1987.
After a carefree stint as Peace Corps volunteers in Cameroon, Mattie and Jo's friendship is destroyed by Jo's life-threatening involvement with tragic victims of a Mideast conflict. (Fiction)

Smith, Robert Kimmel.   *Jane's House*, Morrow, 1983.
When Paul Klein remarries after his wife's sudden death, Hilary, sixteen, and Bobby, ten, reluctantly accept bright, independent businesswoman Ruth. (Fiction)

■ Selected for "Still Alive: The Best of the Best, 1960–1974"

▲ Selected for "The Best of the Best Books, 1970–1983"

♦ Selected for "Nothin' But the Best: Best of the Best Books for Young Adults, 1966–1986"

Smith, Rukshana. *Sumitra's Story*, Coward, 1983.
Sumitra, an East Indian girl, is torn between her traditional home, loving but repressive, and the English society, which offers freedom as well as prejudice. (Fiction)

Smith, W. Eugene, and Smith, Aileen Mioko. *Minamata*, Holt, 1975.
Using their cameras, the Smiths have recorded the horrors of industrial pollution that has killed or disabled more than 800 people in a Japanese town. (Nonfiction)

Snyder, Zilpha Keatley. *Fabulous Creature*, Atheneum, 1981.
James Fielding almost causes the death of a magnificent stag he has gentled. (Fiction)

_____. *Libby on Wednesday*, Delacorte, 1991.
Membership in the small class of Future Writers of America helps previously home-educated Libby overcome the shock of entering eighth grade in public school. (Fiction)

Sorrentino, Joseph. *Up from Never*, Prentice-Hall, 1971.
The son of a street sweeper, Joe Sorrentino tells of his youth in Brooklyn in the 1940s and of his journey from street punk to Harvard graduate. (Nonfiction)

Soto, Gary. *Baseball in April and Other Stories*, Harcourt, 1991.
These short stories reflect the funny and touching side of growing up Latino in Fresno, California, including one about Gilbert, who decides to emulate a character in a popular movie by finding a teacher and becoming a karate expert. (Fiction)

Southerland, Ellease. *Let the Lion Eat Straw*, Scribner, 1979.
Choosing marriage over a musical career that promises escape from the poverty she has always known, Abeba Williams fights to achieve a decent life for her husband and children. (Fiction)

Southhall, Ivan. *Long Night Watch*, Farrar, 1984.
During World War II a young sentry, failing in his duty, causes the death of all but a few of the religious refugees on an isolated island in the South Pacific. (Fiction)

Speare, Elizabeth George. *Sign of the Beaver*, Houghton, 1983.
A proud, resourceful American Indian boy deigns to help Matt survive the raw Maine wilderness winter when he is left alone to guard a newly built cabin. (Fiction)

Spiegelman, Art. *Maus: A Survivor's Tale*, Pantheon, 1986.
In a comic book of revolutionary graphic design, a cartoonist juxtaposes his frustration with his father's insensitivity today and his father's desperate struggle to stay alive forty years earlier during the Holocaust. (Fiction)

_____. *Maus: A Survivor's Tale II: And Here My Troubles Began*, Pantheon, 1992.
This graphic novel, the sequel to *Maus*, re-creates Vladek and Anja's agonizing struggles to survive in a concentration camp. (Fiction)

Spielman, Ed. *Mighty Atom: The Life and Times of Joseph L. Greenstein*, Viking, 1980.
The biography of Yosselle (Joe) Greenstein, born in 1893 in a Jewish ghetto in Poland, an asthmatic and sickly child, who trained himself to become the world's strongest man. (Nonfiction)

Spinelli, Jerry. *Maniac Magee*, Little, Brown, 1991.
"Maniac, Maniac he's so cool." The orphan Jeffrey Lionel Magee blitzes into the town of Two Mills and changes it forever. (Fiction)

_____. *There's a Girl in My Hammerlock*, Simon & Schuster, 1992.
Whoever heard of a girl on a wrestling team? She might get hurt. Besides, it's embarrassing and dumb! (Fiction)

Staples, Suzanne Fisher. *Shabanu: Daughter of the Wind*, Knopf, 1990.
Torn between allegiance to her family and her growing independence and strength, Shabanu tells the story of her life as a member of a nomadic tribe in the Pakistani desert. (Fiction)

Steffan, Joseph. *Honor Bound: A Gay American Fights for the Right to Serve His Country*, Villard, 1993.
Revealing he is gay two weeks before his Annapolis graduation, all-American boy Joe Steffan is discharged and begins to fight for the right to serve his country. (Nonfiction)

Steinem, Gloria. *Outrageous Acts and Everyday Rebellions*, Holt, 1983.
The founder and editor of *MS.* magazine writes about her life and work and discusses politics, pornography, and literature from a feminist point of view. (Nonfiction)

Sterling, Dorothy, ed. *We Are Your Sisters: Black Women in the Nineteenth Century*, Norton, 1984.
A documentary history of black women in nineteenth-century America, based on transcripts of interviews with former slaves, memoirs, letters, and other primary sources. (Nonfiction)

Stevenson, Florence. *Curse of the Concullens*, World, 1971.
Beautiful, eighteen-year-old Lucinda Ayers longs to be a governess, but she gets more than she bargained for when she obtains a position with an eccentric Irish family that comes complete with a castle, ghosts, and werewolves. (Fiction)

Stevermer, Carolyn. *River Rats*, Harcourt/ Jane Yolen, 1993.
Tomcat and his teenage friends try to survive after a nuclear holocaust by taking over a Mississippi riverboat, but their lives are endangered when killers come after the boat. (Fiction)

Stewart, Fred. *Mephisto Waltz*, Coward-McCann, 1969.
A dead, diabolical genius inhabits the body of Myles Clarkson, concert pianist; only Myles's wife suspects what has happened but she has no proof. (Fiction)

Stewart, Mary. *Crystal Cave*, Morrow, 1970. ▲
Merlin, the base-born son of royalty in fifth century Britain, uses magic to outwit his enemies until he sets the stage for the birth of Arthur, the future king of Britain. (Fiction)

———. *Hollow Hills*, Morrow, 1973.
In this sequel to *The Crystal Cave*, Merlin conceals and grooms the child Arthur until the time of his coronation. (Fiction)

Stoehr, Shelley. *Crosses*, Delacorte, 1993.
Nancy loves cutting herself; the bloody designs and scars are "cool." Then there are always alcohol and other drugs—all thanks to Katie, the best teacher at school. (Fiction)

Stoll, Cliff. *Cuckoo's Egg: Tracking a Spy through the Maze of Computer Espionage*, Doubleday, 1991.
A young astronomer turns detective as he embarks on the trail of an elusive computer hacker who has managed to break into top secret government and military data banks. (Nonfiction)

Stone, Bruce. *Half Nelson, Full Nelson*, Harper, 1985.
Nelson Gato tells how he faked the kidnapping of his little sister and her friend in an effort to bring about a reconciliation between his wrestler father and his mother, who could no longer stand life in a tacky Florida trailer park. (Fiction)

Strasser, Todd. *Friends till the End*, Delacorte, 1981. ♦
David thinks he has problems—with soccer, his girlfriend, parents, and college plans—until he meets Howie, the new guy in school, who has leukemia. (Fiction)

———. *Rock 'n' Roll Nights*, Delacorte, 1982.
Determined to make it to the top in rock music, Gary Specter plays lead guitar and sings with his group almost every night. (Fiction)

Strauss, Gwen. *Trail of Stones*, Knopf, 1991.
These dark and dramatic retellings of fairy tales in poetic monologues are accompanied by equally stark drawings. (Fiction)

Strieber, Whitley. *Wolf of Shadows*, Knopf, 1985.
In their attempt to survive after a nuclear war, a woman and her daughter join and learn from a wolf pack led by Wolf of Shadows. (Fiction)

Styron, William. *Confessions of Nat Turner*, Random, 1967.
While awaiting execution, the instigator of the 1831 slave rebellion in Virginia reconstructs the agonizing events of his life that led to insurrection and murder. (Fiction)

Sullivan, Charles, ed. *Children of Promise: African-American Literature and Art for Young People*, Abrams, 1992.
A choice sampling of art and literature conveys the image of African Americans over the past 200 years. (Nonfiction)

Sullivan, Jack, ed. *Penguin Encyclopedia of Horror and the Supernatural*, Viking, 1986.
Surpassing the typical reference book, this collection of articles leads the reader from Stephen King to *The Birds* to Prokofiev. (Nonfiction)

Sullivan, Tom, and Gill, Derek L. T. *If You Could See What I Hear*, Harper, 1975.
Tom Sullivan refused to let blindness interfere with school or sports, his marriage, his career, or his life. (Fiction)

Summers, Ian, ed. *Tomorrow and Beyond: Masterpieces of Science Fiction Art*, Workman, 1979.
A magical mystery tour through the imaginative images used to illustrate speculative fiction. (Nonfiction)

■ Selected for "Still Alive: The Best of the Best, 1960–1974"

▲ Selected for "The Best of the Best Books, 1970–1983"

♦ Selected for "Nothin' But the Best: Best of the Best Books for Young Adults, 1966–1986"

Sussman, Alan N. *Rights of Young People: The Basic ACLU Guide to a Young Person's Rights*, Avon, 1977.
This legal bible for those less than age eighteen states what the law allows and what it prohibits, emphasizing differences in state laws, and offers advice on legal defense. (Nonfiction)

Sutcliff, Rosemary. *Road to Camlann: The Death of King Arthur*, Dutton, 1983.
King Arthur strives to preserve the Round Table as Mordred plots against him and as gossip about Lancelot and Guinevere intensifies. (Fiction)

Swanson, Walter S. J. *Deepwood*, Little, Brown, 1981.
A young man's desire for sexual fulfillment and personal freedom challenges his moral values and his devoted relationship to an older woman. (Fiction)

Swarthout, Glendon. *Bless the Beasts and Children*, Doubleday, 1970. ■ ▲ ♦
Five misfits in an Arizona boys' camp sneak out on a daring escapade to save a herd of buffalo from bloodthirsty gun-toting tourists. (Fiction)

Sweeney, Joyce. *Center Line*, Delacorte, 1984.
Fearing for their safety, five teenage brothers steal their abusive, alcoholic father's car and run away from home. (Fiction)

Switzer, Ellen. *How Democracy Failed*, Atheneum, 1975.
Personal reminiscences of Germany under Hitler from people who were then only teenagers. (Nonfiction)

Szabo, Joseph. *Almost Grown*, Crown/ Harmony, 1978.
More than ninety provocative photographs and a number of telling poems written by teen-agers themselves express the concerns and feelings, the highs and the lows, of kids who are "almost grown." (Nonfiction)

Szulc, Tad. *Bombs of Palomares*, Viking, 1967.
Four H-bombs lost over Spain in 1966 created potentially explosive social and political situations. (Nonfiction)

Talbert, Marc. *Dead Birds Singing*, Little, Brown, 1985.
Left alone because of a tragic accident, Matt must face the reality of losing the last of his family—his mother and sister—and cope with his feelings for the drunken driver who killed them. (Fiction)

Tan, Amy. *Joy Luck Club*, Putnam, 1990.
Chinese American daughters find conflict, love, and connection with their mothers, who are haunted by their early lives in China. (Fiction)

Tang, Hsi-yang. *Living Treasures: An Odyssey through China's Extraordinary Nature Reserves*, Bantam, 1988.
A beautifully photographed description of the wildlife and landscapes of China's stunning natural reserves. (Nonfiction)

Tapert, Annette, ed. *Lines of Battle: Letters from U.S. Servicemen, 1941-45*, Times Books, 1987.
Letters from the battle lines of World War II convey a sense of adventure, loneliness, and tragedy. (Nonfiction)

Taylor, Clark. *House That Crack Built*, Chronicle, 1993.
Following the same pattern as the children's nursery rhyme, this bleak picture book shows the strung-out addicts, the crack lord's mansion, the hungry baby of a crack addict. (Fiction)

Taylor, David. *Zoo Vet: Adventures of a Wild Animal Doctor*, Lippincott, 1977.
An authority on treating wild animals describes unusual cases from his veterinary practice around the world. (Nonfiction)

Taylor, Gordon. *Biological Time Bomb*, World, 1968.
The biological revolution is at hand and in the offing are memory-erasing drugs, choice of sex in offspring, reconstructed organisms, and the indefinite postponement of death. (Nonfiction)

Taylor, Mildred D. *Let the Circle Be Unbroken*, Dial, 1981.
In this sequel to *Roll of Thunder, Hear My Cry*, the Logan family survives the Depression, a murder trial, and the jailing of a son. (Fiction)

_____. *Road to Memphis*, Dial, 1991.
On the eve of World War II, Cassie Logan is finishing high school and dreaming of college when a violent racial incident forces her to help a good friend escape to the north. (Fiction)

Taylor, Theodore. *Sniper*, Harcourt, 1990.
A gunman begins killing the big cats the week Ben, fifteen, is left in charge of the family's animal preserve. (Fiction)

_____. *Weirdo*, Harcourt, 1993.
Disfigured in a plane crash and called Weirdo by the locals, Chip seeks refuge in the swamp with his recovering alcoholic artist father. There he befriends Samantha, and the two teens find themselves threatened by murderous bear poachers. (Fiction)

Teague, Robert. *Letters to a Black Boy,* Walker, 1968.

A former college football star (now a New York television newscaster) voices the frustrations of being considered a Negro rather than an individual. (Nonfiction)

Teitz, Joyce. *What's a Nice Girl like You Doing in a Place like This?,* Coward, 1972.

Women talk candidly about their careers and ambitions, their challenges and dreams. (Nonfiction)

Telander, Rick. *Heaven Is a Playground,* St. Martin's, 1977.

The inspirational story of the dreams, hopes, and frustrations of talented black urban youths whose love of basketball is their lifeline to the future. (Nonfiction)

Tepper, Sheri S. *Beauty,* Doubleday, 1992.

In this modern retelling of the fairy tale, Beauty avoids the sleeping spell and trips through time into different worlds, searching for beauty and love. (Fiction)

Terkel, Studs. *American Dreams: Lost and Found,* Pantheon, 1980.

Sharing their innermost hopes and dreams through interviews with Studs Terkel is a cross section of Americans ranging from celebrities such as Joan Crawford, Bill Veeck, and Coleman Young to steelworker Ed Sadlowski and sixteen-year-old Linda Haas. (Nonfiction)

———. *"The Good War": An Oral History of World War Two,* Pantheon, 1984.

This vibrant Second World War oral history offers wonderfully readable tales that are alive, spontaneous, and personal as Americans from all walks of life recall their involvement and participation. (Nonfiction)

Terris, Susan. *Nell's Quilt,* Farrar, 1987.

Not knowing how to resist her parents' plans for her marriage, Nell stitches her lost dreams of college and independence into a quilt—all the while literally wasting away. (Fiction)

Terry, Douglas. *Last Texas Hero,* Doubleday, 1982.

A humorous, bawdy, and explicit look at the life of a college freshman and All-American football hero, told in the inspiring words of Homer Jones. (Fiction)

Terry, Wallace. *Bloods: An Oral History of the Vietnam War by Black Veterans,* Random, 1984.

From their own perspective, twenty black soldiers give graphically detailed accounts of the Vietnam War and the emotional after effects. (Nonfiction)

Tevis, Walter. *Queen's Gambit,* Random, 1983.

In the orphanage where she lived Beth learned the game of chess, beginning an obsession that took her all the way to the top. (Fiction)

Thesman, Jean. *Rain Catchers,* Houghton, 1992.

Abandoned by her mother and growing up in a household of women, Grayling, at fourteen, must deal with love, death, and her relationship with her mother. (Fiction)

———. *When the Road Ends,* Houghton, 1993.

Can four abandoned strangers—a twelve-year-old, a teenager, a silent child, and a brain-injured woman—come together as a loving family? (Fiction)

Thomas, Joyce Carol. *Marked by Fire,* Avon/Flare, 1982.

When tragedy strikes Abby, her proud black rural Oklahoma community gathers around to protect and save her from harm. (Fiction)

Thomas, Kurt, and Hannon, Kent. *Kurt Thomas and Gymnastics,* Simon & Schuster, 1980.

This portrayal of Kurt Thomas's life provides an insight into the world of men's gymnastics—the training, dedication, and life-style necessary to reach the level of Olympic competition. (Nonfiction)

Thomas, Lewis. *Youngest Science: Notes of a Medicine Watcher,* Viking, 1983.

These autobiographical musings by the author of *Lives of a Cell* appeal because of their "celebration and a warning about the nature of man and the future of life on our planet." (Nonfiction)

Thompson, Estelle. *Hunter in the Dark,* Walker, 1979.

The only witness to the kidnapping of a child who is later murdered, blind teacher Philip Blair determines to find the criminal. (Fiction)

■ Selected for "Still Alive: The Best of the Best, 1960–1974"

▲ Selected for "The Best of the Best Books, 1970–1983"

♦ Selected for "Nothin' But the Best: Best of the Best Books for Young Adults, 1966–1986"

Thompson, Jean. *House of Tomorrow,* Harper, 1967. ■
In a home for unwed mothers Jean overcomes despair and faces many decisions about her future and that of her unborn child. (Nonfiction)

Thompson, Joyce. *Conscience Place,* Doubleday, 1984.
The Place, an idyllic, protected secret settlement for the mutant offspring of nuclear-energy workers, has come to the attention of scientists, who want to use its inhabitants for experimentation. (Fiction)

Thompson, Julian. *Band of Angels,* Scholastic, 1986.
Unaware that government agents are pursuing them with the intent to kill, five teenagers camp in the wilderness to plan a crusade against nuclear war. (Fiction)

Tiburzi, Bonnie. *Takeoff! The Story of America's First Woman Pilot for a Major Airline,* Crown, 1984.
In this autobiography, the first woman pilot for a major U.S. airline shares her love of flying and tells of her challenging and often frustrating climb to success. (Nonfiction)

Tidyman, Ernest. *Dummy,* Little, Brown, 1974.
What defense did a black, illiterate deaf-mute have against a murder charge? His deaf lawyer had to contend not only with his client's inability to communicate but also with an unfeeling court system and circumstantial evidence. (Nonfiction)

Torchia, Joseph. *Kryptonite Kid,* Holt, 1979.
Jerry's letters to his hero, Superman, reveal his sinking into insanity and his discovery of who Superman really is. (Fiction)

Townsend, John. *Good Night, Prof. Dear,* Lippincott, 1971.
Seventeen-year-old Graham Hollis, unhappy with himself and his home life, runs off with Lynn, a waitress, and finds her a surprising and beautiful person. (Fiction)

Townsend, Sue. *Adrian Mole Diaries,* Grove, 1986.
In cryptically funny entries, teenager Adrian worries incessantly about his problems—acne, his parents' separation, sexual urges, and much more. (Fiction)

Trevor, Elleston. *Theta Syndrome,* Doubleday, 1977.
"For God's sake help me" is the desperate telepathic cry of a young woman deep in a coma prolonged by her fear of another attempt on her life. (Fiction)

Trudeau, G. B. *Doonesbury Chronicles,* Holt, 1975.
No one can feel the pulse of the world like Garry Trudeau, whose satirical look at the sixties and early seventies is a real delight. (Nonfiction)

_____. *Doonesbury's Greatest Hits,* Holt, 1978.
Washington politics, student activists, talking to plants, and relations between the U.S. and China are among the popular cartoonist's targets. (Nonfiction)

Trull, Patti. *On with My Life,* Putnam, 1983.
A courageous young cancer victim at fifteen, Patti Trull loses her leg despite numerous treatments and surgery but finds hope as an occupational therapist for other young victims. (Nonfiction)

Turney, David C. *Why Are They Weeping? South Africans under Apartheid,* Stewart, Tabori & Chang, 1990.
One hundred color photographs vividly show the brutal conflict in a troubled and beautiful land. (Nonfiction)

Tyler, Anne. *Slipping-Down Life,* Knopf, 1970.
The story of fat, plain Evie Decker's romance and marriage to a rock singer and their slipping-down life together. (Fiction)

Uchida, Yoshiko. *Invisible Thread,* Messner, 1993.
The author describes growing up in Berkeley as a second-generation Japanese American and her family's humiliating experience in Utah internment camps during World War II. (Nonfiction)

Uhlman, Fred. *Reunion,* Farrar, 1977.
Thirty years later, the Jewish narrator recalls his doomed friendship with the son of a nobleman in Nazi Germany. A poignant and provocative novella. (Fiction)

Ure, Jean. *Plague,* Harcourt/Jane Yolen, 1993.
Returning to London from a wilderness camping trip, Fran finds her family and friends dead from a plague that has engulfed the city. (Fiction)

_____. *See You Thursday,* Delacorte, 1983.
Marianne, a sixteen-year-old British schoolgirl, helps her family's boarder, Abe, a twenty-four-year-old blind music teacher, achieve independence as their friendship grows into love. (Fiction)

Van Devanter, Lynda, and Morgan, Christopher. *Home before Morning: The*

Story of an Army Nurse in Vietnam, Beaufort, 1983. ■ ▲ ♦
Lt. Lynda Van Devanter recounts her experiences as an army surgical nurse in Vietnam and the stress after coming home. (Nonfiction)

Van Leeuwen, Jean. *Seems Like This Road Goes On Forever,* Dial, 1979.
Guided by an empathetic psychologist, the seventeen-year-old daughter of a fundamentalist minister learns to separate her needs from the expectations of her domineering parents. (Fiction)

Van Raven, Pieter. *Great Man's Secret,* Scribner, 1990.
Jerry, a fourteen-year-old student reporter, is sent to interview reclusive writer Paul Bernard and discovers not only Bernard's secret, but also those hidden within others and himself. (Fiction)

_____. *Pickle and Price,* Scribner, 1991.
Pickle, the son of a white prison farm supervisor, and Price, a newly released black convict Pickle has befriended, travel across America. (Fiction)

Vare, Ethlie Ann. *Mothers of Invention: From the Bra to the Bomb: Forgotten Women and Their Unforgettable Ideas,* Morrow, 1988.
Vare presents and praises the often ignored accomplishments of women in areas that include nuclear physics and the invention of the cotton gin. (Nonfiction)

Vinge, Joan D. *Psion,* Delacorte, 1982. ♦
In the year 2417, a poor orphan, taken from the slums to participate in a dangerous experiment, soon finds that his extraordinary telepathic powers endanger his life. (Fiction)

Voigt, Cynthia. *Izzy, Willy-Nilly,* Atheneum, 1986. ♦
Who are your real friends? Izzy struggles to rethink her friendships after losing a leg in a car crash. (Fiction)

_____. *On Fortune's Wheel,* Atheneum, 1991.
Fourteen-year-old Birle's impulsive attempt to stop a stranger from stealing a boat leads to romance and adventure with a young runaway lord. (Fiction)

_____. *Runner,* Atheneum, 1985.
Bullet, a seventeen-year-old cross country runner, finds that compromise is something necessary if an athlete is going to be the best. (Fiction)

_____. *Solitary Blue,* Atheneum, 1983.
Jeff Green's mother left home when he was only seven. When she shows up in his life again Jeff learns some hard lessons about love and caring. (Fiction)

_____. *Sons from Afar,* Atheneum, 1987.
Dicey's brothers, on the brink of growing up, search for the father who deserted them as infants—and find unexpected truths. (Fiction)

_____. *Tell Me If the Lovers Are Losers,* Atheneum, 1982.
Three college roommates—each very different, but gifted—clash and come together as they learn values from one another. (Fiction)

Von Canon, Claudia. *Inheritance,* Houghton, 1983.
A young medical student faces the horrors of the Inquisition in sixteenth-century Spain. (Fiction)

Vonnegut, Kurt. *Jailbird,* Delacorte/Seymour Lawrence, 1979.
Harvard, the New Deal, the Holocaust, World War II, Watergate, two prison terms, and a giant conglomerate—Walter Starbuck, who tries to live by the Sermon on the Mount, experiences them all. Shall the meek inherit the earth? Perhaps on a short-term basis. (Fiction)

Vonnegut, Mark. *Eden Express,* Praeger, 1975.
Kurt Vonnegut's son reflects on his life in the counter culture and his battle with schizophrenia. (Nonfiction)

Wagenheim, Kal. *Clemente!,* Praeger, 1973.
The tragic death of Roberto Clemente, well-known as a great baseball player, revealed the depth of his commitment and concern for others. (Nonfiction)

Wagoner, David. *Road to Many a Wonder,* Farrar, 1974.
Setting out with his wheelbarrow to seek his fortune in western gold fields, Ike Bender marries a high-spirited young woman, and together they travel roads that do indeed lead to many a wonder. (Fiction)

Wain, John. *Free Zone Starts Here,* Delacorte, 1984.
After his younger sister is killed in a plane crash, seventeen-year-old Paul Waterford flies to Lisbon for a memorial service where a dis-

---

■ Selected for "Still Alive: The Best of the Best, 1960–1974"
▲ Selected for "The Best of the Best Books, 1970–1983"
♦ Selected for "Nothin' But the Best: Best of the Best Books for Young Adults, 1966–1986"

turbing night makes him aware of his own imperfections. (Fiction)

Walker, Alice.   *In Search of Our Mothers' Gardens: Womanist Prose,* Harcourt, 1984.
Thirty-five essays examine Walker's development as a human being, writer, and woman. (Nonfiction)

Walker, Margaret.   *Jubilee,* Houghton, 1966.
Life at the time of the Civil War as experienced by Vyry, daughter of a Negro slave and the white plantation owner. (Fiction)

Wallace, Duncan R.   *Mountebank,* Houghton, 1972.
Lee, who wants to be a writer, is drawn to Nonno, the prankster, as they enter prep school together. (Fiction)

Wallin, Luke.   *Redneck Poacher's Son,* Bradbury, 1981.
The son of a redneck poacher in an Alabama swamp, Jesse hates—perhaps enough to kill—his father, whom he blames for his mother's death. (Fiction)

Walsh, John, and Gannon, Robert.   *Time Is Short and the Water Rises,* Dutton, 1967.
"Operation Gwamba: The story of the rescue of 10,000 animals from certain death in a South American rain forest" (Subtitle). (Nonfiction)

Walsh, M. M. B.   *Four-colored Hoop,* Putnam, 1976.
Surviving the cruelty of the reservation, Mildred Shoot-Eagle becomes a feared mystic and medicine woman and revenges herself on the white man. (Fiction)

Watson, James.   *Double Helix: A Personal Account of the Discovery of the Structure of DNA,* Atheneum, 1968.
A young scientist gives an inside view of how he and a colleague pursuing fame and the Nobel Prize managed to discover the structure of DNA, the molecule of heredity. (Nonfiction)

Watson, Lyall.   *Dreams of Dragons: Riddles of Natural History,* Morrow, 1987.
Random numbers, movement of water, chance, and the pulse of the earth are among the subjects of essays that extol the magic and wonder of science and the world. (Nonfiction)

Webb, Sheyann, and Nelson, Rachel West.   *Selma, Lord, Selma: Girlhood Memories of the Civil-Rights Days,* Univ. of Alabama Press, 1980. ♦
A recollection of the events of the 1965 civil rights movement in Selma, Alabama, where Sheyann, eight, and Rachel, nine, faced nightsticks, dogs, and mounted police, alongside Dr. Martin Luther King, Jr., and other adults who fought to achieve the right to vote. (Nonfiction)

Weiss, Ann E.   *Who's to Know? Information, the Media and Public Awareness,* Houghton, 1991.
Putting the public's right to know in historical perspective, Weiss illustrates how business, advertising, special interest groups, politics, and the media shape and manipulate the news and information Americans receive. (Nonfiction)

Wells, Evelyn.   *I Am Thinking of Kelda,* Doubleday, 1974.
Kelda's story moves from New York sweat shops to a pioneer farm in Kansas and finally to California, where she is captivated by a new form of entertainment called movies. (Fiction)

Wells, Rosemary.   *Through the Hidden Door,* Dial, 1987.
A bullied prep school student discovers his inner strengths as he helps the school misfit excavate a mysterious ruin. (Fiction)

_____.   *When No One Was Looking,* Dial, 1980.
Fourteen-year-old Kathy thrives on the pressure to become a tennis star until the death, possibly murder, of a competitor forces her to question her ambition and her future. (Fiction)

Wersba, Barbara.   *Carnival in My Mind,* Harper/Charlotte Zolotow, 1982.
Harvey Beaumont is fourteen, five feet tall, and in love for the first time—with a twenty-year-old, six-foot would-be actress. (Fiction)

_____.   *Country of the Heart,* Atheneum, 1975.
A brief, poignant romance between a dying older woman who is a famous poet and a young man who aspires to be a writer. (Fiction)

_____.   *Run Softly, Go Fast,* Atheneum, 1970. ▲ ♦
Written in diary form, this is the story of nineteen-year-old David Marks and his attempt to reconcile his love-hate relationship with his father. (Fiction)

_____.   *Tunes for a Small Harmonica,* Harper, 1976.
Sixteen-year-old J. F. McAllister, a constant source of worry to everyone, masters the harmonica and then uses her talents to help her poetry teacher with whom she is in love. (Fiction)

West, Jessamyn.   *Massacre at Fall Creek,* Harcourt, 1975.
Seventeen-year-old Hannah Cape was only one person affected by the first trial (in 1824) of white men accused of murdering Indians. (Fiction)

Westall, Robert. *Devil on the Road,* Greenwillow, 1979.
In a time fantasy set in present day England, John Webster travels from a barn with strange symbols and an unusual cat to a trial three hundred years in the past, where he fights to save a young woman sentenced to die for being a witch. (Fiction)

———. *Futuretrack 5,* Greenwillow, 1984.
The story of Henry Kitson, one of a small group responsible for keeping the highly computerized, manipulative, twenty-first-century British society functioning, and Keri, the London bike-riding champion of Futuretrack 5. (Fiction)

———. *Kingdom by the Sea,* Farrar, 1992.
It's 1942, and Harry has just become a war orphan. Will he and the stray dog he takes up with be able to survive on their own? (Fiction)

———. *Stormsearch,* Farrar, 1993.
Tim's summer vacation turns into a quest when an antique model ship, washed up on the beach after a terrible storm, brings with it secrets of love and death. (Fiction)

———. *Wind Eye,* Greenwillow, 1978.
The members of a professor's family are transported, via an old boat said to have belonged to St. Cuthbert, back into medieval times—where the not too friendly monk touches each of their lives. (Fiction)

———. *Yaxley's Cat,* Scholastic, 1991.
Renting the wrong vacation cottage proves to be an almost fatal mistake for a mother and two teenagers, especially after a stray cat moves in and starts digging around in the garden. (Fiction)

Wetherby, Terry, ed. *Conversations: Working Women Talk about Doing a "Man's Job,"* Les Femmes, 1978.
Twenty-two women talk about their experiences in such traditionally male-dominated jobs as welder, carpenter, butcher, grain elevator operator, and chairperson of the board. (Nonfiction)

Wharton, William. *Birdy,* Knopf, 1979.
In a V.A. hospital, Birdy, prompted by his friend Al, reviews his bird-obsessed youth and discovers freedom without flight. (Fiction)

———. *Midnight Clear,* Knopf, 1982.
A group of unseasoned teenage soldiers standing guard in an old chalet in the Ardennes Forest in December 1944 experience first hand the irony and tragedy of war when they desperately try to set up peaceful communications with a similar group of Germans. (Fiction)

Whipple, Dorothy. *Is the Grass Greener?: Answers to Questions about Drugs,* Luce, 1971.
In question and answer form, a physician reports with total objectivity on the facts about drugs of all kinds, the laws, the uses, and the ways to confront the problem. (Nonfiction)

White, Ellen Emerson. *Long Live the Queen,* Scholastic, 1990.
Abducted by terrorists, Megan, the president's daughter, realizes her survival is completely up to her. (Fiction)

White, Robb. *Deathwatch,* Doubleday, 1972. ■ ▲ ♦
Ben's hunting expedition for bighorn sheep becomes a deathwatch in the desert—with hope of survival forty-five miles away! (Fiction)

White, Ruth. *Weeping Willow,* Farrar, 1993.
Life in idyllic 1950s Virginia is difficult for Tiny Lambert as she struggles to emerge whole from her stepfather's brutal attention. (Fiction)

White, Ryan, and Cunningham, Ann Marie. *Ryan White: My Own Story,* Dial, 1992.
Teenager Ryan White not only fights AIDS but also prejudice and his own fears in a personal account about the medical disaster facing all of us. (Nonfiction)

Whitney, Phyllis. *Hunter's Green,* Doubleday, 1968.
Returning to Athmore for a reconciliation with her husband, Eve North finds herself the pawn in a deadly game of chess with the black rook out to destroy her. (Fiction)

Wibberley, Leonard. *Mouse on Wall Street,* Morrow, 1969.
Gloriana, ruler of Grand Fenwick, conqueror of the United States, sender of the first rocket to the moon, now is possessed by a "Midas touch" which almost wrecks the simple economy of her country. (Fiction)

Wieler, Diana. *Bad Boy,* Delacorte, 1993.
AJ and Tulley have been best friends both on and off the ice for years, but AJ's discovery of Tulley's secret threatens their friendship and AJ's control over his own behavior. (Fiction)

■ Selected for "Still Alive: The Best of the Best, 1960–1974"
▲ Selected for "The Best of the Best Books, 1970–1983"
♦ Selected for "Nothin' But the Best: Best of the Best Books for Young Adults, 1966–1986"

Wiesenthal, Simon. *Murderers among Us,* McGraw-Hill, 1967.
A survivor of the concentration camps searches out and brings to justice Adolf Eichmann, a Gestapo officer; Karl Silberbauer, who arrested Anne Frank; and some 900 other Nazi murderers. (Nonfiction)

Wilcox, Fred A. *Waiting for an Army to Die: The Tragedy of Agent Orange,* Random, 1983.
Based on interviews with Vietnam veterans and on government documents, this comprehensive look at the effects of the defoliant Agent Orange points to callous disregard for its victims. (Nonfiction)

Wilford, John Noble. *Riddle of the Dinosaur,* Knopf, 1986.
The science editor of the *New York Times* has produced a humorous and readable history of paleontology, including surprising new discoveries that have revolutionized dinosaur theory. (Nonfiction)

Wilhelm, Kate. *Where Late the Sweet Birds Sang,* Harper, 1976.
When humankind is faced with annihilation by the sterilizing effects of pollution and plague, cloning becomes the only hope of man's continued existence—or is it? (Fiction)

Wilkinson, Brenda. *Ludell and Willie,* Harper, 1977. ▲
Two high school seniors from a poor, black Georgia community fall in love but are separated because of family tragedy. (Fiction)

Willard, Nancy. *Things Invisible to See,* Knopf, 1985.
Mystical visions, romance, and the struggle of making choices are intertwined in the story of twins Ben and Willie and Clare Bishop after Ben's stray ball paralyzes Clare. (Fiction)

Willeford, Charles. *I Was Looking for a Street,* Countryman, 1988.
A writer's memoir of his survival from age eight when he was orphaned to his life on the road as a teenager during the Great Depression. (Nonfiction)

Willey, Margaret. *Bigger Book of Lydia,* Harper, 1983.
Lydia Bitte is small and unhappy and her rock-musician boyfriend calls her Littlebit. She acquires a new perspective when she meets Michelle, who has anorexia. (Fiction)

———. *Finding David Dolores,* Harper, 1986.
"Oh God, I whispered. At last I've found someone." Thirteen-year-old Arly experiences the intensity of a first crush when she secretly follows handsome, older David Dolores. (Fiction)

———. *Saving Lenny,* Bantam/Starfire, 1991.
When Jesse falls in love with handsome, mysterious Lenny, she willingly gives up everything for him—family, friends, and college. (Fiction)

Williams, Juan. *Eyes on the Prize: America's Civil Rights Years, 1954-1965,* Viking, 1987.
A history of the dramatic events of the years between the Supreme Court's ruling against segregated schools in 1954 and the approval of the Voting Rights Act of 1965. (Nonfiction)

Williams, Martin. *Where's the Melody?,* Pantheon, 1966.
A listener's introduction to jazz with record notes. (Nonfiction)

Williams, Michael. *Crocodile Burning,* Dutton/Lodestar, 1993.
Joining the cast of a play about apartheid headed for the New York stage, Seraki leaves his native Soweto, where life under white rule has become unbearable. (Fiction)

Williams, Ted, and Underwood, John. *My Turn at Bat: The Story of My Life,* Simon & Schuster, 1969.
One of baseball's greatest hitters, Ted Williams, explains himself and his controversial career with honesty and frankness. (Nonfiction)

Williams-Garcia, Rita. *Fast Talk on a Slow Track,* Dutton/Lodestar, 1992.
Denzel Watson has always been a star; now he faces his first taste of failure the summer before his freshman year at Princeton. (Fiction)

Wilson, Budge. *Leaving,* Putnam/Philomel, 1993.
Nine stories about growing up female reveal the roller coaster of teenage emotions. (Fiction)

Wilson, David Henry. *Coachman Rat,* Carroll & Graf, 1990.
When the clock tolls midnight, the rat that the fairy godmother had turned into a coachman accidentally remains human in all but physical form; will he be as inhumane as the people he encounters? (Fiction)

Wilson, F. Paul. *Dydeetown World,* Baen, 1990.
Private detective Sigmundo Dreyer takes on the underworld and corporate crime when he helps a client in this futuristic hard-boiled detective saga. (Fiction)

Wilson, Robert Charles. *Gypsies,* Doubleday/Foundation, 1990.
Fifteen-year-old Michael suddenly realizes his mom shares his unusual psychic ability, and now they must flee for their lives. (Fiction)

Windsor, Patricia. *Summer Before*, Harper, 1973.
Alexandra fights her way back to reality with the help of her parents and a psychiatrist, after the death of her special friend Bradley. (Fiction)

Winthrop, Elizabeth. *Knock, Knock, Who's There?*, Holiday, 1979.
While Sam and Michael try to cope with their father's death, they discover that their mother has a problem even more devastating to their lives. (Fiction)

Winton, Tim. *Lockie Leonard, Human Torpedo*, Little, Brown/Joy Street Books, 1993.
Lockie gets thrown out of class his first day at his new high school—a good start, he decides. Things look even better when the prettiest girl in school takes an interest in him. (Fiction)

Wirths, Claudine G., and Bowman-Kruhm, Mary. *I Hate School: How to Hang In and When to Drop Out*, Harper, 1986.
This self-help manual for potential dropouts offers usable, nonpreachy suggestions for improving academic performance and coping with problems. (Nonfiction)

Wisler, G. Clifton. *Red Cap*, Dutton/Lodestar, 1992.
Starvation, disease, and despair destroy the lives of Union soldiers at Andersonville. How can Ransom, a thirteen-year-old prisoner of war, expect to survive? (Fiction)

Wolf, David. *Foul! The Connie Hawkins Story*, Holt, 1972.
Slum beginnings and a college basketball scandal could not keep Connie Hawkins from becoming a superstar with the Phoenix Suns. (Nonfiction)

Wolfe, Tom. *Right Stuff*, Farrar, 1980.
Wolfe provides a fascinating and often irreverant history of manned space flight from the late 1940s exploits of Chuck Yeager to the NASA missions of John Glenn, Alan Shepard, and Gus Grissom—all of whom had the right stuff. (Nonfiction)

Wolff, Tobias. *This Boy's Life: A Memoir*, Atlantic Monthly Press, 1990.
A witty, wrenching autobiography of Wolff's coming-of-age with a loving mother and a cruel stepfather. (Nonfiction)

Wolff, Virginia Euwer. *Mozart Season*, Holt, 1992.
Allegra Shapiro plays Mozart on her violin with the same intensity that she plays softball; her decision to enter a music competition turns her twelfth summer into the "Mozart season." (Fiction)

_____. *Probably Still Nick Swansen*, Holt, 1988.
Slow but proud special education student Nick Swansen must deal with the pain of rejection and lingering guilt over his sister's death. (Fiction)

Wood, Bari. *Killing Gift: A Novel*, Putnam, 1975.
Does Jennifer Gilbert really have the psychic power to kill? (Fiction)

Woodson, Jacqueline. *Maizon at Blue Hill*, Delacorte, 1993.
After winning a scholarship to a mostly white boarding school, Maizon is forced to confront issues of racism, friendship, and fitting in. (Fiction)

Woolley, Persia. *Child of the Northern Spring*, Poseidon, 1987.
The first book in an Arthurian trilogy views life through the eyes of lively fifteen-year-old Guinevere. (Fiction)

_____. *Queen of the Summer Stars*, Poseidon, 1991.
Young Queen Guinevere is torn between loyalty to her king and love for his closest companion, Lancelot, in this sequel to *Child of the Northern Spring*. (Fiction)

Wrede, Patricia C. *Dealing with Dragons*, Harcourt/Jane Yolen, 1991.
Unconventional Cimorene, fed up with her dull life as a princess, runs away and joins the dragons. A fun book that turns fairy tales upside down. (Fiction)

_____. *Searching for Dragons*, Harcourt/Jane Yolen, 1993.
Princess Cimorene and Mendabar, king of the Enchanted Forest, triumph over wizards to rescue Kazul, the king of the dragons. (Fiction)

Wyden, Peter. *Day One: Before Hiroshima and After*, Simon & Schuster, 1985.
The author not only chronicles the making of the atomic bomb and its first use, but also fol-

---

■ Selected for "Still Alive: The Best of the Best, 1960–1974"
▲ Selected for "The Best of the Best Books, 1970–1983"
◆ Selected for "Nothin' But the Best: Best of the Best Books for Young Adults, 1966–1986"

lows the aftermath to the present day. (Nonfiction)

Wyss, Thelma Hatch. *Here at the Scenic-Vu Motel,* Harper, 1988.
Living too far away to be bused to the local high school, a coed group of teens room at a motel, with seventeen-year-old Jake in charge and by no means ready for such awesome responsibilities. (Fiction)

Yeager, Chuck, and Janos, Leo. *Yeager: An Autobiography,* Bantam, 1985.
Air Force General Chuck Yeager, World War II ace and first man to break the sound barrier, candidly shares the drama of his life and career. (Nonfiction)

Yolen, Jane. *Briar Rose,* Tor, 1993.
Grandmother Gemma always told the story of Briar Rose, and after she dies, her granddaughter discovers that Gemma was a real-life Sleeping Beauty—a Holocaust survivor. (Fiction)

_____. *Dragon's Blood,* Delacorte, 1982.
In an original and engrossing fantasy, Jakkin's freedom is ensured when the dragon he steals and secretly trains wins its first fight. (Fiction)

_____. *Gift of Sarah Barker,* Viking, 1981.
Vivacious Sarah and stalwart Abel create havoc in a quiet, modest Shaker community when they fall in love. (Fiction)

_____. *Heart's Blood,* Delacorte, 1984.
Jakkin wants only to possess and train his own red dragon—until his love for Akki leads him into the maze of Austarian politics. (Fiction)

_____, **and Greenberg, Martin H., eds.** *Vampires: A Collection of Original Stories,* HarperCollins, 1992.
Meet the vampire of your dreams—in the mall, in a neighbor's garden, or haunting the streets at night. (Fiction)

Young, Al. *Snakes,* Holt, 1970.
MC, a young, black ghetto musician, makes the stormy journey through adolescence with the help of his grandmother, a hit record, and his friends. (Fiction)

Young, Jean. *Woodstock Craftsman's Manual,* Praeger, 1972.
This how-to book covers everything from beads to batik. (Nonfiction)

_____. *Woodstock Craftsman's Manual 2,* Praeger, 1973.
In this second how-to volume, crafts such as needlepoint, appliqué, quilting, songwriting, and woodblock printing are covered along with how to make stained glass, bronze jewelry, sandals, and videotapes. (Nonfiction)

Zambreno, Mary Frances. *Plague of Sorcerers,* Harcourt/Jane Yolen, 1993.
A magic plague is infecting the wizards in the land. Only sixteen-year-old Jermyn can break the spell, with the help of an overprotective skunk. (Fiction)

Zassenhaus, Hiltgunt. *Walls: Resisting the Third Reich—One Woman's Story,* Beacon, 1974.
Refusing to be intimidated by the Nazi regime in Germany, Hiltgunt uses her knowledge of the Scandinavian language to help, at some risk to herself, the Scandinavian prisoners in Germany. (Nonfiction)

Zelazny, Roger. *Doorways in the Sand,* Harper, 1976.
Interstellar espionage with two zany alien agents, disguised as a wombat and a kangaroo, and an acrophobic earthman hero. (Fiction)

Zerman, Melvyn Bernard. *Taking on the Press: Constitutional Rights in Conflict,* Harper/Crowell, 1986.
The Black Panthers, Vietnam, and nuclear secrets are only some of the legal issues explained in Zerman's lively, entertaining book. (Nonfiction)

Zindel, Paul. *Begonia for Miss Applebaum,* Harper, 1990.
Henry and Zelda use a cash card to help their offbeat favorite teacher with her homeless friends. (Fiction)

_____. *Confessions of a Teenage Baboon,* Harper, 1977.
Sixteen-year-old Chris Boyd gains self-confidence and control over his life after a tragic encounter with a thirty-year-old misfit who befriends lonely teenagers. (Fiction)

_____. *Effects of Gamma Rays on Man-in-the-Moon Marigolds,* Harper, 1971. ▲ ◆
An alcoholic mother stifles the lives of her two teenage daughters—one who is bordering on madness and the other who is a sensitive, loving creature. (Nonfiction)

_____. *Pardon Me, You're Stepping on My Eyeball!,* Harper, 1976.
Marsh Mellow, an offbeat teenager with an alcoholic mother and a missing father, begins to accept himself when Edna, a new acquaintance, decides to shed her aloofness and help him. (Fiction)

_____. *Pigman and Me,* HarperCollins/ Charlotte Zolotow, 1993.
Zindel recounts his bizarre adventures growing up when his neighbor's father becomes his personal "pigman" and teaches him to cope with his rootless family. (Nonfiction)

_____. *Pigman's Legacy*, Harper, 1980.
John and Lorraine befriend an old man who is
hiding from the IRS in the Pigman's house, and
through the hilarious and poignant experiences
they share with him they discover the legacy of
love that the Pigman left. (Fiction)

Zolotow, Charlotte, ed. *Early Sorrow: Ten
Stories of Youth*, Harper, 1986.
Themes range from the end of a special relationship to the loss of a special item, from the
death of a loved one to a loss of self, in these
stories about the first sorrows of youth.
(Fiction)

■ Selected for "Still Alive: The Best of the Best, 1960–1974"
▲ Selected for "The Best of the Best Books, 1970–1983"
♦ Selected for "Nothin' But the Best: Best of the Best Books for Young Adults, 1966–1986"

BEST BOOKS FOR YOUNG ADULTS

The Books by Year

1966 SELECTIONS

Abel, Elie   *Missile Crisis*
Asimov, Isaac   *Fantastic Voyage*
Bach, Richard   *Biplane*
Barker, S. Omar   *Little World Apart*
Boyd, Malcolm   *Are You Running With Me, Jesus?*
Brooks, Earle, and Brooks, Rhoda   *Barrios of Manta*
Capps, Benjamin   *Woman of the People*
Clifford, Francis   *Naked Runner*
Dufresne, Frank   *My Way Was North*
Durrell, Gerald   *Two in the Bush*
Friel, Brian   *Philadelphia, Here I Come!*
Fuller, John G.   *Incident at Exeter*
Gallery, Daniel   *Stand by-y-y to Start Engines*
Gilman, Dorothy   *Unexpected Mrs. Pollifax*
Hallet, Jean-Pierre   *Congo Kitabu*
Hollinger, Carol   *Mai Pen Rai Means Never Mind*
Lindall, Edward   *Northward the Coast*
MacLean, Alistair   *When Eight Bells Toll*
Manry, Robert   *Tinkerbelle*
Nader, Ralph   *Unsafe at any Speed*
Parks, Gordon   *Choice of Weapons*
Plimpton, George   *Paper Lion*

Russell, Bill, and McSweeney, William   *Go Up for Glory*
Ryan, Cornelius   *Last Battle*
Sherman, D.R.   *Brothers of the Sea*
Walker, Margaret   *Jubilee*
Williams, Martin   *Where's the Melody?*

1967 SELECTIONS

Amosov, Nikolai   *Open Heart*
Armstrong, Charlotte   *Gift Shop*
Bagley, Desmond   *Landslide*
Ball, John Dudley   *Cool Cottontail*
Cole, Ernest, and Flaherty, Thomas   *House of Bondage*
Conot, Robert   *Rivers of Blood, Years of Darkness*
Hardy, William Marion   *U.S.S. Mudskipper: The Submarine That Wrecked a Train*
Hartog, Jan De   *Captain*
Head, Ann   *Mr. and Mrs. Bo Jo Jones*
Inouye, Daniel Ken, and Elliot, Lawrence   *Journey to Washington*
Kuznetsov, Anatolli Petrovich   *Babi Yar*
Levitt, Leonard   *African Season*
Lord, Walter   *Incredible Victory*
Maas, Peter   *Rescuer*
Mather, Melissa   *One Summer in Between*

Olsen, Jack   *Black is Best: The Riddle of Cassius Clay*

Peters, Ellis   *Black is the Colour of My True-Love's Heart*

Potok, Chaim   *Chosen*

Ridgway, John M., and Blyth, Chay   *Fighting Chance*

Rosten, Leo   *Most Private Intrigue*

Schaap, Richard   *Turned On: The Friede-Crenshaw Case*

Sheehan, Susan   *Ten Vietnamese*

Simak, Clifford D.   *Werewolf Principle*

Styron, William   *Confessions of Nat Turner*

Szulc, Tad   *Bombs of Palomares*

Thompson, Jean   *House of Tomorrow*

Walsh, John, and Gannon, Robert   *Time Is Short and the Water Rises*

Wiesenthal, Simon   *Murderers Among Us*

1968 SELECTIONS

Bagley, Desmond   *Vivero Letter*

Bradford, Richard   *Red Sky at Morning*

Braithwaite, Edward   *Paid Servant*

Cleaver, Eldridge   *Soul on Ice*

Collins, Larry, and Lapierre, Dominique   *Or I'll Dress You in Mourning*

Courlander, Harold   *African, a Novel*

David, Jay, ed.   *Growing Up Black*

Davies, Hunter   *Beatles: The Authorized Biography*

Durrell, Gerald   *Rosy Is My Relative*

Kellogg, Majorie   *Tell Me That You Love Me, Junie Moon*

Kramer, Jerry   *Instant Replay; the Green Bay Diary of [the author]*

Kuper, Jack   *Child of the Holocaust*

Leslie, Robert   *Bears and I: Raising Three Cubs in the North Woods*

Lynd, Alice   *We Won't Go*

MacInnes, Helen   *Salzburg Connection*

Parks, David   *G.I. Diary*

Portis, Charles   *True Grit: A Novel*

Sanderson, Ivan   *Uninvited Visitors: A Biologist Looks at UFO's*

Schulz, Charles   *Peanuts Treasury*

Taylor, Gordon   *Biological Time Bomb*

Teague, Robert   *Letters to a Black Boy*

Watson, James   *Double Helix: A Personal Account of the Discovery of the Structure of DNA*

Whitney, Phyllis   *Hunter's Green*

1969 SELECTIONS

Ball, John Dudley   *Johnny Get Your Gun*

Bradbury, Ray   *I Sing the Body Electric!*

Brown, Turner, Jr.   *Black Is*

Cohn, Nik   *Rock from the Beginning*

Crichton, Michael   *Andromeda Strain*

Decker, Sunny   *Empty Spoon*

Durrell, Gerald   *Birds, Beasts, and Relatives*

Ferris, Louanne   *I'm Done Crying*

Gaines, William, and Feldstein, Albert, eds.   *Ridiculously Expensive MAD*

Granatelli, Anthony   *They Call Me Mister 500*

Hay, Jacob, and Keshishian, John M.   *Autopsy for a Cosmonaut*

King, Coretta Scott   *My Life with Martin Luther King, Jr.*

Kunen, James Simon   *Strawberry Statement: Notes of a College Revolutionary*

Lester, Julius   *Search for the New Land*

Lowenfels, Walter, ed.   *Writing on the Wall: 108 American Poems of Protest*

Michaels, Barbara   *Ammie, Come Home*

Moody, Anne   *Coming of Age in Mississippi: An Autobiography*

Olsen, Jack   *Night of the Grizzlies*

Potok, Chaim   *Promise*

Stewart, Fred   *Mephisto Waltz*

Wibberley, Leonard   *Mouse on Wall Street*

Williams, Ted, and Underwood, John   *My Turn at Bat: The Story of My Life*

1970 SELECTIONS

Angelou, Maya   *I Know Why the Caged Bird Sings*

Birmingham, John   *Our Time Is Now: Notes from the High School Underground*

Blum, Ralph   *Simultaneous Man*

Bouton, Jim   *Ball Four: My Life and Hard Times Throwing the Knuckleball in the Big Leagues*

Brenner, Joseph H., Coles, Robert, M.D., and others   *Drugs and Youth: Medical, Psychiatric and Legal Facts*

Chisholm, Shirley   *Unbought and Unbossed*

Cousteau, Jacques-Yves, and Cousteau, Philippe   *Shark: Splendid Savage of the Sea*

Dorman, Michael   *Under 21: A Young People's Guide to Legal Rights*

Dowdey, Landon, comp.   *Journey to Freedom: A Casebook with Music*

Dribben, Judith   *Girl Called Judith Strick*

Eisen, Jonathan, ed.   *Altamont: Death of Innocence in the Woodstock Nation*

Fall, Thomas   *Ordeal of Running Standing*

Finney, Jack   *Time and Again*

Gaylin, Willard, M.D.   *In the Service of Their Country: War Resisters in Prison*

Goro, Herb   *Block*

Greenberg, Joanne   *In This Sign*

Gregory, Susan   *Hey, White Girl!*

Hammer, Richard   *One Morning in the War: The Tragedy at Son My*

Hedgepeth, William, and Stock, Dennis
Alternative: Communal Life in New
America
Hillerman, Tony   Blessing Way
Hough, John   Peck of Salt: A Year in the
Ghetto
Howard, Jane   Please Touch: A Guided Tour
of the Human Potential Movement
Jordan, June, ed.   Soulscript: Afro-American
Poetry
Kavaler, Lucy   Freezing Point: Cold as a
Matter of Life and Death
Kim, Richard   Lost Names: Scenes from a
Korean Boyhood
Meriwether, Louise   Daddy Was A Number
Runner
O'Leary, Brian   Making of an Ex-Astronaut
Segal, Erich   Love Story
Shaw, Arnold   World of Soul: Black
America's Contribution to the Pop Music
Scene
Stewart, Mary   Crystal Cave
Swarthout, Glendon   Bless the Beasts and
Children
Tyler, Anne   Slipping-Down Life
Wersba, Barbara   Run Softly, Go Fast
Young, Al   Snakes

1971 SELECTIONS

Anonymous   Go Ask Alice
Balducci, Carolyn   Is There a Life after
Graduation, Henry Birnbaum?
Barjavel, Rene   Ice People
Brand, Stewart   Last Whole Earth Catalog
Brown, Dee   Bury My Heart at Wounded
Knee: An Indian History of the American
West
Campbell, Hope   No More Trains to
Tottenville
Cousteau, Jacques-Yves, and Diole, Philippe
Life and Death in a Coral Sea
Gaines, Ernest J.   Autobiography of Miss Jane
Pittman
Goulart, Ron   What's Become of Screwloose?
and Other Inquiries
Guffy, Ossie, and Ledner, Caryl   Ossie: The
Autobiography of a Black Woman
Henderson, Zenna   Holding Wonder
Heyerdahl, Thor   Ra Expeditions
Hinton, S. E.   That Was Then, This Is Now
Houriet, Robert   Getting Back Together
Houston, James   White Dawn
Jordan, June   His Own Where
LaVallee, David   Event 1000
Lawick-Goodall, Jane Van   In the Shadow of
Man
Lydon, Michael   Rock Folk: Portraits from
the Rock 'n Roll Pantheon
Michaels, Barbara   Dark on the Other Side

Moore, Gilbert   Special Rage
Nolen, William   Making of a Surgeon
Parks, Gordon   Born Black
Pierce, Ruth   Single and Pregnant
Plath, Sylvia   Bell Jar
Postman, Neil, and Weingartner, Charles
Soft Revolution: A Student Handbook for
Turning Schools Around
Powers, Thomas   Diana: The Making of a
Terrorist
Renvoize, Jean   Wild Thing
Sorrentino, Joseph   Up from Never
Stevenson, Florence   Curse of the Concullens
Townsend, John   Good Night, Prof. Dear
Whipple, Dorothy   Is the Grass Greener?:
Answers to Questions about Drugs
Zindel, Paul   Effects of Gamma Rays on
Man-in-the-Moon Marigolds

1972 SELECTIONS

Allen, Terry, ed.   Whispering Wind; Poetry
by Young American Indians
Blue, Vida, and Libby, Bill   Vida: His Own
Story
Blum, Ralph   Old Glory and the Real-Time
Freaks
Carlson, Dale   Mountain of Truth
Conrat, Maisie, and Conrat, Richard
Executive Order 9066: The Internment of
110,000 Japanese Americans
Crichton, Michael   Terminal Man
Del Rey, Lester   Pstalemate
Durham, Marilyn   Man Who Loved Cat
Dancing
Elfman, Blossom   Girls of Huntington House
Fair, Ronald   We Can't Breathe
Fast, Howard   Hessian
Friedman, Philip   Rage
Giovanni, Nikki   Gemini
Graham, Robin Lee, and Gill, Derek L.T.
Dove
Hall, Lynn   Sticks and Stones
Herbert, Frank   Soul Catcher
Holland, Isabelle   Man Without a Face
Krents, Harold   To Race the Wind: An
Autobiography
Lee, Mildred   Fog
Mathis, Sharon Bell   Teacup Full of Roses
O'Brien, Robert C.   Report from Group 17
Potok, Chaim   My Name is Asher Lev
Scaduto, Anthony   Bob Dylan
Schiff, Ken   Passing Go
Sheehan, Carolyn, and Sheehan, Edmund
Magnifi-Cat
Smith, Dennis   Report from Engine Co. 82
Teitz, Joyce   What's A Nice Girl Like You
Doing in a Place Like This?
Wallace, Duncan R.   Mountebank
White, Robb   Deathwatch

Wolf, David   *Foul! The Connie Hawkins Story*

Young, Jean   *Woodstock Craftsman's Manual*

1973 SELECTIONS

Aldridge, James   *Sporting Proposition*

Bickham, Jack M.   *Katie, Kelly and Heck*

Carlson, Dale   *Girls Are Equal Too: The Women's Movement for Teenagers*

Carrighar, Sally   *Home to the Wilderness*

Castaneda, Carlos   *Journey to Ixtlan: The Lessons of Don Juan*

Childress, Alice   *Hero Ain't Nothin' but a Sandwich*

Clarke, Arthur C.   *Rendezvous with Rama*

Cooper, Henry S. F., Jr.   *Thirteen: The Flight That Failed*

Freemantle, Brian   *Good-bye to an Old Friend*

Friedman, Myra   *Buried Alive: The Biography of Janis Joplin*

Giovanni, Nikki   *My House: Poems*

Glasser, Ronald J.   *Ward 402*

Gray, Martin, and Gallo, Max   *For Those I Loved*

Greenburger, Ingrid   *Private Treason: A German Memoir*

Guy, Rosa   *Friends*

Habenstreit, Barbara   *"To My Brother Who Did a Crime. . .": Former Prisoners Tell Their Stories in Their Own Words*

Harris, Marilyn   *Hatter Fox*

Hillerman, Tony   *Dance Hall of the Dead*

Huffaker, Clair   *Cowboy and the Cossack*

James, P. D.   *Unsuitable Job for a Woman*

Lawson, Donna   *Mother Nature's Beauty Cupboard: How to Make Beautiful, Money-Saving Natural Cosmetics and Other Beauty Preparations*

Lieberman, James E., and Peck, Ellen   *Sex & Birth Control: A Guide for the Young*

Logan, Jane   *Very Nearest Room*

Maas, Peter   *Serpico*

Maynard, Joyce   *Looking Back: A Chronicle of Growing Up Old in the Sixties*

Michaels, Barbara   *Witch*

O'Brien, Tim   *If I Die In a Combat Zone, Box Me Up and Ship Me Home*

Peck, Robert Newton   *Day No Pigs Would Die*

Robertson, Dougal   *Survive the Savage Sea*

Schwarz-Bart, Andre   *Woman Named Solitude*

Stewart, Mary   *Hollow Hills*

Wagenheim, Kal   *Clemente!*

Windsor, Patricia   *Summer Before*

Young, Jean   *Woodstock Craftsman's Manual 2*

1974 SELECTIONS

Adams, Richard   *Watership Down*

Angelou, Maya   *Gather Together in My Name*

Baldwin, James   *If Beale Street Could Talk*

Benchley, Nathaniel   *Bright Candles: A Novel of the Danish Resistance*

Blum, Ralph, and Blum, Judy   *Beyond Earth: Man's Contact with UFO's*

Cherry, Mike   *On High Steel: The Education of an Ironworker*

Cormier, Robert   *Chocolate War: A Novel*

Craven, Margaret   *I Heard the Owl Call My Name*

Demas, Vida   *First Person, Singular*

Fields, Jeff   *Cry of Angels*

Frazier, Walt, and Berkow, Ira   *Rockin' Steady: A Guide to Basketball & Cool*

Greenfield, Josh, and Mazursky, Paul   *Harry & Tonto*

Hamilton, Virginia   *M. C. Higgins, the Great*

Herriot, James   *All Things Bright and Beautiful*

Herzog, Arthur   *Swarm*

Holman, Felice   *Slake's Limbo*

Jacopetti, Alexandra   *Native Funk and Flash: An Emerging Folk Art*

Jacot, Michael   *Last Butterfly*

Johnston, Jennifer   *How Many Miles to Babylon? A Novel*

Le Guin, Ursula K.   *Dispossessed*

Levit, Rose   *Ellen: A Short Life Long Remembered*

MacCracken, Mary   *Circle of Children*

Mathis, Sharon Bell   *Listen for the Fig Tree*

Niven, Larry, and Jerry, Pournelle   *Mote in God's Eye*

Page, Thomas   *Hephaestus Plague*

Read, Piers Paul   *Alive: The Story of the Andes Survivors*

Rose, Louise Blecher   *Launching of Barbara Fabrikant*

Samuels, Gertrude   *Run, Shelly, Run!*

Scoppettone, Sandra   *Trying Hard to Hear You*

Sleator, William   *House of Stairs*

Slesar, Henry   *Thing at the Door*

Tidyman, Ernest   *Dummy*

Wagoner, David   *Road to Many a Wonder*

Wells, Evelyn   *I Am Thinking of Kelda*

Zassenhaus, Hiltgunt   *Walls: Resisting the Third Reich—One Woman's Story*

1975 SELECTIONS

Ali, Muhammad, and Durham, Richard   *Greatest: My Own Story*

Beck, Calvin   *Heroes of the Horrors*

Bell, David, M.D.   *Time to Be Born*

Bleier, Rocky, and O'Neill, Terry *Fighting Back*

Cavagnaro, David, and Cavagnaro, Maggie *Almost Home: A Life-style*

Coleman, Lonnie *Orphan Jim*

Davis, Mildred *Tell Them What's Her Name Called*

Dixon, Paige *May I Cross Your Golden River?*

Ellison, Harlan *Deathbird Stories: A Pantheon of Modern Gods*

Ferazani, Larry *Rescue Squad*

Gilman, Dorothy *Clairvoyant Countess*

Giovanni, Nikki *Women and the Men*

Higgins, Jack *Eagle Has Landed*

Hinton, S. E. *Rumblefish*

Holland, Isabelle *Of Love and Death and Other Journeys*

Horan, James David *New Vigilantes*

Hotchner, A. E. *Looking for Miracles: A Memoir about Loving*

Hunter, Kristin *Survivors*

Kerr, M. E. *Is That You, Miss Blue?*

Lockley, Ronald *Seal Woman*

Lund, Doris Herold *Eric*

MacLaine, Shirley *You Can Get There from Here*

MacLean, Alistair *Circus*

Montandon, Pat *Intruders*

O'Brien, Robert C. *Z for Zachariah*

Peck, Richard *Representing Super Doll*

Platt, Kin *Headman*

Powers, John R. *Do Black Patent Leather Shoes Really Reflect Up?*

Roueche, Berton *Feral*

Ryden, Hope *God's Dog*

Sargent, Pamela *Women of Wonder: Science Fiction Stories by Women about Women*

Scortia, Thomas N., and Robinson, Frank G. *Prometheus Crisis*

Sherman, D. R. *Lion's Paw*

Simak, Clifford D. *Enchanted Pilgrimage*

Smith, W. Eugene, and Smith, Aileen Mioko *Minamata*

Sullivan, Tom, and Gill, Derek L. T. *If You Could See What I Hear*

Switzer, Ellen *How Democracy Failed*

Trudeau, G. B. *Doonesbury Chronicles*

Vonnegut, Mark *Eden Express*

Wersba, Barbara *Country of the Heart*

West, Jessamyn *Massacre at Fall Creek*

Wood, Bari *Killing Gift: A Novel*

1976 SELECTIONS

Angelou, Maya *Swingin' & Singin' & Gettin' Merry Like Christmas*

Archer, Jeffrey *Not a Penny More, Not a Penny Less*

Boston Women's Health Book Collective *Our Bodies, Ourselves: A Book by and for Women*

Bova, Ben *Multiple Man: A Novel of Suspense*

Bradley, William Warren *Life on the Run*

Bridgers, Sue Ellen *Home Before Dark*

Claire, Keith *Otherwise Girl*

Clarke, Arthur C. *Imperial Earth*

Conford, Ellen *Alfred G. Graebner Memorial High School Handbook of Rules and Regulations: A Novel*

Derby, Pat, and Beagle, Peter *Lady and Her Tiger*

Eagan, Andrea Boroff *Why Am I So Miserable if These Are the Best Years of My Life? A Survival Guide For the Young Woman*

Fuller, John G. *Ghost of Flight 401*

Gordon, Sol, and Conant, Roger *You! The Teenage Survival Book*

Guest, Judith *Ordinary People*

Guy, Rosa *Ruby*

Haley, Alex *Roots*

Hobbs, Anne, and Specht, Robert *Tisha: The Story of a Young Teacher in the Alaskan Wilderness*

Konecky, Edith *Allegra Maud Goldman*

Konigsburg, E. L. *Father's Arcane Daughter*

Kovic, Ron *Born on the Fourth of July*

Le Guin, Ursula K. *Very Far Away from Anywhere Else*

Levin, Ira *Boys From Brazil*

Lueders, Edward, and St. John, Primus, comps. *Zero Makes Me Hungry: A Collection of Poems For Today*

MacCracken, Mary *Lovey: A Very Special Child*

Margolies, Marjorie, and Gruber, Ruth *They Came to Stay*

Mazer, Norma Fox *Dear Bill, Remember Me?*

Meltzer, Milton *Never to Forget: The Jews of the Holocaust*

Mojtabai, A. G. *400 Eels of Sigmund Freud*

Moody, Raymond A., Jr. *Life After Life: Investigation of a Phenomenon, Survival of Bodily Health*

Patterson, Sarah *Distant Summer*

Peck, Richard *Are You in the House Alone?*

Pohl, Frederik *Man Plus*

Samson, Joan *Auctioneer*

Schulke, Flip *Martin Luther King, Jr.: A Documentary . . . Montgomery to Memphis*

Walsh, M. M. B. *Four-colored Hoop*

Wersba, Barbara *Tunes for a Small Harmonica*

Wilhelm, Kate *Where Late the Sweet Birds Sang*

Zelazny, Roger *Doorways in the Sand*

Zindel, Paul   *Pardon Me, You're Stepping on My Eyeball!*

1977 SELECTIONS

Rolling Stone Illustrated History of Rock and Roll

Anson, Jay   *Amityville Horror*

Atwood, Ann   *Haiku-Vision: In Poetry and Photography*

Banks, Lynne Reid   *Dark Quartet: The Story of the Brontes*

Begley, Kathleen   *Deadline*

Brancato, Robin   *Winning*

Bredes, Don   *Hard Feelings*

Brooks, Terry   *Sword of Shannara*

Cook, Robin   *Coma*

Cormier, Robert   *I Am the Cheese*

Dolan, Edward F.   *How To Leave Home—and Make Everybody Like It*

Elfman, Blossom   *House for Jonnie O.*

Garani, Gary, and Schulman, Paul   *Fantastic Television*

Garfield, Brian   *Recoil*

Gedge, Pauline   *Child of the Morning*

Hall, Elizabeth   *Possible Impossibilities: A Look at Parapsychology*

Hayes, Billy, and Hoffer, William   *Midnight Express*

Heyman, Anita   *Exit from Home*

Highwater, Jamake   *Anpao: An American Indian Odyssey*

Horwitz, Elinor   *Madness, Magic, and Medicine: The Treatment and Mistreatment of the Mentally Ill*

Houston, James   *Ghost Fox*

Huygen, Wil, and Poortvliet, Rien   *Gnomes*

Jenner, Bruce, and Finch, Philip   *Decathlon Challenge: Bruce Jenner's Story*

Koehn, Ilse   *Mischling, Second Degree: My Childhood in Nazi Germany*

Kopay, David, and Young, Perry   *David Kopay Story: An Extraordinary Self-Revelation*

Larrick, Nancy, ed.   *Crazy to Be Alive in Such a Strange World: Poems About People*

Lipsyte, Robert   *One Fat Summer*

Mazer, Harry, and Mazer, Norma Fox   *Solid Gold Kid*

McCaffrey, Anne   *Dragonsinger*

McCartney, Linda   *Linda's Pictures: A Collection of Photographs*

McConnell, Joan   *Ballet as Body Language*

Mohr, Nicholasa   *In Nueva York*

Peck, Richard   *Ghosts I Have Been*

"Pele," Edson A. do Nascimento, and Fish, Robert   *My Life and the Beautiful Game: The Autobiography of Pele*

Petty, Richard   *King of the Road*

Powers, John R.   *Unoriginal Sinner and the Ice-Cream God*

Rather, Dan, and Herskowitz, Mickey   *Camera Never Blinks: Adventures of a TV Journalist*

Robinson, Spider   *Callahan's Crosstime Saloon*

Rothenberg, Mira   *Children with Emerald Eyes: Histories of Extraordinary Boys and Girls*

Ruby, Lois   *Arriving at a Place You've Never Left*

Schwarzenegger, Arnold, and Hall, Douglas Kent   *Arnold: The Education of a Bodybuilder*

Sharpe, Roger C.   *Pinball!*

Sussman, Alan N.   *Rights of Young People: The Basic ACLU Guide to a Young Person's Rights*

Taylor, David   *Zoo Vet: Adventures of a Wild Animal Doctor*

Telander, Rick   *Heaven Is a Playground*

Trevor, Elleston   *Theta Syndrome*

Uhlman, Fred   *Reunion*

Wilkinson, Brenda   *Ludell and Willie*

Zindel, Paul   *Confessions of a Teenage Baboon*

1978 SELECTIONS

Adoff, Arnold, ed.   *Celebrations: A New Anthology of Black American Poetry*

Arrick, Fran   *Steffie Can't Come Out to Play*

Ash, Brian, ed.   *Visual Encyclopedia of Science Fiction*

Blankfort, Michael   *Take the A Train*

Burnford, Sheila   *Bel Ria*

Campbell, Wright R.   *Where Pigeons Go to Die*

Curtis, Edward S.   *Girl Who Married a Ghost, and Other Tales from the North American Indian*

De Larrabeiti, Michael   *Borribles*

Duncan, Lois   *Killing Mr. Griffin*

Elder, Lauren, and Streshinsky, Shirley   *And I Alone Survived*

Francke, Linda Bird   *Ambivalence of Abortion*

Fuller, John G.   *Poison That Fell from the Sky*

Glass, Frankcina   *Marvin & Tige*

Guy, Rosa   *Edith Jackson*

Hamilton, Eleanor   *Sex with Love: A Guide for Young People*

Hautzig, Deborah   *Hey, Dollface*

Hayes, Kent, and Lazzarino, Alex   *Broken Promise*

Holliday, Laurel, ed.   *Heart Songs: The Intimate Diaries of Young Girls*

Ives, John   *Fear in a Handful of Dust*

Jones, Adrienne   *Hawks of Chelney*

Kelly, Gary F.   *Learning about Sex: The Contemporary Guide for Young Adults*

Kerr, M. E.   *Gentlehands*

King, Stephen   *Night Shift*

Leekley, Sheryle, and Leekley, John   *Moments: The Pulitzer Prize Photographs*

LeFlore, Ron, and Hawkins, Jim   *Breakout: From Prison to the Big Leagues*

Leitner, Isabella   *Fragments of Isabella: A Memoir of Auschwitz*

Levenkron, Steven   *Best Little Girl in the World*

London, Mel   *Getting into Film*

Mazer, Harry   *War on Villa Street: A Novel*

McFarlane, Milton C.   *Cudjoe of Jamaica: Pioneer for Black Freedom in the New World*

McIntyre, Vonda N.   *Dreamsnake*

McKinley, Robin   *Beauty: A Retelling of the Story of Beauty and the Beast*

Messing, Shep, and Hirshey, David   *Education of an American Soccer Player*

Meyer, Carolyn   *C. C. Poindexter*

Nabokov, Peter   *Native American Testimony: An Anthology of Indian and White Relations/First Encounter to Dispossession*

Peck, Richard   *Father Figure: A Novel*

Ryan, Cheli Duran, ed.   *Yellow Canary Whose Eye Is So Black*

Saleh, Dennis   *Rock Art: The Golden Age of Record Album Covers*

Scoppettone, Sandra   *Happy Endings Are All Alike*

Smith, Martin Cruz   *Nightwing*

Szabo, Joseph   *Almost Grown*

Trudeau, G. B.   *Doonesbury's Greatest Hits*

Westall, Robert   *Wind Eye*

Wetherby, Terry, ed.   *Conversations: Working Women Talk about Doing a "Man's Job"*

1979 SELECTIONS

Anderson, Wayne   *Flight of Dragons*

Bachman, Richard   *Long Walk*

Bridgers, Sue Ellen   *All Together Now: A Novel*

Comfort, Alex, and Comfort, Jane   *Facts of Love: Living, Loving and Growing Up*

Cormier, Robert   *After the First Death*

Craig, John   *Chappie and Me: An Autobiographical Novel*

Culin, Charlotte   *Cages of Glass, Flowers of Time*

Davis, Terry   *Vision Quest*

Dickinson, Peter   *Tulku*

Forman, James D.   *Ballad for Hogskin Hill*

Girion, Barbara   *Tangle of Roots*

Guy, Rosa   *Disappearance: A Novel*

Hanckel, Frances, and Cunningham, John   *Way of Love, A Way of Life: A Young Person's Introduction to What it Means to Be Gay*

Hartman, David, and Asbell, Bernard   *White Coat, White Cane*

Helms, Tom   *Against All Odds*

Hinton, S. E.   *Tex*

Ipswitch, Elaine   *Scott Was Here*

Jenkins, Peter   *Walk Across America*

Kaplan, Helen Singer   *Making Sense of Sex: The New Facts about Sex & Love for Young People*

Keane, John   *Sherlock Bones: Tracer of Missing Pets*

Leffland, Ella   *Rumors of Peace*

LeRoy, Gen   *Cold Feet*

Macaulay, David   *Motel of the Mysteries*

Marsh, Dave   *Born to Run: The Bruce Springsteen Story*

Mazer, Harry   *Last Mission*

Mazer, Norma Fox   *Up in Seth's Room*

McCoy, Kathy, and Wibbelsman, Charles   *Teenage Body Book*

Meyer, Carolyn   *Center: From a Troubled Past to a New Life*

Myers, Walter Dean   *Young Landlords*

Nicol, Clive W.   *White Shaman*

Pascal, Francine   *My First Love & Other Disasters*

Peyton, K. M.   *Prove Yourself a Hero*

Reed, Kit   *Ballad of T. Rantula*

Sandler, Martin   *Story of American Photography: An Illustrated History for Young People*

Say, Allen   *Ink-Keeper's Apprentice*

Sebestyen, Ouida   *Words by Heart*

Seed, Suzanne   *Fine Trades*

Southerland, Ellease   *Let the Lion Eat Straw*

Summers, Ian, ed.   *Tomorrow and Beyond: Masterpieces of Science Fiction Art*

Thompson, Estelle   *Hunter in the Dark*

Torchia, Joseph   *Kryptonite Kid*

Van Leeuwen, Jean   *Seems Like This Road Goes On Forever*

Vonnegut, Kurt   *Jailbird*

Westall, Robert   *Devil on the Road*

Wharton, William   *Birdy*

Winthrop, Elizabeth   *Knock, Knock, Who's There?*

1980 SELECTIONS

Adams, Douglas   *Hitchhiker's Guide to the Galaxy*

Auel, Jean   *Clan of the Cave Bear*

Bach, Alice   *Waiting for Johnny Miracle*

Barlow, Wayne Douglas, and Summers, Ian   *Barlow's Guide to Extraterrestrials*

Bode, Janet   *Kids Having Kids: The Unwed Teenage Parent*

Bogle, Donald   *Brown Sugar: Eighty Years of America's Black Female Superstars*

Boissard, Janice   *Matter of Feeling*

Bradshaw, Gillian   *Hawk of May*

Brancato, Robin F.   *Come Alive at 505*

Brown, Dee   *Creek Mary's Blood*

Brown, Michael   *Laying Waste: The Poisoning of America by Toxic Chemicals*

Butterworth, W. E.   *LeRoy and the Old Man*

Calvert, Patricia   *Snow Bird*

Cohen, Barbara   *Unicorns in the Rain*

Curtis, Patricia   *Animal Rights: The Stories of People Who Defend the Rights of Animals*

De Veaux, Alexis   *Don't Explain: A Song of Billie Holiday*

Due, Linnea A.   *High and Outside*

Garfield, Brian   *Paladin*

Hall, Lynn   *Leaving*

Haugaard, Erik Christian   *Chase Me, Catch Nobody!*

Hayden, Torey L.   *One Child*

Hogan, William   *Quartzsite Trip*

King, Stephen   *Firestarter*

Laure, Jason, and Laure, Ettagale   *South Africa: Coming of Age Under Apartheid*

Le Guin, Ursula K.   *Beginning Place*

Lee, Mildred   *People Therein*

MacLeish, Roderick   *First Book of Eppe: An American Romance*

Maiorano, Robert   *Worlds Apart: The Autobiography of a Dancer From Brooklyn*

Matthew, Christopher   *Long-Haired Boy*

Miller, Frances A.   *Truth Trap*

Oneal, Zibby   *Language of Goldfish*

Paterson, Katherine   *Jacob Have I Loved*

Pfeffer, Susan Beth   *About David*

Prince, Alison   *Turkey's Nest*

Prochnik, Leon   *Endings: Death, Glorious and Otherwise, as Faced by Ten Outstanding Figures of Our Time*

Sagan, Carl   *Cosmos*

Sallis, Susan   *Only Love*

Sebestyen, Ouida   *Far From Home*

Shreve, Susan   *Masquerade*

Silverberg, Robert   *Lord Valentine's Castle*

Spielman, Ed   *Mighty Atom: The Life and Times of Joseph L. Greenstein*

Terkel, Studs   *American Dreams: Lost and Found*

Thomas, Kurt, and Hannon, Kent   *Kurt Thomas and Gymnastics*

Webb, Sheyann, and Nelson, Rachel West   *Selma, Lord, Selma: Girlhood Memories of the Civil-Rights Days*

Wells, Rosemary   *When No One Was Looking*

Wolfe, Tom   *Right Stuff*

Zindel, Paul   *Pigman's Legacy*

1981 SELECTIONS

Alexander, Lloyd   *Westmark*

Bauer, Steven   *Satyrday: A Fable*

Bell, Ruth, ed.   *Changing Bodies, Changing Lives: A Book for Teens on Sex and Relationships*

Blume, Judy   *Tiger Eyes*

Booher, Dianna Daniels   *Rape: What Would You Do If . . .?*

Bridgers, Sue Ellen   *Notes for Another Life*

Bykov, Vasil   *Pack of Wolves*

Chester, Deborah   *Sign of the Owl*

Childress, Alice   *Rainbow Jordan*

Dolan, Edward F.   *Adolf Hitler: A Portrait in Tyranny*

Duncan, Lois   *Stranger with My Face*

Eckert, Allan   *Song of the Wild*

Grace, Fran   *Branigan's Dog*

Guy, David   *Football Dreams*

Hentoff, Nat   *Does This School Have Capital Punishment?*

Herring, Robert   *Hub*

Hoover, H. M.   *Another Heaven, Another Earth*

Hughes, Monica   *Keeper of the Isis Light*

Jacobs, Anita   *Where Has Deedie Wooster Been All These Years?*

Jaffe, Rona   *Mazes and Monsters*

Janeczko, Paul B., ed.   *Don't Forget to Fly*

Jones, Diana Wynne   *Homeward Bounders*

Kerr, M. E.   *Little Little*

Knowles, John   *Peace Breaks Out*

Koehn, Ilse   *Tilla*

Krementz, Jill   *How It Feels When A Parent Dies*

Kullman, Harry   *Battle Horse*

Lawson, Don   *United States in the Vietnam War*

Levoy, Myron   *Shadow Like a Leopard*

Mann, Peggy, and Hersh, Gizelle   *"Gizelle, Save the Children!"*

Marzollo, Jean   *Halfway Down Paddy Lane*

Mayhar, Ardath   *Soul Singer of Tyrnos*

Mazer, Harry   *I Love You, Stupid!*

Murphy, Barbara Beasley, and Wolkoff, Judie   *Ace Hits the Big Time*

Myers, Walter Dean   *Hoops*

———   *Legend of Tarik*

Namioka, Lensey   *Village of the Vampire Cat*

Peck, Richard   *Close Enough to Touch*

Peterson, P. J.   *Would You Settle For Improbable?*

Reader, Dennis J.   *Coming Back Alive*

Santoli, Al   *Everything We Had: An Oral History of Vietnam War as Told By 33 American Soldiers Who Fought It*

Senn, Steve   *Circle in the Sea*

Sheldon, Mary *Perhaps I'll Dream of Darkness*
Skurzynski, Gloria *Manwolf*
Snyder, Zilpha Keatley *Fabulous Creature*
Strasser, Todd *Friends Till the End*
Swanson, Walter S.J. *Deepwood*
Taylor, Mildred D. *Let the Circle Be Unbroken*
Wallin, Luke *Redneck Poacher's Son*
Yolen, Jane *Gift of Sarah Barker*

1982 SELECTIONS

Alexander, Lloyd *Kestrel*
Banks, Lynne Reid *Writing on the Wall*
Bradley, Marion Zimmer *Hawkmistress!*
Brancato, Robin F. *Sweet Bells Jangled Out of Tune*
Butterworth, Emma Macalik *As the Waltz Was Ending*
Clapp, Patricia *Witches' Children: A Story of Salem*
Cohen, Barbara, and Lovejoy, Bahija *Seven Daughters and Seven Sons*
Davis, Daniel S. *Behind Barbed Wire: Imprisonment of Japanese Americans During World War II*
Dragonwagon, Crescent, and Zindel, Paul *To Take a Dare*
Duncan, Lois *Chapters: My Growth as Writer*
Epstein, Sam, and Epstein, Beryl *Kids in Court: The ACLU Defends Their Rights*
Ford, Richard *Quest for the Faradawn*
Garden, Nancy *Annie on My Mind*
Girion, Barbara *Handful of Stars*
Glenn, Mel *Class Dismissed! High School Poems*
Goldston, Robert *Sinister Touches: The Secret War Against Hitler*
Hamilton, Virginia *Sweet Whispers, Brother Rush*
Hellman, Peter, and Meier, Lili *Auschwitz Album: A Book Based Upon an Album Discovered By Concentration Camp Survivor, Lili Meier*
Irwin, Hadley *What About Grandma?*
Kazimiroff, Theodore L. *Last Algonquin*
Lawrence, Louise *Calling B for Butterfly*
Lehrman, Robert *Juggling*
Lester, Julius *This Strange New Feeling*
Llywelyn, Morgan *Horse Goddess*
Lynn, Elizabeth A. *Sardonyx Net*
Magorian, Michelle *Good Night, Mr. Tom*
Magubane, Peter *Black Child*
McKinley, Robin *Blue Sword*
Murphy, Jim *Death Run*
Naylor, Phyllis Reynolds *String of Chances*
Oneal, Zibby *Formal Feeling*
Park, Ruth *Playing Beatie Bow*

Peterson, P. J. *Nobody Else Can Walk It For You*
Pierce, Meredith Ann *Darkangel*
Riley, Jocelyn *Only My Mouth Is Smiling*
Robeson, Susan *Whole World in His Hands: A Pictorial Biography of Paul Robeson*
Schell, Jonathan *Fate of Earth*
Searls, Hank *Sounding*
Sebestyen, Ouida *IOU's*
Simon, Nissa *Don't Worry, You're Normal: Teenager's Guide to Self Health*
Strasser, Todd *Rock 'n' Roll Nights*
Terry, Douglas *Last Texas Hero*
Thomas, Joyce Carol *Marked by Fire*
Vinge, Joan D. *Psion*
Voigt, Cynthia *Tell Me If the Lovers Are Losers*
Wersba, Barbara *Carnival in My Mind*
Wharton, William *Midnight Clear*
Yolen, Jane *Dragon's Blood*

1983 SELECTIONS

Adler, C. S. *Shell Lady's Daughter*
Arrick, Fran *God's Radar*
Asimov, Isaac, and Others, eds. *Creations: The Quest for Origins in Story and Science*
Bell, Clare *Ratha's Creature*
Boulle, Pierre *Whale of the Victoria Cross*
Briggs, Raymond *When the Wind Blows*
Chambers, Aidan *Dance on My Grave*
Cormier, Robert *Bumblebee Flies Anyway*
Crutcher, Chris *Running Loose*
Faber, Doris *Love and Rivalry: Three Exceptional Pairs of Sisters*
Ferry, Charles *Raspberry One*
Fretz, Sada *Going Vegetarian: A Guide for Teen-agers*
Gaan, Margaret *Little Sister*
Gaines, Ernest J. *Gathering of Old Men*
Geras, Adele *Voyage*
Golden, Frederic *Trembling Earth: Probing and Predicting Quakes*
Goldman, Peter, and Fuller, Tony *Charlie Company: What Vietnam Did to Us*
Gordon, Suzanne *Off Balance: The Real World of Ballet*
Greenberg, Joanne *Far Side of Victory*
Hamilton, Virginia *Magical Adventures of Pretty Pearl*
Hayden, Torey L. *Murphy's Boy*
Heidish, Marcy *Secret Annie Oakley*
Holman, Felice *Wild Children*
Hughes, Monica *Hunter in the Dark*
Janeczko, Paul B., ed. *Poetspeak: In Their Work, about Their Work*
Kerr, M. E. *Me Me Me Me Me: Not a Novel*
Korschunow, Irina *Night in Distant Motion*
Krementz, Jill *How It Feels to Be Adopted*

Lasky, Kathryn   *Beyond the Divide*
Lee, Tanith   *Red as Blood; or, Tales from the Sisters Grimmer*
Liang, Heng, and Shapiro, Judith   *Son of the Revolution*
Madaras, Lynda, and Madaras, Area   *What's Happening to My Body? A Growing Up Guide for Mothers and Daughters*
Mason, Robert C.   *Chickenhawk*
Mazer, Norma Fox   *Someone to Love*
McGuire, Paula   *It Won't Happen to Me: Teenagers Talk about Pregnancy*
Newton, Suzanne   *I Will Call It Georgie's Blues*
Nicholls, Peter   *Science in Science Fiction*
Page, Tim   *Nam*
Paulsen, Gary   *Dancing Carl*
Pollack, Dale   *Skywalking: The Life and Times of George Lucas*
Reese, Lyn   *I'm on My Way Running: Women Speak on Coming of Age*
Richards, Arlene Kramer, and Willis, Irene   *Under 18 and Pregnant: What to Do If You or Someone You Know Is*
Santiago, Danny   *Famous All over Town*
Sargent, Pamela   *Earthseed*
Severin, Tim   *Sinbad Voyage*
Singer, Marilyn   *Course of True Love Never Did Run Smooth*
Skurzynski, Gloria   *Tempering*
Slepian, Jan   *Night of the Bozos*
Smith, Robert Kimmel   *Jane's House*
Smith, Rukshana   *Sumitra's Story*
Speare, Elizabeth George   *Sign of the Beaver*
Steinem, Gloria   *Outrageous Acts and Everyday Rebellions*
Sutcliff, Rosemary   *Road to Camlann: The Death of King Arthur*
Tevis, Walter   *Queen's Gambit*
Thomas, Lewis   *Youngest Science: Notes of a Medicine Watcher*
Trull, Patti   *On with My Life*
Ure, Jean   *See You Thursday*
Van Devanter, Lynda, and Morgan, Christopher   *Home before Morning: The Story of an Army Nurse in Vietnam*
Voigt, Cynthia   *Solitary Blue*
Von Canon, Claudia   *Inheritance*
Wilcox, Fred A.   *Waiting for an Army to Die: The Tragedy of Agent Orange*
Willey, Margaret   *Bigger Book of Lydia*

1984 SELECTIONS

Abercrombie, Barbara   *Run for Your Life*
Alexander, Lloyd   *Beggar Queen*
Anthony, Piers   *On a Pale Horse*
Ashabranner, Brent   *To Live in Two Worlds: American Indian Youth Today*
Avi   *Fighting Ground*

Bond, Nancy   *Place to Come Back To*
Bunting, Eve   *If I Asked You, Would You Stay?*
Burch, Jennings Michael   *They Cage the Animals at Night*
Carter, Alden R.   *Growing Season*
Conover, Ted   *Rolling Nowhere*
Crichton, Michael   *Electronic Life: How to Think about Computers*
Dear, William   *Dungeon Master: The Disappearance of James Dallas Egbert III*
Durkin, Barbara Wernecke   *Oh, You Dundalk Girls, Can't You Dance the Polka?*
Durrell, Gerald, and Durrell, Lee   *Amateur Naturalist*
Fox, Paula   *One-Eyed Cat*
Gale, Jay   *Young Man's Guide to Sex*
Gallo, Donald R., ed.   *Sixteen: Short Stories by Outstanding Writers for Young Adults*
Godden, Rumer   *Thursday's Children*
Greenberg, Jan   *No Dragons to Slay*
Hall, Lynn   *Uphill All the Way*
Hamilton, Virginia   *Little Love*
Harris, Rosemary   *Zed*
Highwater, Jamake   *Legend Days*
Hirshey, Gerri   *Nowhere to Run: The Story of Soul Music*
Janeczko, Paul B., ed.   *Strings: A Gathering of Family Poems*
Jones, Diana Wynne   *Archer's Goon*
Kohner, Hanna   *Hanna and Walter: A Love Story*
Kurtis, Bill   *Bill Kurtis on Assignment*
Lasky, Kathryn   *Prank*
MacKinnon, Bernie   *Meantime*
Magorian, Michelle   *Back Home*
Mahy, Margaret   *Changeover: A Supernatural Romance*
Manchester, William   *One Brief Shining Moment: Remembering Kennedy*
Mazer, Norma Fox   *Downtown*
McCullough, Frances, ed.   *Love Is Like the Lion's Tooth: An Anthology of Love Poems*
Montalbano, William D., and Hiaasen, Carl   *Death in China*
Paton Walsh, Jill   *Parcel of Patterns*
Paulsen, Gary   *Tracker*
Sachs, Marilyn   *Fat Girl*
Schirer, Eric W., and Allman, William F.   *Newton at the Bat: The Science in Sports*
Simon, Neil   *Brighton Beach Memoirs*
Sleator, William   *Interstellar Pig*
Southhall, Ivan   *Long Night Watch*
Sterling, Dorothy, ed.   *We Are Your Sisters: Black Women in the Nineteenth Century*
Sweeney, Joyce   *Center Line*
Terkel, Studs   *"The Good War": An Oral History of World War Two*
Terry, Wallace   *Bloods: An Oral History of the Vietnam War by Black Veterans*

Thompson, Joyce   *Conscience Place*
Tiburzi, Bonnie   *Takeoff! The Story of America's First Woman Pilot for a Major Airline*
Wain, John   *Free Zone Starts Here*
Walker, Alice   *In Search of Our Mothers' Gardens: Womanist Prose*
Westall, Robert   *Futuretrack 5*
Yolen, Jane   *Heart's Blood*

1985 SELECTIONS

Angell, Judie   *One-way to Ansonia*
Ballard, J. G.   *Empire of the Sun*
Bridgers, Sue Ellen   *Sara Will*
Brin, David   *Postman*
Brooks, Bruce   *Moves Make the Man*
Burchard, Sue   *Statue of Liberty: Birth to Rebirth*
Burns, Olive Ann   *Cold Sassy Tree*
Card, Orson Scott   *Ender's Game*
Carter, Alden R.   *Wart, Son of Toad*
Conrad, Pamela   *Prairie Songs*
Couper, Heather, and Pelham, David   *Universe*
Cross, Gillian   *On the Edge*
Dahl, Roald   *Boy: Tales of Childhood*
Dickson, Margaret   *Maddy's Song*
Edelman, Bernard   *Dear America: Letters Home from Vietnam*
Edmonds, Walter D.   *South African Quirt*
Ferris, Timothy   *Spaceshots: The Beauty of Nature Beyond Earth*
Foster, Rory C.   *Dr. Wildlife: A Northwoods Veterinarian*
Gallagher, Hugh Gregory   *FDR's Splendid Deception*
Greenbaum, Dorothy, and Laiken, Deidre S.   *Lovestrong*
Halberstam, David   *Amateurs*
Hall, Lynn   *Just One Friend*
Hermes, Patricia   *Solitary Secret*
Highwater, Jamake   *Ceremony of Innocence*
Howker, Janni   *Badger on the Barge and Other Stories*
Irwin, Hadley   *Abby, My Love*
Janeczko, Paul B., ed.   *Pocket Poems: Selected for a Journey*
Jones, Douglas C.   *Gone the Dreams and Dancing*
Kerr, M. E.   *I Stay near You*
Kincaid, Jamaica   *Annie John*
Lawrence, Louise   *Children of the Dust*
Lisle, Janet Taylor   *Sirens and Spies*
Mason, Bobbie Ann   *In Country*
Matsubara, Hisako   *Cranes at Dusk*
McKinley, Robin   *Hero and the Crown*
Meltzer, Milton   *Ain't Gonna Study War No More*
Michaels, Barbara   *Be Buried in the Rain*

Miller, Jonathan, and Pelham, David   *Facts of Life*
Nomberg-Prztyk, Sara   *Auschwitz: True Tales From a Grotesque Land*
North, James   *Freedom Rising*
Oneal, Zibby   *In Summer Light*
Palmer, David R.   *Emergence*
Parnall, Peter   *Daywatchers*
Paulsen, Gary   *Dogsong*
Peck, Richard   *Remembering the Good Times*
Phipson, Joan   *Hit and Run*
Pierce, Meredith Ann   *Woman Who Loved Reindeer*
Rodowsky, Colby   *Julie's Daughter*
Ryerson, Eric   *When Your Parent Drinks Too Much: A Book for Teenagers*
Sleator, William   *Singularity*
Smith, Mary-Anne Tirone   *Book of Phoebe*
Stone, Bruce   *Half Nelson, Full Nelson*
Strieber, Whitley   *Wolf of Shadows*
Talbert, Marc   *Dead Birds Singing*
Voigt, Cynthia   *Runner*
Willard, Nancy   *Things Invisible to See*
Wyden, Peter   *Day One: Before Hiroshima and After*
Yeager, Chuck, and Janos, Leo   *Yeager: An Autobiography*

1986 SELECTIONS

Angelou, Maya   *All God's Children Need Traveling Shoes*
Appel, Allen   *Time After Time*
Archer, Jules   *Incredible Sixties: The Stormy Years That Changed America*
Arnosky, Jim   *Flies in the Water, Fish in the Air: A Personal Introduction to Fly Fishing*
Atwood, Margaret   *Handmaid's Tale*
Avi   *Wolf Rider*
Bess, Clayton   *Tracks*
Blume, Judy   *Letters to Judy: What Your Kids Wish They Could Tell You*
Bodanis, David   *Secret House: 24 Hours in the Strange and Unexpected World in Which We Spend Our Nights and Days*
Branscum, Robbie   *Girl*
Brooks, Bruce   *Midnight Hour Encores*
Brooks, Terry   *Magic Kingdom for Sale—Sold!*
Callahan, Steven   *Adrift: Seventy-Six Days Lost at Sea*
Calvert, Patricia   *Yesterday's Daughter*
Caras, Roger   *Mara Simba: The African Lion*
Card, Orson Scott   *Speaker for the Dead*
Cohen, Susan, and Cohen, Daniel   *Six-pack and a Fake I.D.*
Collier, James Lincoln   *When the Stars Begin to Fall*
Cooney, Caroline B.   *Don't Blame the Music*

Crutcher, Chris   Stotan!
Dahl, Roald   Going Solo
Dana, Barbara   Necessary Parties
Dann, Patty   Mermaids
Derby, Pat   Visiting Miss Pierce
Fante, John   1933 Was a Bad Year
Fine, Judylaine   Afraid to Ask: A Book for Families to Share About Cancer
Finnegan, William   Crossing the Line: A Year in the Land of Apartheid
Gingher, Marianne   Bobby Rex's Greatest Hit
Greenberg, Joanne   Simple Gifts
Greene, Constance C.   Love Letters of J. Timothy Owen
Grunwald, Lisa   Summer
Guy, David   Second Brother
Hall, Lynn   Solitary
Hambly, Barbara   Dragonsbane
Hill, Susan   Woman in Black
Hunter, Mollie   Cat, Herself
Jones, Diana Wynne   Howl's Moving Castle
Kerr, M. E.   Night Kites
Koertge, Ron   Where the Kissing Never Stops
Korman, Gordon A.   Son of Interflux
Lamb, Wendy, ed.   Meeting the Winter Bike Rider and Other Prize Winning Plays
Lasky, Kathryn   Pageant
LeVert, John   Flight of the Cassowary
Levoy, Myron   Pictures of Adam
Lopez, Barry   Arctic Dreams: Imagination and Desire in a Northern Landscape
Mahy, Margaret   Catalogue of the Universe
Mandela, Winnie   Part of My Soul Went With Him
Mazer, Harry   When the Phone Rang
Moll, Richard   Public Ivys: A Guide to America's Best Public Undergraduate Colleges and Universities
Naylor, Phyllis Reynolds   Keeper
Okimoto, Jean Davies   Jason's Women
Parini, Jay   Patch Boys
Patent, Dorothy Hinshaw   Quest for Artificial Intelligence
Pei, Lowry   Family Resemblances
Ramati, Alexander   And the Violins Stopped Playing: A Story of the Gypsy Holocaust
Rinaldi, Ann   Time Enough for Drums
Rostkowski, Margaret I.   After the Dancing Days
Rylant, Cynthia   Fine White Dust
Sanders, Scott R.   Bad Man Ballad
Spiegelman, Art   Maus: A Survivor's Tale
Sullivan, Jack, ed.   Penguin Encyclopedia of Horror and the Supernatural
Thompson, Julian   Band of Angels
Townsend, Sue   Adrian Mole Diaries
Voigt, Cynthia   Izzy, Willy-Nilly
Wilford, John Noble   Riddle of the Dinosaur
Willey, Margaret   Finding David Dolores

Wirths, Claudine G., and Bowman-Kruhm, Mary   I Hate School: How to Hang In & When to Drop Out
Zerman, Melvyn Bernard   Taking on the Press: Constitutional Rights in Conflict
Zolotow, Charlotte, ed.   Early Sorrow: Ten Stories of Youth

1987 SELECTIONS

Allen, Maury   Jackie Robinson: A Life Remembered
Anson, Robert Sam   Best Intentions: The Education and Killing of Edmund Perry
Bacon, Katherine Jay   Shadow and Light
Benedict, Helen   Safe, Strong, and Streetwise
Bosse, Malcolm   Captives of Time
Bradshaw, Gillian   Beacon At Alexandria
Bridgers, Sue Ellen   Permanent Connections
Bull, Emma   War For the Oaks
Card, Orson Scott   Seventh Son
Carter, Alden R.   Sheila's Dying
Carter, Peter   Bury the Dead
Cole, Brock   Goats
Collins, Max Allan   Dark City
Conrad, Pamela   What I Did For Roman
Cross, Gillian   Chartbreaker
Crutcher, Chris   Crazy Horse Electric Game
Cullen, Brian   What Niall Saw
Davis, Jenny   Good-bye and Keep Cold
Dolmetsch, Paul, and Mauricette, Gail, eds.   Teens Talk About Alcohol and Alcoholism
Dorris, Michael   Yellow Raft in Blue Water
Einstein, Charles, ed.   Fireside Book of Baseball 4th ed.
Feinstein, John   Season on the Brink: A Year With Bob Knight and the Indiana Hoosiers
Ferris, Jean   Invincible Summer
Fink, Ida   Scrap of Time: And Other Stories
Freedman, Russell   Indian Chiefs
Gallo, Donald R., ed.   Visions: Nineteen Short Stories by Outstanding Writers for Young Adults
Gibbons, Sheila   Ellen Foster
Gies, Miep, and Gold, Alison Leslie   Anne Frank Remembered: The Story of Miep Gies, Who Helped to Hide the Frank Family
Gordon, Ruth, ed.   Under All Silences: Shades of Love: An Anthology of Poems
Gordon, Sheila   Waiting for the Rain
Hamlin, Liz   I Remember Valentine
Haskins, James   Black Music in America: A History Through Its People
Hearne, Betsy   Love Lines: Poetry in Person
Hentoff, Nat   American Heroes: In and Out Of School
Howker, Janni   Isaac Campion
Jacques, Brian   Redwall

Janeczko, Paul B., ed.   *Going Over to Your Place: Poems for Each Other*

Johnson, LouAnne   *Making Waves: The Story of a Woman in This Man's Navy*

Kerr, M. E.   *Fell*

Klass, Perri Elizabeth   *Not Entirely Benign Procedure: Four Years as a Medical Student*

Klass, Sheila Solomon   *Page Four*

Kogan, Judith   *Nothing But the Best: The Struggle for Perfection at the Juilliard School*

Koontz, Dean R.   *Watchers*

Korman, Gordon A.   *Semester in the Life of a Garbage Bag*

Kropp, Lloyd   *Greencastle*

Kuklin, Susan   *Reaching for Dreams: A Ballet from Rehearsal to Opening Night*

L'Engle, Madeleine   *Many Waters*

Lackey, Mercedes   *Arrows of the Queen*

Leder, Jane M.   *Dead Serious: A Book About Teenagers and Teenage Suicide*

Levitin, Sonia   *Return*

Llewellyn, Chris   *Fragments From the Fire: The Triangle Shirtwaist Company Fire of March 25, 1911*

MacLean, John   *Mac*

Mahy, Margaret   *Tricksters*

Marshall, Kathryn   *In the Combat Zone: An Oral History of American Women in Vietnam, 1966-1975*

Mazer, Harry   *Girl of His Dreams*

Mazer, Norma Fox   *After the Rain*

McKillip, Patricia A.   *Fool's Run*

Meltzer, Milton, ed.   *American Revolutionaries: A History in Their Own Words, 1750-1800*

Meyer, Carolyn   *Denny's Tapes*

———   *Voices of South Africa: Growing Up in a Troubled Land*

Michelson, Maureen R., ed.   *Women & Work: Photographs and Personal Writings*

Naylor, Phyllis Reynolds   *Unexpected Pleasures*

———   *Year of the Gopher*

Palmer, Laura   *Shrapnel in the Heart: Letters and Remembrances from the Vietnam Memorial*

Paulsen, Gary   *Crossing*

Peck, Richard   *Princess Ashley*

Pfeffer, Susan Beth   *Year Without Michael*

Pullman, Philip   *Ruby in the Smoke*

Rendell, Ruth   *Heartstones*

Salassi, Otto R.   *Jimmy D., Sidewinder, and Me*

Salzman, Mark   *Iron & Silk*

Shilts, Randy   *And the Band Played On: Politics, People, and the AIDS Epidemic*

Sleator, William   *Boy Who Reversed Himself*

Smith, Mary-Anne Tirone   *Lament for a Silver-eyed Woman*

Tapert, Annette, ed.   *Lines of Battle: Letters from U.S. Servicemen, 1941-45*

Terris, Susan   *Nell's Quilt*

Voigt, Cynthia   *Sons From Afar*

Watson, Lyall   *Dreams of Dragons: Riddles of Natural History*

Wells, Rosemary   *Through the Hidden Door*

Williams, Juan   *Eyes on the Prize: America's Civil Rights Years, 1954-1965*

Woolley, Persia   *Child of the Northern Spring*

1988 SELECTIONS

Ashabranner, Brent   *Always to Remember: The Vietnam Veterans Memorial*

Bova, Ben   *Welcome to Moonbase*

Brown, Rita Mae   *Starting from Scratch: A Different Kind of Writers' Manual*

Cable, Mary   *Blizzard of '88*

Cagin, Seth   *We Are Not Afraid: The Story of Goodman, Schwerner, and Chaney and the Civil Rights Campaign for Mississippi*

Cleary, Beverly   *Girl from Yamhill: A Memoir*

Coman, Carolyn   *Body & Soul: Ten American Women*

Cormier, Robert   *Fade*

Deaver, Julie Reece   *Say Goodnight, Gracie*

Edgerton, Clyde   *Floatplane Notebooks*

Feldbaum, Carl B., and Bee, Ronald J.   *Looking the Tiger in the Eye: Confronting the Nuclear Threat*

Flanigan, Sara   *Alice*

Fleischman, Paul   *Joyful Noise: Poems for Two Voices*

Freedman, Russell   *Lincoln: A Photobiography*

Gelman, Rita Golden   *Inside Nicaragua: Young People's Dreams and Fears*

Giddings, Robert   *War Poets*

Gordon, Jacquie   *Give Me One Wish*

Greenberg, Joanne   *Of Such Small Differences*

Greene, Marilyn, and Provost, Gary   *Finder: The Story of a Private Investigator*

Hailey, Kendall   *Day I Became an Autodidact: And the Advice, Adventures, and Acrimonies That Befell Me Thereafter*

Haing, Ngor, and Warner, Roger   *Cambodian Odyssey*

Hambly, Barbara   *Those Who Hunt the Night*

Hamilton, Virginia   *Anthony Burns: The Defeat and Triumph of a Fugitive Slave*

———   *In the Beginning: Creation Stories from Around the World*

Haskins, James, and Benson, Kathleen   *60's Reader*

Hillerman, Tony   *Thief of Time*
Hinton, S. E.   *Taming the Star Runner*
Hoffman, Alice   *At Risk*
Hoover, H. M.   *Dawn Palace: The Story of Medea*
Hotze, Sollace   *Circle Unbroken*
Janeczko, Paul B., ed.   *Music of What Happens: Poems That Tell Stories*
Kennedy, William P.   *Toy Soldiers*
Kingsolver, Barbara   *Bean Trees*
Knudson, R. R., and Swenson, May, eds.   *American Sports Poems*
Koertge, Ron   *Arizona Kid*
Komunyakaa, Yusef   *Dien Cai Dau*
Kozol, Jonathon   *Rachel and Her Children: Homeless Families in America*
Langone, John   *AIDS: The Facts*
Lopes, Sal, ed.   *Wall: Images and Offerings From the Vietnam Veterans Memorial*
Mackay, Donald A.   *Building of Manhattan*
Madaras, Lynda   *Lynda Madaras Talks to Teens about AIDS: An Essential Guide for Parents, Teachers, and Young People*
Mahy, Margaret   *Memory*
Mazer, Norma Fox   *Silver*
McKinley, Robin   *Outlaws of Sherwood*
Meltzer, Milton   *Rescue: The Story of How Gentiles Saved the Jews in the Holocaust*
Mills, Judie   *John F. Kennedy*
Morrison, Lillian, selector   *Rhythm Road: Poems to Move You*
Myers, Walter Dean   *Fallen Angels*
—— *Scorpions*
Noonan, Michael   *McKenzie's Boots*
Paulsen, Gary   *Island*
Pringle, Terry   *Preacher's Boy*
Pullman, Philip   *Shadow in the North*
Riddles, Libby   *Race Across Alaska: The First Woman to Win the Iditarod Tells Her Story*
Rinaldi, Ann   *Last Silk Dress*
Ritter, Lawrence S.   *Babe: A Life in Pictures*
Rochman, Hazel, ed.   *Somehow Tenderness Survives: Stories of Southern Africa*
Rogasky, Barbara   *Smoke and Ashes: The Story of the Holocaust*
Ruskin, Cindy   *Quilt: Stories From the NAMES Project*
Rylant, Cynthia   *Kindness*
Scholl, Hans, and Scholl, Sophie   *At the Heart of the White Rose: Letters and Diaries of Hans and Sophie Scholl*
Severin, Tim   *Ulysses Voyage: Sea Search for the Odyssey*
Sleator, William   *Duplicate*

Tang, Hsi-yang   *Living Treasures: An Odyssey Through China's Extraordinary Nature Reserves*
Vare, Ethlie Ann   *Mothers of Invention: From the Bra to the Bomb: Forgotten Women and Their Unforgettable Ideas*
Willeford, Charles   *I Was Looking For a Street*
Wolff, Virginia Euwer   *Probably Still Nick Swansen*
Wyss, Thelma Hatch   *Here at the Scenic-Vu Motel*

1990 SELECTIONS*

Amos, James   *Memorial: A Novel of the Vietnam War*
Anderson, Joan   *American Family Farm*
Andronik, Catherine M.   *Quest for a King: Searching for the Real King Arthur*
Armor, John, and Wright, Peter   *Manzanar*
Banfield, Susan   *Rights of Man, The Reign of Terror: The Story of the French Revolution*
Block, Francesca Lia   *Weetzie Bat*
Bode, Janet   *New Kids on the Block: Oral Histories of Immigrant Teens*
Brooks, Bruce   *No Kidding*
—— *On the Wing*
Busselle, Rebecca   *Bathing Ugly*
Carson, Jo   *Stories I Ain't Told Nobody Yet: Selections from the People Pieces*
Carter, Alden R.   *Up Country*
Childress, Mark   *V for Victor*
Cohen, Susan, and Cohen, Daniel   *When Someone You Know Is Gay*
Cole, Brock   *Celine*
Conrad, Pamela   *My Daniel*
Conway, Jill Ker   *Road from Coorain*
Crew, Linda   *Children of the River*
Crutcher, Chris   *Chinese Handcuffs*
Davis, Lindsey   *Silver Pigs*
Deuker, Carl   *On the Devil's Court*
Dickinson, Peter   *Eva*
Duder, Tessa   *In Lane Three, Alex Archer*
Duncan, Lois   *Don't Look Behind You*
Grant, Cynthia D.   *Phoenix Rising; or, How to Survive Your Life*
Green, Connie Jordan   *War at Home*
Hayslip, Le Ly, and Wurts, Jay   *When Heaven and Earth Changed Places: A Vietnamese Woman's Journal from War to Peace*
Helprin, Mark   *Swan Lake*
Hobbs, Will   *Bearstone*

*In 1989 the list was renamed "Best Books for Young Adults—1990" to conform to the standard set by the Newbery-Caldecott Awards: the 1990 list consists of books published in 1989. Thus, from 1990 forward, the year indicated on the list becomes the year the list is issued and includes titles published the previous year.

Hodges, Margaret   *Making a Difference: The Story of an American Family*

Homes, A. M.   *Jack*

Horner, John R., and Gorman, James   *Digging Dinosaurs*

Hudson, Jan   *Sweetgrass*

Janeczko, Paul B.   *Brickyard Summer*

Klass, David   *Wrestling with Honor*

Klein, Norma   *No More Saturday Nights*

Krementz, Jill   *How It Feels to Fight for Your Life*

Kuklin, Susan   *Fighting Back: What Some People Are Doing about AIDS*

Laird, Elizabeth   *Loving Ben*

Lanker, Brian   *I Dream a World: Portraits of Black Women Who Changed America*

Levitin, Sonia   *Silver Days*

Macaulay, David   *Way Things Work*

Maguire, Gregory   *I Feel Like the Morning Star*

Marsden, John   *So Much to Tell You*

McCullough, Frances, ed.   *Earth, Air, Fire & Water*

McKibben, Bill   *End of Nature*

Meltzer, Milton   *Benjamin Franklin: The New American*

_____   *Voices from the Civil War: A Documentary History of the Great American Conflict*

Mickle, Shelley Fraser   *Queen of October*

Miller, Jim Wayne   *Newfound*

Moeri, Louise   *Forty-third War*

Monk, Lorraine   *Photographs that Changed the World*

Murphy, Pat   *City, Not Long After*

Murrow, Liza Ketchum   *Fire in the Heart*

Namioka, Lensey   *Island of Ogres*

Naughton, Jim   *My Brother Stealing Second*

Nelson, Theresa   *And One for All*

Newth, Mette   *Abduction*

Norman, David, and Milner, Angela   *Dinosaur*

Paulsen, Gary   *Voyage of the Frog*

_____   *Winter Room*

Pevsner, Stella   *How Could You Do It, Diana?*

Pinkwater, Jill   *Buffalo Brenda*

Pringle, Terry   *Fine Time to Leave Me*

Rhodes, Richard   *Farm: A Year in the Life of an American Farmer*

Saul, John   *Creature*

Shannon, George   *Unlived Affections*

Sieruta, Peter D.   *Heartbeats and Other Stories*

Smith, K.   *Skeeter*

Staples, Suzanne Fisher   *Shabanu: Daughter of the Wind*

Tan, Amy   *Joy Luck Club*

Taylor, Theodore   *Sniper*

Turney, David C.   *Why Are They Weeping? South Africans under Apartheid*

Van Raven, Pieter   *Great Man's Secret*

White, Ellen Emerson   *Long Live the Queen*

Wilson, David Henry   *Coachman Rat*

Wilson, F. Paul   *Dydeetown World*

Wilson, Robert Charles   *Gypsies*

Wolff, Tobias   *This Boy's Life: A Memoir*

Zindel, Paul   *Begonia for Miss Applebaum*

1991 SELECTIONS

Abdul-Jabbar, Kareem, and McCarthy, Mignon   *Kareem*

Agard, John, comp.   *Life Doesn't Frighten Me at All*

Anderson, Scott   *Distant Fires*

Ansa, Tina McElroy   *Baby of the Family*

Appel, Allen   *Till the End of Time*

Avi   *True Confessions of Charlotte Doyle*

Baldwin, J., ed.   *Whole Earth Ecolog: The Best of Environmental Tools and Ideas*

Bell, Clare   *Ratha and Thistle-chaser*

Bennett, James   *I Can Hear the Mourning Dove*

Blake, Jeanne   *Risky Times: How to be AIDS-Smart and Stay Healthy*

Bode, Janet   *Voices of Rape*

Brooks, Polly Schoyer   *Beyond the Myth: The Story of Joan of Arc*

Cannon, A. E.   *Shadow Brothers*

Carter, Peter   *Borderlands*

Caseley, Judith   *Kisses*

Chestnut, J. L.   *Black in Selma: The Uncommon Life of J. L. Chestnut, Jr.*

Chetwin, Grace   *Collidescope*

Clarke, J.   *Heroic Life of Al Capsella*

Clements, Bruce   *Tom Loves Anna Loves Tom*

Crispin, A. C.   *Starbridge*

Cushman, Kathleen, and Miller, Montana   *Circus Dreams*

Doherty, Berlie   *White Peak Farm*

Donofrio, Beverly   *Riding in Cars with Boys*

Embury, Barbara   *Dream Is Alive: A Flight of Discovery Aboard the Space Shuttle*

Ferris, Jean   *Across the Grain*

Freedman, Russell   *Franklin Delano Roosevelt*

Freedman, Samuel G.   *Small Victories: The Real World of a Teacher, Her Students & Their High School*

Friedman, Ina R.   *Other Victims: First-Person Stories of Non-Jews Persecuted by the Nazis*

Fuer, Elizabeth   *Paper Doll*

Gallo, Donald R., ed.   *Speaking for Ourselves: Autobiographical Sketches by Notable Authors of Books for Young Adults*

Gilmore, Kate   *Enter Three Witches*
Hall, Barbara   *Dixie Storms*
Hamanaka, Sheila   *Journey*
Hamilton, Virginia   *Cousins*
Harrison, Sue   *Mother Earth Father Sky*
Haskins, James   *Black Dance in America*
Hendry, Frances Mary   *Quest for a Maid*
Ho, Minfong   *Rice Without Rain*
Hudson, Jan   *Dawn Rider*
Human Rights in China   *Children of the Dragon: The Story of Tiananmen Square*
James, J. Alison   *Sing for a Gentle Rain*
Janeczko, Paul B., ed.   *Place My Words Are Looking For: What Poets Say About and Through Their Work*
Jordan, Robert   *Eye of the World*
Katz, William Loren   *Breaking the Chains: African American Slave Resistance*
Kilworth, Garry   *Foxes of Firstdark*
Kisor, Henry   *What's That Pig Outdoors? A Memoir of Deafness*
Klause, Annette Curtis   *Silver Kiss*
Koertge, Ron   *Boy in the Moon*
Korman, Gordon A.   *Losing Joe's Place*
Larson, Gary   *Prehistory of The Far Side: A 10th Anniversary Exhibit*
Lauber, Patricia   *Seeing Earth from Space*
Levin, Betty   *Brother Moose*
Lord, Bette Bao   *Legacies: A Chinese Mosaic*
Martin, Valerie   *Mary Reilly*
McCorkle, Jill   *Ferris Beach*
Meltzer, Milton   *Columbus and the World Around Him*
Myers, Walter Dean   *Mouse Rap*
Naar, Jon   *Design for a Livable Planet*
Naidoo, Beverley   *Chain of Fire*
Naylor, Phyllis Reynolds   *Send No Blessings*
O'Brien, Tim   *Things They Carried*
Parks, Gordon   *Voices in the Mirror: An Autobiography*
Paulsen, Gary   *Woodsong*
Pershall, Mary K.   *You Take the High Road*
Pierce, Meredith Ann   *Pearl of the Soul of the World*
Popham, Melinda Worth   *Skywater*
Pullman, Philip   *Tiger in the Well*
Ray, Delia   *Nation Torn: The Story of How the Civil War Began*
Rylant, Cynthia   *Couple of Kooks and Other Stories about Love*
———   *Soda Jerk*
Sanders, Dori   *Clover*
Schami, Rafik   *Hand Full of Stars*
Sleator, William   *Strange Attractors*
Snyder, Zilpha Keatley   *Libby on Wednesday*
Soto, Gary   *Baseball in April and Other Stories*
Spinelli, Jerry   *Maniac Magee*
Stoll, Cliff   *Cuckoo's Egg: Tracking a Spy Through the Maze of Computer Espionage*

Strauss, Gwen   *Trail of Stones*
Taylor, Mildred D.   *Road to Memphis*
Van Raven, Pieter   *Pickle and Price*
Voigt, Cynthia   *On Fortune's Wheel*
Weiss, Ann E.   *Who's to Know? Information, the Media and Public Awareness*
Willey, Margaret   *Saving Lenny*
Woolley, Persia   *Queen of the Summer Stars*
Wrede, Patricia C.   *Dealing with Dragons*

1992 SELECTIONS

Aaron, Henry, and Wheeler, Lonnie   *I Had a Hammer*
Adams, Douglas, and Carwardine, Mark   *Last Chance to See*
Anastos, Phillip   *Illegal: Seeking the American Dream*
Arter, Jim   *Gruel and Unusual Punishment*
Avi   *Nothing but the Truth: A Documentary Novel*
Bing, Leon   *Do or Die*
Bode, Janet   *Beating the Odds: Stories of Unexpected Achievers*
Brooks, Bruce   *Predator!*
Buss, Fran Leeper, and Cubias, Daisy   *Journey of the Sparrows*
Cannon, A. E.   *Amazing Gracie*
Cary, Lorene   *Black Ice*
Choi, Sook Nyul   *Year of Impossible Goodbyes*
Cooper, J. California   *Family*
Corman, Avery   *Prized Possessions*
Cormier, Robert   *We All Fall Down*
Counter, S. Allen   *North Pole Legacy: Black, White & Eskimo*
Crichton, Michael   *Jurassic Park*
Crutcher, Chris   *Athletic Shorts: 6 Short Stories*
Davis, Jenny   *Checking on the Moon*
Durham, Michael S.   *Powerful Days: The Civil Rights Photography of Charles Moore*
Fleischman, Paul   *Borning Room*
Fluek, Toby Knobel   *Memories of My Life in a Polish Village, 1930-1949*
Fox, Paula   *Monkey Island*
Freedman, Russell   *Wright Brothers: How They Invented the Airplane*
Fussell, Samuel Wilson   *Muscle: Confessions of an Unlikely Bodybuilder*
Gaiman, Neil, and Pratchett, Terry   *Good Omens: The Nice and Accurate Prophecies of Agnes Nutter, Witch*
Glenn, Mel   *My Friend's Got This Problem, Mr. Candler*
Hall, Lynn   *Flying Changes*
Hathorn, Libby   *Thunderwith*
Hayden, Torey L.   *Ghost Girl: The True Story of a Child Who Refused to Talk*
Hayes, Daniel   *Trouble with Lemons*

Henry, Sue   *Murder on the Iditarod Trail*

Higa, Tomiko   *Girl with the White Flag: An Inspiring Tale of Love and Courage in War Time*

Hobbs, Will   *Downriver*

Honeycutt, Natalie   *Ask Me Something Easy*

Jones, Diana Wynne   *Castle in the Air*

Kingsolver, Barbara   *Animal Dreams*

Kotlowitz, Alex   *There Are No Children Here: The Story of Two Boys Growing Up in the Other America*

Kuklin, Susan   *What Do I Do Now? Talking about Teenage Pregnancy*

Lauber, Patricia   *Summer of Fire: Yellowstone, 1988*

Lee, Tanith   *Black Unicorn*

Lipsyte, Robert   *Brave*

Lyons, Mary E.   *Sorrow's Kitchen: The Life and Folklore of Zora Neale Hurston*

MacLachlan, Patricia   *Journey*

McCaffrey, Anne   *Pegasus in Flight*

McCammon, Robert R.   *Boy's Life*

Montgomery, Sy   *Walking with the Great Apes: Jane Goodall, Dian Fossey, Birute Galdikas*

Morpurgo, Michael   *Waiting for Anya*

Murphy, Jim   *Boy's War: Confederate and Union Soldiers Talk about the Civil War*

Myers, Walter Dean   *Now Is Your Time! The African-American Struggle for Freedom*

Orlev, Uri   *Man from the Other Side*

Paterson, Katherine   *Lyddie*

Paulsen, Gary   *Cookcamp*

———   *Monument*

Plummer, Louise   *My Name Is Sus5an Smith: The 5 is Silent*

Rappaport, Doreen   *American Women: Their Lives in Their Words*

Rinaldi, Ann   *Wolf by the Ears*

Savage, Georgia   *House Tibet*

Shusterman, Neal   *What Daddy Did*

Spiegelman, Art   *Maus: A Survivor's Tale II: And Here My Troubles Began*

Spinelli, Jerry   *There's a Girl in My Hammerlock*

Sullivan, Charles, ed.   *Children of Promise: African-American Literature and Art for Young People*

Tepper, Sheri S.   *Beauty*

Thesman, Jean   *Rain Catchers*

Westall, Robert   *Kingdom by the Sea*

White, Ryan, and Cunningham, Ann Marie   *Ryan White: My Own Story*

Williams-Garcia, Rita   *Fast Talk on a Slow Track*

Wisler, G. Clifton   *Red Cap*

Wolff, Virginia Euwer   *Mozart Season*

Yolen, Jane, and Greenberg, Martin H., eds.   *Vampires: A Collection of Original Stories*

1993 SELECTIONS

Armstrong, Jennifer   *Steal Away*

Arrick, Fran   *What You Don't Know Can Kill You*

Avi   *Blue Heron*

Beattie, Owen, and Geiger, John   *Buried in Ice: The Mystery of a Lost Arctic Expedition*

Berry, James   *Ajeemah and His Son*

Block, Francesca Lia   *Cherokee Bat and the Goat Guys*

Bonner, Cindy   *Lily*

Brooks, Bruce   *What Hearts*

Brooks, Martha   *Two Moons in August*

Bunting, Eve   *Jumping the Nail*

Campbell, Eric   *Place of Lions*

Caseley, Judith   *My Father, the Nutcase*

Cooney, Caroline B.   *Flight #116 Is Down*

Cooper, Louise   *Sleep of Stone*

Cormier, Robert   *Tunes for Bears to Dance To*

Craig, Kit   *Gone*

Currie, Elliott   *Dope and Trouble: Portraits of Delinquent Youth*

Davis, Terry   *If Rock and Roll Were a Machine*

Dickinson, Peter   *AK*

Doherty, Berlie   *Dear Nobody*

Duncan, Lois   *Who Killed My Daughter? The True Story of a Mother's Search for Her Daughter's Murderer*

Edelman, Marian Wright   *Measure of Our Success: A Letter to My Children and Yours*

Ferry, Charles   *Binge*

Ford, Michael Thomas   *100 Questions and Answers about AIDS: A Guide for Young People*

Forman, James D.   *Becca's Story*

Freedman, Russell   *Indian Winter*

Garland, Sherry   *Song of the Buffalo Boy*

Gould, Steven   *Jumper*

Gravelle, Karen, and Peterson, Leslie   *Teenage Fathers*

Gregory, Kristiana   *Earthquake at Dawn*

Grisham, John   *Pelican Brief*

Gurney, James   *Dinotopia: A Land Apart from Time*

Guy, Rosa   *Music of Summer*

Hall, Barbara   *Fool's Hill*

Haskins, James   *One More River to Cross: The Stories of Twelve Black Americans*

Hesse, Karen   *Letters from Rifka*

Hobbs, Will   *Big Wander*

Hoffman, Alice   *Turtle Moon*

Horrigan, Kevin   *Right Kinds of Heroes: Coach Bob Shannon and the East St. Louis Flyers*

Hotze, Sollace   *Acquainted with the Night*

Johnson, Earvin "Magic"   *What You Can Do to Avoid AIDS*

Johnson, Scott   *One of the Boys*

Jones, Diana Wynne   *Sudden Wild Magic*

Kaye, Geraldine   *Someone Else's Baby*

Kimble, Bo   *For You, Hank: The Story of Hank Gathers and Bo Kimble*

Kincaid, Nanci   *Crossing Blood*

Kittredge, Mary   *Teens with AIDS Speak Out*

Koertge, Ron   *Harmony Arms*

Koller, Jackie French   *Primrose Way*

Lackey, Mercedes   *Bardic Voices: The Lark and the Wren*

Laird, Elizabeth   *Kiss the Dust*

Lyons, Mary E.   *Letters from a Slave Girl: The Story of Harriet Jacobs*

Magorian, Michelle   *Not a Swan*

Marlette, Doug   *In Your Face: A Cartoonist at Work*

McKissack, Patricia C., and McKissack, Fredrick   *Sojourner Truth: Ain't I a Woman?*

Meyer, Carolyn   *Where the Broken Heart Still Beats: The Story of Cynthia Ann Parker*

Mowry, Jess   *Way Past Cool*

Murphy, Jim   *Long Road to Gettysburg*

Myers, Walter Dean   *Righteous Revenge of Artemis Bonner*

———   *Somewhere in the Darkness*

Nelson, Theresa   *Beggar's Ride*

Parks, Rosa, and Haskins, Jim   *Rosa Parks: My Story*

Paulsen, Gary   *Haymeadow*

Pfeffer, Susan Beth   *Family of Strangers*

Powell, Randy   *Is Kissing a Girl Who Smokes Like Licking an Ashtray?*

Pullman, Philip   *Broken Bridge*

Reaver, Chap   *Little Bit Dead*

Reidelbach, Maria   *Completely Mad: A History of the Comic Book and Magazine*

Reiss, Kathryn   *Time Windows*

Rice, Robert   *Last Pendragon*

Rinaldi, Ann   *Break with Charity: A Story about the Salem Witch Trials*

Robertson, James I.   *Civil War! America Becomes One Nation*

Rylant, Cynthia   *Missing May*

Salisbury, Graham   *Blue Skin of the Sea*

Scieszka, Jon   *Stinky Cheese Man and Other Fairly Stupid Tales*

Sherman, Josepha   *Child of Faerie, Child of Earth*

Simon, Neil   *Lost in Yonkers*

Steffan, Joseph   *Honor Bound: A Gay American Fights for the Right to Serve His Country*

Stevermer, Carolyn   *River Rats*

Stoehr, Shelley   *Crosses*

Taylor, Clark   *House That Crack Built*

Taylor, Theodore   *Weirdo*

Thesman, Jean   *When the Road Ends*

Uchida, Yoshiko   *Invisible Thread*

Ure, Jean   *Plague*

Westall, Robert   *Stormsearch*

———   *Yaxley's Cat*

White, Ruth   *Weeping Willow*

Wieler, Diana   *Bad Boy*

Williams, Michael   *Crocodile Burning*

Wilson, Budge   *Leaving*

Winton, Tim   *Lockie Leonard, Human Torpedo*

Woodson, Jacqueline   *Maizon at Blue Hill*

Wrede, Patricia C.   *Searching for Dragons*

Yolen, Jane   *Briar Rose*

Zambreno, Mary Frances   *Plague of Sorcerers*

Zindel, Paul   *Pigman and Me*

The Best of the Best

by Preconference

STILL ALIVE

Selections from 1960 to 1974

Adams, Richard   *Watership Down*

Adamson, Joy   *Born Free*

Angelou, Maya   *Gather Together in My Name*

_____ *I Know Why the Caged Bird Sings*

Anonymous   *Go Ask Alice*

Asimov, Isaac   *Fantastic Voyage*

Baldwin, James   *If Beale Street Could Talk*

Borland, Hal   *When the Legend Dies*

Boston Women's Health Collective, eds.   *Our Bodies, Ourselves: A Book by and for Women*

Braithwaite, E. R.   *To Sir, with Love*

Brautigan, Richard   *Trout Fishing in America*

Brown, Claude   *Manchild in the Promised Land*

Burnford, Sheila   *Incredible Journey*

Carson, Rachel   *Silent Spring*

Castaneda, Carlos   *Journey to Ixtlan: The Lessons of Don Juan*

Childress, Alice   *Hero Ain't Nothin' but a Sandwich*

Clarke, Arthur C.   *2001: A Space Odyssey*

Cleaver, Eldridge   *Soul on Ice*

Cormier, Robert   *Chocolate War*

Craven, Margaret   *I Heard the Owl Call My Name*

Crichton, Michael   *Andromeda Strain*

Dunning, Stephen, ed.   *Reflections on a Gift of Watermelon Pickle*

Elfman, Blossom   *Girls of Huntington House*

Fast, Howard   *April Morning*

Frazier, Walt, and Beckow, Ira   *Rockin' Steady: A Guide to Basketball and Cool*

Friedman, Myra   *Buried Alive: The Biography of Janis Joplin*

Gaines, Ernest   *Autobiography of Miss Jane Pittman*

Gaines, William, and Feldstein, Albert, eds.   *Ridiculously Expensive Mad*

Graham, Robin Lee, and Gill, Derek T.   *Dove*

Green, Hannah   *I Never Promised You a Rose Garden*

Griffin, John   *Black like Me*

Guy, Rosa   *Friends*

Hall, Lynn   *Sticks and Stones*

Harris, Marilyn   *Hatter Fox*

Head, Ann   *Mr. and Mrs. Bo Jo Jones*

Heinlein, Robert   *Stranger in a Strange Land*

Heller, Joseph   *Catch-22*

Herbert, Frank   *Dune*

Herriot, James   *All Creatures Great and Small*

Herzog, Arthur   *Swarm*

Hinton, S. E.   *Outsiders*

_____ *That Was Then, This Is Now*

Jackson, Shirley   *We Have Always Lived in the Castle*

Kellogg, Marjorie   *Tell Me That You Love Me, Junie Moon*

Kesey, Ken   *One Flew over the Cuckoo's Nest*

Keyes, Daniel   *Flowers for Algernon*

Knowles, John   *Separate Peace*

Krentz, Harold   *To Race the Wind: An Autobiography*
Lee, Harper   *To Kill a Mockingbird*
Maas, Peter   *Serpico*
Meriwether, Louise   *Daddy Was a Number Runner*
Moody, Anne   *Coming of Age in Mississippi: An Autobiography*
Neufeld, John   *Lisa Bright and Dark*
Peck, Robert Newton   *Day No Pigs Would Die*
Plath, Sylvia   *Bell Jar*
Potok, Chaim   *Chosen*
Read, Piers Paul   *Alive: The Story of the Andes Survivors*
Robertson, Dougal   *Survive the Savage Sea*
Samuels, Gertrude   *Run, Shelley, Run!*
Schulz, Charles   *Peanuts Treasury*
Scoppettone, Sandra   *Trying Hard to Hear You*
Sleator, William   *House of Stairs*
Solzhenitsyn, Alexander   *One Day in the Life of Ivan Denisovich*
Swarthout, Glendon   *Bless the Beasts and Children*
Thompson, Jean   *House of Tomorrow*
Vonnegut, Kurt, Jr.   *Slaughterhouse Five; or, The Children's Crusade*
Westheimer, David   *My Sweet Charlie*
——— *Von Ryan's Express*
White, Robb   *Deathwatch*
Wigginton, Eliot   *Foxfire Book*
X, Malcolm, and Haley, Alex   *Autobiography of Malcolm X*
Zindel, Paul   *Pigman*

THE BEST OF THE BEST BOOKS
Selections from 1970 to 1983

Adams, Richard   *Watership Down*
Alexander, Lloyd   *Westmark*
Ali, Muhammed, and Durham, Richard   *Greatest: My Own Story*
Angelou, Maya   *I Know Why the Caged Bird Sings*
Anonymous   *Go Ask Alice*
Arrick, Fran   *Tunnel Vision*
Auel, Jean   *Clan of the Cave Bear*
Baldwin, James   *If Beale Street Could Talk*
Bell, Ruth   *Changing Bodies, Changing Lives: A Book for Teens on Sex and Relationships*
Bethancourt, T. Ernesto   *Tune in Yesterday*
Bleier, Rocky, and O'Neill, Terry   *Fighting Back*
Blume, Judy   *Forever*
Boston Women's Health Book Collective   *Our Bodies, Ourselves*, 2d ed.
Brancato, Robin   *Winning*
Bridgers, Sue Ellen   *Notes for Another Life*

Brown, Dee   *Bury My Heart at Wounded Knee: An Indian History of the American West*
Childress, Alice   *Hero Ain't Nothin' but a Sandwich*
Christopher, John   *Empty World*
Conroy, Pat   *Great Santini*
Cormier, Robert   *After the First Death*
——— *Chocolate War: A Novel*
——— *I Am the Cheese*
Due, Linnea A.   *High and Outside*
Duncan, Lois   *Killing Mr. Griffin*
——— *Stranger with My Face*
Elder, Lauren, and Streshinsky, Shirley   *And I Alone Survived*
Elfman, Blossom   *Girls of Huntington House*
Garden, Nancy   *Annie on My Mind*
Glenn, Mel   *Class Dismissed! High School Poems*
Greenberg, Joanne   *In This Sign*
Greene, Bette   *Summer of My German Soldier*
Guest, Judith   *Ordinary People*
Guy, Rosa   *Edith Jackson*
——— *Friends*
Hamilton, Virginia   *Sweet Whispers, Brother Rush*
Harris, Marilyn   *Hatter Fox*
Hayden, Torey L.   *One Child*
Hinton, S. E.   *Tex*
Hogan, William   *Quartzsite Trip*
Holland, Isabelle   *Man without a Face*
Holman, Felice   *Slake's Limbo*
Johnston, Norma   *Keeping Days*
Jordan, June   *His Own Where*
Kerr, M. E.   *Dinky Hocker Shoots Smack*
King, Stephen   *Carrie*
Le Guin, Ursula   *Farthest Shore*
——— *Tombs of Atuan*
——— *Very Far Away from Anywhere Else*
Leitner, Isabella   *Fragments of Isabella: A Memoir of Auschwitz*
Levenkron, Steven   *Best Little Girl in the World*
Lipsyte, Robert   *One Fat Summer*
MacCracken, Mary   *Circle of Children*
MacDougall, Ruth   *Cheerleader*
Mazer, Harry   *Last Mission*
Mazer, Norma Fox   *Up in Seth's Room*
McCaffrey, Anne   *Dragonsong*
McCoy, Kathy, and Wibbelsman, Charles   *Teenage Body Book*
McIntyre, Vonda N.   *Dreamsnake*
McKinley, Robin   *Beauty: A Retelling of the Story of Beauty and the Beast*
——— *Blue Sword*
Meltzer, Milton   *Never to Forget: The Jews of the Holocaust*
Niven, Larry   *Ringworld*
O'Brien, Robert C.   *Z for Zachariah*

Oneal, Zibby *Formal Feeling*
_____ *Language of Goldfish*
Peck, Richard *Are You in the House Alone?*
_____ *Father Figure: A Novel*
_____ *Ghosts I Have Been*
Pierce, Meredith Ann *Darkangel*
Plath, Sylvia *Bell Jar*
Platt, Kin *Headman*
Powers, John *Last Catholic in America: A Fictionalized Memoir*
Robertson, Dougal *Survive the Savage Sea*
Samuels, Gertrude *Run, Shelley, Run!*
Santoli, Al *Everything We Had: An Oral History of the Vietnam War as Told by 33 American Soldiers Who Fought It*
Schulke, Flip, ed. *Martin Luther King, Jr.: A Documentary . . . Montgomery to Memphis*
Scoppettone, Sandra *Trying Hard to Hear You*
Sleator, William *House of Stairs*
Stewart, Mary *Crystal Cave*
Swarthout, Glendon *Bless the Beasts and Children*
Taylor, Mildred *Roll of Thunder, Hear My Cry*
Wersba, Barbara *Run Softly, Go Fast*
White, Robb *Deathwatch*
Wilkinson, Brenda *Ludell and Willie*
Zindel, Paul *Effects of Gamma Rays on Man-in-the-Moon Marigolds*

NOTHIN' BUT THE BEST

Selections from 1966 to 1986

Adams, Douglas *Hitchhiker's Guide to the Galaxy*
Angelou, Maya *I Know Why the Caged Bird Sings*
Bell, Ruth *Changing Bodies, Changing Lives: A Book for Teens on Sex and Relationships*
Blume, Judy *Forever*
Brancato, Robin *Winning*
Bridgers, Sue Ellen *All Together Now*
Briggs, Raymond *When the Wind Blows*
Callahan, Steven *Adrift: Seventy-Six Days Lost at Sea*
Card, Orson Scott *Ender's Game*
Childress, Alice *Hero Ain't Nothin' but a Sandwich*
_____ *Rainbow Jordan*
Clark, Mary Higgins *Where Are the Children?*
Cormier, Robert *After the First Death*
_____ *Chocolate War*
Crutcher, Chris *Running Loose*
_____ *Stotan!*
Duncan, Lois *Killing Mr. Griffin*
Edelman, Bernard, ed. *Dear America: Letters Home from Vietnam*

Fox, Paula *One-Eyed Cat*
Gallo, Donald R., ed. *Sixteen: Short Stories by Outstanding Writers for Young Adults*
Garden, Nancy *Annie on My Mind*
Garfield, Brian *Paladin*
Greenberg, Joanne *In This Sign*
Guest, Judith *Ordinary People*
Guy, Rosa *Disappearance*
_____ *Friends*
Head, Ann *Mr. and Mrs. Bo Jo Jones*
Hinton, S. E. *Outsiders*
_____ *Tex*
_____ *That Was Then, This Is Now*
Hogan, William *Quartzsite Trip*
Holland, Isabelle *Man without a Face*
Holman, Felice *Slake's Limbo*
Irwin, Hadley *Abby, My Love*
Kazimiroff, Theodore L. *Last Algonquin*
Kerr, M. E. *Gentlehands*
_____ *Night Kites*
Keyes, Daniel *Flowers for Algernon*
King, Stephen *Night Shift*
Koehn, Ilse *Mischling, Second Degree: My Childhood in Nazi Germany*
Lipsyte, Robert *One Fat Summer*
MacKinnon, Bernie *Meantime*
Mason, Bobbie Ann *In Country*
Mazer, Harry *Last Mission*
McCaffrey, Anne *Dragonsong*
McIntyre, Vonda N. *Dreamsnake*
McKinley, Robin *Beauty: A Retelling of Beauty and the Beast*
Myers, Walter Dean *Hoops*
Naylor, Phyllis Reynolds *Keeper*
Newton, Suzanne *I Will Call It Georgie's Blues*
Peck, Richard *Are You in the House Alone?*
_____ *Ghosts I Have Been*
Plath, Sylvia *Bell Jar*
Potok, Chaim *Chosen*
Richards, Arlene Kramer, and Willis, Irene *Under 18 and Pregnant: What to Do If You or Someone You Know Is*
Robeson, Susan *Whole World in His Hands: A Pictorial Biography of Paul Robeson*
Rolling Stone Illustrated History of Rock and Roll
Segal, Erich *Love Story*
Silverberg, Robert *Lord Valentine's Castle*
Sleator, William *House of Stairs*
_____ *Interstellar Pig*
Strasser, Todd *Friends till the End*
Swarthout, Glendon *Bless the Beasts and Children*
Van Devanter, Lynda, and Morgan, Christopher *Home before Morning: The Story of an Army Nurse in Vietnam*
Vinge, Joan D. *Psion*
Voigt, Cynthia *Homecoming*
_____ *Izzy, Willy-Nilly*

_____ *Runner*
_____ *Solitary Blue*
Walker, Alice   *In Search of Our Mothers'
   Gardens: Womanist Prose*
Webb, Sheyann, and Nelson, Rachel West
   *Selma, Lord, Selma: Girlhood Memories of
   the Civil-rights Days*

Wersba, Barbara   *Run Softly, Go Fast*
White, Robb   *Deathwatch*
Zindel, Paul   *Effects of Gamma Rays on
   Man-in-the-Moon Marigolds*
_____ *Pigman*

APPENDIX

BBYA Policies and Procedures

YOUNG ADULT LIBRARY SERVICES ASSOCIATION
BEST BOOKS FOR YOUNG ADULTS
POLICIES AND PROCEDURES

Charge

To select from the year's publications significant adult and young adult books; to annotate the selected titles.

Purpose of the List

The list presents books published in the past 16 months that are recommended reading for young adults (12 to 18).

It is a general list of fiction and nonfiction titles selected for their proven or potential appeal to the personal reading tastes of the young adult.

Such titles should incorporate acceptable literary quality and effectiveness of presentation. Standard selection criteria consonant with the ALA Library Bill of Rights shall be applied.

Fiction should have characterization and dialog believable within the context of the novel or story.

Nonfiction should have an appealing format and a readable text. Although the list attempts to present a variety of reading tastes and levels, no effort will be made to balance the list according to subject or area of interest.

Target Audience

The list is prepared for the use of young adults themselves and annotations will be written to attract the young adult reader.

These policies and procedures took effect with the Best Books for Young Adults Committee that selected the list, Midwinter 1993.

Eligibility Time Frame

The committee will consider and vote on books published within their assigned calendar year, January 1 to December 31, in addition to those published between September 1 and December 31 of the previous year. Both field and committee nominations will be accepted for books that meet the published criteria.

Nominations may be accepted from the field and committee up to November 1 of that calendar year.

Managing the List

A book's nominator may, by October 1, remove from nomination any title that person nominated. These titles removed from nomination may be placed back in nomination by other committee members.

A book that is removed from the list during the year may be renominated for the next year's list as long as that book meets the publishing criteria.

Discussing the List

After observer comments, the chair will provide each book's nominator with the first opportunity to address that title if he/she so desires.

Committee Members

Members are appointed by the vice-president/president-elect of YALSA for a one-year term renewable for a two-year consecutive term. Members are expected to attend all committee meetings and read widely from books eligible for nomination. Reappointment is not automatic, but instead is based upon participation.

Members will be appointed on a staggered basis so that the ideal committee will have five new members appointed each year. Each term begins at the conclusion of one Midwinter and ends at the conclusion of Midwinter at the end of the term. Members who have served two consecutive terms may not be reappointed to the committee for five years from the conclusion of their last term.

If someone resigns, the current president of the Association appoints a new person to fill that particular term.

There are fifteen personal committee members. The editor of the "Books for Youth" section of *Booklist* is a nonvoting member of the committee and serves as a consultant.

Chair

The chair is appointed by the vice-president/president-elect for a one-year term and, as such, has the right to vote, to validate titles (by a vote) for consideration on the list, and to enter into discussion of titles. It should be understood, however, that the primary responsibility of the chair is facilitator of the committee's charge, including all business matters. The chair should only discuss a title after other committee members have had an opportunity to speak so as not to unduly influence the decision.

An administrative assistant will be appointed in consultation with the committee chair by the president-elect of YALSA. This administrative assistant will assist the chair in duties that may include the following: maintaining the nominations' database, tabulating votes, and other such duties assigned by the chair. The administrative assistant is a nonvoting member of the committee.

Voting Procedures

Final selections are made at the Midwinter Meeting during an intensive series of meetings. After comments from observers and discussion by committee members, a vote is taken to determine if a title should be included on the final list.

A book must receive a minimum of nine "yes" votes to be placed on the final list regardless of the number of the fifteen-member committee present and voting. Only members attending the Midwinter Meeting will be allowed to vote. Members can only vote on books they have read. If a committee member must leave before the final vote, that member must give a signed ballot to the chair, who will designate a voting proxy for the absent member. The final vote will be counted by the consultant and the administrative assistant.

After the final discussion and selection, titles are then annotated by the committee. These annotations are completed at the last meeting of the committee.

Availability of Lists for General Distribution

The first list of titles nominated will be made available at the Annual Conference and will be mailed to interested individuals or institutions if they send a self-addressed stamped envelope to the YALSA office with their requests.

The final list of nominations will be available after November 1 and again will be mailed out upon request with a SASE. Committee members and the chair can also make these copies available on request, but because of the volume of copying, the YALSA office should be the main contact.

At Midwinter, lists with an addendum will be available to observers, along with nomination forms and rules for observers.

All committee meetings will be open to ALA members as long as they are willing to follow the guidelines set up for observers. Before the committee discusses each suggested title, an opportunity will be given to observers to make short comments about the books (two to four minutes per title) but the chair reserves the right to cut short the discussion if necessary.

Publishers' representatives are requested to refrain from participating in discussion or making comments about their own books.

While comments from individuals outside the organization are certainly encouraged and necessary for discussion, according to ALA policies 7.4.1 and 7.4.3 only registered ALA members may participate in committee meetings. Comments from nonmembers must be channeled through registered ALA members.

The final list of selected titles will be available, as a press release, from the ALA public information office the morning following the committee's last meeting. The YALSA office will mail press releases to interested persons on request.

Miscellaneous

1. No nominations should be accepted unless they are submitted on an official nomination form. The chair should respond to all nominations not received on the proper form.
2. If possible, a nomination form should be reproduced in *Journal of Youth Services in Libraries* (JOYS). Nomination forms should be made widely available and notices of where to obtain them should be printed in all the standard professional publications.

Approved by YALSA Board, July 1991

Works Cited

Aaron, Henry, and Lonnie Wheeler. *I Had a Hammer*. New York: HarperCollins, 1991.

Aaseng, Nathan. *Baseball: It's Your Team*. Minneapolis: Lerner, 1985.

Abrahamson, R. F., and Betty Carter. "What We know about Nonfiction and Young Adult Readers and What We Need to Do about It." *Publishing Research Quarterly* 8 (Spring 1992): 41–54.

Alexander, Lloyd. *Beggar Queen*. New York: Dutton, 1984.

_____. *Kestrel*. New York: Dutton, 1982.

_____. *Westmark*. New York: Dutton, 1981.

_____. Letter to Evelyn Shaevel, 20 May 1982.

American Library Association. *ALA Handbook of Organization, 1972–73*. Chicago: The Association, 1973.

_____. *ALA Handbook of Organization, 1973–74*. Chicago: The Association, 1974.

_____. *ALA Handbook of Organization, 1983–84*. Chicago: The Association, 1984.

American Library Association, Press Release, 2 Feb. 1955. In Michael C. Madden, "An Analysis of the American Library Association's Annual List 'Best Books for Young Adults,' 1930–1967," Master's thesis, University of Chicago, 1967.

Angelou, Maya. *I Know Why the Caged Bird Sings*. New York: Random, 1970.

Anson, Jay. *The Amityville Horror*. New York: Prentice-Hall, 1977.

Atwood, Margaret. *The Handmaid's Tale*. Boston: Houghton, 1986.

Avi. Letter to Evelyn Shaevel, 23 May 1987.

Baker, Jerri. Letter to Jan Freeman, 19 May 1979.

Beagle, Peter. *The Last Unicorn*. New York: New American Library, 1991.

Beattie, Owen, and John Geiger. *Buried in Ice: The Mystery of a Lost Arctic Expedition*. New York: Scholastic, 1992.

Bethancourt, T. Ernesto. *The Me Inside of Me*. Minneapolis: Lerner, 1985.

Black, Nancy. "Review of *Face at the Edge of the World* by Eve Bunting." In *School Library Journal* 32 (Dec. 1985): 98.

Block, Francesca Lia. *Weetzie Bat*. New York: Harper/Charlotte Zolotow, 1989.

Blume, Judy. *Forever*. Scarsdale: Bradbury, 1975.

Bodart, Joni. "View from the Inside: How the Best Books for Young Adults Committee Really Works." *Top of the News* 38 (Fall 1981): 77.

Briggs, Raymond. *When the Wind Blows*. New York: Schoken 1982.

Brin, David. *The Postman*. New York: Bantam, 1985.

Broderick, Dorothy M. "Good, Better, Best Or the Saga of YASD's Best Books Selection." *VOYA* 12 (Apr. 1989): 17–18.

———. "Here's News." *VOYA* 10 (April 1987): 6–7.

Brooks, Bruce. *On the Wing*. New York: Scribner, 1989.

———. *What Hearts*. New York: HarperCollins/Laura Geringer, 1992.

Brooks, Terry. *Sword of Shannara*. New York: Random, 1977.

Bunting, Eve. *Face at the Edge of the World*. New York: Clarion, 1985.

Burleson, Nanette P. "Terry Davis' Vision." Unpublished paper, Texas Woman's University, 1993.

Butterworth, W. E. *LeRoy and the Old Man*. New York: Four Winds, 1980.

———. Letter to Evelyn Shaevel, 14 May 1981.

Byars, Betsy. *The Blossoms Meet the Vulture Lady*. New York: Delacorte, 1986.

Callahan, Steven. *Adrift: Seventy-Six Days Lost at Sea*. Boston: Houghton, 1986.

Caras, Roger A. *Mara Simba: The African Lion*. New York: Holt, 1985.

———. Letter to Evelyn Shaevel, 14 May 1982.

Carner, Charles. American Library Association Press Release, 1 Mar. 1964.

Carter, Betty, Hollis Lowery-Moore, and Barbara Samuels. "Readers' Choices: A Comparison of Critical Comments." *The ALAN Review* 20 (Spring 1993): 52–55.

Cary, Mary Ruth Metcalf. "An Analysis of the Critical Reception and the Age Level Designations for the 1993 Best Books For Young Adults List." Professional paper, Texas Woman's University, 1993.

Caseley, Judith. *My Father, the Nutcase*. New York: Knopf/Borzoi, 1992.

Childress, Alice. *A Hero Ain't Nothin' but a Sandwich*. New York: Coward, 1973.

Clark, Mary Higgins. *Where Are the Children?* New York: Dell, 1976.

Clements, Bruce. *Tom Loves Anna Loves Tom*. New York: Farrar, 1990.

Cook, Robin. *Coma*. New York: Little, Brown, 1977.

Cooper, Ilene. "Review of *Count Me In* by Christine McDonnell." *Booklist* 81, no. 22 (Aug. 1985): 81.

Cormier, Robert. *The Chocolate War: A Novel*. New York: Pantheon, 1974.

———. *I Am the Cheese*. New York: Pantheon, 1977.

Cousteau, Jacques-Yves, and Philippe Cousteau. *Shark: Spendid Savage of the Sea*. New York: Doubleday, 1970.

Craig, John. *Chappie and Me: An Autobiographical Novel*. New York: Dodd, 1979.

———. Letter to Jan Freeman, 8 May 1980.

Davis, Terry. *If Rock and Roll Were a Machine*. New York: Delacorte, 1993.

———. *Vision Quest*. New York: Viking, 1979.

Donelson, Ken, and Alleen Pace Nilsen. *Literature for Today's Young Adults*. Chicago: Scott, Foresman, 1980.

Eaglen, Audrey B. "A Pox on Some of Your Houses." *School Library Journal* 34 (Jan. 1988): 45.

Edelman, Bernard, ed. *Dear America: Letters Home from Vietnam*. New York: Norton, 1985.

Edelman, Marian Wright. *The Measure of Our Success: A Letter to My Children and Yours*. Boston: Beacon, 1992.

Edgerton, Cathi. Letter to Mike Printz, Mar. 1985.

Estes, Sally. "Review of *Face at the Edge of the World* by Eve Bunting." *Booklist* 81, no. 13 (1 Mar. 1985): 102.

Fante, John. *1933 Was a Very Bad Year*. Santa Barbara, Calif.: Black Sparrow, 1985.

Ferber, Edna. *Cimarron*. Boston: G. K. Hall, 1981.

Ferris, Timothy. *Spaceshots: The Beauty of Nature Beyond Earth*. New York: Pantheon, 1984.

Ferry, Charles. *Binge*. Rochester, Mich.: DaisyHill, 1992.

Fields, Jeff. *A Cry of Angels*. New York: Atheneum, 1974.

———. Letter to Eleanor K. Pourron, 11 Nov. 1975.

Ford, Richard. *Quest for the Faradawn*. New York: Delacorte/E. Friede, 1982.

Forman, Jack. Letter to Betty Carter, 15 Apr. 1993.

Frank, Pat. *Alas Babylon*. Philadelphia: Lippincott, 1959.

Freedman, Russell. *Lincoln: A Photobiography*. New York: Clarion, 1988.

Gaan, Margaret. Letter to Evelyn Shaevel, 23 Nov. 1984.

Gallo, Donald R., ed. *Sixteen: Short Stories by Outstanding Writers for Young Adults*. New York: Delacorte, 1984.

Garfield, Brian. *Recoil*. New York: Morrow, 1977.

Gedge, Pauline. *Child of the Morning*. New York: Dial, 1977.

Gerani, Gary, and Paul Schulman. *Fantastic Televison*. New York: Harmony, 1977.

Gingher, Marianne. *Bobby Rex's Greatest Hit*. New York: Atheneum, 1986.

Goodman, Rhonna A. Letter to Betty Carter, 30 Mar. 1993.

Gordon, Jacquie. "A Spark in Tippecanoe: Case Study of a Book That Would Not Die." *SIGNAL* 14 (Winter 1990): 10–12.

Greenberg, Joanne. *Far Side of Victory.* New York: Holt, 1983.

——. *In This Sign.* New York: Holt, 1970.

——. *Of Such Small Differences.* New York: Holt, 1988.

——. *Simple Gifts.* New York: Holt, 1986.

——. Letter to Evelyn Shaevel, 24 May 1984.

Guy, Rosa. *The Friends.* New York: Holt, 1973.

Hall, Lynn. *Just One Friend.* New York: Scribner, 1985.

Hayden, Torey L. *Sunflower Forest.* New York: Putnam, 1967.

Head, Ann. *Mr. and Mrs. Bo Jo Jones.* New York: Putnam, 1966.

Hermes, Patricia. *A Solitary Secret.* San Diego: Harcourt, 1985.

Hesse, Karen. *Letters from Rifka.* New York: Holt, 1992.

Hinton, S. E. *The Outsiders.* New York: Viking, 1967.

Horwitz, Elinor. *Madness, Magic, and Medicine: The Treatment and Mistreatment of the Mentally Ill.* New York: Lippincott, 1977.

Horwitz, Joshua. *Only Birds and Angels Fly.* New York: Harper, 1985.

Human Rights in China. *Children of the Dragon: The Story of Tiananmen Square.* New York: Macmillan/Collier, 1990.

Huygen, Wil, and Rien Poortvliet. *Gnomes.* New York: Abrams, 1976.

"Involving Young Adults in Fiction Selection." *Top of the News* 40 (Winter 1984): 163–70.

James, Will. *Lone Cowboy.* New York: Scribners, 1929.

Janeczko, Paul, ed. *Poetspeak: In Their Work, about Their Work.* New York: Bradbury, 1983.

Jackson, Winifred B. "Selecting Adult Books for Young People." *Top of the News* 5 (Dec. 1948): 5–6, 31.

Jeffrey, Penny. Letter to YASD Board of Directors, 19 Dec. 1978.

——. Letter to Betty Carter, 15 Apr. 1993.

Kerr, M. E. *Him She Loves?* New York: Harper, 1984.

King, Stephen. *Night Shift.* New York: Doubleday, 1978.

Koehn, Ilse. *Mischling, Second Degree: My Childhood in Nazi Germany.* New York: Greenwillow, 1977.

Kollasch, Matthew. "Professionalism and BBYA: A Lengthy Problem." *Wilson Library Bulletin* 66 (Sept. 1991): 68–69, 137.

Lackey, Mercedes. *Bardic Voices: The Lark and the Wren.* New York: Baen, 1992.

LaFaille, Eugene. Letter to Betty Carter, 19 Apr. 1993.

Larrick, Nancy, ed. *Crazy to Be Alive in Such a Strange World: Poems about People.* New York: Evans, 1977.

——. Letter to Jack Forman, 2 June 1978.

Lawson, Donna. *Mother Nature's Beauty Cupboard: How to Make Beautiful, Money-Saving Natural Cosmetics and Other Beauty Preparations.* New York: Crowell, 1973.

"Letters." *Top of the News* 36 (Fall 1979): 18.

Levoy, Myron. *Three Friends.* New York: Harper, 1984.

Lipsyte, Robert. *One Fat Summer.* New York, Harper, 1977.

Littke, Lael. *Shanny on Her Own.* San Diego: Harcourt, 1985.

Llywelyn, Morgan. *The Horse Goddess.* Boston: Houghton, 1982.

——. Letter to Evelyn Shaevel, 27 May 1983.

Lopez, Barry. *Arctic Dreams: Imagination and Desire in a Northern Landscape.* New York: Scribner, 1986.

——. Letter to Evelyn Shaevel, 7 July 1987.

MacRae, Cathi. "The Young Adult Perplex." *Wilson Library Bulletin* 63 (Nov. 1988): 98–99, 135.

Madden, Michael C. "An Analysis of the American Library Association's Annual List 'Best Books for Young Adults,' 1930–1967." Master's thesis, University of Chicago, 1967.

"Major Activities of the YASD Board." *Journal of Youth Services in Libraries* 4 (Fall 1990): 8.

——. *Journal of Youth Services in Libraries* 4 (Fall 1991): 9.

Marlette, Doug. *In Your Face: A Cartoonist at Work.* Boston: Houghton, 1992.

Mazer, Harry, and Norma Fox Mazer. *The Solid Gold Kid.* New York: Delacorte, 1977.

McCartney, Linda. *Linda's Pictures: A Collection of Photographs.* New York: Knopf, 1976.

McCue, Michael, and Evie Wilson. "Book You—Book Now: A Survival Preconference." *Top of the News* 32 (Nov. 1975): 30–33.

McDonnell, Christine. *Count Me In.* New York: Viking, 1986.

McKissack, Patricia C., and Fred McKissack. *Sojourner Truth: Ain't I a Woman?* New York: Scholastic, 1992.

Minudri, Regina. Letter to Betty Carter, 14 Apr. 1993.

Mohr, Nicholasa. *In Nueva York.* New York: Dial, 1976.

Naar, Jon. *Design for a Livable Planet.* New York: HarperCollins, 1990.

Nelson, Brenda. Letter to YASD, 17 May 1968.

Norvell, George. *The Reading Interests of Young People.* East Lansing: University of Michigan Press, 1973.

Palmer, David R. *Emergence.* New York: Bantam, 1984.

Peck, Richard. *Ghosts I Have Been.* New York: Viking, 1977.

Petty, Richard. *King of the Road.* New York: Macmillan, 1977.

Plath, Sylvia. *The Bell Jar.* New York: Harper, 1971.

Platt, Kin. *Headman.* New York: Morrow, 1975.

Porter, E. Jane. "Research Report." *Language Arts* 52 (Oct. 1975): 1025.

Pourron, Eleanor. Letter to Betty Carter, 25 Mar. 1993.

_____, and Sue Tait. Letter to YASD Board, 10 Jan. 1979.

Powell, Randy. *Is Kissing a Girl Who Smokes Like Licking an Ashtray?* New York: Farrar, 1992.

Printz, Mike. Letter to Betty Carter, 20 Apr. 1993.

Rather, Dan, and Herskowitz, Mickey. *The Camera Never Blinks: Adventures of a TV Journalist.* New York: Morrow, 1977.

Rice, Robert. *The Last Pendragon.* New York: Walker, 1992.

Richards, Arlene Kramer, and Irene Willis. *Under 18 and Pregnant: What to Do if You or Someone You Know Is.* New York: Lothrop, 1983.

Robeson, Susan. *Whole World in His Hands.* New York: Citadel, 1982.

Rochman, Hazel. "Review of *The Me Inside of Me* by T. Ernesto Bethancourt." *Booklist* 82 (15 Jan. 1986): 75.

Rodgers, Rabo. *The Rainbow Factor.* Boston: Houghton, 1985.

The Rolling Stone Illustrated History of Rock and Roll. Rev. Ed. New York: Rolling Stone, 1980.

Russell, Bill, and William McSweeney. *Go Up for Glory.* New York: Coward-McCann, 1966.

Ryerson, Eric. *When Your Parent Drinks Too Much: A Book for Teenagers.* New York: Facts On File, 1984.

Salvadore, Maria B. "Review of *Abby, My Love* by Hadley Irwin." *School Library Journal* 31 (May 1985): 102.

Schwarzenegger, Arnold, and Douglass Kent Hall. *Arnold: The Education of a Bodybuilder.* New York: Simon & Schuster, 1977.

Scieszka, Jon. *The Stinky Cheese Man and Other Fairly Stupid Tales.* New York: Viking, 1992.

Shoemaker, Joel. Letter to 1994 BBYA Committee Members, 26 Mar. 1993.

_____. Letter to Betty Carter, 13 Apr. 1993.

Shute, Neville. *On the Beach.* New York: Morrow, 1957.

Simpson, Elaine. Letter to Audrey Biel, 21 Jan. 1964.

Sleator, William. *House of Stairs.* New York: Dutton, 1974.

Spencer, Pam. Letter to Betty Carter, 12 May 1993.

_____. Telephone interview by Betty Carter. 21 May 1993.

Spielman, Ed. *Mighty Atom: The Life and Times of Joseph L. Greenstein.* New York: Viking, 1980.

_____. Letter to Evelyn Shaevel, 1 June 1981.

Stark, Li. "Review of *Just One Friend* by Lynn Hall." *School Library Journal* 32 (Dec. 1985): 88.

Stoll, Cliff. *Cuckoo's Egg: Tracking a Spy Through the Maze of Computer Espionage.* New York: Doubleday, 1989.

Striber, Whitley. *Wolf of Shadows.* New York: Knopf, 1985.

Sutton, Roger. "Best Books for Young Adults." *School Library Journal* 30 (Mar. 1984): 125.

_____. "Even Restaurants Have Menus." *School Library Journal* 31 (Aug. 1985): 36.

Swarthout, Glendon. *Bless the Beasts and Children.* New York: Doubleday, 1970.

Taylor, Clark. *The House That Crack Built.* Chicago: Chronicle, 1992.

Taylor, Deborah. Letter to Betty Carter, 23 Apr. 1993.

_____. Letter to YALSA Board, 31 Mar. 1993.

Tenny, Dixie. *Call the Darkness Down.* New York: Atheneum, 1984.

Thesman, Jean. *When the Road Ends*. Boston: Houghton, 1992.

Thompson, Jean. *House of Tomorrow*. New York: Harper, 1967.

Trahan, Marian L. Letter to Mildred Batchelder, 16 May 1960.

Trosper, Penelope Lou Apple. "Holdings of the 1991 Best Books for Young Adult List Titles by Northeast Texas Library System Members Who Belong to Online Computer Library Center." Professional paper, Texas Woman's University, 1993.

Uhlman, Fred. *Reunion*. New York: Farrar, 1977.

"Up for Discussion." *VOYA* 8 (Aug. 1985): 169–71.

Van Devanter, Lynda, and Christopher Morgan. *Home before Morning: The Story of an Army Nurse in Vietnam*. New York: Beaufort, 1983.

Walsh, Jill Patton. *Parcel of Patterns*. New York: Farrar, 1983.

Walsh, John, and Robert Gannon. *Time Is Short and the Water Rises*. New York: Dutton, 1967.

Ward, Margaret. Letter to Young People's Reading Round Table, 19 July 1945. Quoted in Michael C. Madden "An Analysis of the American Library Association's Annual List 'Best Books for Young Adults,' 1930–1967," Master's thesis, University of Chicago, 1967.

Watson, James. *Double Helix: A Personal Account of the Discovery of the Structure of DNA*. New York: Atheneum, 1968.

Washington State Young Adult Review Group (WASHYARG). Letter to YALSA Board, 24 Feb. 1993.

Wersba, Barbara. *Run Softly, Go Fast*. New York: Atheneum, 1970.

Westall, Robert. *Yaxley's Cat*. New York: Scholastic, 1991.

White, Robb. *Deathwatch*. New York: Doubleday, 1972.

Woody, Jacquie Brown. Letter to Betty Carter, 1 June 1993.

Young, Jean. *Woodstock Craftsman's Manual*. New York: Praeger, 1972.

Young Adult Library Services Association. *A Manual for the Chair of the Best Books for Young Adults Committee*. Chicago: Young Adult Services Library Services Association, n. d.

Zindel, Paul. *The Effect of Gamma Rays on Man-in-the-Moon Marigolds*. New York: Harper, 1971.

———. *The Pigman*. New York: Harper, 1968.

Zvirin, Stephanie. "Review of *Abby, My Love* by Hadley Irwin." *Booklist* 81, no. 13 (1 Mar. 1985): 945.

INDEX